CHIEF RABBI HERTZ

Also by Derek Taylor

History

The Golden Age of British Hotels (with David Bush)
Fortune, Fame and Folly – The Caterer 1878–1978
Jewish Education 1981–1982 (Editor)
Jewish Education 1982–1983 (Editor)
Ritzy – British Hotels 1837–1987
British Chief Rabbis 1664–2007
Hospitality: A Portrait: The British Hospitality Association 1907–2007
Don Pacifico: The Acceptable Face of Gunboat Diplomacy
Jewish Parliamentarians (with Greville Janner)
Solomon Schonfeld: A Purpose in Life
The Sunderland Beth Hamedresh 1889–1999 (with Harold Davis)
Thank You for Your Business: The Jewish Contribution to the British Economy

Hotel Management

Hotel and Catering Sales Promotion
How to Sell Banquets
Profitable Hotel Reception (with Richard Thomason)
Sales Management for Hotels
Hotel and Catering Sales: A Complete Guide
Hotel and Restaurant Advertising (with Hugh Taylor)
Effective Hotel Sales and Marketing

Chief Rabbi Hertz

The Wars of the Lord

DEREK TAYLOR

VALLENTINE MITCHELL
LONDON • CHICAGO

First published in 2015 by Vallentine Mitchell

Catalyst House
720 Centennial Court, Centennial Park
Elstree, WD6 3SY UK

814 N. Franklin Street
Chicago
IL 60610, USA

www.vmbooks.com

British Library Cataloguing in Publication Data:
An entry can be found on request

ISBN 978 0 85303 918 1 (cloth)
ISBN 978 0 85303 968 6 (paper)
ISBN 978 0 85303 919 8 (ebook)

Library of Congress Cataloging-in-Publication Data:
An entry can be found on request

For
Simon and Deborah
Hugh and Katie
Tim and Suzy
Kate and David

Contents

List of Illustrations

Foreword

I have one advantage over some of those who have written recently about Chief Rabbi Hertz. I was there for part of his time. My family had been supporters of the United Synagogue since its inception in 1870. My father had sung in the choir in the West End's Central Synagogue as a child and, in later life, served for fifteen years as its warden. His brother was head of the Board of Shechita and a warden at Dunstan Road Synagogue in Golders Green. On my mother's side, the Freedmans were wardens of a number of London synagogues. The patriarch was Joseph Freedman, who subsidized the printing costs of the one-volume edition of Hertz's commentary on the *Chumash* and chaired the United Synagogue Building Committee for some years in the 1930s.

We were not part of the Cousinhood, those interlocking families of rich Jews who had developed so strongly in the nineteenth century and were the powers in the Anglo-Jewish establishment. Joseph Freedman had started his business life as a pedlar in the Welsh valleys, and had made a fortune out of hire-purchase in his furniture shops between the wars. It was rumoured in the family that he had turned down the offer of a knighthood, when they were being sold in Lloyd George's time. He was said to have considered £10,000 too much to pay, even though his partner, Sir Julien Cahn, received the honour in Ramsay Macdonald's time.

Joseph Freedman was a deeply religious man. The Yom Kippur evening service lasts two to three hours, followed by nine or more hours during the following day. My great-grandfather would stand for the whole service. When he was too old to do that, he delegated the responsibility to my father, who was not best pleased to have the honour.

The United Synagogue was the financial headquarters of all their synagogues. The Central had a surplus on its annual balance sheet, as it was a rich congregation, but most of this surplus was sent to the United Synagogue Head Office to be used to pay the deficits of smaller and poorer congregations. Beyond its financial role, though, the United Synagogue had very little influence and also asked for little. When a congregation needed a new rabbi, that synagogue's Honorary

Officers would make their selection. If the choice was acceptable to the Chief Rabbi – and normally there was no reason why it shouldn't be – the appointment was confirmed. The United Synagogue looked after the cemeteries as well, but otherwise played only a small role in the running of its member congregations.

The relationships between the local Honorary Officers and the Rabbi depended on the qualities of both. A strong rabbi would have more influence than a timid one. Even when the Honorary Officers dominated the proceedings, however, the religious running of the synagogue normally remained the rabbi's province.

Where the rabbi wanted a greater say in the running of the synagogue, there could be conflict. Revd Isaac Livingstone and my grandfather in the wardens' box at Dunstan Road were reputed to have had many severe arguments. My father, at the Central, disliked the rabbi's undergraduate sense of humour, but they got on well enough otherwise. Some years after Hertz's death I was elected to the Board of Management at the Central, and the Board dealt with non-religious matters without the rabbi even being invited to attend.

The attitude towards the Chief Rabbi was one of the greatest respect. He would come to the Central on the first day of the Festival of Succot and would be treated with the utmost deference. It was an honour to have him in our midst. Where the role of the United Synagogue was considered purely bureaucratic, the Chief Rabbi was acknowledged as the spiritual leader of the community and his eminence was a source of pride to the vast majority of United Synagogue members.

The congregants in the Dunstan Road and Central synagogues had, largely, been born in Britain. Before the 1939 war they had badly wanted to be accepted as Englishmen, even though many public schools had a quota, limiting the number of Jewish children they would accept. There were also hotels which wouldn't take Jewish clients, restaurants which had no vacant tables if your name was Cohen, and golf clubs which had quotas as well. And, for some, the quota was zero. Soon after Hertz died, a number of Jews bought Coombe Hill Golf Club in Surrey because there was no other way of becoming a member. As the new owners, though, they did accept Christian members.

The general attitude of British-born Jews was epitomized in the 1960s in a sketch in the revue *Beyond the Fringe*. Britain was still a class-ridden society and the revue lampooned every aspect of that culture. In one sketch the cast discussed ancestry and dismissed one of their members, Jonathan Miller, as being beyond the Pale, because he was a Jew. Miller protested that he wasn't actually a Jew, but only Jew-ish! The community generally used that term to refer to itself. At the time they would never dream of wearing a yarmulke, or skull cap, in the street. They preferred to keep their Jewish heads down and continue to aim for acceptance in the wider world.

Nevertheless, most Jewish families had until relatively recently been very Orthodox. If they hadn't felt deeply about their religion, they would have converted. That would have ended the discrimination that in many other countries led to pogroms, unfair taxation, expulsion and exclusion from the trade guilds. That they held on to their Judaism, in spite of all this, explains their survival as Jews.

The desire both to be accepted as fully English and to observe the rules of Judaism created a dilemma. It was difficult to be both before the multiculturalism of the present day, and it was the observance of the rules of Judaism that tended to suffer. In very many cases, the son was less religious than his father and the grandson less religious than both.

This was the British world to which Hertz came in 1913. One of the older generation of Jews who had escaped the pogroms at the back end of the nineteenth century was my paternal grandfather, a master tailor from Poland who could only write his name. The refugee immigrants had increased the number of British Jews nearly tenfold over thirty years, and they came from much more Orthodox backgrounds than the core British community. In America, the flood had largely turned in favour of the Reform movement, with their more assimilated form of Judaism. In 1913, Hertz, who was born in the Austro-Hungarian Empire, had to face the challenge of keeping the refugees in the British Orthodox section of the community within the faith, and his responsibility for this extended throughout the British Empire. It was a massive achievement that he largely did so.

I would like to thank Lord Sacks, for kindly agreeing to write the introduction to this book. I also owe many thanks to Dr Jeremy Schonfield for giving me access to photographs, photocopies of some of the documents now in the Hertz archive, and for a very great deal of excellent advice. I am also much indebted to Elkan Levy. The United Synagogue kindly gave me permission to consult their records at the London Metropolitan Archives. The Hartley Library staff at the University of Southampton, who hold the full Hertz archive, were equally helpful. The librarian of the London School of Jewish Studies, Erla Zimmels, was always able to find the books I needed and *The Times* and the *Jewish Chronicle* archives were invaluable. I would also like to acknowledge the contribution of Rabbi Dr Abraham Levy, Rabbi Dov Kaplan, Charles Tucker, Jack Lopian, Lionel Kopelowitz, Lionel Ziman, my ever patient editor, Heather Marchant, and my wife, Diane, whose support is remarkable, as the home is dominated for months on end by long-dead historical characters.

Views on the life of Chief Rabbi Hertz have been subject to much debate over the years. I, naturally, take full responsibility for any errors made in writing his biography.

Introduction

Emeritus Chief Rabbi, Lord Jonathan Sacks

This book tells the story of a remarkable religious leader who lived through epoch-making times. Rabbi Dr J.H. Hertz was Chief Rabbi of Britain and its Overseas Dominions from 1913 to 1946, leading British Jewry through two world wars, the Balfour Declaration, the rise of Hitler and the sometimes desperate attempt to save Jewish lives at a time when, in the words of Chaim Weizmann the world was 'divided into places where the Jews cannot live and places they may not enter'.

Such times would have tested the mettle of lesser figures, but Hertz was fully equal to the challenge. There are leaders who are peacemakers and diplomats. No one ever accused Hertz of being among their ranks. Combative, self-confident, utterly unafraid to speak his mind, sturdy in appearance, trenchant in language, he was and saw himself as a defender of the faith, fighting the wars of the Lord. The Talmud contrasts Moses, who held 'let the law pierce the mountain' ('let the chips fall where they may') with his brother Aaron who 'loved peace, and pursued peace' even if it meant making a golden calf. Hertz was undeniably in the camp of Moses.

Throughout his long term in office, British Jewry was in a state of considerable flux. On the one hand there were the recent Yiddish-speaking arrivals from Eastern Europe, who tended to see the Anglo-Jewish establishment as more Anglo (even Anglican) than Jewish. They did not recognize the authority of the Chief Rabbi, and were sceptical of the halakhic credentials of the Beth Din (the Court of the Chief Rabbi) at least until the appointment of Dayan Yehezel Abramsky in 1934. The irony is that Hertz himself was a fluent Yiddish speaker, and that, leading one of the main groups not recognizing his authority, Agudah, was the man who eventually became his son-in-law, Rabbi Dr Solomon Schonfeld. Hertz was able to give significant support to Schonfeld in his daring rescue of European Jews, among them many rabbis, during the Holocaust years.

In the opposite direction there was the growing assertiveness of non-Orthodox groups within the community, specifically the movement called Liberal Judaism (the Reform movement in Britain until the late 1920s was far more conservative than its counterparts in Germany and America). Though the Liberal movement was small, it contained significant figures like Claude Montefiore and Lily Montagu from the old-established Anglo-Jewish families.

However, as is often the case and as Derek Taylor's study makes painfully clear, the most significant opposition Hertz faced was within his own ranks of the British-Jewish mainstream. On one famous occasion he was forced publicly to distance himself from the Board of Deputies of which he was an ecclesiastical authority. Throughout the early decades of the twentieth century the Board was hostile to Zionism, which it saw as damaging to the public perception of Jews as loyal citizens of Britain. The president of the board, David Alexander, together with Claude Montefiore, head of the Anglo-Jewish Association, published a letter in *The Times* expressing their opposition to the Balfour Declaration. Hertz, a Zionist like his counterpart in the Spanish and Portuguese Jewish Congregation, Chakham Moses Gaster, was forced to write a letter in sharp dissent, stating that Alexander and Montefiore did not represent the views of Anglo-Jewry as a whole. It was an argument that Hertz won, both with the community (mainly because the president of the board had not consulted its members) and the government.

His longest standing disputes though were with a senior lay leader of the United Synagogue, Robert Waley Cohen. The story of their relationship, well chronicled by Taylor, reads almost like a novelist's account of a dysfunctional Jewish family. Somehow Hertz and Waley Cohen could not get on. Their attempts at amicable friendship resembled Hertz's description of the British government's implementation of the Balfour Declaration: not only had they failed to try, they had tried to fail.

They differed in many ways. Waley Cohen, lax in his own Jewish practice, constantly sought to blur the boundaries between Orthodox and Reform, which Hertz refused to let him do. Waley Cohen believed in Erastianism, the principle that secular authority was superior to religious, so that even in a synagogue body, lay leaders should hold ultimate control. Hertz, knowing that Judaism was not the Anglican Church, disagreed and rightly insisted on rabbinic authority in religious matters. The most combustible element in their relationship, though, was their respective characters. They were both authoritarian personalities. Neither was given to accepting dissent graciously (it was famously said of Hertz that he never neglected a peaceful solution when all other means had failed).

Of the two, Hertz clearly emerges as the more likeable, partly because he always acted on the basis of principle, and partly because he had a sense of humour that Waley Cohen lacked. Taylor recounts the story that when Hertz met George VI in 1940, the king asked what Hertz thought about the war. Hertz is said to have replied that the allies would eventually win, but that it might not be a bad idea for the king to put some of the colonies in his wife's name.

Hertz was a rabbi of the type that the Chief Rabbinate seems consistently to have selected. He was well-educated both Jewishly and secularly, widely read, able to speak brilliantly to both Jewish and non-Jewish audiences and admired by both. He was equally at home with rabbis, politicians, royalty and bishops. He was an international figure, becoming the first Chief Rabbi to undertake a pastoral tour of the Canadian, South African, Australian and New Zealand Jewish communities, a trip that took eleven months and involved forty-two communities. He was also, thanks to the birth of the BBC in 1922, the first Chief Rabbi to become a successful broadcaster.

Hertz's interventions were carefully considered and generally successful. He led the campaign to defeat the League of Nations' attempt to alter the calendar, which would have had disastrous ramifications for the observance of Shabbat. He worked on this with the Jewish historian Cecil Roth. Their memos were headed: 'From CR to CR re. CR', from Chief Rabbi to Cecil Roth about Calendar Reform. He was fearless in bringing the plight of German and Austrian Jewry to the attention of the government. And he successfully resisted Waley Cohen's several attempts to create a kind of Orthodox–Reform hybrid.

His most lasting achievement, though, was literary. His brilliant anthology, *A Book of Jewish Thoughts*, initially produced for Jewish servicemen and women during the First World War, was a superb production, testimony to his wide and eclectic reading. It brought spiritual sustenance to many and was produced in its hundreds of thousands. His *Commentary to the Pentateuch*, blending the best of traditional and modern scholarship and directly addressing many of the challenges to Jewish faith, was one of the greatest of its kind in the modern age. Widely read throughout English-speaking Jewry, it is still used by many congregations today.

It was not to everyone's taste. Many on the right wing of the community were displeased with his recourse to non-Jewish sources. Hertz's reply to this was to invoke Maimonides' dictum, 'Accept the truth from whatever source it comes.' Gaster wrote a mean-spirited review, calling it 'dilettantism'. It was undeniably a product of its age, an answer to the kind of biblical criticism that Solomon Schechter called 'the higher anti-Semitism'. Hertz's literary output, Taylor says, exceeded all the other British Chief Rabbis combined, and it was deftly done.

One other work which is worthy of mention is his *Commentary to the Prayer Book*. Strangely, this never caught on, yet it was until 2006 the only systematic commentary to the prayers by a British Chief Rabbi and like the Chumash it drew on Hertz's extensive scholarship and finely-honed editorial skills.

Much ink has been spilled over the question of Hertz's own interpretation of Judaism. Some, instancing the fact that he was ordained by the Jewish Theological Seminary of America, today a non-Orthodox institution, have argued that he was really a Masorti/ Conservative rather than an Orthodox Jew. That is clearly nonsense. The Seminary was, at the time, Orthodox, and no one fought longer or harder for the fundamentals of Orthodoxy than Hertz: the divine revelation and mosaic authorship of the Torah, the eternity of both the written and oral law, and the non-negotiable authority of Halacha, Jewish law. Hertz criticized non-Orthodox Judaism in a series of devastating lectures published as *The New Paths*, focusing on the challenge of his day, Liberal Judaism. There was no Masorti Judaism in Britain in his lifetime, and the Reform movement was small and still highly traditional.

Some cite in evidence the fact that he was willing to attend the opening of a new social hall in a Reform synagogue in 1934. As he made clear at the time, however, the reason he did so was that after the rise of Hitler he considered the rescue of Jews from Germany took priority over everything else, and – having experienced the almost disastrous sabotage of the Balfour Declaration by leaders of the Jewish community themselves – he did not want to provide any evidence of disunity at that singular time. He resisted, however, all attempts at creating joint Orthodox–Reform initiatives in any substantive field such as Jewish education or the training of religious leaders.

From the opposite perspective Hertz is sometimes accused of setting in motion a rightward shift within the community by appointing figures like Dayan Abramsky to the Beth Din (Hertz's initial choice was Rabbi Yechiel Yaakov Weinberg, who felt unable to leave the German-Jewish community in its hour of crisis). One of the most interesting observations in this book is Taylor's assertion that it was not the Chief Rabbi who enhanced the authority of the dayanim of the Beth Din, but Waley Cohen himself, precisely to *curtail* the power of the Chief Rabbi. If true, this is a supreme instance of the law of unintended consequences.

What is astonishing in this work is the kind of battles Hertz was forced to fight within the United Synagogue itself for the sovereignty of Jewish law and rabbinic authority. The language used by Hertz's opponents is little short of astounding. For instance, when Hertz ruled – following a principle of Jewish law no one has disputed since the days of Paul and the birth of Christianity – that a non-Jew who had not undergone circumcision could not be counted as a Jew in Jewish law, the Hampstead Synagogue called his decision an 'inquisition'. Waley Cohen called it 'priestly dictatorship'.

The writer of these lines – no stranger to controversy himself – can testify that in the twenty-two years in which he held the office held by Hertz, not once did the lay leadership of the United Synagogue challenge the authority of the Chief Rabbinate, nor was there ever the slightest hint of such a thing. I suspect, in short, that Hertz fought and won a battle not only for his time but for all time. He established the primacy of the rabbinate in Britain, which is why in my own travels around the Jewish world I sense a respect for the rabbinate in Britain and throughout the Commonwealth which is not always present in the United States, where lay leaders often exercise far more power.

In truth, though, the most impressive independent testimony to the greatness of Chief Rabbi Hertz is the fact that non-Orthodox Jews often claim to be following in his footsteps. Hertz was the single most fearless defender of Orthodoxy in the twentieth century, as anyone who has read his Chumash Commentary or his *Affirmations of Judaism* knows. Yet his defence was so eloquent, so compelling, so broad in its intellectual sweep and so uplifting in its formulation that it is easy to understand why those whose beliefs he challenged would wish to claim him as one of their own. It could not be done in his lifetime, when no one was in any doubt what he stood for. It could only be done two or three generations later. Perhaps Hertz, with his rich sense of humour, is looking down in amusement from Heaven.

Hertz fought the battles of the Lord in an age when a great many British Jews were lax in practise and uncertain in the principles of their faith. Like every Chief Rabbi before and since, it was his task to defend the citadel of Judaism in law and creed and he did so with unrivalled vigour and panache. He was an outstanding Chief Rabbi and Derek Taylor has written a fine account of his life and work. Faithful Jews know that we are dwarves on the shoulders of giants. Hertz was one such giant, and we in British Jewry stand high today because of what he did and was.

Emeritus Chief Rabbi, Lord Jonathan Sacks
Shevat 5773

of Jewish law and rabbinic authority [illegible] kingdom, as used by [illegible] Hertz's opponents [illegible] of [illegible]. For instance, when [illegible] [illegible] followed, in [illegible] [illegible] Jewish law and [illegible] on the days of Chal and the birth of [illegible] [illegible] [illegible] [illegible] [illegible] circumstances [illegible] [illegible] [illegible] Jewish [illegible] the [illegible] [illegible] suited his occasion [illegible] [illegible] [illegible] Cohen called [illegible] [illegible].

Hertz was [illegible] [illegible] [illegible] [illegible] [illegible] [illegible] [illegible] [illegible] [illegible] [illegible] [illegible] the field [illegible] not [illegible] [illegible] [illegible] [illegible] [illegible] great [illegible], the authority of the Chief Rabbinate, [illegible] [illegible] even the slightest hint of such [illegible] [illegible] that [illegible] and would [illegible] [illegible] [illegible] [illegible] [illegible] [illegible] [illegible] [illegible] [illegible] [illegible] [illegible] [illegible] [illegible] [illegible] [illegible] [illegible] around the Jewish [illegible] [illegible] respect for the [illegible] in Britain and throughout the Commonwealth [illegible] [illegible] [illegible] in the United States [illegible] [illegible] leadership often [illegible] [illegible] [illegible] [illegible].

In death, the [illegible] [illegible] [illegible] [illegible] [illegible] to the greatness of Chief Rabbi Hertz [illegible] [illegible] [illegible] [illegible] [illegible] [illegible] [illegible] [illegible] [illegible] [illegible] [illegible] [illegible] [illegible] [illegible] [illegible] [illegible] [illegible] [illegible] of Orthodoxy in [illegible] [illegible] [illegible] [illegible] [illegible] [illegible] [illegible] [illegible] [illegible] [illegible] [illegible] [illegible] [illegible] [illegible] intellectual sweep and [illegible] looking down [illegible] [illegible] [illegible].

Hertz fought the battles of the Lord [illegible] [illegible] [illegible] [illegible] British Jewry [illegible] [illegible] [illegible] and uncertain [illegible] [illegible] [illegible] [illegible] [illegible] [illegible] Chief Rabbi [illegible] [illegible] [illegible] [illegible] [illegible] [illegible] [illegible] [illegible] [illegible] [illegible] [illegible] [illegible] [illegible] [illegible] [illegible] [illegible] [illegible] Chief Rabbi and [illegible] [illegible] [illegible] [illegible] account of his life and work [illegible] [illegible] [illegible] [illegible] [illegible] [illegible] [illegible] [illegible] [illegible] [illegible] [illegible] [illegible] British Jewry [illegible] [illegible] [illegible] of what [illegible].

Jonathan Sacks, Chief Rabbi [illegible]
[illegible]

Chapter One

In the Beginning

To understand where Chief Rabbi Joseph Herman Hertz was coming from, you have to go back a long way.

Over the centuries there had developed three views on how Judaism might survive. The first was to divorce Jewish communities completely from neighbouring cultures to protect them from being infected by non-Jewish ideas and practices, as they had been by the Greeks and Romans. The Jews would retire into a shell from which the opposing ideologies would be totally excluded and this remains the view, to a greater or lesser extent, in the ultra-Orthodox world.

The second method was to abide strictly by Jewish law, but to try to benefit from whatever seemed good in the cultures of the countries where the Jews lived. In modern times this approach was developed by Rabbi Samson Raphael Hirsch of Frankfurt in the nineteenth century. His core teaching is known as *Torah im Derech Eretz* – Torah with the way of the land – and was the position of the founder of the British Union of Orthodox Hebrew Congregations, Rabbi Dr Victor Schonfeld. The British United Synagogue came eventually to follow broadly the practices of such continental communities.

The third view was to adjust Judaism to the modern world. In those who supported this approach there was also a desire to, as they saw it, modernize the religion. They took the view that, in modern times – in whichever century that was – aspects of the original Jewish law needed to be amended. There have been many of these splinter groups.

The battle is still raging, but Hertz was a key figure in it at the time of his ministry as the Chief Rabbi of Britain and the British Empire. His influence as an upholder of Orthodoxy was immense. Efforts are still being made, however, to prove that he was, at heart, a Conservative rabbi, to give additional legitimacy to the present day position of those who have moved away from the traditional Orthodox approach. 'Conservative' roughly corresponds in America to British Reform.

Certainly, Hertz received his *semicha*, his rabbinical diploma, in New York in an America where the majority of Jews are today no longer Orthodox. In Britain, however, about 70 per cent still belong to Orthodox communities. One of the major reasons for this dichotomy is Chief Rabbi Joseph Herman Hertz.

He was born in Rubrin in Austria-Hungary, now Zemplinski-Siroka in eastern Slovakia, on Tuesday, 25 September 1872. The day for his circumcision would have coincided with the first day of the New Year and it is certainly possible that the ceremony was carried out in the family's synagogue as part of the service. His early years were spent in Austria-Hungary but before his barmitzvah the family emigrated to America where they had relatives.

Simon Hertz, his father, had been a small-scale plum farmer in Austria-Hungary. He probably leased a plum orchard crop from a farmer and made slivovitz, a powerful liqueur, from the juice. It was a good business if you were left in peace, but there was a lot of anti-Semitism in Simon's neighbourhood and he felt that the family would prosper better in New York.

Simon Hertz had studied at the Hildesheimer rabbinical seminary in Eisenstadt, south of Vienna, and was a deeply learned and pious man. He also developed into a very good poet. Uniquely for the time, the curriculum at the seminary included secular subjects. Simon Hertz's ability and knowledge were confirmed by Rabbi Hildesheimer in a recommendation in 1866: 'The candidate for the Rabbinate, Mr Simon Hertz from Palin ... who has spent three months with me in order to acquire rabbinic training and practice that he possesses sufficient knowledge of the Rabbinic Sciences in order to fulfil the rabbinic functions.'[1]

A further commendation in 1867 added that 'he possesses a rich rabbinic knowledge as he has proved by his excellent results of the examinations'.[2]

Simon Hertz became 'one of the best-known pedagogues and one of the most facile Hebrew writers and poets in Hungary'.[3] Indeed, his Hebrew grammar has just been reprinted in America. Theologically, he believed in benefiting from knowledge of the modern world, so long as nothing took precedence over the Talmud. His obituary in the *Jewish Chronicle* recorded: 'His character was marked by deep piety, while he was distinguished for his wide interests in matters literary and scientific.'[4] That would be the theological position of his son, Joseph, as well. As he said in later years: 'In my earliest youth a father's loving care initiated me into the sanctuary of Biblical and Rabbinical lore'.[5]

Although Simon brought up his seven children – three sons and four daughters – to be Orthodox, he wanted them to become professionals, rather than follow a religious career. He had found it difficult enough in New York to earn his living as a teacher. His eldest became a lawyer and his third son a dentist, but Joseph, his second son, wanted to be a rabbi. His father didn't stand in his way and, to obtain the rabbinic diploma, Joseph elected to join a group of students at a newly formed seminary in New York, presided over by Rabbi Sabato Morais.

Hertz's adolescent years were spent on New York's East Side. The family were poor and Hertz always remembered playing in the street with the spray of the water hydrants during the hot weather. Eventually he was able to attend the College of the City of New York: 'an institution which catered specifically for what would now be termed the "underprivileged" of the City'.[6] He received his BA from the college in 1891 when he was seventeen.

Morais' views were in the Hildesheimer tradition. He was a Sephardi, Italian and strictly Orthodox. He came to America in 1851 at the suggestion of Sir Moses Montefiore in London, and later served as the minister of the Mikveh Israel synagogue in Philadelphia for forty-five years. He was a strong humanitarian, a friend of Joseph Mazzini in Italy, and a member of the American Union League, which campaigned for the freedom of the slaves.

In the latter part of the nineteenth century the Orthodox rabbinate in America looked to Europe for leadership. That was where the major *yeshivot*, seminaries, and the great Talmudic brains were to be found. There had been a considerable change in Jewish thinking in the nineteenth century as a result of the movement known as the Enlightenment. This had the effect of freeing the Jews to participate in the life of the countries where they lived, often for the first time.

Some now felt that advantage should be taken of the access to modern thought, and an attempt should be made to synthesize the benefits of Talmudic and secular knowledge, of which science was considered the most important. The others felt that trying to synthesize the Talmud and modern culture would lead to threats to the eternal truths of the Oral and Written law. That if you gave an inch, you would eventually give a mile. To prevent such modern influences weakening traditional practice, many continued to set up communities which lived their lives divorced from the modern world.

Those who rejected both approaches became known as Liberal in Germany and Reform in America. Their rabbis decided to change the Orthodox basis of observance, which is that one must obey the *din* – the 'law' comprising the age-old precepts of the Written and Oral law.

In America, the Reformers decided that the *din*, centuries old, was out-of-date, and that modern man was quite capable of making up his own mind about which traditions to obey and which to ignore.

In 1875 the Hebrew Union College had been created in Cincinnati to train Reform rabbis. Its principal, Rabbi Isaac Mayer Wise, initially hoped that a compromise could be found between the Reform and Orthodox positions. He, eventually, became convinced that the Reform position was best for the modern world of the late nineteenth century and, at a conference in Pittsburgh in 1885, which he chaired, supported what became known as the Pittsburgh Platform.

The changes that this approved were fundamental; for example the assembly held that *kashrut*, the dietary laws, were foreign to their present mental and spiritual state. It asserted that only moral laws should be obeyed and that any that were not adapted to the views and habits of modern civilization should be rejected.

The Reform movement gained a large number of adherents. It had one enormous advantage for many of its members: it removed the feelings of guilt that so many felt at their own laxity in obeying traditional laws. In the books of Leviticus and Deuteronomy long passages describe the punishments the Almighty would inflict on the Jewish people if they did not keep His commandments. These graphic passages inspired fear in all those who believed in punitive suffering.

If, however, the laws were pronounced no longer applicable, then there was no problem in not obeying them. This was a side effect, and a particularly fortuitous one, for those laymen and women who were troubled by their self-perceived religious shortcomings. It also made it much easier to fit in with the norms of American society.

It was after the Pittsburgh Platform that the 63-year-old Morais, in 1886, decided to start his Jewish Theological Seminary (JTS). Morais had fought for the Reform movement to remain Orthodox in its practices, while still adopting sermons in English and transforming its members from immigrants to Americans. After the publication of the Pittsburgh Platform he gave up the fight, finally satisfied that the Reform movement and the Orthodox could never have the same theological outlook. He was horrified by the Pittsburgh Platform's threat to traditional Judaism.

So, at his relatively advanced age, he determined to start his own seminary to produce rabbis who would defend Orthodox practices. It was housed in the Sephardi Shearith Israel Synagogue building, with a curriculum based on the famous European *yeshivot* at Breslau, Budapest and at Berlin, where Hildesheimer's seminary had moved.

It was this new college in New York that Hertz joined at its inception in 1886. There was a class of ten, and the course would last eight years before the granting of *semicha*. Hertz became the first student to graduate from the seminary in 1894, in the same year that he was awarded a PhD from Columbia for a thesis on the philosopher James Martineau. An impressive number of Yeshiva-trained rabbis signed Hertz's *semicha* certificate, the Hattarat Horaah. Thirty-five years later he would receive the Columbia medal for outstanding service.

Morais wanted his students to be well aware of other cultures. He insisted that they combine religious studies with a course at the College of the City of New York. Hertz's work on James Martineau was considered good enough to be published in the *Columbia University Contributions to Philosophy, Psychology and Education*.

Hertz sent his thesis to Martineau who replied in a long letter from London in 1898. Martineau, who was not Jewish, argued that the main difference between his views and those of Hertz lay in: 'the standards by which we test; the systems presented to us for judgement: yours being epistemological, requiring proof of every position as a condition of assent; mine being moral, i.e. according to its place on the scale of rightness; truth being the ideal of the one; goodness of the other'.[7]

It was, of course, the rabbinic position that the law had been set down in the Talmud and all that remained was its interpretation as the world progressed.

From the outset Morais wanted a strictly Orthodox seminary. One of the senior members of the original staff, Rabbi Bernard Drachman, pointed out some years later when the seminary moved from its original theological position, that: 'Although a certain proportion of the organizing delegates and participating rabbis belonged to the Conservative way of Judaism, the principles of the Seminary, as declared in its Charter of Incorporation, granted by the legislature of the State of New York on May 9th 1886, were those of uncompromising adherence to the tenets of Orthodox Judaism.'[8]

The charter laid down the objectives of the college very clearly: the preservation in America of the knowledge and practice of historical Judaism as ordained in the law of Moses and expanded by the Prophets and Sages of Israel in biblical and Talmudic writings.

Morais was fully supported by his fellow Sinaists, Alexander Kohut, the Professor of Talmud, and Bernard Drachman, both from the very Orthodox Breslau *yeshiva* in Poland. Morais and Kohut died, though, before the end of the century and Drachman resigned in 1909. Drachman was a staunch supporter of Orthodox practice, having given up one pulpit already because the congregation chose to introduce mixed seating. He then served the New York Park East Synagogue for fifty-five years.

Hertz was deeply inspired by Morais. He recorded the situation when Morais started the Seminary:

> All around him were 'rabbis' who were fanatically advocating the tearing up of Jewish life by the roots; endeavouring to banish the Sabbath, the Hebrew language, and the Sefer Torah itself from the synagogue. To such revolution in religion, Sabato Morais was the lifelong inveterate foe, as persistent and as unyielding as the rocks; proclaiming that the precepts of the Torah were high above the peradventure of inclination, the whim of the demagogues, or the fashion of the hour.[9]

In the years to come, the Jewish Theological Seminary did not work out as Morais had wanted. Today it is the foremost college for the teaching of what is now known in the United States as Conservative Judaism, its theology having changed drastically over time from its original charter.

Hertz was faithful to the traditional Orthodox teachings of Morais, and referred to Morais as the leader of Orthodox Judaism in America. The British equivalent of those Conservatives today are probably to be found in the Masorti movement, some of whose spokespersons try to claim Hertz for their own. Where, however, the college was originally designed to be a bridge between Reform and Orthodoxy, it has now moved far more towards Reform thinking. Although there were efforts to merge the Seminary with the Orthodox Yeshiva Yitzchak Elchanan in 1902 and 1926, they came to nothing.

The supporters of strict Orthodoxy came to find themselves isolated in the Jewish Theological Seminary. For example, Drachman had been brought up to be a Reform rabbi but decided that Orthodoxy was the path he wanted to follow. After the death of Morais, Drachman continued to serve the Jewish Theological Seminary, but found that his settled Orthodox views were becoming less popular within the faculty, under its new head, Solomon Schechter.

> The weakening of both Jewish loyalty and scholarship grieved him and caused him no end of anxiety. If he spoke up against it at faculty conference to a Board and President predetermined upon a fundamental change in policy, his insistence must have been painful. In getting rid of him, they were 'dropping the pilot' shaking off the voice of their own Orthodox conscience.[10]

Hertz proved himself a diligent student. He had a great capacity for remembering what he had read, and he read avidly. In his future extensive library his friends would marvel at his ability to put his hand on any text without hesitation. His message was inspired by the teaching of Morais.

> We were thrilled by the clear, clarion notes of his call to the Wars of the Lord; by his passionate and loyal stand that the Divine Law was imperative, unchangeable, eternal. He made rigorous demands ... [for] ... the courage to stand alone, if need be, in the fight against unrighteousness and un-Judaism.[11]

Hertz signed up for the war and saw it in those terms. He was the first to graduate from the Seminary. As Bernard Drachman recalled: 'Well do I remember how young Hertz felt the spirit of the ceremony. His face paled as he stood before me to receive the solemn charge from the pulpit.'[12]

As Hertz said on that graduation day in 1894: 'We are fighting a holy war ... we shall be accused of clogging the wheels of Progress, of stemming the tides of Advance, of aiming to haul our brethren back into the exclusiveness of the Ghetto.'[13]

Hertz had chosen where to take his stand. If, in future, he was often one of only a small band, it never dismayed him. He was in the war for the duration.

The influence on Hertz of his years at the Jewish Theological Seminary is generally agreed, but authors like Elton and Freud-Kandel deal primarily with the strictly intellectual aspects of the subject. Admittedly, this is a rabbi, assessing different and contradictory approaches to Judaism, a man of God and one who would become a senior figure in the religious life of Judaism in the twentieth century. A rabbi, however, is required to be a teacher, not a saint. The word 'rabbi' means teacher. Hertz didn't see himself as involved just in an intellectual discussion. His Judaism was: 'An insistence on "thou shalts" and "thou shalt nots" in life.'[14]

All his life Hertz would be a volunteer for the war which would rage between the proponents of different views of what was the correct Jewish approach to the challenges of the twentieth century. The mass of the evidence is that Hertz was prepared to be a bare-fisted fighter for what he believed in. Not an advocate or a supporter, but a battler. He would be prepared to take on anybody, and any body, to win the day. In future he would cross swords with the Boer government in South Africa, the Czar, the League of Nations, the Nazis, the Communists, the Liberal, Reform and ultra-Orthodox Jews, and the Honorary Officers of the British United Synagogue.

Nobody gets into so many battles unless he enjoys fighting. A timid man, a follower, or a man with an inferiority complex doesn't have such an agenda. In reviewing Hertz's life, it is necessary to remember that he was a tough man, not a member of a drawing-room movement or a club in academe. He also recognized the need to balance the loyalty that Orthodox Jews owed to the Halacha with that which they owed to their country. If the two clashed, Hertz might, on occasions, put the country first, even against opposition from senior Talmudic authorities. It would happen in England during the two world wars.

He never spared himself. One of his closest friends when he eventually settled in Britain was the witty Revd Ephraim Levine, always known as Ephy, the long-serving minister at the prestigious New West End synagogue in London. Levine, a Cambridge graduate and a brilliant orator, said of Hertz that: 'He was a painstaking worker, never satisfied till he had found the exact words that could express his meaning ... He often confessed that the gravity of his message and the burden of cares under which he laboured, demanded verbal precision.'[15] He also pointed out that, as far as Hertz was concerned, 'any infringement of the rights of the individual or of the community must be ruthlessly prosecuted'.[16]

After the death of Morais the battle for theological supremacy between the Orthodox members of the faculty and those who wanted the benefit of the new secular knowledge was initially won by the Orthodox. The financial position of the Seminary, however, deteriorated until it was unsustainable. It was the academic Cyrus Adler who persuaded Jacob Schiff, a New York banker and one of the senior leaders of American Jewry, to rescue it in 1902 and become President of its Board of Trustees. Adler had a PhD in Semitics from Johns Hopkins University where he taught the subject, but he was not a rabbi. He would still become acting president of the JTS in 1915 and president from 1924.

The money came from Reform sources and Schiff used it to provide the JTS with a building and to arrange a $500,000 endowment fund. Schiff still wanted a bridge between the Orthodox and Reform approaches and it was agreed with Adler that the main condition for his largesse was that Solomon Schechter be appointed president. They both considered him the best candidate to achieve their objective. With a charter from New York State, the new Jewish Theological Seminary of America was incorporated in October 1901 and reopened in September 1902.

Schechter had been born in Romania and was a child prodigy in Talmudic scholarship. He had been brought to London by Claude Montefiore as his Hebrew tutor and had gone on to lecture at Cambridge. Montefiore was related to Sir Moses Montefiore, the undisputed leader of British Jewry in his time. Schechter was responsible for the contents of the Cairo Genizah being removed to the university.

This was a room at the Ben Ezra synagogue in Old Cairo that could be entered only through an opening high up a wall. Through that opening were thrown hundreds of thousands of papers, which are still being studied at Cambridge and elsewhere. This vast repository of material in Hebrew could not be thrown away because Jewish texts are considered sacred. Thus Schechter ensured the survival of a mass of medieval literature that might otherwise have been lost, and brought it to Britain.

Theologically, Schechter believed it essential to bind the different strands of Judaism into one whole. If that meant compromise, he felt it was worth it to keep Judaism alive and well in the twentieth century; he would find, however, that the Orthodox were not prepared to compromise, even if the majority of American Jews would accept the concept.

Schechter believed that the Halacha was formed and had evolved on the basis of the behaviour of the people. This idea that the law evolved, based on national consensus, is not traditional and, eventually, Schechter and the more Orthodox parties parted company. Hertz, however, saw Schechter as far more Orthodox than he was painted. He described his approach as: 'to assert and establish loyalty to the Torah, to foster Jewish religious life in the home; and to maintain the traditional character of our Liturgy, with Hebrew as the language of prayer.'[17] In that approach the two men were aligned.

Hertz's position throughout his life was crystal clear: 'Judaism stands or falls with its belief in the historical actuality of the Revelation at Sinai'.[18] He was a Sinaist; he believed the Almighty gave the Torah to Moses on the mountain and that it was immutable. While this view would be questioned in future at the Jewish Theological Seminary, the institution was still Orthodox enough in 1913 for Hertz to accept an invitation to deliver the invocation at the founding meeting of the United Synagogue of America, which was Schechter's brainchild.

When Hertz graduated from the JTS he needed to find a community. This was not easy because the philosophy of the Seminary did not fit in with that of most established American congregations. To begin with, the JTS was diametrically opposed to the Reform position, which was why Rabbi Morais had set it up in the first place. On the other hand, its philosophy was not considered Orthodox enough for the substantial number of immigrants who wanted to follow the rules of the congregations they had left behind in Eastern Europe.

That left only a few communities which fitted the 1894 JTS outlook. One of these was the Adath Yeshurun congregation in Syracuse in New York State, which in 1893 was looking for a teacher and lecturer who could speak good English. Hertz had given sermons at the synagogue before he graduated. Morais believed that his students should have opportunities to hone their skills in the pulpit and Hertz had given his first sermon at the Sephardi synagogue in Philadelphia, Morais' old congregation, in 1890 when he was only 18 years old.[19] He was now the successful applicant for the Syracuse vacancy and it was there, on 5 June 1894, that he was inducted into his first pulpit. He was just 21 years old.

When Hertz accepted the Syracuse pulpit the congregation believed in the Written and Oral law, but were prepared to take advantage of the fruits of modern learning. Initially their views suited Hertz very well. He settled down and even took a course in Arabic at Syracuse University. In 1896 he started the first Zionist Society in the community. In 1898 he had the congregation become a founding member of the Orthodox Jewish Congregational Union, which included fifty of the more traditional synagogues, all of whom were satisfied to take on board modern scientific discoveries. There were thirteen executive committee members, of whom Hertz became one.

Hertz would speak at the Young Israel movement Sabbath services and he lectured on Friday nights in English, and on Saturday mornings in Yiddish, appealing to the two different audiences. He also served on the Advisory Board of Ministers at the JTS. As a result he became very popular: 'Dr Hertz, while in Syracuse, has won the esteem of all classes, non-Jew, Reformers and Russian Orthodox alike.'[20]

At the end of 1897, however, Adath Yeshurun decided to make a major change in its practices: it agreed to have mixed seating rather than separate male and female areas.

This created a serious dilemma for Hertz. The innovation was contrary to Orthodox law and, after much heart searching, Hertz decided that he could not remain the synagogue minister if this was to be their approach. In the years that followed, the Syracuse community also started to read major prayers in English rather than Hebrew, and even introduced an organ. Hertz would never have agreed to these changes either. By April 1898 he had resigned and answered an advertisement for a vacancy at the Witwatersrand Old Hebrew Congregation in Johannesburg in South Africa.

One of those referees he chose to provide him with a reference, wrote 'with his conservatism, there is little prospect for advancement under the conditions prevailing in this country'.[21] Hermann Adler, the British Chief Rabbi, who found most of the South African rabbis for the communities, was very supportive: 'I was pleased to hear ... that you are a zealous and devoted adherent of Orthodox Judaism'.[22] Over the next ten years, Hertz's experiences in South Africa would be crucial for his development as a minister and laid the foundations for the methods he would adopt throughout his rabbinic career.

Hertz considered that his teachers 'steeled me against the scorn and opposition that dog the steps of him who is determined to be an *unhesitating* witness of the Torah'.[23] He said this in 1933 when he was celebrating twenty years as Chief Rabbi in Britain, so clearly he didn't change his central beliefs during his lifetime.

NOTES

1. Dr Jeremy Schonfield private family archive.
2. Ibid.
3. Obituary, *Jewish Chronicle*, 28 March 1913.
4. Ibid.
5. Joseph Herman Hertz, *Sermons, Addresses and Studies*, Vol.1 (London: The Soncino Press, 1938), p.18.
6. Aubrey Newman, *Lecture on the Centenary of the Birth of Joseph Hertz* (London: United Synagogue, 1972), p.2.
7. Letter from Martineau to Hertz, Jeremy Schonfield private family archive.
8. Bernard Drachman, *The Unfailing Light. Memoirs of an American Rabbi* (New York: The Rabbinical Council of America, 1948), p.181.
9. Hertz, *Sermons, Addresses and Studies*, Vol.3, p.361.
10. Drachman, *The Unfailing Light*, p.181.
11. Hertz, *Sermons, Addresses and Studies*, Vol.3, p.361.
12. Cyrus Adler (ed.), *The Jewish Theological Seminary of America* (New York: Jewish Theological Seminary of America, 1939), p.43.
13. Hertz, *Sermons, Addresses and Studies*, Vol.3, p.368.
14. Ibid., Vol.1. p.19.
15. Revd Ephraim Levine in Isidore Epstein (ed.), *Joseph Herman Hertz: In Memoriam* (London: Soncino Press, 1947), p.24.
16. Ibid.
17. Hertz, *Sermons, Addresses and Studies*, Vol.1, p.88.
18. Joseph Herman Hertz, *Pentateuch & Haftorahs* (Hindhead: Soncino Press, 1960), p.402.
19. Hertz, *Sermons, Addresses and Studies*, Vol.1, p.310.
20. Editorial, *Jewish Chronicle*, 26 August 1898.
21. Benjamin J. Elton, *Britain's Chief Rabbis and Religious Character of Anglo-Jewry, 1880–1970* (Manchester: Manchester University Press, 2009), p.201.
22. Hertz, *Sermons, Addresses and Studies*, Vol.1, p.19.
23. Ibid., p.201.

Chaper Two

The Witwatersrand Old Hebrew Congregation

Hertz stayed in South Africa until 1909 when he was 36. When he arrived in 1898 he soon discovered that Johannesburg was more like the Wild West than New York. It had been barren land until gold was discovered, and had only been proclaimed a town in 1886. From the outset it had attracted Jews, though the initial president of the first congregation said that it was hardly possible to find three very religious Jews among the community.

South Africa as a whole was still a pioneer country. It was divided into four main provinces: Cape Province and Natal were run by the British and the Transvaal and the Orange Free State were independent republics. The Transvaal was the creation of the Boers in South Africa, who had left the Cape Province in the 1830s and 1840 to try to find more productive agricultural land, and more independence from the British in Southern Africa. The Boers were originally Dutch, but the country had been conquered by the British in 1806, which was confirmed by the Treaty of Vienna in 1815. Jews had arrived in the Cape Province in the first half of the century and their first minister was Revd Joel Rabinowitz who served the Cape Town community from as early as 1859 to 1882.

All the ministers of the Cape Town community, Tikvath Israel, came from England, usually on the recommendation of the British Chief Rabbi, acting in consultation with a lay committee. They were perfectly acceptable scholars; Alfred Bender for instance, who served in Cape Town for many years, was a Cambridge graduate, but English-born Jews in Victorian times were not encouraged to get *semicha* and the title of Rabbi was seldom earned.

Bender was the son of a Dublin rabbi and had served at the Upper Berkeley Street synagogue in London. This had split from the Orthodox camp in the mid-nineteenth century, but Bender still had no difficulty in being accepted by the Orthodox Cape Town community's main synagogue when he applied to join them. Their services, though, were the same as the Orthodox Great Synagogue in London rather than Upper Berkeley Street. Bender might have been nicknamed 'the priest' by the more observant local immigrant community from Eastern Europe, but he was very highly regarded and his sermons were even printed in local newspapers.

Bender introduced batmitzvahs, confirmations for girls, and he was awarded a Chair at the South Africa College which later became the University of Cape Town. He did nothing, however, to encourage the study of Hebrew at the university and most of the Jewish students read Engineering or Law. Bender did not seek to be Chief Rabbi of South Africa, and the Jews throughout the country chose to look to the Chief Rabbi in London for their ultimate religious guidance.

There was normally little cooperation at the time between the Jewish communities in Johannesburg and Cape Town. Bender would serve in Cape Town for forty-two years until he died in 1937. Being a rabbi in South Africa in those days was an arduous occupation. Often the ministers would have to travel hundreds of miles to remote communities to perform a *brit* (circumcision), or conduct a barmitzvah. It was very much a labour of love.

Gold was discovered on the Witwatersrand in 1885, and by 1887 there were estimated to be 100 Jews in Johannesburg. A year later there were 500, and when Hertz was appointed, between 10,000 and 12,000.[1] They made up about 10 per cent of the population of the town. Between 1881 and 1910 40,000 Jews came to South Africa from Eastern Europe.

The community had been started effectively by Joel Rabinowitz. After Cape Town he qualified as an assayer and came to Johannesburg, where he agreed to try to find the money to build a new synagogue. He raised £700 very quickly and was proposed as the temporary minister in 1888. As would happen, however, with other rabbis many times in the future, he fell out with the lay leaders; on this occasion over pay and conditions. The result was a breakaway movement which was called the Witwatersrand United Hebrew Congregation, but within a couple of years Rabinowitz was back in Cape Town.

After another breakaway in 1891, the Johannesburg Hebrew Congregation was formed. This time the split occurred because the original Witwatersrand United Hebrew Congregation had employed a minister, Revd Mark Harris, whose views tended toward Reform. The Johannesburg Hebrew Congregation membership was primarily from very observant Lithuanian and Russian communities and, as was the case in London at the time, the new immigrants tended to look down on the standards of Orthodoxy of the original English members of the congregation. Anything associated with Reform was anathema to the newcomers. Their new synagogue was opened in 1892 by President Kruger, though it was regretted that he refused to cover his head during the service.

Harris' religious tendencies came under fire as the years went by, and in March 1898 he resigned from what was now called the Witwatersrand Old Hebrew Congregation. When it was agreed that Harris should leave, he promised not to start another congregation but broke his word. Instead he helped to found the Rand Modern Hebrew Congregation, which catered for those with a similar outlook to his own.

When Harris left, the Witwatersrand synagogue advertised in the *Jewish Chronicle*[2] in London and in the *American Hebrew*[3] for a replacement. They offered a salary of £750 a year (the equivalent of £65,000 today) plus a free house and £1,000 of life insurance. They wanted a rabbi with *semicha* and a university education, who was also a *mohel* (capable of circumcising male babies), under 45, married and, preferably, with some American experience. To lay all their cards on the table, they felt it necessary to point out that they did have a mixed choir, which it was considered Jewish law did not permit.

The Witwatersrand community would, of course, have found it hard to find a rabbi with *semicha* in Britain. The British Chief Rabbinate reserved the title of 'Rabbi' for themselves. Equally a rabbi would be unlikely to come forward from the British Empire and, while there were any number in Europe, they were not going to be English and the English language would be foreign to them. An American rabbi might overcome both difficulties.

When Nathan Marcus Adler from Hanover was appointed British Chief Rabbi in 1844, one of the conditions was that he would learn to speak English in a year, which he did. In America the South African synagogue set up a committee in New York to try to find a suitable candidate. It consisted of both an Orthodox and a Reform rabbi, the president of the B'nai B'rith charitable organization, an editor of a Jewish paper and a famous lawyer.

There were quite a number of applicants but the committee recommended Hertz, even though, at the outset, he appeared to be far too young. He also wasn't married although he had the other qualifications. With the High Holydays on the horizon, he was informed on 11 August 1898 that he had been selected and hurried to sail for Southampton on 13 August. On the eve of Rosh Hashanah he arrived in Johannesburg.

If the streets of New York were not paved with gold, neither were they in the heart of South Africa's mining industry. In fact, Hertz found even the creature comforts were largely missing. The more fortunate inhabitants in the early days had lived in thatched mud huts, though there were some wood and iron buildings. If the walls were brick lined, it was a sign of opulence.

Jews shared with others the discomforts of pioneering life and the mining-camp atmosphere. Hotel accommodation was scarce and expensive. The housing shortage was acute. Men remembered sleeping for months on the counters of their shops, before they managed to acquire better quarters.[4]

Ten years later, things had improved to some extent but Hertz, writing to friends in America in October 1899, was still uncertain what he had taken on:

> I seem to be having it all my own way out here, you say. Well, up to a certain point that is true. Transvaal is but another name for opportunity, and the fact is, more opportunities for doing something have presented themselves to me during the last 12 months than would have been the case during as many years in America ... however there are two circumstances which well-nigh neutralise the advantage of my position, as well as the advances I have made during the last year: First, the uncertainty of Transvaal life. Everything is in flux. Now this uncertainty pervades every department of life. For example, I cannot for the life of me tell whether the next year will see me unanimously elected Chief Rabbi of the Federated Jewish Congregations of the Transvaal (and ultimately of South Africa) or whether a year from today I may not begin to see that there is absolutely no scope for me on the subcontinent as a rabbi. The people of Johannesburg are young, given to inordinately admiring a thing today only to throw it aside as a stale toy on the morrow. The great current of life, of work, of activity is forever tearing you along ... The climate is an enervating one; its unspeakable beauties even, because so changeless, pall; it is without even mild winters, with their invigorating cold. More than once I have blamed the sun for my troubles, and may one fine day succeed in convincing myself that this climate was never intended for white men.[5]

What Hertz could understand was the large number of immigrants from Eastern Europe in Johannesburg. Here were the same people he had known in New York: impoverished, Yiddish speaking and trying to scratch a living in a totally foreign environment. They were cordially disliked by the other sections of the general community where, among other objections, it was feared that their perceived standards of cleanliness would be likely to trigger an epidemic of one kind or another.

Hertz knew the reality of the situation. The immigrant's week centred on the Sabbath, where their rags would be set aside, they would smarten themselves up in their Shabbat finery and arrive in synagogue almost indistinguishable from their more prosperous brethren. They were equally patronized, however, by the more affluent section of their own community, who felt they brought them into disrepute by association.

The bad publicity the 'Peruvians', as they were called, attracted was made worse by the illegal trade in drink in which they were supposed to be deeply involved. Like any other community, the Jews did have their black sheep and Hertz would set out to make the true facts clear to the general public in the years to come, and to attack the miscreants within the Jewish community. His latter efforts would make him another set of enemies; but then Hertz never sought cheap popularity.

He arrived in time for the Witwatersrand Old Hebrew Congregation's tenth anniversary. He was installed on 21 September 1898 four days before his 26th birthday. In his inaugural sermon Hertz made his own position very clear: 'He would preach no easy Judaism, no fashionable Judaism, but the Judaism which demanded of every true child of Israel unconditional obedience to the law given by Moses as an eternal inheritance ... our motto shall be the Torah and nothing but the Torah.'[6]

That was what he had been taught at the Jewish Theological Seminary and that was what he stood for: unconditional obedience to the law given to Moses. The sermon went down very well, as did almost all the addresses Hertz gave during his lifetime. He was an inspiring speaker, but he did not set out to entertain the audience from the pulpit. His great friend, Ephraim Levine, a very fine preacher in his own right, wrote a memorial essay after Hertz died. He said: 'yet one often misses the human touch, and the emotional appeal and the homely atmosphere'.[7] As Hertz was always battling in the Morais way, he would give fighting sermons against prejudice, backsliding, Progressives, immorality and oppression: 'We shall not imitate those of our brethren who "choose their path" and, as a consequence, even in prayer, separate themselves from the community and thus divide the House of Israel against itself.'[8]

A homely atmosphere and a spirit of compromise were unlikely to be part of the message when Hertz was on his feet. His preaching almost immediately drew large audiences: The *Jewish Chronicle* correspondent reported that Hertz was the most talked about man in Johannesburg, and that he had only been able to get a seat to listen to one of Hertz's sermons after he had tried four times. The audience was even standing in the aisles and doorways.[9]

If there was to be competition for who would be the most notable spiritual leader in Johannesburg, the alternative choice was David Wasserzug of the Johannesburg Hebrew Congregation. Wasserzug was not in Hertz's forceful and combative league, but neither did he want to be. He had gone to Jews' College in London in 1877 and had stayed until 1891, collecting a BA from London University and a great deal of Talmudic knowledge. He did not receive a *semicha*, though, and after a period as the minister in Cardiff, he accepted a call to Port Elizabeth and went on from there to the Johannesburg Hebrew Congregation.

Wasserzug was reserved, modest and scholarly. He quietly went about his work, helping to educate the children and improve his congregation. He was a good speaker, if not a rousing orator in the Hertz mould. Within a comparatively short time after his arrival in Johannesburg, Hertz would be labelled 'The Fighting Parson' by the press, an appellation which Wasserzug would not have enjoyed.

As there was no reason to dislike Hertz, who had only just arrived, the fact that Wasserzug, the other Orthodox minister in the town and the Reform minister from the Rand Modern Hebrew Congregation did not attend his installation illustrates the highly competitive nature of the Johannesburg communities. The Reform community disintegrated shortly afterwards.

This competition among the Johannesburg congregations was never really resolved in Hertz's years in the country. They remained split by internal politics, different national origins and the minutiae of different *minhagim* (customs). Apart from the absence of the ministers, though, the congregation who witnessed the ceremony was packed full of Johannesburg notables, both Jewish and non-Jewish. The British Consul came to the inauguration, as well as representatives of the Wesleyan, Dutch Reformed and Congregational churches.

Hertz soon found that the Boer government in the Transvaal – which included Johannesburg – was at loggerheads with the British high commissioner in Cape Town. The Dutch Protestant Boers were naturally anxious to maintain their own culture. They had won their independence at great personal cost many years before and they wanted to keep it. So they had instituted a policy of restricting the offices of state to their own people.

The non-Dutch Uitlanders, literally foreigners, who could be Catholics, Jews or any non-Boer, were discriminated against in other ways as well. They weren't persecuted, and indeed the Boers had a very high regard for Jews, because they both revered the Bible and the Jews were seen as the people of the Bible. In Johannesburg in 1887 the Boers had provided land for a cemetery and for a synagogue in 1888. Nevertheless, Hertz found himself at the outset of his ministry in the middle of a major row between the Boer government and the Uitlanders about abolishing the disabilities affecting them.

At the time legislation barred Uitlanders from military posts and they couldn't officially be appointed president or state secretary or serve as a magistrate. They couldn't be elected to the parliament, the Volksraad, and they were not allowed to supervise natives or mines. Russians and Romanian immigrants couldn't vote and Jews and Catholics couldn't teach in state-subsidized schools.

In practice, however, though the offices of state were officially barred to Jews, there were too few people available who could serve the state effectively, and consequently the regulations were often ignored. As Kruger would tell Hertz: 'If you are an honest and able public servant, I shall never ask you what your religious views are'.[10]

Most of the Jews were far too busy trying to make a living or looking for gold to bother about the restrictions. The leaders of the community, however, thought them unfair. They had lobbied the government on many occasions to change the enfranchisement rules, but they had been put off time and again. They would continue to lobby amid obstruction and indifference.

It might have been expected that Hertz would take time to settle down and get to know the territory before deciding his approach to the local problems. This was, however, never to be Hertz's way. Almost immediately he called a meeting to protest at the government's regulations. Then, in November 1898, just two months after he had been installed, Hertz was invited to speak at a meeting to mark the tenth anniversary of the founding of Johannesburg. He had every excuse to be bland and non-controversial. He could have explained that he was new to the country, was more than happy to defer to his elders and betters, didn't want to rock any boats and wanted to learn more before committing himself.

Again, this simply wasn't his approach. As he would show fifteen years later in London, soon after he became Chief Rabbi, he preferred to take his place on the community's bridge at the first opportunity. He attacked the disabilities and at another mass meeting in June 1899 he called his address 'The Jew as a patriot – a plea for the removal of the civil disabilities of the Jews in the Transvaal.' In particular he was concerned about the denial of naturalization to Jews born in Russia and Romania. He said:

> I know that this law is practically a dead letter. And I would much rather live in Johannesburg or Pretoria where I am subjected to a great many disabilities on paper, than live in Paris or Vienna, where a Jew enjoys all the rights, privileges, and prerogatives of his fellow citizens – on paper. All honour to the sect that's better than its creed and all honour to the nation that is better than its constitution.[11]

But, he went on: 'In a free state, it is not the Christian that rules the Jew, neither is it the Jew that rules the Christian. It is justice that rules ... we want no liberties. We want liberty.'

It was Hertz's view that: 'Because Russia had robbed Jews of the rights of man and had hounded the Jew from abject misery to serfdom, it was no reason why a state which called itself civilized should follow such an inhuman example.'[12]

> Let President Kruger demand of the Catholic burgher, of the Jewish burgher, everything he has a right to demand of his other burghers. We would willingly give all, all. Willingly, joyfully, would we sacrifice everything with the exception of our faith, our principles, our truth and our honour ... Let us unanimously this night record our conviction that the Republic will only become a Republic when it places all denominations on a footing of equality.[13]

It was clear that Hertz was already a powerful speaker and was showing a considerable reluctance to keep his head down and let the laymen lead in his stead.

As early as December 1898, Hertz had been invited to preach in Pretoria and was granted an interview afterwards by Kruger which lasted for two hours. Hertz wanted to protest about the restrictions. The 63-year-old Kruger told the 26-year-old Hertz that there were three reasons why the disabilities could not be altered: 'Jews were not patriots; they could not be soldiers; and they were cowards.'[14] In the war that was coming, the president would be proved wrong on all three counts. In all, some 2,800 South African Jews fought for the British in the Boer War and 150 were killed. Many others were loyal to the Boer government and fought on the Boer side.

Hertz considered that he was received by the president with courtesy, but felt that nothing had been achieved. This wasn't entirely true because, within forty-eight hours, Kruger decided to try to introduce a greater degree of tolerance. But in this he was unsuccessful, as the Volksraad, the parliament, voted against his proposals.

Kruger did not deal gently with protesters. With justification he had initially dealt harshly with opponents of all kinds after the abortive Jameson Raid from 29 December 1895 to 2 January 1896, which had been organized by the mining interests as a coup d'état to overthrow the Boer government. The raid was a disastrous flop and, in 1896, no fewer than sixty-four reformers had been imprisoned, including seven Jews. One prominent Jewish mining engineer, Lionel Phillips, had even been sentenced to death, but was released after six months.

The whole subject of reform was highly contentious. The problem for the Boers was that they had carved the country out of the wilderness after great efforts, which involved heavy sacrifices in men and possessions. The native Zulus had not welcomed the invaders. Now the Boers were in danger of being outnumbered by foreign immigrants. They felt that if they treated the Uitlanders equally, they would lose power because they were, as early as 1895, the smaller section of the population by a ratio of 4:7.

Hertz had internal problems too. He was immediately attacked by his own Honorary Officers for leading the delegation to Kruger. They also objected to the singing of *God Save the Queen* at an earlier protest meeting and said that a rabbi shouldn't be involved in political matters. It was not the most auspicious beginning to his ministry, but his actions did make it very clear that Hertz had no intention of being a minor cog in the system and did not see himself as a deferential employee. One of his critics had written to the *Jewish Chronicle* in London:

> The only jarring note in the whole political concert, as far as the Jews were concerned, was the appearance of the Rev. Dr J.H. Hertz at a large meeting of Uitlanders. When I tell you that the meeting concluded by singing God Save the Queen and Rule Britannia, and this in a foreign state, you will agree with me that such a gathering was not the place for a rabbi. Although I am a British citizen, I consider it very bad taste, to use a mild expression, to force our National Anthem down the throats of foreigners and I strongly disapprove of a rabbi speaking at gatherings of the kind mentioned.[15]

For those Honorary Officers of the United Synagogue who would clash with Hertz in Britain in the years to come, a study of the letter he sent in reply to the *Jewish Chronicle*, dated 11 January 1900, might well have been worth remembering.[16]

First, they would have been forewarned that Hertz didn't mince his words. 'I am, by this time, accustomed to vile attacks by the Pretoria gang' he said of the government. Second, they would have known his views on the role of Honorary Officers: 'The President and Committee [of the synagogue] are commercial managers and not keepers of my conscience.'[17]

Third, they would have understood his views on the involvement of rabbis in political matters: 'By education, by training, by attainments, by post and by position, I am entitled to lead my community and constitute myself as the court of last appeal as to whether a certain course of mine be right or wrong.'[18] Hertz did feel he was qualified to be both judge and jury.

Many years later, when other United Synagogue critics of Hertz found they had underestimated their man, they should have equally regretted failing to take note of another point he made in 1900. Hertz wrote: 'These gentlemen all start with the assumption that of the entire community, the Rabbi alone has no conscience ... he, unguided, is always wrong; they, purse-proud, respectable (or disreputable) nonentities are always right.'[19]

Hertz went on to point out that he had attended a meeting of Americans in Johannesburg and nobody had commented when they sang *The Star Spangled Banner*. The writer of the original letter to the *Jewish Chronicle* complained that Hertz's contribution made the negotiations of the Jewish community with the Boers more difficult. Hertz replied that they had got nothing from past negotiations and that, after his own speech, President Kruger had at least tried to have religious emancipation introduced by the parliament. Moreover, the government had proposed dropping the exclusion clause which prevented Russian Jews from voting.

When Hertz was attacked, he always fought back vigorously and woe betide the critic who had not done his homework thoroughly before getting to his feet. Hertz would set out to destroy alternative arguments with credible facts. If his pronouncements did not always measure up to this criteria, they would still be delivered with skill and passion. As he said himself in later years 'the usual epithet flung at me is "bigot" which is rather feeble. The late Dr Deutsch ... as far back as 1911 spoke of me as "Torquemada"'.[20]

On the subject of whether a rabbi should allow himself to become involved in politics, Hertz had the example of one of his mentors, Rabbi Dr Benjamin Szold, back in the United States, who had worked hard for the freeing of American slaves. Hertz made his own position very clear in the letter: 'For my part I have all along consistently and conscientiously acted counter to this fundamental tenet of English Judaism.'[21] He had every intention of interfering in politics if he felt he should. Ten years later, nobody would have remembered his comments but they were still very pertinent. If Hertz held those views when he was 28 years old, it was unlikely that further promotion, experience and maturity would lead him to change them.

Throughout his South African ministry, Hertz was learning about English Jews. He recognized that in their energy, public spirit and administrative matters they formed the backbone of the various Johannesburg congregations, even if they were outnumbered by migrants from Russia, Lithuania or Germany.

The British government's position in their discussions with the Boers was that they could not allow total equality in the British controlled part of the country, and simultaneously submit to British immigrants not being given the same privileges in the Transvaal. So in May 1897, just a year before the arrival of Hertz, they had appointed a new high commissioner, Sir Alfred Milner. It was he who opened negotiations with Kruger to have the enfranchisement rules changed.

During 1899 the British government continued to insist on their suzerainty over the Transvaal and, in September, it was decided to increase the military strength in Natal. There was, however, no movement or compromise on either side and war was declared in October 1899. Those who had shown themselves opposed to the Boer government were, of course, immediately highly suspect. Four days before the war broke out, Hertz wrote to his friend, Henrietta Szold, Benjamin Szold's daughter, in America: 'Naturally the city is depopulated, given over to silence, solitude and starvation. As for myself, I am tolerably safe; with an American flag flying over my house, an American passport in my vest pocket, a pistol in my trouser pocket ... I have furthermore provisions enough stored in my house to last a company of five for nearly six months.'[22]

Henrietta Szold would go on to found Hadassah, the Women's Zionist organization in America, and become the head of Youth Aliyah when Hitler came to power, an organization whose objective was to encourage young people to emigrate to Palestine.

When the war started, about 10,000 of the 12,000 Jews in Boer areas fled by train out of the Transvaal and down to Cape Town. Hertz didn't want to desert his new congregation in Johannesburg and, as he was an American citizen, his case had to be handled by the Boer government with circumspection. Feelings naturally ran high: 'Commandant Schutte, the military commander of Johannesburg, informed me, in his private capacity, that he would not be held responsible for my safety, or even my life.'[23]

As early as 11 December 1899 Kruger resolved to take action. He declared Hertz an enemy of the state and said that he could either withdraw his complaints about discrimination or leave the country within forty-eight hours.

For Hertz the logical decision was clear. As he told the *Jewish Chronicle*: 'chaperoned by the Acting Public Prosecutor of the Witwatersrand Goldfields, and armed with a free first class railway ticket issued by the government, I reached Lourenço Marques',[24] a Portuguese colony. The Acting Public Prosecutor would become a good friend in future years: General Jan Smuts.

First class ticket or not, the train consisted only of cattle trucks. By coincidence, another passenger on the train was Winston Churchill. When Hertz finally became Chief Rabbi in London, Churchill would be a key figure until he fell out of favour in the 1930s, and Hertz's early contact with him would have been an advantage. They were met at Lourenço Marques by Samson Marks, the Reuters representative, who had been told to look after them. There would be plenty of publicity.

Hertz only stayed a week in Lourenço Marques:

> Here I found Jewish conditions bad enough, but was not disappointed. As only one or two Jewish people have their families living with them, there is neither shochet, congregation nor Beit Chayim [cemetery] in Lourenço Marques. My astonishment, on the contrary, was great when I found a prominent businessman a Shabbat observer, and another, a subscriber to the Jewish Quarterly Review.[25]

In the time at his disposal he used the local press to call a meeting:

> The attendance was good, and the thermometer not very much above 95 degrees. I impressed upon them the necessity of doing three things. First, immediately to elect a committee to interview the Governor General of the province for the purpose of receiving a grant of land for a cemetery; that this committee have power to add to its number and as soon as possible constitute itself into a congregation.[26]

His last recommendation was to go to work to protect Jewish women and girls, which was: 'rendered necessary by the fact that of late the term "Jewess" has become a byword and a hissing on the East Coast of Africa ... the phrase "the immemorial chastity of the Jewess" is something less than a name, and more even than a mockery'.

Hertz was well under 30 and giving out instructions like a commanding general. He also took the opportunity to divide the synagogue services into six parts, so that some could be according to the Sephardi format and some like the Ashkenazi, 'so as to suit the two jealous wrangling parties'.[27] His expertise at finding diplomatic solutions, though, was applied only where halakhically possible, and this would remain a constant in the years to come. What was striking was his readiness to take the lead and hand down judgements where he really had no authority to do so. What carried him through was the power of his leadership and the brilliance of his oratory.

He then travelled to Durban in Natal and 'it was only on the boat that I began to feel the "bitterness of exile" and the full significance of the term, "Rand Refugee"'.[28] On reaching Durban, together with Churchill, he found the Jewish Relief Committee doing excellent work: 'in aid of all Jewish persons in distress' and he went to work to help them.

Durban was in that part of South Africa still run by the British and, as such, it attracted many refugees from the Boer territory. Most of the refugees were destitute and living in tents. One joked that he had never previously lived in a *sukkah* (the temporary shelter built for the festival of Succot), as laid down in the *din*, but now he was. Hertz moved on 1,000 miles to Cape Town, the capital of Cape Province, where the produce market down by the docks had been converted into a refugee camp. There had only been 500 Jews in Cape Town in 1875 but the numbers had increased to 4,000 before the war and had now been swollen by the newcomers to 10,000 in all.

The refugees were given 5p a day from the charity funds if they were desperate and an extra 2½p for kosher meat. Hertz arranged a synagogue service under his auspices, though as he had no official position, this may not have gone down well with some of the Cape Town ministers. His mastery of Yiddish would probably have been greater than Alfred Bender's, endearing the newcomer more to the immigrant section of the community.

Back in Johannesburg, David Wasserzug continued to minister to the remnants of the community that hadn't fled. Although he was British, he refused to leave the town and went on conducting services three times a day. The Witwatersrand Old Hebrew Congregation closed for a few months without Hertz, but reopened after Purim 1900. The Chevra Kadishah, responsible for preparing the Jewish dead for burial, now took on the additional responsibility of providing the ambulance corps for Johannesburg. The diminished community raised over £1,200 to help the Jewish poor, and came to services, even if they needed to carry pistols as well as *talitot* (prayer shawls). Shops and houses had to be barricaded, though, and business dropped to practically nothing.

Meanwhile Hertz maintained a high profile in Cape Province. He was also invited to speak at a meeting in the Durban Town Hall in January 1900. His subject was the fight for Catholic and Jewish emancipation in the Transvaal and the Mayor took the chair. It was the first Jewish lecture to the citizens of Natal. He also kept in touch with the community in Johannesburg, writing to the *Jewish Chronicle* in February to praise the Chevra Kadishah for operating the ambulance service in the city.[29]

The Boer War was short but vicious. The Boers never had a chance because Lord Roberts, the British commander, would have an army of 500,000 and the Boers had 88,000. Admittedly, the ability of the Boer snipers to cut down the redcoats led to the introduction of khaki uniforms for the first time, but British reinforcements were obtainable without too much difficulty.

The Boers had attacked first and had a number of initial successes. They knew the country and, as farmers, were good shots. They were, however, not professional soldiers and were outgunned and outnumbered. Field Marshall Roberts occupied Bloemfontein in February and entered Johannesburg at the end of May. This was not, however, the end of the war, as the Boers carried on with guerrilla operations until 1902. For their part the British burnt and laid to waste Boer farms to prevent supplies getting to their army in the field.

They also deprived the Boers of the infrastructure they needed to fight the war. Small towns lost their shops and supplies, and camps were created to house Boer families compulsorily, called Concentration Camps. Within these large numbers died from disease, including many women and children. The countryside and the economy were ruined and, after the war, there were lengthy periods of economic depression. Only gradually were the refugees in the Cape Province allowed to return to their homes, after they had been subject to security checks.

When Roberts took Johannesburg, Hertz went back to his shattered community. He had taken the opportunity to visit the family in America in the early spring and went via London where he gave an interview to the *Jewish Chronicle*.[30]

The main topics discussed were not of a religious nature, although the reporter noted that 'he has always displayed an aggressive orthodoxy'. The newspaper was, primarily, interested in whether it was true that the South African Jewish financiers had caused the Boer War, as they were being accused of doing in some quarters. Hertz named a large number of South African financiers who were not Jewish and pointed out that many who were born Jewish had converted to Roman Catholicism.

He had a weaker case when the subject of the illicit liquor trade was raised. He admitted that considerable numbers of Jews were involved, but said they were unduly prominent because the government detectives concentrated on them. This was because other nationalities would 'use a stiletto' in retaliation and were not prepared to bribe the police to drop the charges. Hertz said the Jews were not violent, and as they had often been prepared to pay off the detectives, had become the favoured target.

When he was in America, Hertz recognized the strength of pro-Boer sentiment. He nevertheless publicly denounced the Boer government as a corrupt oligarchy and said there was no religious liberty in South Africa. This was an exaggeration, but when an American rabbi reported that in New York, it certainly helped the British cause.

In spite of the war he was chosen to be one of the South African delegates to the Fourth Zionist Congress in London in August 1900. His credentials included an essay which appeared in a synagogue magazine written in Syracuse in 1897 which he had called 'After the Congress – a résumé and a retrospect'. Hertz would remain an enthusiastic Zionist all his life and a powerful member of the Mizrachi, the religious Zionists.

Another international figure, who agreed to represent the South African Zionists, was Haham (Sephardi Chief Rabbi) Moses Gaster, one of the few British Jewish leaders prepared to support Theodor Herzl, and this would have been the first time that he and Hertz had met. After the war ended, Hertz reported on the congress at the Annual General Meeting (AGM) of the South African Zionists in July 1901.

Johannesburg was then still under martial law and special permission had to be granted for the assembly. The *Jewish Chronicle* reported that Hertz 'held the audience spellbound' and 'ended to great applause with a touching appeal for help and assistance' for East European Jews.[31] Milner arranged for Jews to receive permits to attend synagogue and Jewish soldiers in the army were given leave to go to synagogue on the High Holydays.

The Zionist programme was not without its critics. 'Some questions aroused the wrath and indignation of Dr Hertz and for some ten minutes the proceedings were decidedly unpleasant and undignified.'[32] Indeed 'the result was a scene of tremendous confusion and uproar', though it ended with votes of confidence in Hertz and his colleagues being passed nem con. By now he had been in South Africa for less than three years. He was still under 30 years old but he was already a prominent and contentious public figure.

It was also in July 1901 that David Wasserzug decided that he'd had enough and would go home. He had indeed more than done his duty to his community during the war, but the country was still in a sorry state and the peace and quiet of a London community was sufficient to draw him away from South Africa. Replete with handsome cheques from a rightly grateful congregation, he left to become the minister at the Dalston synagogue in London where he became equally highly regarded until his death in 1918.

Queen Victoria passed away in 1901 and the new heir apparent, later George V, made a wide-ranging tour of the Empire in that year. When he arrived with his wife in Natal, Hertz wrote to Henrietta Szold: 'I presented an address to the Royal Pair in the name of Natal, Orange River Colony and Transvaal Jewries … to your iconoclastically democratic mind it were vain to dwell at length on the various gorgeous functions connected with the visit.'[33]

He was now mixing with royalty. He was impressed too. He said that spending fifteen minutes with the beautiful Princess May, later Queen Mary, 'was almost enough to take the oath of allegiance on the spot … As for myself, I managed to squeeze in a sermon, a Zionist mass meeting, a banquet in my honour, and two other Jewish meetings of some use to Natal Judaism during the busy week'.[34]

Here was a young American rabbi in Alfred Bender's city and the Cape Town minister's reaction was likely to be frosty, though he also would have given an address to the royal visitors on behalf of the Cape Town community. Hertz didn't make enemies just in Cape Town though. When he went back to Johannesburg after the war he was not at all happy about the behaviour of a number of the lay leaders of his congregation.

According to A.H. Jessel KC, the chairman of the selection committee for a new British Chief Rabbi in 1911, Hertz acted with great firmness. Some of the lay leaders were involved in illicit liquor trading, some in illicit diamond buying and some were smugglers. There were even white slavers, involved in prostitution. Hertz told them that if they didn't stop, he would denounce them from the pulpit of the synagogue. Hertz had them all turned out from leading the community. In addition, there were efforts to prevent known Jewish criminals who had fled to Cape Town from being granted permission to return to Johannesburg. Some of those he upset would do their best to get their own back when the campaigning started to replace Chief Rabbi Hermann Adler ten years later.

Hertz's reputation did not suffer when he took on powerful lay leaders: 'His presence in Cape Town at the time was a great help, and his eloquence both in the pulpit and on the platform attracted enthusiastic audiences.'[35]

Hertz was a great Zionist supporter, but Bender was not. He did not attend the Fourth Zionist Congress on behalf of the Cape Town community and, like most English Jews at the time, he saw the concept as far-fetched. The additional downside was the possibility that the Jews' loyalty to Britain would be questioned. While in Cape Town 'Dr Hertz played an outstanding role as an advocate of Zionism'.[36] Bender would become more Zionist as the years went by, but there would still be opposition to choosing him to open a new Zionist hall in 1907.

It would also be Hertz who, in 1902, was invited by its Eastern European community to consecrate the very Orthodox Roeland Street Synagogue in Cape Town. In Hertz the congregation were gaining a man with *semicha* who came originally from Central Europe. Bender was a good scholar but he didn't have *semicha*. The Eastern Europeans chose one of their own, which would not have pleased Bender either.

In 1903 another very able rabbi came to South Africa. Judah Leo Landau (1865–1942) received his *semicha* in Vienna and served as minister of the British community in North Manchester for three years from 1900. He then accepted a call to the Jewish Hebrew Congregation in Johannesburg in 1903. Thereafter, hints of personal rivalries often emerged and of a struggle for power between the two individuals. Both Hertz and Landau had ambitions to be the senior spiritual voice in the Transvaal and, if possible, in South Africa. Beneath the surface there was considerable antagonism.

When there was any question in the future of a Chief Rabbi for South Africa, the Cape Town community would not accept any nominee other than someone from their own city. Bender, their minister, was a man whose efforts for charity were outstanding and whose devotion to his synagogue was unwavering for over forty years. As late as 1928 at the AGM of the Cape Town community: 'Speakers at the meeting protested strongly against what they termed "assumption and continued use" of the title Chief Rabbi, by Dr Judah Leo Landau of Johannesburg. It was stated that the matter is likely to arouse dissension between the two chief communities in South Africa.'[37]

It was a pity that the senior South African rabbis were involved in a power struggle, but there is no doubt that this was the case. They represented their communities and these were split among the originally British, the Germans and the Eastern European immigrants. Landau was a very good influence on South African Jewry for nearly forty years and he worked closely and in harmony with Hertz in many areas, but synagogue politics continued to be a serious obstacle to achieving unity. 'For at least 10 years there had been unfruitful negotiations between the WOHC and the JHC regarding the amalgamation of the two congregations.'[38]

This would happen only after Hertz's departure.

NOTES

1. Gustav Saron and Louis Hotz, *The Jews of South Africa: A History* (London: Oxford University Press, 1955), p.150.
2. *Jewish Chronicle*, 18 March 1898.
3. *American Hebrew*, 17 July 1898. Cutting from the Jeremy Schonfield private family archive.
4. Saron and Hotz, *The Jews of South Africa*, p.151.
5. Alexandra Lee Levin, *Letters from South Africa* (New York: Herzl Press, 2005). Jeremy Schonfield private family archive.
6. 'Jottings from South Africa', *Jewish Chronicle*, 21 October 1898, p.26.
7. See Revd Ephraim Levine in Isidore Epstein (ed.), *Joseph Herman Hertz, In Memoriam* (London: Soncino Press, 1947), p.26.
8. Meir Persoff, *Faith Against Reason: Religious Reform and the British Chief Rabbinate, 1840–1990* (London and Portland, OR: Vallentine Mitchell, 2008), p.162.
9. 'Jottings from South Africa', *Jewish Chronicle*, 28 October 1898.
10. Saron and Hotz, *The Jews of South Africa*, p.199.
11. Ibid., p.186.
12. Ibid., p.199.
13. 'Jottings from South Africa', *Jewish Chronicle*, 18 January 1946, p.20.
14. Joseph Herman Hertz, Letter to Henrietta Szold. Jeremy Schonfield private family archive.
15. *Jewish Chronicle*, 9 February 1900, in Levin, *Letters from South Africa*, p.11.
16. Ibid.
17. Ibid.
18. Ibid.
19. Jeremy Schonfield private family archive.
20. Joseph Herman Hertz, *Affirmations of Judaism* (London: Oxford University Press/ Humphrey Milford, 1927), p.171.
21. Levin, *Letters from South Africa*. Jeremy Schonfield private family archive.
22. *Jewish Chronicle*, 9 February 1900. Levin, *Letters from South Africa*, p.11.
23. Ibid.
24. Ibid.
25. Ibid.
26. Ibid.
27. Letter in Jeremy Schonfield private family archive.
28. Ibid.
29. 'The Zionist Movement', *Jewish Chronicle*, 16 August 1901, p.14.

30. *Jewish Chronicle*, 9 February 1900. Levin, *Letters from South Africa*, p.11.
31. Ibid., p.14.
32. Ibid.
33. Letter to Henrietta Szold. Jeremy Schonfield private family archive.
34. Ibid.
35. Saron and Hotz, *The Jews of South Africa*, p.39.
36. Ibid., p.272.
37. *Jewish Telegraphic Agency*, 18 September 1928.
38. Great Park Synagogue history, http://www.greatpark.co.za./pages/Great%20Park%20 Synagogue%20History.

Chapter Three

The Battle to Live, Breathe and Grow, 1902–12

After the war, from Milner's point of view, the first task was to rebuild the Transvaal, which had suffered greatly in the conflict: As he recalled when he left South Africa in 1905:

> The one thing essential, the one thing imperative, when we took over this country, a total wreck with half its population in exile, with no Administrative machinery whatever, and as far as the plant of government was concerned, with the scantiest equipment of any civilised country in the world, was to make it a going concern as soon as possible.[1]

The situation was indeed grim.

> The destitution among the victims of war, who had lost their farms, their homesteads, their means of livelihood and their anchorage, led to a depression … contemporary records speak of the increased demand upon charity and of the urgent need for communal expansion and reconstruction in every field, social, educational and cultural.[2]

'In the Transvaal and the Orange Free State there was hardly a farmhouse standing and in large areas the livestock had been almost exterminated.'[3]

This was the challenge faced by Milner and, from the high commissioner's point of view, supportive religious leaders like Hertz could be very useful allies. He appointed him to his Consultative Committee in 1901 and would remember his contribution in the future. He further told the Jewish community as a whole that they were welcome to hold public office. A Central Refugee Committee was then set up to deal with applications from the refugees to be allowed to return to Johannesburg, and Hertz spent a lot of time on it. By the end of the war permits for 45,000 had been granted in all.

Hertz realized that one of the criticisms of the Jewish community in South Africa was that most of its members had arrived only in time to take advantage of the mineral wealth of the country. They had not built it up, as had the original settlers. While in general this was true, there were exceptions, and Hertz set out to publicize these early contributions, from whatever source, in the years to come.

At the South African Zionist conference in 1905 he even recalled the Portuguese King Henry the Navigator who, in 1438, had appointed the Jew Jehude Cresques as director of the National Naval Academy. It was their ships which first found and started to colonize the country. The navigator of the convoy was also Jewish.

Another of Milner's objectives was to unite the country. Hertz was sure that this was equally desirable for the Jewish community, but the question was what form this unity should take. He discussed the problem at length with his English lay leader, the property magnate, Max Langerman. They quickly decided that, as they had contacts with the Anglo-Jewish Association (AJA) in London, the simplest answer would be to form a South African branch of that association.

This was agreed with London, but then Hertz had second thoughts. He disliked the fact that the AJA members were not elected, and came to prefer the other Jewish British organization, the Board of Deputies. At a meeting in April 1903 he explained his reasoning, but found himself in the middle of a major row with the Zionists. He was unwilling to give way: 'I, though an ardent Zionist and Vice President of that Federation, could not concede, as there was certainly an important section of Johannesburg Jews who were not, and were not likely to become, Zionists.'[4]

The South African Zionists at the meeting did not want to see another organization of any kind created to represent the South African Jews. They recognized it would reduce their own power and they argued fiercely that no other committee should be formed. Hertz pointed out that what was needed was a body that could represent everybody. Heckling from the floor became louder and louder.

At this point Hertz decided that, as the audience were mostly immigrants, they probably didn't understand the detailed arguments that were being put to them in English. He, therefore, went to the podium and made an impassioned speech in favour of the concept of the Board of Deputies in Yiddish. That swung the mood of the attendees behind him and it was agreed that the Board of Deputies concept would be adopted. Hertz's Yiddish was that fluent and though his future career would be largely spent with the Jewish upper crust leadership in Britain's United Synagogue, his roots in the world of Eastern European Orthodoxy were firmly laid.

Hertz was appointed to the new Board's committee, which was given the responsibility of writing the constitution. The decision did not, however, stop the Zionists from opposing the new body for a long time thereafter. This put Hertz into a quandary. As the vice-president of the Zionist Federation and the future secretary of the Board of Deputies, there was a very definite conflict of interest.

Another meeting was held in July 1903 to take the Board of Deputies concept further and Milner, the high commissioner, was invited to speak. The Zionists asked him not to attend as they didn't want the proponents of a Board of Deputies to receive such illustrious support. Milner, however, was in favour of a Board of Deputies and spoke strongly in support of it to a vast audience, which numbered some 2,500, at the Wanderers Hall. He called it: 'so natural, so above board and so calculated to serve many useful purposes'.[5] He said: 'This great community has its own religion; it has its own race tradition and race loyalty. There is absolutely nothing incompatible in this with the most thoroughgoing British patriotism.'[6]

Hertz spoke again, and this time he supported the much maligned Russian Jews. He pointed out that the accusations that had been appearing in the press for the past four years, that they were massively involved in illegal drink trafficking, was not born out by the facts. He reported that only 5 per cent of those charged between the beginning of 1901 and the meeting had been Jews. He relied on their names to identify their religion, but his conclusion, however unscientific, was very well received. It was a strong defence, but many poor Jews had definitely been attracted to the illegal drink trade out of economic necessity. Hertz also asked for Yiddish to be accepted as a European language, which Milner now supported: 'Quite prepared to believe that Yiddish is a European language; and much more after what I heard from the eloquent lips of Dr Hertz.'[7]

The books of immigrant Jewish companies were often kept in Yiddish and, if this were to be prohibited, it would be very difficult for the immigrants to produce their accounts properly. The internal conflict in the Jewish community, though, was indeed over the status of Yiddish. The Orthodox used it and believed it to be the Jewish language. The 'English' Jews despised it as a debased jargon. It was not surprising that Hertz considered Milner's speech: 'such as for ever to linger in the memory of those who were privileged to hear it'.[8]

Hertz was appointed secretary of the new body but it was a tortuous business to build up the organization. As Hertz said at the first AGM: 'The great portion of the year passed before the various details of scope, constituency and representation were finally agreed upon'.[9]

As far as scope was concerned, Hertz never let the fact that he was thousands of miles away from Europe affect his involvement with Jewry world-wide. For example, in 1904 he complained vigorously about the situation in Austria, where Jewish children were sometimes kidnapped and put into monasteries so that they could be converted.

The Board did much good work on a wide range of issues. They obtained approval for a Yiddish interpreter to be available at the High Court, and set up a committee to try and ensure that only qualified *mohelim* carried out circumcisions. As with so many public organizations, the main burden of the work fell upon a few individuals, and within a year or two there was even talk of winding up the committee because many members didn't turn up for meetings.

The reasons suggested for this lack of support were that: 'The Chairman of the year had proved unsatisfactory; there had been bad blood between leading personalities on the executive, especially between Langerman and Hertz ... there was also sharp disagreements between some of the constituent bodies. In general there was a lack of clarity as to the scope of the Board's work.'[10]

The arguments between Hertz and Langerman centred on the question of whether the Zionists or the Board should be the lead organization for the community. Among the constituent bodies there was also the question of who had the ultimate authority for the Board's actions. Then there was the competition between the various Johannesburg synagogues, and an infinite capacity to take offence, which is often a feature of synagogue politics.

Hertz would see the same conflicts emerging in the 1930s with refugees from the Nazis. The British government would then find it difficult to decide which Jewish body represented the views of the community, as the World Jewish Congress, the Board of Deputies and others fought for the senior role. As a consequence of the Transvaal arguments, in 1905 a new constitution was devised and Hertz stood down as secretary, although he remained a member ex officio, together with Rabbi Landau. He also remained a keen Zionist. After Theodor Herzl died in 1904, the new president of the World Zionist Organization, David Wolfsohn, came to South Africa in 1907. As he could address the Zionist supporters only in German, it was Hertz who was called upon to translate. He was fluent in both German and Yiddish. German had been spoken at home in his childhood.

As the years went by, the Jewish community in South Africa would provide many leaders in civic government and the great majority of these would play a full part in their community's affairs. They were powerful men and the rabbis needed firm characters and personalities to avoid becoming mere appendages of the synagogue administration. The congregations were conscious of their image in the country; many fine synagogues were built to lend the communities additional respectability and, architecturally, to parade their virtues.

Most of the rabbis complained, however, that the shuls were there more for show than for worship, but this was not true of many of the Orthodox immigrant congregations. They remained wedded to studying the Torah. The experience Hertz gained from dealing with these different types of community would be invaluable to him in London, where he would find exactly the same challenges.

In 1904 the Cape Town community decided to start their own Board of Deputies. This was against the wishes of the Revd Alfred Bender, who felt that the existing cordial relations between the Cape government and the Jewish community were quite adequate for their needs. By 1905, however, the Zionists themselves recognized that many of the problems facing South African Jewry, notably naturalization, were hardly in their bailiwick. Hertz turned his attention to other community activities and, in 1907, accepted a position at Transvaal University College as their Professor of Philosophy. As such he gave a course of lectures on Hebrew and became even better known outside the community.

The Jews in the Transvaal were widely distributed. In 1904, it was estimated that they numbered 15,000 of whom only 3,000 were members of congregations. So communities tended to be small outside the major cities. Hertz always tried to make himself available to help them.

The new government encouraged Jewish education and new schools were opened. In the Jewish government school, the Transvaal Administration left the choice of teachers to Claude Montefiore in London, ignoring his own radical views on Judaism. However, the number of Jewish children always well exceeded the capacity of the Jewish schools to cope. Even at the major Jewish school the general attitude of the parents was also not constructive. At the prize giving in 1903 the Headmaster had to admit that of over 400 pupils, only 100 attended the religion classes.

For many, the teaching at Roman Catholic Schools had more to offer; they taught musical instruments, how to speak English well, the refinements of etiquette and they prepared the students for the professions.

Throughout his time as Chief Rabbi in London, Hertz would try to tackle this problem of the inadequate numbers of places in Jewish schools and their poor public image. It would be his future son-in-law, Rabbi Solomon Schonfeld, who would lay the foundations for a complete change of attitude by the British community to Jewish schools, but this would come to fruition only towards the end of the twentieth century.

One of the most serious educational problems was the inability of many of the immigrant girls to speak English and when, in 1904, Hertz brought his new wife to South Africa, she started classes to remedy the situation.[11] By the time they moved on, there were 250 children in the Jewish school in Johannesburg and 220 in the Jewish school in Pretoria.

Hertz had a hectic year in 1904. In 1903 he had consecrated the new synagogue in Klerksdorp and in March 1904 the new synagogue in Bloemfontein. In June he was discussing the future of the Johannesburg Jewish Orphanage, which was full and needed larger premises. In May, at the synagogue's AGM, it was said from the platform that he 'continues to enjoy the esteem of the entire community', and that his salary would be increased.[12]

In midsummer he was on holiday in New York with his family and on 19 July went with his sister to supper with his relatives, the Freed family. Rose Freed had been a friend of his since childhood, and she wrote to a friend about the evening:

> Dr Hertz is a short, dark, bearded individual, wearing glasses (not spectacles). He has travelled extensively all over Europe – England etc. – and of course knows a great deal about Africa and everything else. Two years ago, I met him twice at the home of his sister ... He called last night at 5.30pm and did not leave until – 11.30. He is a good interesting talker who speaks a great deal, very much like Professor Callison – but this is a minister! and very little taller than I am.[13]

Rose Freed came from an Orthodox family and was one of eight sisters. She was also related to Dayan Jacob Reinowitz who had served on the London Beth Din in Adler's time. Her father had died when he was only 36, so the girls were brought up by their mother. Unusually for those days, Rose had a BA in Domestic Science from Columbia University. She was also beautiful, with dark hair and dark blue eyes.[14] She was a very intelligent woman and had become a settlement worker when she graduated. From 1902 until her wedding, she was the Head of the Domestic Art department of the Educational Alliance, one of the largest Jewish educational bodies at the time.

After the supper evening they went off with friends to an amusement park a few days later, and Hertz proposed shortly afterwards. With a pulpit awaiting his return in Johannesburg he had to act decisively and a month later they were married. He had known Rose a long time though, and when they were betrothed, the *New York Herald* reported that the marriage was 'the culmination of a courtship ... begun when they were children'.[15]

'The invitations were confined to the relatives and a few intimate friends.'[16] The wedding took place on 30 August at the Jewish Theological Seminary's synagogue, and was conducted by Bernard Drachman. The president of the seminary, Solomon Schechter, was one of the *unterfuhrers*, who escorted the bride: 'She wore a pretty gown of white net over white satin, made with insertions of lace and trimmed with white satin ribbon. Her veil of tulle was fastened with lilies of the valley and sprays of myrtle.'[17]

Since neither the Freeds nor the Hertz family were wealthy: 'a buffet luncheon was served in one of the large classrooms at the Seminary'[18] but: 'there was a patriotic display of American flags and bunting, flowers and palms'.[19]

In the future Rose Hertz would always be popular. She was, however, a modern American girl and not wedded to the Victorian world. It was a time when most women were not highly educated and it has often been the case that when the wives of senior members of a congregation find that the *rebbetzin* is their intellectual superior, it results in a good deal of jealousy. Throughout her marriage to Hertz, however, Rose was a major asset to him. She was always prepared to be involved in good works, she supported him fully and she was elegant and charming. She was to be an ideal wife for the next twenty-five years. They would have six children – three boys born in South Africa and three girls in England.

For their honeymoon the couple left for Britain on the *Deutschland*, a massive 16,000 ton, four-funnel, 2,000-passenger, Hamburg-American steamship that had held the Blue Riband for the fastest crossing of the Atlantic in just over five days. As far, however, as a peaceful honeymoon crossing was concerned, the ship had the nickname 'The Cocktail Shaker', due to the excessive vibrations the engines caused when working flat out.

They recovered in London where Rose visited the fine book shops. When she tried in vain to find a simple book about Judaism, she suggested to her new husband that he write one. From that idea would come *The Book of Jewish Thoughts*. They went on to spend

Yom Kippur in Amsterdam. They left for South Africa on the Union Castle RMS *Saxon* on 24 September and arrived in a more leisurely fashion in Johannesburg on 14 October, being greeted at the station by a goodly turnout from the Witwatersrand Old Hebrew Congregation. Hertz told the welcoming committee that he would, as was his custom, continue to give a discourse every Friday evening and also lecture on occasional Sabbath mornings.

The ultra-Orthodox congregation sent a deputation to their home to present them with a silver Kiddush cup, which was in the nature of a peace offering. Hertz had often preached at the synagogue in Yiddish when he had first arrived, but the relationship had cooled thereafter. The problem was that Hertz was more in favour of larger communities than religious exclusivity. As long as the members were halakhically Jewish and accepted Orthodoxy, Hertz was not over critical about their level of observance.

For Rose it was all very new. The 'express' train from Cape Town to Johannesburg had taken forty-eight hours to cover 1,000 miles, and her new home in Joel Road on the Barnato Estate, with its eight rooms: 'furnished beautifully, simply and well', made her feel as if she was still on holiday. The protocol of calling on congregants she found irksome: 'did you ever believe that my principal mission in life would be to pay calls?'[20] It was not the academic life she had enjoyed in New York.

Rose: 'assumed charge of the Hebrew and Religion classes in connection with Dr Hertz's school'.[21] She always referred to him in letters as Dr Hertz, but it was very much a love match: 'Doesn't this whole affair seem like a fairy tale? And we are just as happy as the folks in fairy tales.'[22]

Milner retired due to overwork in 1905, when South Africa was still trying to emerge from the post-war economic crisis. By 1906 the Hertz family were settled down in their new surroundings. Rose was well content. As she had written home a few years before: 'If ever I were to leave Africa, I would long for this house, for the quiet, peace and repose.' The marriage had turned out very well: 'my only wish to you is that your married life will prove to you as happy as mine is to me, and that your husband will be as kind, considerate and gentle to you as my husband is to me'.[23]

The Hertz's first child, Samuel Moses, had arrived safely in 1906. He was six pounds in weight with navy blue eyes like his mother, and while Rose had a bad time afterwards, she was soon on the mend: 'For four weeks after the arrival of baby I saw absolutely no one and now that people know that I am seeing visitors, they keep flocking in every afternoon. Yesterday afternoon ten ladies called.'[24]

The arrival of Samuel led Hertz to consider whether he really wanted to stay in South Africa for the rest of his career. In that year he applied for the pulpit at the New West End Synagogue in London, vacant after the death of the minister, Rabbi Simeon Singer. Because of Singer's fame as the creator of the ubiquitous Singer prayer book, it was a senior position in the United Synagogue ministerial hierarchy, but Hertz was not chosen to replace him, nor was Alfred Bender of Cape Town who also applied.

The rabbi and his wife continued to be welcome visitors everywhere and Rose reported on staying at the best homes in the land. Hertz's sister, Sadie, with whom he would remain close to the end of his life, became matron of the new Jewish Orphanage. Fourteen months after the birth of Samuel came Leon in 1907, and in October 1909 Daniel was born.

Hertz had founded the first Talmud Torah school and Rose wrote that he was also: 'teaching History of Education and Logic and next year he expects to tackle Psychology'[25] at the Technical Institute. He would lecture on Jewish themes to the young people and could attract audiences of up to 500 Jews and non-Jews to listen to him. In 1908, however, the campus was moved to Pretoria and Hertz felt he had to give up the chair as a consequence.

By this time he was beginning to struggle in Johannesburg. He had been unable to persuade his congregation to attend Shabbat-morning prayers in reasonable numbers, although his Friday-night services still attracted a large audience. It was also becoming clear that the physical location of the Witwatersrand synagogue was becoming less fashionable and that the Johannesburg Hebrew congregation was more conveniently situated, as the Jews moved to a pleasanter part of the town. Landau, though, had his own problems. As early as 1905 he said of his own congregation: 'All their Judaism is shrunk within the walls of the synagogue which is empty even on Sabbath and Festivals from one Day of Atonement to the next. For them their synagogue is simply a monument.'[26]

He still, however, had a more attractive location than Hertz, who had an uphill struggle to compete. It was not always friendly competition either. As always there was a hard core of observant Jews, but the largest percentage of these were to be found in the Beth Hamedresh Hechadash synagogue. This had the ultra-Orthodox rabbi, Moses Mirvish, one of whose family would become the British Chief Rabbi 100 years later. In the Mirvish shul nobody was clean-shaven and copies of the Talmud were to found on the tables for study.

Among the ministers throughout South Africa there remained strong competition. Although their congregations accepted Hermann Adler as their spiritual authority in London, they were still not about to appoint a South African Chief Rabbi, other than their own minister. There continued to be the three major contenders: Hertz himself, a hero during the Boer War and influential in the development of many Jewish institutions in the Transvaal; Rabbi Landau representing the German migrants in the Johannesburg Hebrew Congregation and Alfred Bender, the long-serving and extremely charitable minister, who remained prominent in Cape Town.

Hertz had no wish to give up the struggle to unite the two Johannesburg congregations, but he was having little success in achieving his objective. Judah Landau at the Johannesburg Hebrew Congregation saw it as equally desirable, but with himself as the senior rabbi. Alfred Bender in Cape Town, together with his congregation, had no intention of taking second place to a non-British rabbi in the Transvaal. The hostilities between the communities in Johannesburg were reported to be particularly bitter. The lay leaders jockeyed for power as well.

Ten years after he had written home to America in 1899 about his prospects, Hertz had not been: 'unanimously elected Chief Rabbi of the Federated Jewish Congregations of the Transvaal (and ultimately of South Africa)'. It was far more likely that he had come to the conclusion that: 'there is absolutely no scope for me on the subcontinent as a rabbi'.[27] The lack of scope he assessed by his own high standards, but communities like Cape Town and rabbis like Landau and Bender would continue to block any attempt at integration.

At which point, thousands of miles away in New York, the Orach Chaim (path of life) congregation suffered a tragedy. Their charismatic rabbi, Rabbi Joseph Asher, who was a friend of Hertz, died at the early age of 37. The Orach Chaim had been founded in 1879, not to be a large synagogue, but in order for the congregants to be able to study Talmud every day. Originally occupying a room over a saloon, it had soon moved to the more fashionable 54th Street and, in 1898, it had become a founder-congregation of the American Union of Orthodox Jewish Congregations.

Asher was born in Manchester, went to Manchester Grammar School and then to Cambridge. He came from a rabbinic family. As there was little chance that he would be encouraged by Nathan Marcus Adler, the Chief Rabbi, to obtain *semicha* in Britain, he went to Kovno in Lithuania and qualified at that great *yeshiva*. His achievement would not, however, have been popular with Adler, so Asher decided to make his way in New York, where he was appointed by Orach Chaim.

It was reported at the time that: 'we hear that ... there is a congregation called the Orach Chaim, whose members are enormously wealthy and completely German ... and who gather daily after the afternoon prayers ... to enjoy Torah study'.[28]

It had been in existence for many years. The *Jewish Messenger* had reported in 1880: 'The congregation ... is greatly extending its influence and securing the objective for which it was organized ... not the foundation of a huge congregation and the building of a handsome synagogue, but the daily study and practice of the law.'[29] Asher, who was also very Orthodox, was the ideal appointment. In addition to occupying the pulpit, he became the professor of homiletics at the Jewish Theological Seminary, teaching students the art of writing and delivering sermons.

This was now the synagogue that considered Hertz Orthodox enough to become its minister. He may have been recommended to Orach Chaim by the Jewish Theological Seminary, which was also still strictly Orthodox at the time, and his father would have been well known to the community as well. Hertz was in two minds whether to accept the call. On the one hand, the request to replace Asher was an honour. On the other, he could still hope to achieve at least some of his outstanding objectives in South Africa.

The South African Board of Deputies was still establishing itself, he was unhappy about the level of Jewish education available in the country and the unification of the South African community remained unfinished business. There was talk of building a new wing for the orphanage, the *Shechita* Board had been re-established, a Home for the Aged was being promoted and the Talmud Torah was buying its own building. There was still much work to do.

Hertz was also concerned that he might fall between two stools. He might be rejected by Orach Chaim while his Witwatersrand congregation would learn that he was prepared to leave. He pointed out to Orach Chaim that he had been elected unanimously in Syracuse and had twice been re-elected unanimously at Witwatersrand. He wanted to know his chances of success if he applied for Orach Chaim. He supported his candidacy by pointing out that: 'through continual self tuition I have become more or less at home in all branches of Jewish learning'.[30]

Orach Chaim assured him that, if he agreed to let his name go forward, no other rabbi would be considered until Hertz had decided whether to accept the position or not. With that in mind Hertz decided to tell Witwatersrand that he had been offered the position. He explained that: 'Johannesburg was outside the sweep of Jewish spiritual currents.'[31]

After all, he had explored many avenues to become accepted in different milieus. For example, he had become a freemason in 1903 and would be appointed to the rank of Past District Grand Chaplain in the South Africa Grand Lodge in October 1911. Although he would not continue actively in the craft when he left the country, his credentials among the brethren internationally were firmly established. There was also the question of whether he wanted Rose to have to live in a rough, frontier community and to bring up their children there.

In April he was granted leave by the WOHC to go to Europe for some months to deal with a throat complaint. The Honorary Officers had asked Orach Chaim to withdraw the call as they were so anxious to keep Hertz, but the American congregation had no reason to do this; Hertz came well recommended and practised their level of Orthodoxy.

When, again, Hertz's own level of Orthodoxy is associated with the Conservative stance of the Jewish Theological Seminary today, it needs to be remembered that the Orach Chaim congregation would never have contemplated accepting a rabbi who held the institution's current Conservative convictions. He would have been rejected out of hand as allied to the Reform.

Before Hertz left for Europe, the Witwatersrand Old Hebrew Congregation gave him a handsome cheque for his travels, and he told the congregation that he might well turn down the Orach Chaim offer. The decision, he suggested, would be made in consultation with his father whom he was visiting for Passover in New York. The true situation was somewhat different. His father was becoming increasingly mentally erratic from the effects of arteriosclerosis.

On the boat to New York, Hertz wrote to Rose, agonizing over the risky decision he now had to make. Orach Chaim was a relatively unknown quantity and if they were undoubtedly Orthodox, then so had Syracuse been when he joined them. If they could change, then so could Orach Chaim. Their top offer was $3,500 a year, about £700 at the rate of exchange applying at the time. He had persuaded them to increase their original offer of $3,000 but he was being paid better than that in Johannesburg.

In addition to his salary, the Witwatersrand synagogue paid the rent on his house and his life insurance premiums. There were also often gifts from the congregants when he officiated at circumcisions, weddings or in the homes of mourners. During the economic depression in South Africa his salary had been reduced to £780, but it was now back to £900. He needed it all; in addition to Rose, there were now three young sons to support.

In considering his possible departure from the South African ministry, he had to face facts:

> Let us not deceive ourselves. I have no congregation in Johannesburg; you need loyalty, enthusiasm, members – and all these Landau has, not I. Spiritual bondage for your bread. No appreciation for your work, how many of the leaders turned up to my presentation? The masses were there but they don't shape the politics of the community. They can't ward off insults and humiliations your leaders are ever ready to heap on you.[32]

In addition there was the distance from their families and the calculation that: 'if they took a holiday in New York in 1912 it would use up the savings of years'.[33] The original promise of Johannesburg had soured: 'Objections and bitter pills remain. One, the triumph of Landau. You cannot have one half as mean an opinion of that liar, lunatic and hypocrite that I have.'[34]

The constant battle in South Africa now choked him: 'Rose, I want to live, breathe and grow – none of these things can I any longer do in Johannesburg.'[35] The letter offers a rare insight into the realities of a religious career. So many of the official versions are carefully planned, edited, checked and measured, but great rabbis are just as human as anyone else. It is possible that Hertz was just depressed at the size of the challenge, but it's more likely that the letter correctly reflects the problems that faced him throughout his life. Certainly, he would have had to deal with more insults and humiliations.

There is no doubt that the Witwatersrand congregation were proud of the academic record of their rabbi, his public service and his wonderful oratory. They were not, however, prepared to devote more of their time to prayer and study, and the lay leaders judged people primarily from the point of view of their wealth and possessions. If the incumbent had neither – and rabbis didn't – then they were not treated with deference if their views did not coincide with those of the Honorary Officers. This would not be the last time Hertz came up against this situation.

When he passed through London, Hertz gave an interview to the *Jewish Chronicle*[36] and reviewed the arguments for and against leaving South Africa. He confessed that he had failed to get decent attendances at the synagogue on Shabbat and was very critical of those young people in Johannesburg who involved themselves in communal activity only to improve their status in the community.

He had also failed to unite the synagogues, so that in the town there was not only his synagogue but also Landau's: 'the Beth Hamedresh, five smaller synagogues and any number of minyanim'.[37] One congregant, Lionel Phillips, had offered substantial financial backing to the community if they would unite, but even this had been insufficient incentive to achieve the objective.

Hertz could point to the success of his work in creating the Deputies, the Talmud Torah and the Jewish Ladies Communal League, which had led to the building of the Jewish Orphanage. He had become the honorary chaplain of the Rand Rifles, acting chairman of the Jewish Citizens Law & Order League, and vice-president of the Transvaal Philosophical Society. At the same time he had seen Zionism decline in popularity and many members of his own congregation move to the suburbs. His community now numbered about 300.

Hertz's major criticism, however, was of the Reform movement, which had started in Germany and spread widely in America. Hertz said that the result of this was that: 'many a nationalist, no less than Reform Jewry, sadly need[s] conversion to Judaism'.[38] He went on: 'I am more than ever convinced of the total and absolute unsoundness of the entire Reform movement in Judaism.'

In the end Hertz decided to accept the New York offer. When he left, there was a reception and he was complimented that: 'you have for fully thirteen years – the best and most vigorous of your life – unflinchingly, unceasingly and most eloquently taught us how best to preserve and cherish the holy religion of our fathers'.[39]

In thanking the congregation, Hertz explained his own way of thinking which had not been without its resulting problems: 'When he had satisfied his own conscience as to what was right, he cared nothing for thanks, nothing for advice, and nothing for any pressure that any individual, organization or society tried to exert upon him ... they had made his parting more bitter than it would have been in ordinary circumstances.'[40]

Although his comments were published in London, they seem to have had little effect on those British Jewish communal leaders who had other plans for Hertz's future.

It was agreed by Orach Chaim that he would be paid from July but arrive in September. In fact, he wanted to be installed as the grand chaplain in the Grand Lodge of South Africa that autumn, and didn't arrive to take up his post until December 1911. It was also in 1911 that the University of the Cape of Good Hope awarded him an MA. The *Baltimore Jewish Comment* reported: 'Dr Joseph H. Hertz arrives to assume the pulpit of Congregation Orach Chaim. Full of energy and altogether a live wire, he will no doubt make things hum in New York.'[41]

Orach Chaim had a condition for membership of which Hertz approved. In his inaugural address he told them: 'no other English-speaking congregation in the world, to my knowledge, insists on strict Sabbath observance as the indispensable prerequisite for admission to its membership.'[42]

It was very different from the synagogue in Syracuse. Hertz knew that a rabbi had initially to accept the *minhag* (customs) of the congregation he was to serve, but if the *minhag* was changed, as it had been in Syracuse, he might have to leave, if the result was to introduce a practice outside the *din*. As he said in his inaugural sermon in January 1912: 'The assumption of the leadership of such a congregation presupposes a definite kinship of spirit and a virtual identity of aims between the covenanting parties.'[43]

When he later moved on to become the Chief Rabbi in Britain, he would find a different situation again. In Britain the congregations he would lead were all in favour of the Oral Law. They just didn't follow it very enthusiastically. Hertz could live with this. He was not responsible for the conscience of the members of the community. He was responsible only for ensuring that the policy of the body he led was totally supportive of the *din*. As he said in his inaugural address: 'I will be no hesitating or stammering witness to the truth' [of Orthodox Judaism].[44] He would repeat that sentiment on other occasions.

He had harsh words for those who didn't adopt the same attitude. When he was inducted at Orach Chaim he made it clear in his sermon that he still adhered to the task Rabbi Morais had inculcated in all the Jewish Theological Seminary graduates. As he said: 'It is in this city where, in my earliest years, the inextinguishable beauty of the religion, seized me.' As the *Jewish Chronicle* pointed out at the time, Hertz's acceptance of the Orach Chaim pulpit: 'has deprived South African Jewry of a preacher of remarkable power'.[45]

Hertz was still fighting the Orthodox corner. He went on: 'For over sixty years Orthodox Judaism has in America been subjected to a running fire of ridicule, blasphemy and merciless warfare by the leaders of the liberalizing, the revolutionary wing of our faith. And these children of progress deny us the right to defend ourselves. I shall look to you for loyal help in my conflict with illiberal liberalism.'[46]

He was, however, still certain that Judaism needed to take advantage of new discoveries in non-Jewish cultures following the Enlightenment and Emancipation: 'The spiritual quarantine forced upon us throughout the Middle Ages can no longer be maintained'.[47]

The two Johannesburg communities did decide to amalgamate in 1914 and Landau was appointed Chief Rabbi of the Amalgamated

Congregations. The attempt, however, to expand this into the title of Chief Rabbi of South Africa did not gain widespread acceptance. Cape Town, in particular, retained its independence.

NOTES

1. Gustav Saron and Louis Hotz, *The Jews of South Africa: A History* (London: Oxford University Press, 1955), p.226.
2. 'Jottings from South Africa', *Jewish Chronicle*, 13 May 1904, p.17.
3. Saron and Hotz, *The Jews of South Africa*, p.226.
4. Ibid., p.231.
5. 'Jottings from South Africa', *Jewish Chronicle*, 28 August 1903, p.17.
6. Saron and Hotz, *The Jews of South Africa*, p.239.
7. Ibid., p.240.
8. Ibid., p.239.
9. Ibid., p.241.
10. Ibid., p.243.
11. Ibid., p.221.
12. Ibid., p.242.
13. Letter from Rose Freed to Stella Klugherz, 20 July 1904, Jeremy Schonfield private family archive.
14. Irene Hertz-Majerczik, *Through Life My Way* (Ra'anana: Docostory, 2003), p.71.
15. *New York Herald*, 31 August 1904. Cutting from Jeremy Schonfield private family archive.
16. Ibid.
17. Ibid.
18. Ibid.
19. Letter home, 26 November 1904, Jeremy Schonfield private family archive.
20. Ibid.
21. Ibid.
22. Ibid.
23. Letter of Rose Hertz, 14 February 1906, Jeremy Schonfield private family archive.
24. Letter of Rose Hertz, 19 April 1906, Jeremy Schonfield private family archive.
25. Ibid.
26. Saron and Hotz, *The Jews in South Africa*, p.283.
27. Jeremy Schonfield private family archive.
28. Jonathan Sarna (ed.), *People Walk on their Heads: Moses Weinberger's Jews and Judaism in New York* (New York: Holmes Meir Publishing, 1982).
29. *Jewish Messenger*, 28 May 1880.
30. File 44/6, J.H. Hertz Archive, Hartley Library, University of Southampton.
31. Ibid.
32. Letter, 2 May 1911 in Ibid.
33. File 44/6, J.H. Hertz Archive. Hartley Library, University of Southampton.
34. Ibid.
35. Ibid.
36. 'South Africa', *Jewish Chronicle*, 7 April 1911.
37. Ibid.
38. Ibid.
39. 'South Africa', *Jewish Chronicle*, 22 December 1912, p.14.
40. Ibid.
41. *Baltimore Jewish Comment*, 12 January 1912, cutting in Jeremy Schonfield private family archive.

42. Joseph Herman Hertz, *Early and Late: Addresses, Messages, and Papers* (Hindhead: Soncino Press, 1943), p.127.
43. Ibid.
44. Derek Taylor, *British Chief Rabbis, 1664–2006* (London and Portland, OR: Vallentine Mitchell, 2007), p.348.
45. 'South Africa', *Jewish Chronicle*, 15 March 1912.
46. Hertz, *Early and Late*, p.132.
47. Benjamin J. Elton, *Britain's Chief Rabbis and the Religious Character of Anglo-Jewry, 1880–1970* (Manchester: Manchester University Press, 2009), p.203.

Chapter Four

Chief Rabbi, 1912

The death of Hermann Adler in 1911 initiated interminable debates about his successor. Adler, himself, had hoped that he would be succeeded by his son, Alfred, but the young man had died a few months before his father, when he was only 34. Up to then, all the Chief Rabbis, since Aaron Hart in 1705, had been related to Haham Zevi Ashkenazi of Amsterdam, but now that 200-year-old record was to be broken.

Hermann Adler had been brought up to give spiritual guidance to a small, well-integrated Jewish community. By training and upbringing he had little experience of the mass of Eastern European immigrants who had flooded into the country because of discriminatory Russian legislation and catastrophic pogroms. Adler, himself, recognized that his successor must be able to talk their language, even if it was Yiddish. In 1904 71 per cent of Orthodox Jewish weddings in Britain involved at least one immigrant.

The Honorary Officers of the United Synagogue also realized that they would need a spiritual leader with a track record of success in talking to and understanding the newcomers. He would have to have come from the same background and if he didn't measure up to Adler as an elegant English gentleman, the Honorary Officers considered themselves quite capable of filling that role for him.

The first question to be decided, however, was whether to have a Chief Rabbi at all. There was a great deal of opposition to the office. To begin with, the religious leaders of the Orthodox refugee communities in the East End were very much against it. They felt that it had no traditional place in Judaism and that it diminished their own authority within their communities.

The latter objection was seldom voiced, but the reality emerging from the existence of the office was pretty obvious. As they had never recognized the Chief Rabbi anyway, however, they were really just attacking the prime position of the United Synagogue in deciding on the successful candidate. Their fallback position was that they would at least want a man of great piety, strict Orthodoxy, a rigid observer of the Shulchan Aruch and a great Talmudist.

Such a range of skills does not seem unreasonable for a Chief Rabbi, but even if he lived up to the job specification, the question of ultimate authority would still rankle with the East End. It was said of Adler that he was: 'as much at home in the Athenaeum as in the synagogue'[1] but his comfort zone did not reach as far as the East End. Coming from another viewpoint, the United Synagogue ministers also wanted more say within their own communities, instead of all the final authority resting with the Chief Rabbinate.

They asked for a rabbinical consistory to be set up to assist him, admittedly with the Chief Rabbi as president, but with decisions to be made by a simple majority of the members. It was a power play and the *Jewish Chronicle* commented that the Chief Rabbi would then: 'be assisted out of existence'.[2]

The United Synagogue ministers knew that the tradition in Orthodox communities on the Continent was for the rabbi of the congregation to make religious decisions as necessary. The British system was, internationally, almost unique. The office of Chief Rabbi had developed over many years since provincial congregations first started asking for Rabbi Aaron Hart's rulings in the early eighteenth century. Hart was the rabbi of the Great Synagogue in London and, as the provincial communities couldn't afford their own rabbi, they had to ask for help and rulings from someone from outside.

One opponent of the office was Revd Dr Joseph Hochman, the successful candidate against Hertz in 1906 for minister of the London New West End Synagogue. He was also co-editor of the *Jewish Review* and he wrote in May 1912 that he believed the Chief Rabbi served to deprive congregations of all powers and the minister of all influence. For a few years Hochman was to prove a nuisance to the Chief Rabbi. His views tended towards Reform, to the irritation of his own more Orthodox members, and his opposition to Hertz went so far as to refuse Hertz's future request that his ministers be bearded, as is traditional in Ashkenazi congregations. Hochman cut off his own beard in protest at the suggestion.

While previous Chief Rabbis had had little difficulty in looking after the religious affairs of a few synagogues, the challenge of controlling a major organization had not been required of them, and it was more difficult. One major weapon the Chief Rabbi had possessed, the power of pronouncing *cherem* (a form of excommunication), had been abolished as too draconian. He would have to achieve his ends through moral authority.

The Honorary Officers of the United Synagogue were chosen by the council members, who were elected by the synagogues they represented. It was a democratic process but, in reality, the leadership had always been, primarily, in the hands of a small group of rich, intermarried Jewish families. These were much later labelled 'The Cousinhood' and the United Synagogue president was one of them, Lord Rothschild, bearer of the most famous name in Jewry. The lay leaders were unquestionably in charge of financial matters.

The United Synagogue attitude to the East End, however, was typified by a comment by Lord Rothschild at a meeting of the delegates charged with electing a Chief Rabbi in January 1912. He said that the new Chief Rabbi should set out to prevent the teaching and spread of what he considered the slang and jargon of Yiddish. When Rothschild came to consider Hertz's candidacy, he was probably unaware of the rabbi's efforts to ensure that the South African government acknowledged Yiddish as a proper European language.

Like America or South Africa, there were a number of great families in the community, wielding all the influence that their wealth could bring to bear. In Britain, they partly belonged to the original Sephardi immigrants, who had been the first to arrive in the country in the seventeenth century from Holland. These families kept much to themselves in religious matters and had nothing to do with the United Synagogue. Nevertheless, they were considered the aristocracy of the community because of their longevity of tenure in Britain.

It was a Sephardi leader, Sir Moses Montefiore, the most influential Jew in Britain for much of the nineteenth century, who made sure that the Chief Rabbinate kept the religious power in its own hands. After the unexpected breakaway which had led to the creation of the leftward-leaning West London Synagogue of British Jews in 1840, Montefiore didn't want to give authority to any minister who might stray from the strictly Orthodox path. He included all the ministers in that category, setting out to ensure that there would be no other breaches in the dike.

Chief Rabbi Nathan Marcus Adler (1844–90) had set out the rules for all those synagogues that acknowledged his authority in Britain and abroad. These included the necessity for the Chief Rabbi to confirm all candidates for office. He also had to give his approval for the creation of any new congregation or synagogue. By 1871 there were twenty-one provincial and fifteen colonial synagogues that benefited from his work, even though they didn't contribute to its cost.

Hermann Adler, who succeeded his father, was prepared on occasion to use his authority with a firm hand to maintain the status quo. He rejected a number of proposed changes to the liturgy, told Hochman off for his views, and refused to allow Revd Morris Joseph to take the pulpit at Hampstead because of his neo-Reformist approach. Joseph went off to serve as minister at Upper Berkeley Street, the foremost Reform synagogue in London, thus suggesting that Adler might have assessed the true thinking of the cleric correctly.

Joseph once said of the Jewish community that they were averse to change even though very frequently they did not believe in or support what they accepted. What he overlooked was that most British Jews realized that they were incompetent to understand the theological arguments for change, and felt safer relying on the Chief Rabbi to lay down the law.

It was in the middle of what would eventually be a two-year process to decide on a new Chief Rabbi, that Hertz came through London in December 1911, on his way back to America from South Africa. As he told the American *Jewish Morning Journal*[3] unspecified 'friends' had approached him and suggested he put his name forward for the post. Subsequently he had met Lord Rothschild and Lord Swaythling, head of the Federation of Synagogues. As a result he had received an official invitation in February 1912 to come to England to give a number of sermons, so that he could get to know the congregations and they could learn more about him.

Hertz was effectively being invited to apply to succeed Adler as the Chief Rabbi of the United Synagogue, and those many congregations in the British Empire which acknowledged the Chief Rabbi's leadership. It was a heady prospect after accepting a single pulpit in New York but, apart from his academic record, his experience in South Africa had looked well on his curriculum vitae. He had, in addition, worked in a community with a large number of immigrant European Jews in Johannesburg and had the advantage that he spoke Yiddish fluently.

During his visit to Britain, Hertz had the opportunity of learning about the people he would lead. Reviewing his life for the *Dictionary of National Bibliography*, Israel Finestein wrote years later that, at the time:

> Hertz was a short, broadly built man with a purposeful gait. His full beard did not hide his firm features or his genial smile among his many personal friends or with young people. It was said of him that he had a brusque manner and kindly nature ... Hertz

> [did not] always take adequate account of the limited value of abrasiveness as an instrument of communal debate.[4]

Perhaps one reason why these outbreaks of abrasiveness were misunderstood, though, was that Hertz was always inclined to fight fire with fire. He was accustomed to finding himself outgunned in public by men who were richer and more powerful than he was. To compete, he would if necessary use invective and scorn, as well as intellectual argument and rage to attack his opponents.

He also soon found out that the ministers of United Synagogue shuls in Britain were in need of a lot of help: 'Hertz assumed office over a ministry that was ill-paid, poorly regarded and divided.'[5] They were treated with scant respect and were normally firmly under the thumb of their lay leaders. He must have soon realized that, if he became Chief Rabbi, he would be the only one who could stand up to the laymen and fight his ministers' corner. In the future he: 'attacked the trend in Anglo-Jewry to "cringe and fawn" to those leaders'. He wanted: 'an end to the "dictatorial parnass" ... In some communities the Minister seems to have no rights which the laymen feel bound to respect'.[6]

Whether his opposition reflected the example of the prophets, the suzerainty of European rabbis in their ghettos, or just the independence of Uncle Sam's citizens, is a moot point. For whatever reason, if United Synagogue ministers found it difficult to 'challenge its masters' Hertz certainly did not. He was also unhappy about the paucity of English Jewish religious scholars. 'There are few departments of human endeavour to which modern Jewry has contributed fewer men than it has to Jewish learning ... and whatever has been accomplished in this field, very little of it indeed has been done by Jews of English birth and training.'[7]

There was precedent in Britain for rocking boats. The unsuccessful attempt by the Sephardi Mahamad to dismiss their Haham, Moses Gaster, fifteen years before, would have been well known to Hertz; it had been public knowledge and had featured in the *Jewish Chronicle* week after week in 1896. The Sephardi members had rejected the advice of their Elders and voted for the Haham to continue in office. Gaster was a controversial character and a strong Zionist. In the battle for the national home he would find Hertz a new and welcome supporter.

In South Africa, Hertz had always been prepared to stand his ground and, although there had been some bitter disagreements, his approach had resulted in him being highly regarded even by most, though not all, of his opponents. He knew his abrasiveness and his religious authority were always going to be among his few weapons in achieving his objectives. It was also soon obvious that British Jewish lay leaders had seldom respected any signs of weakness in their ministers. He also had additional weapons: he could influence his flock by the power of his oratory and his writing.

From the outset, however, Hertz's primary source of authority, if he became Chief Rabbi, lay in the 1835 Constitution of the Board of Deputies and the 1870 Deed of Foundation of the United Synagogue. The Board of Deputies had represented the British community with the government of the day almost since its inception in 1760. Within the Board, when it came to who was in charge on questions of Jewish law, their constitution was absolutely clear: 'The guidance of the Board on religious matters (inclusive of matters relating to marriages and matters involving questions affecting the religious customs and usages of the Jews) shall remain as heretofore with the Ecclesiastical Authorities, to whom all such matters shall be referred.'

There could be argument about whether a particular matter came under the heading of 'religious customs and usages of the Jews' but, if it did, as far as the Board of Deputies was concerned, it had always been up to the Chief Rabbi to make the final decision. Indeed, as already noted, as long ago as 1847, Nathan Marcus Adler, as Chief Rabbi, had written the Laws and Regulations for all the Ashkenazi Synagogues of the British Empire, with the full support of the acknowledged lay leader, Sir Moses Montefiore.

The Deed of Foundation of the United Synagogue bolstered the Chief Rabbi's position still further. This laid down that: 'The form of worship in each of the Constituent Synagogues, and all the religious observances in the Constituent Synagogues, and all matters connected with the religious administration of the United Synagogue ... shall ... be under the supervision and control of the Chief Rabbi.'

There was an occasion in 1894 when the subject of musical instruments in synagogue came before the council of the United Synagogue. It was resolved that in such matters, it was strictly the Chief Rabbi's responsibility to make decisions; but even if the Chief Rabbi was the final judge, it was possible to argue that a matter was not strictly religious, as far as 'observance' or 'administration' were concerned. Such attempts would be made in the future.

These rules were much more supportive of Hertz's authority than had been those in force in Syracuse and South Africa. Hertz would also have realized that, once he was appointed, he would possess the ultimate public relation weapon: in extremis, he could resign the office on religious grounds. The international opprobrium, not just in the British Jewish community but in the Empire as well, which this would inevitably bring down upon the heads of the United Synagogue Honorary Officers, would be unsustainable.

So it would prove in the future, almost until his death. His opponents might try to go behind his back, withdraw their financial support for his objectives, or deny his authority if they were not part of the United Synagogue. If they were within that organization, however, they had to accept that the Chief Rabbi had ultimate authority.

When Hertz considered the make-up of the community, in terms of its Orthodoxy, the picture was again unlike his previous experience. Where the Reform movement had made great strides in the United States, it was a totally different situation in Britain. The British Reform communities were as near Orthodox as made little difference. For example, where Hertz had felt it necessary to resign from the Orthodox Syracuse congregation because of the mixed seating issue, the Reform Upper Berkeley Street Synagogue, by far the largest in the country, had rejected the proposal in 1905.

There were stout defenders of Orthodox practice within Upper Berkeley Street. Members of prominent Jewish families, like Mrs Lionel Lucas, were said to be prepared to denounce any hint of concession or change. It was, in fact, largely due to her influence that Reform ritual allowed so little alteration. Many felt that the retention of the old service was a matter of life and death to her.

Progress in building up the Reform movement had been painfully slow. There had been no new congregation formed since Bradford in 1873, forty years before. At that time the *Jewish Chronicle* reported:

> We may state that the members of the new congregation [Upper Berkeley Street] deny altogether the impeachment of having renounced the Oral Law. Professor Marks [their rabbi] and Mr Elkin [the warden] in the earlier days of the Reform, strenuously maintained the general fidelity of the congregation to the Jewish tradition ... there is probably less discrepancy between the Jews forming what are called Orthodox congregations and Jews who are members of the Reformed Congregation of London than is apparent within the bosom of a single denomination of Christians ... [The Reformed Synagogue] cannot be characterized other than as a secession.[8]

Indeed, its members were known as the Secessionists. This was not remotely the position of the supporters of the Pittsburgh Platform.

In Britain in 1910 it was further remarked upon that attendances were dropping in Reform synagogues; they had long ago abandoned morning and evening weekday services as they couldn't attract sufficient worshippers. Even when they shortened the Shabbat service by half an hour and said more prayers in English, the movement still languished as a proportion of the British Jewish community. The Reform members were, numerically, insignificant.

There had also been a further breakaway movement a few years before. The children of two stalwarts of the community, Claude Montefiore, Sir Moses' great nephew, and Lily Montagu, Lord Swaythling's daughter, had set up the Jewish Religious Union in 1902. It developed into the Liberal movement, dissatisfied with what they perceived as the neo-Orthodoxy of the Reform. Both founders came from impeccably Orthodox family roots: Sir Moses Montefiore, the acknowledged leader of British Jewry in the middle of the nineteenth century, and Sir Samuel Montagu (later Lord Swaythling), the founder of the Federation of Synagogues. The Orthodox apple had, however, fallen a very long way from the bough.

The philosophy advocated by Claude Montefiore was even more revolutionary than the Pittsburgh Platform. Montefiore questioned a whole range of basic Talmudic laws. He rejected divine authority, particularly as the source of the Hebrew scriptures, he denied that Moses had received the law from the Almighty on Mount Sinai, he introduced mixed seating, didn't believe in *kashrut* or circumcision and thought there should be closer links with the Church of England. He also did not support Zionism or the restoration of a Jewish state, and so his strictures went on.

At the first Liberal Passover service, there was an organ, much use of English instead of Hebrew and substantial changes in the traditional liturgy; for instance, there was no additional service, the *Hallel* prayers were said partly in English, as were the blessings when congregants were called up to the reading of the Torah.

Only about a fifth of that initial congregation were men and, although the Liberal plan was to draw young people back to the synagogue, the large majority of the congregation were elderly women. Nevertheless, as Montefiore was a member of the Jewish establishment, an excellent self-publicist and a considerable scholar, he did eventually attract a lot of well-to-do youngsters to his banner. He would become an extreme irritant to Hertz, who totally rejected his theology, but, irritant or not, the Liberal movement also remained numerically unimportant. In 1915 they only had 400 members. At the same time, on a personal basis, Hertz and Montefiore enjoyed each other's company, even if, for years, Hertz would attack the Liberals' philosophy far more than that of the Reform

In 1912 the Liberals appointed their first minister, Rabbi Israel Mattuck, an American who had been ordained at the Hebrew Union College. Originally a Lithuanian, Mattuck was intellectually able enough to go to Harvard. He would serve the Liberal congregation till 1947 before becoming emeritus minister, handing the leadership over to his son-in-law Leslie Edgar.

Of far greater significance than the impact of Reform and Liberal Jews, was that of the enormous influx of refugees who had fled to Britain after 1880 as a result of the pogroms in Eastern Europe and the May Laws in Russia. They had totally transformed the demographics of the community, enlarging it from around 35,000 in the middle of the nineteenth century to nearer 300,000 in 1913.

As elsewhere, like America, the new migrants were mostly Yiddish-speaking, impoverished and brought up in the Orthodox Jewish worlds of Lithuania, Poland, Romania and Russia. To try to improve their finances and conditions, Lord Swaythling had drawn a considerable number of their small communities into a new body called the Federation of Synagogues, and had Lord Rothschild of the United Synagogue approved as their honorary president.

He made sure that the Federation acknowledged the authority of the Chief Rabbi in principle, but individual *shtiebels* (small synagogues) usually clung to the traditions they had brought from Eastern Europe. These included the role of the rabbi to make halakhic decisions on matters affecting the community and its constituents.

The effect of the refugees on the United membership was that, while in 1880 there were ten synagogues and about 2,500 male seat holders, there were now 6,000. By 1911, however, the fifty-one Federation synagogues actually had more seat holders in London than the United Synagogue, but the latter had the money, the historical legitimacy and the upmarket image. When it came to an election, it was also not going to be a question of one member, one vote. The United Synagogue decided that the number of votes in electing a new Chief Rabbi would be allocated according to the financial support the office of the Chief Rabbinate received from each synagogue.

Even though the Federation had more seat holders, out of a total of 431 votes, the United Synagogue decided it would retain 314. The Orthodox provincial Manchester communities, who were not members of the United Synagogue, would have a total of seven votes and Leeds one. This method of allocating votes was rejected by the Federation, who withdrew from the process in disgust. The United

Synagogue Honorary Officers wouldn't give in and they had one very sound argument. The Chief Rabbi's office needed a substantial budget and in spite of the fact that the Federation had promised to pay its way, their agreed contribution to the costs had not been forthcoming.

On 6 March 1912 the Federation appointed their own first minister, Rabbi Dr Meir Tsevi Jung, who, like Hertz, was an Austro-Hungarian by birth. He was installed in June. The Federation offered to pay for Jung to serve on the United Synagogue Beth Din but this was rejected. They also offered to carry out their own *shechita* supervision but this was turned down as well. Jung and Hertz approved the Hildesheimer approach to education, though, and the Federation minister introduced secular studies to the curriculum at the newly created Yeshiva Etz Haim in London, which had the support of the Federation.

The United Synagogue Honorary Officers wanted to improve conditions for Jewish immigrants in the East End. Applying the tradition of Jewish charitable support for their coreligionists, they were keen to help the newcomers adjust to moving to a new country. They wished to help them climb out of the desperate poverty in which so many of them lived. With dismay, though, they also recognized that the newcomers tended to undermine the efforts the core community had strenuously made over the years, to prove that they were as British as the rest of the population. The immigrants, all too obviously, were not.

The core community wanted to be popular with their fellow-citizens but, without meaning to, the immigrants aroused antagonism from their neighbours. They were accused of undercutting the wages of the workers in the East End, even if that wasn't true, and raising rents because of their own needs for accommodation, which enabled landlords to take advantage of a higher level of demand than supply. The newcomers were, admittedly, foreigners and they did have a different culture. There was a degree of anti-Semitism involved as well. Eventually, the Balfour government passed an Aliens Act in 1905 which was specifically designed to reduce the influx of Jewish immigrants.

The agenda for the core community was to make their coreligionists typical British citizens as quickly as possible. The *shtiebel* members, however, had their own programme. They knew they were denigrated for their foreign habits and their poverty. They were, on a good day, considered second-class citizens. There was really only one way in which they could prove their superiority to the earlier settlers: their standards of religious observance would be higher than their detractors. They could be – and often were – holier than thou. They were sincere God-fearing families, but their higher standard of obedience to Jewish law grated on the members of the United Synagogue, with their often laxer approach.

One way in which the grandees of the core community could fight back was by emphasizing the importance of ethics and morals over the observance of religious practices; this was a popular stance with many United Synagogue members. Again, those who felt this way might well have sincerely believed in their religious position, but a side effect was to enable them to justify their laxity as a modern improvement on the wide range of *mitzvot* (commandments). The immigrants would say it was perfectly possible, indeed obligatory, to uphold both.

If the immigrants considered United Synagogue members insufficiently observant, the ultimate shortcomings of the newcomers in the eyes of the Jewish establishment was that they seemed foreign, ignorant, common and vulgar. At the outset few of them could read or write English, had little schooling outside the religious *cheder* (religious schools), and didn't know the customs of polite English society. Early initiatives, like the Jews' Free School in the East End, had aimed to help correct this situation and, by 1900, the school had 4,000 pupils and was the largest in the country. The objective, however, was not to produce Talmudic scholars. It was limited to teaching the pupils how to hold down a job in later life, though a number of the school's graduates did well academically and in the professions.

Hertz would have had no difficulty in picking holes in the religious behaviour of most of the United Synagogue members. Where, for example, a condition of membership of the Orach Chaim congregation in New York had been the full observance of the Sabbath, the absence of such a commitment was no barrier either to membership of the United Synagogue or, indeed, a senior role in it. Hertz had, however, learned in his youth from Rabbi Sabato Morais, not to spend his time criticizing the level of practice of the Orthodox. Success was achieved if they married within the faith and did not defect to the Reform. These were the main concerns of the American Orthodox.

In South Africa, of course, Hertz's main problem was not the influence of the Reform movement, but what he called the outright laxity of so many of his community. On Hertz's list of British priorities, though, preventing defections was going to be one of his most important objectives.

On the whole, the rabbis in the East End were better Talmudists than other factions could muster. After all, they had *semicha* and that was more than could be said for almost all of the United Synagogue clerics. If ministers did earn their *semicha* – a few were awarded the qualification in Europe and even two by Adler – they were not allowed to use the title. The United Synagogue weekly services were laid out in Singer's Prayer Book. The editor, Simeon Singer, had *semicha* but is still identified as the Revd Simeon Singer and not as Rabbi.

The hidden agenda for applying the title only to the Chief Rabbi remained the determination to maintain the seniority of his position. In the middle of the nineteenth century there had been the occasional movement in the provinces to set up an alternative to the London authority. The regulation giving all the ministers the lesser title of Reverend helped undermine such opposition to the status quo.

Arguments about standards of observance between East End Jews and the United Synagogue had come into the public eye over the question of *kashrut* when it was suggested that the East End *Kashrut* authorities were subject to bribery and they sued the United Synagogue in Liverpool in 1904 for making such a suggestion. It was a public relations disaster for both sides, but it did result in an agreement that an ultra-Orthodox rabbi would become a member of the Chief Rabbi's law court, the Beth Din.

The United Synagogue continued to rely, in religious matters, only on their Chief Rabbi. At Hertz's inauguration in the Great Synagogue, Lord Rothschild would say 'I give into your care and safe custody our ancient law and our religious guidance'. Hertz had no reason to believe that this was anything other than an official and agreed approach that the Honorary Officers of the United Synagogue would adopt, underwritten by the constitution. They had signed up to accept the strictly Orthodox faith as the foundation of their organization. Many of their successors would not have the same religious point of view.

In the past, however, Adler had had few religious disagreements with Lord Rothschild as the United Synagogue president; Rothschild didn't take a great deal of interest in religious matters. United Synagogue Honorary Officers, nevertheless, fully expected that, if they chose, they would have little difficulty in having their own way with whoever they decided would succeed Adler.

Hertz's approach to theology was, in any case, in line with the United Synagogue membership. He believed, as the vast majority of them did, that there was no need to divorce the community from the modern world. While he accepted that there were aspects of modern culture which could never be acceptable to Orthodox Judaism, he considered that there might be some parts of it which Judaism could usefully absorb. The yardstick for Hertz would continue to be whether, in accepting change, there would be any weakening to the immutable laws of the Talmud, that were, as far as Hertz was concerned, sacrosanct.

If he decided that the laws of the Talmud were unaffected, he would consider the new discoveries on their merits.

When Hertz's proposed visit to London became known, Leopold Greenberg, editor of the *Jewish Chronicle*, became the principal press commentator on the long-drawn-out saga. Hermann Adler had died in July 1911, but it would be April 1913 before Hertz was installed in his place. Rothschild announced the vacancy officially in May 1912.

Hertz was a largely unknown quantity to the vast majority of the community in Britain. As Greenberg wrote dryly: 'If he is thought of as a likely candidate, his choice would come perilously within the region in which "sporting chances" play a large part.'[9]

There were other potential candidates. Dr Joseph Alexander was a possibility. He was British and serving as the minister in Melbourne, Australia. He even came back to Britain and gave a sermon, but was generally dismissed thereafter as not having the necessary strength of personality for the job. There was also Dr Joseph Hyamson, an excellent dayan, who had been looking after the Chief Rabbi's responsibilities since Adler's death. Greenberg said in print that appointing Hyamson would be an over-promotion. There was eventually a shortlist of six candidates, of whom three were rejected as too old for the role.

The Executive Committee of the United Synagogue was trying to make the right decisions, not only on the candidate but also on the Chief Rabbi's brief. They turned to the decision their predecessors had reached in 1891 when Hermann Adler was appointed: 'These duties are naturally of a complex character and being not exclusively religious may be fairly said to touch upon every point which concerns the religious, moral and general welfare of the community ... there are many other duties which are not enumerated which properly appertain to the office.'[10]

This viewpoint would come under attack on many occasions during Hertz's future ministry. At this stage the Executive Committee was certainly not concerned with limiting the authority of a Chief Rabbi, although it was agreed that, like Nathan Marcus Adler, he would still not be able to pronounce *cherem*. It was a major source of discord in the community when Chief Rabbi Solomon Herschell had done so, denouncing the congregants who had founded the West London Synagogue seventy-five years before.

While they were trying to make up their minds, the Executive Committee had to deal with some special pleading. For example, the Association for Furthering Traditional Judaism in Great Britain – a loose grouping of about twenty United Synagogue ministers with their supporters – that had been in existence since Adler died. They wanted provincial rabbis to have absolute authority over their congregations. The Executive Committee was not impressed with that suggestion.

Hertz arrived in London, together with Rose and their children, Samuel, Leon and Daniel, and gave his first sermon at the Great Synagogue in the City on 4 May 1912. It went down very well, which was not surprising as Hertz laid on the flattery with a trowel. He also spoke ex tempore, was more fluent than Hermann Adler had been, did not have a guttural accent and suggested that the British Jewish community occupied a position incomparably higher and stronger than that of any other Jewry. He described the Great Synagogue as the Cathedral Ashkenazi Synagogue of England and thanked the congregation for the honour they had done him, assuring them that it was one he would not forget to his dying day.

In fact, the British Jewish community didn't compare for a moment, on an intellectual Talmudic basis, with the communities in countries like Lithuania and Poland. British *yeshivot* were puny in terms of the Talmudic talent they attracted. If the criterion was the standard of observance of United Synagogue members, it was again second rate. But the community did exist in peace in the greatest nation in the world at the time. After their experiences in Eastern Europe, it was no wonder that the immigrants called Britain 'The Land of Mercy'.

The following week Hertz was in the pulpit at the Bayswater Synagogue, where Hermann Adler had been the minister for some years. Greenberg went to listen and was impressed: 'Dr Hertz preaches ex tempore with sharp, staccato diction, with none of the Clergyman's manners ... never does he seem lost for a word, a quotation or an illustration and ... when he ended his sermon ... one felt that he had by no means exhausted either his subject or himself.'[11]

Greenberg felt he was very different from Adler: 'It was a forceful sermon; a powerful homily on the value of Jewish self respect.' After which, the next week, just before Shavuot, Hertz went into the East End to preach at the Philpot Street Synagogue in Commercial Road. He spoke to the migrant community in Yiddish and did so again when he went to Manchester to preach at the New Synagogue on the Shabbat after Shavuot. The *Jewish Chronicle* covered the Manchester visit as well: 'The sermon was listened to with profound attention by a crowded congregation ... His health was drunk with much enthusiasm.'[12]

After speaking at the Hampstead Synagogue on 1 June and the Dalston Synagogue on 8 June, Hertz could return to America satisfied that he had made a very good impression. He had had social arrangements made for him as well. For example, on 3 June he had attended a meeting of the Jewish Historical Society of England to listen to a paper on the founders of the South African community in Cape Town. He gathered support wherever he could. He also knew that Orach Chaim didn't want to lose him. They had said: 'If he should not undertake the high office of Chief Rabbi, means would be found on his return to New York for much enlarging the field of his work, to which will be attached even better conditions than those at present prevailing.'[13]

There were, of course, minor criticisms; for instance, his *Haftorah* (weekly reading from the books of the Prophets) at Hampstead was not considered very tuneful, but these were only unimportant carpings. The cantillation in America was different at any rate from that sung in London; the former being the Lithuanian tradition and the latter Central European. What may have been of more concern was a letter in the *Jewish Chronicle* from a reader in Johannesburg, published on 31 May 1912. He wrote of the communal position in the City which Hertz had left: 'You either favour the new shool or the old shool; you are either a Landauist or a Hertzist; and you cannot be a "cross bencher" because the partisan feeling is so suspicious and so strong and withal so unreasonable … the obstinate and unreasoning partisanship is the curse of the community.'[14]

Beneath the stately measured tread of steady community progress and harmony, there was an underlying series of conflicts which were hidden from view as much as possible.

South Africa came up again when critics of Hertz seized on the suggestion, made by the *London Standard* newspaper, that Lord Rothschild had been influenced by the comments of Lord Milner, when they were discussing the appointment. Milner, following his return to England, had become chairman of the mining company, Rio Tinto Zinc, and a director of the Midland Bank. He and Rothschild could have come into contact on many occasions. When Hertz's name came up, who more reasonable for Rothschild to consult than the former high commissioner in South Africa?

As a result of his cordial relations with Hertz in the colony, Milner certainly did his best for a man who had always supported him. Hertz, himself, played it down when he told the New York *Jewish Morning Journal*:

> It would be an insult to English Jews to suggest, apart from the foolishness, that a non-Jew, however eminent he might be, would meddle in purely Jewish religious matters. It might as well be suggested that an influential Jew would force the commendation

> for a bishopric. Of course, Lord Milner might have been asked about my personality and my activities in South Africa while he was High Commissioner there. He might have said a good word about me ... (but) they would not entrust so high an office to anyone without having the most complete knowledge about his suitability. Personally, I have so far been to them not more than a name.[15]

There were still a number of other candidates for the vacancy and in the summer the United Synagogue issued an invitation to a serious heavyweight, Hertz's old teacher, Bernard Drachman. He had first taken the Beth Israel Bikkur Cholim pulpit in Manhattan in 1887 but when the community later decided to abandon the Ladies Gallery, Drachman resigned to considerable consternation. In 1889 he had joined the academic faculty of the Jewish Theological Seminary and stayed for twenty years. It was during that period that he advised Hertz to resign from Syracuse over the same mixed-seating problem.

After Schechter had arrived, the initially strictly Orthodox approach of the Jewish Theological Seminary became more difficult to sustain and Drachman was one of several Orthodox members of staff who were unprepared to put up with the changes. He resigned again. His Orthodox credentials were impeccable and his scholastic achievements included a PhD at Heidelberg, Magna Cum Laude.

As the former Dean of the Jewish Theological Seminary Drachman now considered that he should simply be offered the British Chief Rabbinate, rather than have to win an election. This must have been particularly his view as the main competition came from Hertz, one of his former students. Nevertheless, he came to Britain in October 1912 and gave a number of well-regarded sermons. There were, however, two problems.

First, he accepted an invitation to dinner with Aaron Green, the Hampstead Synagogue minister, but wouldn't eat anything because he suspected the standard of the *kashrut*. Green was very popular, very offended and made his views very public. Then Drachman was invited to speak in the East End and refused to give his sermon in Yiddish because he preferred speaking in classic German. Neither incident helped his cause and his candidature was quietly dropped. Drachman went on to be the second president of the Union of Orthodox Jewish Congregations of America.

The final short list of six candidates for the Chief Rabbinate, was whittled down to Dayan Dr Moses Hyamson and Hertz. At this point the infighting became unpleasant. Indeed, the virulence of the *Jewish Chronicle*'s opposition to Hyamson was well illustrated by a letter they printed from a member of the Hampstead Synagogue, who hoped its contents would be seen as typical of what was going on.

> In view of the decision to hold a contested election for the Rabbinate, may I be permitted to warn the electors next Sunday to be on their guard against the 'log rolling' for the office that is going on. In my congregation I have been urged to do and say what I can in support of the candidature of Dr Hyamson, not because of his superior qualifications for the post but because, so I am informed, there exists a tacit compact and understanding into which he has entered, in exchange for the congregation's support that, in the event of his appointment, he will confine himself to Beth Din work and delegate the work of representing the community to the outside world to our minister, Rev. A.A. Green ... of course, at the same time, there has been some silly talk disseminated about the unfitness of Dr Hertz because he did not, on the occasion of his visit to the synagogue, read the Haphtorah tunefully.[16]

Green wrote to deny that anything of the kind had happened, but mud sticks. The alternative opposition to Hertz continued. He was known to be a keen Zionist and the very Orthodox had, in common with most of the community, opposite views. The East End leaders felt that the Holy Land should become Jewish again only when the Messiah came. The Jewish establishment was equally anti-Zionist, worrying that to advocate a national home for the Jews might suggest that they were not fully loyal to Britain; an accusation by anti-Semites that they had been trying to refute ever since they first came to the country some 250 years before.

Another drawback was that Hertz was not British, which was what Lord Rothschild would have preferred. The problem for Rothschild, however, was that even he recognized that the standard of Talmudic expertise of local Jewish ministers was not adequate for the role of Chief Rabbi. Rothschild would also have taken comfort from the fact that, whatever Hertz's nationality, he had proved his loyalty to the British on many occasions in South Africa.

In fact, at the meeting finally to elect a new Chief Rabbi in February 1913, the letter which Milner had sent to Lord Rothschild was read out. His Lordship had written:

> I knew Dr Hertz quite well in South Africa. I have heard him speak in public several times and have had many conversations

> with him. He is certainly a remarkably able man and a most eloquent speaker. He also gave me personally the impression of great sincerity, and of being a 'good fellow'. His reputation, as far as I was acquainted with it, stood high. Personally, as far as I was able to judge of such a matter, I should say that he was well fitted by character and capacity for even so important a position as that of Chief Rabbi.[17]

From such a man, you could hardly receive higher praise than to be described as a 'good fellow' but Hertz also had his detractors. Writing to friends from South Africa, Rabbi Landau denigrated him as a potential disaster in the role. On the other hand, he was fully supported by Solomon Schechter who was trusted in Britain, as he had been a lecturer in Talmudics and a reader in Rabbinics at Cambridge, and later Professor of Hebrew at University College, London. Schechter had also, of course, brought the contents of the Cairo Genizah to Cambridge.

Schechter remained a name to be conjured with and the changes he had initiated at the Jewish Theological Seminary were not well understood on the other side of the Atlantic. He had been anxious to organize the United Synagogue of America but he wanted the members of the constituent synagogues to cover their heads during services and not to use the Reform prayer book.

Certainly, Schechter was persona grata in many different parts of the religious spectrum. As well as being the head of the Jewish Theological Seminary in New York, he had connections with the extreme left wing in the British Jewish community. Claude Montefiore, feeling that he did not have sufficient Talmudic knowledge, had brought the Romanian from Berlin as his personal teacher. In later years Schechter covered his back by letting it be known that he regretted accepting the position. Schechter's support meant a lot for Hertz. He said of the candidate: 'Dr Hertz is a fine Hebrew scholar ... (his) large experience in pastoral work, an industrious student, an omnivorous reader and endowed with a fine philosophic mind. I believe that unless you have a man of his oratory ... traditional Judaism will soon be a thing of the past.'[18]

This all suited Rothschild well. Talmudic rules were not, he considered, the responsibility of the United Synagogue president. He laid it down, for example, that he did not consider it the responsibility of an Orthodox Jew to discuss the shape and size of a *mikveh* (a ritual bath).[19] At the same time, there is no evidence that it was widely known that Schechter had given the bride away at Hertz's wedding and was, therefore, hardly impartial.

The arguments rumbled on. Eventually a delegation of United Synagogue Honorary Officers, led by Sir Adolph Tuck, decided to call on Lord Rothschild to ask that there be more than one candidate at the forthcoming election. At the meeting Rothschild made his own position very clear when he said that he had made up his mind, the election would take place and unless Dr Hertz was elected, he would resign the presidency of the United Synagogue.

He then told a group of very distinguished officers of the United Synagogue to get out of his office. The delegation, their *amour propre* in tatters, decided, with reluctance, that they could not win in such a confrontation. For a long time any heavyweight contests among the lay leaders had been conducted according to Lord Rothschild Rules. Naturally, such cavalier behaviour gave plenty of ammunition to current and future critics.

When the election meeting to settle the matter was held in February 1913, Hyamson was a candidate, but everyone knew how they were expected to vote. There were 100 delegates, with different numbers of votes, including representatives from Australia, New Zealand and South Africa.

The meeting lasted six hours and Hertz eventually won by 298 to Hyamson's thirty-nine. After the protracted negotiations, Hertz's election was almost unanimous. Hyamson took the vacancy Hertz had left at Orach Chaim and served the community for thirty-one years thereafter. He was also appointed to be the lecturer in Codes at the Jewish Theological Seminary from 1915 to 1940. For a dayan of the United Synagogue to accept such a post, the Jewish Theological Seminary must have remained Orthodox in its outlook during those years.

Before Hertz left New York on the RMS *Mauretania* for his new post in London, the seminary gave him a farewell banquet. Hertz was in no doubt that his new role as Chief Rabbi would present many difficulties. As he said at the dinner: 'You can hardly call it a herculean task because Hercules never had the knotty problems to solve that await me.'[20]

He was entering a high-profile international world but one issue remained unresolved when he departed from Orach Chaim: they wanted him to return the $1,200 travelling expenses which they had paid for him to relocate his family from Johannesburg to New York, and the $1,000 they had laid out for furnishings. Hertz protested that nobody had suggested this before he resigned the pulpit, but the Board of Orach Chaim was adamant.

Hertz couldn't go back to the United Synagogue for more money at this late stage and he was afraid of adverse publicity at the start of his London ministry. So he asked his lawyer brother, Emanuel, in New York to act as his agent and conclude the best deal possible. Emanuel in later life wrote some excellent books on President Lincoln and donated his library of 20,000 books to the Hebrew University in Jerusalem. The result of his negotiations with Orach Chaim was a private agreement for them to accept $1,120 (£230 at the rate of exchange) in full settlement.

On 19 March Simon Hertz died in New York at the age of 66, mourned by his wife, three sons and four daughters. Simon succumbed to arteriosclerosis, which had initially led to irrationality, hallucinations and the loss of his short-term memory. As early as August 1911 when Hertz was temporarily back in South Africa, Emanuel had written of his father's: 'usual intolerance, irrationality, jealousy and quick temper'.[21] It was Simon, though, who had inspired Hertz and he felt his loss severely. The year was stormier than most.

On 14 April Hertz was installed as Chief Rabbi by Lord Rothschild in the Great Synagogue, Rothschild telling him to: 'bring up the congregations of Israel under your charge in conformity with Din Torah', as reported in the *Jewish Chronicle*.

It was a responsibility that Hertz believed the Chief Rabbi should have, and no one was surprised to hear it spelt out with admirable clarity by the president of the United Synagogue. The key points were 'under your charge' and 'in conformity with Din Torah'. Those who wanted to see a united British Jewish community, in agreement on religious practices, either couldn't or refused to see that the Chief Rabbi had no room for compromise on this. He was there to say what the Orthodox law was and ensure that the community acknowledged that it should be obeyed. Individual Jews might fail to keep all the *mitzvot*, but as members of the United Synagogue, there was agreement on what the commandments were.

In this respect Hertz didn't have the flexibility the Pittsburgh Programme had granted its adherents. They had decided that *kashrut* was out-of-date. Hertz was there to spell out the laws of *kashrut*. Claude Montefiore might decide for himself that members of his Liberal movement should be able to make up their own minds on what laws they would obey. Hertz was there to say what an Orthodox Jew's behaviour should be – and in minute detail.

The day of Hertz's installation, 14 April 1913 was very cold. The temperature didn't reach ten degrees all day. The packed congregation at the ancient Great Synagogue in the City of London were in full morning dress and top hats, and probably sorry they couldn't have kept their overcoats on as well. The service was simplified to take into account that

Hertz was in mourning for his father. The Lord Mayor and the Sheriffs of the City of London attended and, unlike the installation in South Africa in 1898, both Morris Joseph for the Reform and Israel Mattuck for the Liberals joined the congregation. In installing Hertz, Rothschild said that religious guidance was his responsibility and these were never going to be just words. It was also what the Deed of Foundation of the United Synagogue said. What would only later become clear, however, was that: 'Whereas the Adlers had been willing to accept domination by the Rothschilds, Joseph Hertz was determined to be no Adler to a man who was himself not a 19th century Rothschild.'[22]

Hertz's inaugural sermon lasted forty minutes and he spoke without notes. The *Times* described the sermon as remarkable, and Hertz positioned himself in the middle-ground of Orthodox practice, which was the United Synagogue traditional balancing point: 'Whether we be traditionalist or revolutionaries, first of all disenthral ourselves, on the one hand, from masterly inactivity or from methods obsolete even in Russia: and, on the other hand, the spell of our remedies which have proved pathetically futile, and worse than futile, in Germany and America.'[23]

Looking back on Hertz's ministry, it is often suggested that he tried harder than his successors to bring the whole British Jewish community together in closer accord, but he never tried to disguise his disagreement with the theories and practices of the Progressives, whether their adherents were relatives of United Synagogue Honorary Officers, contributed to the charities of the community or held offices of power in the committees of British Jews. Hertz knew he was there to state the law, in exactly the same way as the Lord Chief Justice – except that Hertz handed out no punishments for backsliding. In matters of religion there could be no common ground with Progressives.

Hertz had an additional range of problems on his mind: 'Ours is an age of doubt and disillusionment ... theological foundations are rocking ... dreams of humanity are dissolving into thin air, in face of the malicious race hatred that is being fanatically preached ... old sanctions are weakening, home influence waning, and there is an alarming subsidence of the service of worship.'[24]

The situation abroad was often even worse than this. Hertz arrived on the bridge when the Jewish ship of state was battling an increasingly violent gale. Throughout his ministry, Hertz's secular problems would be far greater than those involving theological issues. Fighting the oppression of Jews in many parts of the world, opposing those in the general community who attacked the Bible, and establishing himself as a popular leader of British Jewry, were high priorities.

He arrived in Britain only eight years after the passing of the Aliens Act and only two years after a minor, but unique, pogrom at Tredegar in Wales. The image of the community needed improving and it was a primary task of the Chief Rabbi to present a more acceptable face of Judaism to the general public.

On 22 May Rose gave birth to a daughter, Judith. On 30 June, just a couple of months after his installation, Hertz spoke at the 'International Congress for the Suppression of the Traffic in Women and Children' – the white slave trade.

This was, on the face of it, a non-contentious subject. Everybody at the Congress was against it, although the *Jewish Chronicle* in 1910 had severely criticized Jews who participated in it – and there were a considerable number of these. The new Chief Rabbi could well have been expected to be supportive, and apologetic that a few members of his own community did not have clean hands. If that was what the delegates expected, they were soon to be disabused. Hertz, as usual, began as he meant to continue.

Everybody who counted had been invited: the Archbishop of Canterbury, the Cardinal Archbishop of Westminster, ambassadors, politicians and a wide range of influential leaders. Speaker after speaker denounced the infamous trade and then came the Chief Rabbi's turn. Hertz stood up, and started off in the approved manner with a pledge of the utmost help for the suppression of what he called the new slave trade.

He then went on and attacked the Russian government in withering detail. What is more, he attacked them time and again in the next few years and his accusations received world-wide publicity. When, eventually, the Communists would come to power with a totally anti-religious programme, he would attack them as well and with equal vigour.

Under Czar Nicholas almost all the Jews in Russia were confined to an area of the country called the Pale of Settlement. About 200,000 out of five million Jews – the rich, the merchants and the professionals – were able to live in cities like Moscow. Otherwise, the only Jews who could live where they liked were prostitutes. If a Jewess wanted to go to a Russian University outside the Pale, she, therefore, needed a Yellow Ticket. A document provided by the authorities that identified her as a prostitute.

If the local Russian authorities found that such a student was an honest woman, she might be summarily expelled from her college. Hertz complained that in recent months some authorities had gone further, and insisted that women should justify their Yellow Tickets.

The Russians in the audience at the international congress squirmed and this was, after all, a friendly country whose Czar was a cousin of George V. Letters from Russian apologists to *The Times* in subsequent days protested that Hertz had not been speaking the truth, but they were to learn that Hertz: 'never shrank from denunciation of wrong, no matter whence it emanated'.[25] He wrote a reply to *The Times* in which he showed he had been quoting the leader of the Russian Liberal Party in the parliament – the Duma – as well as several reputable authors and the United States Immigration Report for 1892, page 42! Defenders of the Russian authorities beat a hasty retreat and hoped the fuss would die down.[26]

With Hertz, though, in Britain as in South Africa, fusses seldom did die down. As the biblical prophets had reprimanded under-performing kings, as Jacob Sasportas, the first British Sephardi Haham, had castigated followers of Sabbatai Zevi, the false Messiah in the seventeenth century, as Solomon Herschell had denounced the blood libel in Damascus in the nineteenth century, and as Hermann Adler had upbraided the Church for not speaking out against pogroms, so Hertz was quite prepared to continue in what was becoming a grand old tradition. His view remained: 'Any infringement of the rights of the individual or of the community must be ruthlessly prosecuted.'[27]

He attacked the Russian government but, like Hermann Adler, this time with the authority of Chief Rabbi of the British Empire. His speech received world-wide publicity. In Berlin: 'The German press devoted more space to the sensational and courageous action of the Chief Rabbi than to the proceedings of the Conference itself, and all agreed that Dr Hertz had rendered a great service not only to the Jewish cause, but to the cause of culture in general.'[28]

He had set down his marker that he was not going to restrict his activities to purely religious issues. Nor did he consider it necessary to ask the Honorary Officers of the United Synagogue for their approval before he did so: 'He believed that religion and public life were not mutually exclusive.'[29]

In September 1913 events in Russia led him to solicit the help of the Cardinal Archbishop of Westminster. The Public Prosecutor in St Petersburg had accused a Jew of ritually murdering a Christian child. Would the Cardinal be kind enough to write for publication that accusations of ritual murder had been condemned as without foundation by Popes Innocent IV, Gregory X, Martin V, Paul III and Clement XIV? The Cardinal agreed and wrote 'if crime be committed, it will not be attributed to motives which do not really exist'.[30] A protest meeting was then held in October at which eleven bishops, headed by the Archbishop of York, protested at the murder trial. In November 1913 a wholly Russian jury found Mendel Beilis not guilty.

The cooperation of the Church was immediately reciprocated. The Archbishop of Canterbury was concerned at the treatment of workers by a British company in South America, and wanted the government to set up a Select Committee to enquire into it. The letter he sent to *The Times* was considered to carry additional weight because it contained the Chief Rabbi's signature as well as that of His Grace.

There were going to be a lot of other battles during Hertz's ministry. The new challenges would include Liberal Judaism, Zionism, Nazism, two world wars and increasing assimilation. It was a formidable list but Hertz fought with all his might for what he believed in. The British Jewish historian, Cecil Roth, wrote that he had: 'A boundless courage and an inability to maintain a tactful silence in the face of wrongdoing.'

NOTES

1. Aubrey Newman, *Lecture on the Centenary of the Birth of Joseph Herman Hertz* (London: United Synagogue, 1972), p.1.
2. Mentor, 'The Communal Armchair', *Jewish Chronicle*, 5 April 1912, p.7.
3. *Jewish Morning Journal*, 16 August 1912, Jeremy Schonfield private family archive.
4. Israel Finestein, *New Dictionary of National Biography* (Oxford: Oxford University Press, 2010).
5. David Cesarani, *The Jewish Chronicle and Anglo Jewry, 1841–1991* (Cambridge: Cambridge University Press, 1994), p.113.
6. Joseph Herman Hertz, *Sermons, Addresses and Studies*, Vol. 2 (London: Soncino Press, 1938), p.204.
7. Ibid.
8. Editorial, *Jewish Chronicle*, 13 February 1874.
9. Mentor, *Jewish Chronicle*, 5 April 1912, p.7.
10. Robert Henriques, *Sir Robert Waley Cohen, 1877–1952* (London: Secker and Warburg, 1966), p.340.
11. *Jewish Chronicle*, 17 May 1912.
12. *Jewish Chronicle*, 31 May 1912.
13. Meir Persoff, *Faith Against Reason: Religious Reform and the British Chief Rabbinate, 1840–1990* (London and Portland, OR: Vallentine Mitchell, 2008), p.164.
14. Ibid., p.21.
15. *Jewish Morning Journal*, New York, November 1912. Jeremy Schonfield private family archive.
16. *Jewish Chronicle*, 21 February 1913.
17. Ibid.
18. Aubrey Newman, 'Chief Rabbi Dr Joseph H. Hertz, CH' (London: United Synagogue, 1972), p.6.
19. Ibid., p.4.
20. Jeremy Schonfield private family archive.
21. Ibid.
22. Persoff, *Faith Against Reason*, p.168.
23. Aubrey Newman, *The United Synagogue, 1870–1970* (London: Routledge and Kegan Paul, 1976), p.157.

24. Hertz, *Sermons, Addresses and Studies*, Vol.1, p.5.
25. Revd Ephraim Levine in Isidore Epstein (ed.), *Joseph Herman Hertz, In Memoriam* (London: Soncino Press, 1947), p.30.
26. Editorial, *Jewish Chronicle*, 18 January 1946.
27. Epstein (ed.), *Joseph Herman Hertz*, p.30.
28. J.H. Hertz, *Early and Late: Addresses, Messages, and Papers* (Hindhead: Soncino Press, 1943), p.212.
29. Epstein (ed.), *Joseph Herman Hertz*, p.30.
30. Ibid., p.346.

Chapter Five

The Beginning of the Great War

Hertz's arrival coincided with the appointment of a new treasurer at the United Synagogue: Robert Waley Cohen. Theirs was to be a tempestuous relationship but they would each play their part in achievements which have made the United Synagogue membership the largest single group in the Jewish community to this day.

One of the main objectives of the organization in 1913 was to draw within its orbit as great a proportion as possible of the late nineteenth-century refugees from Europe. In this they were successful. By 1940 the number of synagogues in the London area affiliated to the United Synagogue would increase from sixteen to forty, and their male membership from 5,150 to 12,550.[1] The main reasons for this were not theological; between the wars, the vast majority of the members of the synagogues could just about read their prayers in Hebrew, but had little ability to translate what they were reading. They were far more likely at the outset to understand Yiddish.

Their interest in the minutiae of the *mitzvot* was equally minimal, a considerable proportion of them ate in non-kosher restaurants and many only came to synagogue on Rosh Hashanah and Yom Kippur. What then could be the attraction of the United Synagogue to the immigrants? This was an organization led by members of rich and powerful Jewish families who either hadn't come from the Continent at the end of the nineteenth century or who had set out to eliminate the memory of so doing.

First, it was a burial society. A membership fee included the cost of a plot in the cemetery and your eventual burial. That was always very important; it was often the case that the first thing a new community would set out to create was a cemetery, rather than a grand synagogue. Prayers could be said anywhere while the fees collected from the sale of burial plots would pay for essential communal services.

Second, membership was a status symbol. Compared to the poverty-stricken *shtiebels* in the East End, the United Synagogue offered the opportunity of improving one's image in the Jewish world. It was possible to become an Honorary Officer of the synagogue and sit in a special 'box', like the pew of the Lord of the Manor in a village church. In an official capacity, such as Honorary Officer, one would wear a top hat and often morning dress. Lay members invited to participate in the service would, when returning to their seats, stop at the box to shake the hands of all the Honorary Officers, and to thank them for the opportunity to take part; a privilege in the gift of those in the box.

Barmitzvah boys in synagogues would also often wear top hats and the ministers would wear clerical collars, like the Church of England. The traditional *tallit* (the prayer shawl) was woollen and white, with black stripes. This style was less favoured in United Synagogues where a more fashionable silk variety, favoured by the Sephardi, became popular, still white, but with blue stripes. It was also much smaller, but looked more elegant. The sermons would be in English and there was no general criticism of a member's level of observance of the *din*. A blanket exhortation by the minister to obey more of the *mitzvot* was acceptable, but obedience to the message was not considered mandatory. The warden might attend synagogue on the Shabbat, and then go off to business if his shop was open.

Waley Cohen fitted well into this milieu, in that he was far from observant. He had agreed to become one of the United Synagogue treasurers because he belonged to one of those families in the Jewish community which had a proud record of service to communal organizations. As a member in good standing of that coterie, he expected to be able to mould the United Synagogue to his own way of thinking. After all, the new Chief Rabbi was a lower-middle-class American who had come to London from far-off provincial South Africa and lacked most of Waley Cohen's impeccable British credentials.

Waley Cohen's personal history included the right school – Clifton, with its Jewish boarding house – the right accent, the right connections and a very healthy bank balance. Controlling Hertz would not, initially, have appeared to him to be much of a problem. He tried to patronize the Chief Rabbi over the years and often treated him with condescension. The result would be a regular series of explosions.

At the same time, Waley Cohen was fully capable of bringing some kind of order to a very disparate group of London synagogues, and to give it influence outside the capital. There was invariably tension between those from the original community and those who had recently arrived in the country. When the latter were referred to as 'foreign Jews', there was increased tension.

Hertz had met that situation in South Africa and he wasn't going to let it fester beneath the surface in Britain. He went to Glasgow in March 1913 and attended a service at the South Portland Street Synagogue, whose members were all from recently arrived families. Even so, he told them to learn to live in peace, favourably commenting on the example of the original community. There was a lot of protest, but the point had been made. More than 1,000 people came to South Portland Street to see him, even though he only spoke for a few minutes.

What both Hertz and Waley Cohen had to deal with was the effect of the Adler/Rothschild style of leadership, which had been weak in Adler's declining years and reduced further during the two-year interregnum. There was now what the *Jewish Chronicle* denounced, perhaps in exaggerated terms, as: 'chaos, confusion, overlapping [which] are as rife now as they were then'.[2] The editor considered that the prestige of the community was waning in the country, religious indifference was waxing, and that congregational disputes and bickering were growing apace.

Hertz was pragmatic about the behaviour of his community. He would ensure that his Beth Din would hand down judgements in cases brought to its attention, strictly according to Talmudic law. For years, as Av Beth Din (president) he would regularly preside at their Monday and Thursday meetings. He would come to be accused of being in thrall to ultra-Orthodox rulings of the members of his court, but this was often an excuse for attacking him personally. The condemnation gained credibility over the years, through constant reiteration by those more akin to the thinking of the Progressive movement.

This wasn't how a Beth Din worked. Hertz was not a lawmaker. He had no authority to change the *din* and didn't seek to do so. He was there to see that the law was applied. Waley Cohen, by contrast, emphasized instead the importance of the correct spiritual standards of personal behaviour. If those standards could be decided by him, as the senior figure in the United Synagogue, this might have the effect of justifying his own lack of observance. It would also enable him to avoid the criticism that this very senior officer was not personally observant.

What Waley Cohen underestimated was Hertz's determination never to let that happen. During Hertz's ministry there was certainly a drop in the level of observance compared to previous generations, but Hertz was not going to attempt to change the law, in order to coax those who rejected it to stay within the fold. At the same time, he would try to improve the level of *mitzvah* observance, even if the improvement was slight. With Judaism, there is always tomorrow, a new generation, and the chance to improve.

Waley Cohen would serve as treasurer of the United Synagogue from 1913 to 1918, as vice-president from 1918 to 1942 and as president from 1942 to 1952. For much of this time his position was even more important than it seemed because the president from 1918 to 1942 was Lionel de Rothschild, who was happy to preside, but even happier to leave the running of the organization to Waley Cohen. De Rothschild's passion was horticulture and he created a wonderful garden at Exbury in Hampshire which contained over a million plants, including 1,200 varieties of rhododendron and azaleas. He described himself as a banker by hobby and a gardener by profession. His importance to the United Synagogue lay, primarily, in his name and his banking contacts, if need arose.

Waley Cohen's father was Natty Waley Cohen and the son had many of his father's attributes. Natty was a very successful city businessman who had, almost in his spare time, invented Labour Exchanges and the Cambridge University Appointments Board. He was involved in a large number of charitable activities and had foresight, administrative ability and an original mind. At the same time: 'He had an element in his nature … which in his occasional arrogance, wilfulness, obduracy and cyclonic, uncontrollable temper was almost diabolic.'[3]

Robert Waley Cohen unfortunately inherited the trait. The son was an able and intelligent man. He had a Cambridge degree and had risen in his cousin's oil business, Shell, to be one of its most senior executives. He appointed, trained and nurtured a string of senior Shell management, and to those men he was almost a father and highly regarded. He had made a considerable difference to Shell's profits by sponsoring additional research into the qualities of petroleum, particularly in terms of its composition and the efficiency of engines. In 1919, at the end of the Great War, it would be Waley Cohen who canvassed the oil companies for money to build the Physical Chemistry Laboratory at Cambridge.

The problem with Waley Cohen was that he had been brought up to rule, loved power and seriously disliked dissent once he had made up his mind. Because he had a very good brain, he was able on most occasions to outthink his colleagues and competition. He was not, however, a team man. His will had to be obeyed or he lost his temper time and again.

Hertz and Waley Cohen were, physically, very different. Hertz was quite short and Waley Cohen was very tall and broad. Waley Cohen's supporters would try to put the blame for their arguments on Hertz, but disagreements occurred between Waley Cohen and other members of the community on many occasions. An historian of the United Synagogue says: 'Sir Robert's well-known temper led him quite often into explosive scenes with many who came visiting him on official business.'[4] In later years Waley Cohen's temper would end his senior role in some of the most important commercial companies he led.

As with many new appointments to senior management positions, Hertz was granted a honeymoon period to settle into his new role. This wasn't, however, destined to last long. Both the old community and the recently arrived wanted Hertz on their side, but only as long as he abided by their conditions. Nominally, one reason for his appointment had been his perceived ability to build bridges between the two parties, but both sections wanted the other to give way; the English-born to become more observant and the newcomers to adopt more of the English way of life.

When members of the core community didn't get their own way, some started to try to undermine Hertz, including many of those who hadn't wanted his candidature to be successful in the first place. They were small in number, but: 'There is a coterie who have set themselves to the task of teasing and annoying the Chief Rabbi in every conceivable manner on every possible occasion.'[5]

From both his ancestry and his training, Hertz had his roots in the immigrants' camp. In June 1914, after a pastoral visit to Newcastle, he went on to Glasgow and gave a speech at the Young Men's Institute. He tackled the thorny subject of continental ghettos. When the English-born wanted to criticize the newcomers they would pour scorn on what they called ghettos; those cramped – and therefore often unsanitary – sections of many continental towns where Jews had for centuries been forced to live by government decree.

The attempt was made to link the high level of religious observance in the ghettos with the shortcomings of their physical surroundings, as if the latter were a product of the former. Hertz knew the Ghetto Jews very well from his time in America and South Africa. He talked of them with affection and approval: 'The Ghetto Jew ... was a man – heroic, indomitable, free. In a world of brutal ignorance those Jews were free men, although slaves. They thought their own thoughts, measured their actions by their own standards and lived their own lives totally indifferent to the opinions of the blockheads who tortured them.'[6]

Hertz told the audience they needed emancipation from self-contempt. What he was telling them between the lines was that they shouldn't give up their level of observance in order to fit in better with their Christian surroundings. They didn't have to feel embarrassed by their own standards. This was definitely not the view of the previous Chief Rabbi, Hermann Adler. He had adopted much of the dress of Christian vicars for his own ministers and had even been known to attend national events dressed in a bishop's gaiters. Hertz occasionally followed suit.

The implication that Judaism could be improved by copying Christian practices had, however, little appeal for Hertz. He believed in recognizing the differences between religions, and not being concerned about them. It was significant, however, that a gathering of United Synagogue ministers saw the majority in clerical collars, and very few of them with their heads covered. This was the practice, though, in those days. Rabbinical attitudes have varied in the past, some arguing that covering the head was mandatory only for prayer, study and eating.

At the same time, Hertz inherited the goodwill in the wider community enjoyed by Adler. His predecessor had been related to one of the few Jewish aristocratic families, Henry de Worms, Baron Pirbright. Adler was accepted by the establishment, became a commander of the Royal Victorian Order, and Edward VII had referred to him as 'my Chief Rabbi'. It was, therefore, expected that the new Chief Rabbi would be invited to many significant official events. When Lord Milner opened an important new building in December 1913, Hertz was there. Unlike the conference on White Slavery, there was no necessity on this occasion to be contentious. In May 1914 he was at the Guildhall lunch for a visit of the Danish royal family. In the same month he was a guest at the dinner of the British–German Friendship Society.

It was also in 1914 that Hertz dealt with the question of the long-term composition of his Beth Din.[7] It wasn't just a question of having sufficient rabbis – a Beth Din needs three judges to form a quorum. It was also a question of finding candidates with sufficient expertise. They are very rare because the knowledge they need is extensive.

When there were comparatively few Jews in Britain at the beginning of the nineteenth century, most of the work could be done by the Chief Rabbis – Solomon Herschell and Nathan Marcus Adler, working with occasional help from other selected rabbis. Once the mass of refugees arrived, this minimum staffing became inadequate. When Adler retired in 1879, he left Rabbi Jacob Reinowitz to head the day-to-day working of the court. Reinowitz, who was related to Rose Hertz, had the necessary Talmudic ability to carry the burden. The court gave decisions on questions raised by communities throughout the country and overseas.

When Hermann Adler had taken over from his father, he became the Av Beth Din, but the problem for Adler was that he didn't have sufficient Talmudic knowledge to do the job properly and he knew it. His strength was in representing the Jewish community with the wider public. When Reinowitz died in 1893, Adler appointed Susman Cohen, who was Reinowitz's son-in-law, to replace him. Susman Cohen was equally learned.

When Hertz became Chief Rabbi, twenty years later, the Beth Din consisted of Moses Hyamson, who almost immediately left for America, and Asher Feldman. They had both received their *semichas* from Hermann Adler at Jews' College, whose standards were not considered by the immigrant newcomers to be comparable to those of the great *yeshivot* in Eastern Europe. So a highly respected, Orthodox continental rabbi from the Federation, Avigdor Chaikin, was made a member to placate the immigrants. Hertz also appointed three additional dayanim, Samuel Isaac Hillman, a Glasgow rabbi, Harris Lazarus, who was Susman Cohen's son-in-law, and Yaakov ben Zion Mendelson. The latter two were designated assistant dayanim and Hertz would rely on Hillman for most of the halakhic decisions for the next twenty years.

When Hertz installed Hillman, Lazarus and Mendelson at the Great Synagogue in May 1914, he reminded them what their job had always been: 'to walk in the ways of the Almighty', 'To be a co-worker with G-d' and 'the duty of the dayanim is to keep G-d's charges'. They were there to apply and define the *din*.[8]

In Hermann Adler's time this job specification for dayanim created few problems. There were few demarcation disputes between the lay leaders and the Chief Rabbi. Tricky points of law had been left to Jacob Reinowitz and Susman Cohen. Hertz was happy with the system, but laid down the ground rules afresh in the installation address to the new dayanim.

He started with flattery: 'Today's service is a complete vindication of the statesmanship of the Communal leaders who, years ago, realized the possibilities of the Beth Din as a unifying force in the Community.'[9]

He then listed the court's responsibilities: 'Communal and synagogue matters, affecting the Metropolis, the Provinces and the Colonies, over and above the multiform affairs of Shechitah and Kashrut, together with civil arbitration and quasi-magisterial advice on all matters affecting the life of the people'. As the Av Beth Din, a great deal of authority remained in Hertz's hands. Nobody queried the content of the sermon. What Hertz had said was in accordance with the normal situation at the United Synagogue and the Board of Deputies.

It would only create problems in the apparently unlikely event that the lay leaders should decide to compete for religious authority.

When even more learned dayanim were appointed in the 1930s, Hertz would be accused of falling under their influence, but the situation had, in fact, not changed in the slightest. Whoever was appointed as a dayan, the same responsibility applied. Sometimes, of course, there were different interpretations of specific injunctions, but in those cases it was expected that the most lenient decision would be applied, as the dayanim knew.

Hertz was never going to devote all his time to the smaller details of Jewish practice and individual Beth Din cases. There were far too many fundamental problems facing him. For example, how to get good candidates for the provincial ministry when the post was often advertised at £1.25 a week. Although, in Britain, the Chief Rabbi officially only had responsibility for the United Synagogues in London, most provincial communities would rely on him for judgments and the approval of appointees. By law he had to approve the appointment of *shochetim*, Jewish animal slaughterers, and confirm the right of any new Ashkenazi Jewish community to have a marriage secretary.

The situation with ministers, as a whole, was very unsatisfactory. When Hertz examined the state of his own United Synagogue ministry, he had serious reservations about their job specifications. While their main concern should have been with religious matters, they were often also the secretaries of their synagogues and almost fully occupied with the bureaucratic minutiae of their congregations. There were also too few of them where the Jewish communities were expanding. Revd Moses Abrahams in Leeds was highly regarded, but it was estimated that he had responsibility for as many as 15,000–20,000 Jews throughout the city.

As Hertz complained: 'Anglo-Jewish ministers haven't the time to study, like Continental Rabbis, or long holidays like Americans ... the scandal of a miserly underpaid ministry must cease.'[10] Hertz, however, would fight a long and finally unsuccessful battle to improve those salaries and also the funding for Jews' College. He complained that 'Jews' College is still starved and beggared without bursaries.'[11]

He considered the result catastrophic in the way it affected the Jewish education of the young. As he said when he installed the dayanim: 'Today the great majority of Jewish boys and girls in their adolescent period – in fact nearly all our youth in secondary schools – are left without any religious guidance'.[12] This problem would constantly exercise the Chief Rabbi's mind. The solution lay many years in the future in the time of Chief Rabbi Immanuel Jacobovits, inspired by Rabbi Solomon Schonfeld.

A minor organization, the Conference of Anglo-Jewish Preachers, reflected the views of the Jewish ministers in Britain, but it hadn't met since 1911, just before Chief Rabbi Adler died. It was cross-communal and gathered again in June 1914 with Aaron Green, the Hampstead minister, as president. The organization was not held in much esteem. The *Jewish Chronicle* commented in advance that: 'the idea of the conference had been prostituted to personal ends, to sentiments of petty spite, to mean ambition'.[13]

The main concern of the provincial ministers was for the development of district organizations which would provide them with increased authority. Ministers like Revd Harris Jerevitch from Cardiff complained that, under the present regime, he was unable to speak his mind in the pulpit. As an example he recalled his complaint about card playing at communal social functions, for which he had been criticized.

Of even more concern was that the pay and conditions of provincial ministers were not only poor but made no provision for pensions. Hertz was seriously concerned about this. He had preached at the Central Synagogue in London in 1913 and said that the pay was: 'hardly sufficient to keep body and soul together'.[14] There was a provincial ministers' fund to augment salaries but its resources allowed it to help fewer than twenty clerics. Little had been achieved since the last conference, and the core problem was the inability of provincial communities to find the necessary money.

The community certainly had its challenges. As Revd Aaron Green said from the chair: 'Communities without guidance, danger zones without protection, congregations without ministers, pulpits without preachers, children without proper education, pettiness dominating public questions, strife and disorder disfiguring congregational life and delicate situations created by inefficiency and met with crass ineptitude.'[15]

Not surprisingly, it was agreed at the conference that Hertz would now be appointed president, which moved to his office all the responsibility for correcting the shortcomings. Hertz accepted the appointment with some reluctance because he recognized the intractable problems it involved, but it did have the effect of giving him a greater involvement in provincial shuls, which were not under the aegis of the United Synagogue. In his address to the delegates he stalled about the timetable for achieving their objectives but, as he had only been in office for a year, this was not unreasonable.

As early as January 1914, Rose Hertz gave an interview to the *Jewish Chronicle*. She was circumspect about commenting on the British institutions she had encountered, but pointed out the very different size of the organization needed in New York, where the Jewish population was at least ten times greater than London. As she pointed out, it was necessary in New York to have professionals rather than to rely entirely on volunteers, because the tasks they undertook were often immense. For example, in 1912, they had raised £50,000 for new premises for the Young Women's Hebrew Association, which is equivalent to about £4 million today.

At the same time, Mrs Chief Rabbi, as she had been nicknamed, pointed out that the South Africa Jewish Orphanage had been run entirely by women, and she talked of the English classes she had run for immigrants. She was quite sure it was totally safe to work in the East End of London, and fully intended to play an active part wherever she could.[16] She became honorary vice-president of the Women's International Zionist Organisation, the chair of the Bayswater Jewish Schools Care Committee, and had many other offices within the community.

Tactfully, Rose Hertz did not comment on the office accommodation with which the Chief Rabbi had been provided. The *Jewish Chronicle* was less circumspect. They described his headquarters as a 'makeshift haven in a Whitechapel slum'.[17] By the end of the year, though, they had a large house at 48 Hamilton Terrace, St John's Wood (renumbered 103 in the 1930s) and lived there till he died.

When the Great War broke out, Hertz was faced with two major problems. He was the figurehead of the community, and part of his role was to maintain and improve its image in the eyes of the general public and the Establishment. He also had to prove the loyalty of the community to the Allied cause, about one section of which there were grave doubts. This was the Russian immigrants, who found themselves asked to fight on behalf of a hated homeland, whose regime had persecuted them mercilessly over the centuries.

The Germans realized the possibility of getting the Russian Jews to act as a fifth column against the Czar and, in conjunction with senior Zionists, tried to get the Russian Jews on their side. Hertz had to ensure that the British immigrants remained loyal to Britain. The vast majority did so.

Hertz's other major problem was Zionism. He had supported the movement in South Africa, attended its 1900 congress and had taken a prominent part in its activities. Now, in Britain, he found that the vast majority of the British Jewish leadership wanted nothing to do with it. First, because they felt that to support it was to suggest that they didn't want to remain in Britain and that, therefore, they had divided loyalties. Second, because Zionism was more closely associated with German foreign policy than British.

Hertz was anxious to see the Zionist objectives come to fruition. As long as Palestine was part of the Turkish empire, the chances of achieving these were almost non-existent. The situation changed when Turkey came into the war on the side of Germany. Now it was recognized that their empire would be split up if the Allies won.

As far as the British were concerned, if they won, the main rival in that region would be not Germany, but France. As Britain's main competitor in the area if the French were in control in the Holy Land, they would be too close for comfort to Egypt and the Suez Canal. Protecting the Canal against all-comers was a key plank in British foreign policy, as it was the route to India. During the war there would be two attacks by the Turks on sections of the Suez Canal, which were easily repulsed, but the threat was there. Having an empty Sinai desert to its east, rather than French settlements or a Turkish army, suited Britain well.

German responsibility for the Holocaust in later decades has tended to rewrite that country's position regarding the early days of Zionism. The Kaiser was not against the movement; in 1889 he had visited Jerusalem and met with Theodor Herzl. He immediately became enthused with the philosophy of Zionism and promised to help. Although his enthusiasm waned, as it often did, when he met Herzl again in 1897, it was reignited.

Germany sought to increase its influence in the Middle East by supporting the Turkish regime. The British ambassador in Constantinople later reported to the Foreign Office that the Young Turks movement, which seriously reduced the power of the Turkish Sultan in 1908, was a Jewish/Freemasonry conspiracy. The small Judeo/Moslem community in Constantinople called the Donmeh, was also blamed. They were remnants of a seventeenth-century movement, led originally by Sabbatei Zevi. Hertz would later write to *The Times* to point out that they were scarcely Jews, having left the faith in 1666.

The ambassador's report was accepted by the Foreign Office, however, and in 1911 *The Times* reported that "The leaders of the Zionist movement were Yiddish speaking Jews, all of whom understood German."[18] Hertz fitted the description. It was, of course, true that Zionism had been founded by an Austrian and was headquartered in Berlin. The president of the German Zionist Federation, Max

Bodenheimer, was also a staunch German patriot and Chaim Weizmann was educated in Germany.

The British Foreign Office had a good case for considering that: "Zionism was merely a tool of the German Foreign Office".[19] If Germany had won the war, a national home for the Jews in Palestine would have been a feasible possibility. The German Committee for the Liberation of Russian Jewry issued a mission statement, as soon as the war broke out, to ask Russian Jews to support the axis powers against the Czar on the field of battle, in both word and deed. This was grist to the mill of those Russian anti-Semites who characterized Russian Jews as potential enemies of the state.

The British government knew that immigrant Jews in Britain had good reason for hating the Russian government, and that the Arabs in the Middle East were potential allies against the Turks, hoping for independence from the Turkish Empire which would be more likely to come if the allies won. To counter this, the Germans wanted to start a Jihad against the allies in the Middle East, and the Chairman of the International Zionist Executive in Berlin, Professor Otto Warburg, was an enthusiastic supporter of the idea.

As the Zionists were only a tiny minority in the Middle East, there was every reason for the Foreign Office to support the Arabs rather than the Jews, but if the Germans were supporting the Zionists, the British would want to compete for their help. There was an equally erroneous belief in the Foreign Office that the Jews had international influence, particularly in America. As a consequence, Britain eventually made promises to the Arabs at the same time that they issued the Balfour Declaration, favouring a national home for the Jews in Palestine. This ambivalence would seriously muddy the political waters after the war.

As Zionism was associated with Germany and Austria, Hertz's support for it might well look disloyal. At an early stage in his ministry, he could do without that. The majority of the community leadership put the need to protect their reputations as loyal citizens far ahead of supporting Zionism. Moreover, Russia was a major Allied power. So, if the objectives of the Zionists in Britain, like Hertz and Haham Moses Gaster, were to prevail, they would have to win over the Foreign Office as well as the majority of their own community leadership.

Jews joined up to fight loyally on both sides in the First World War and produced both British and German heroes and casualties. The war memorials at Jewish cemeteries would eventually name the thousands who died in the conflict. A small percentage of the Russian immigrants were initially unwilling to enlist but, when conscription was introduced, they had no option but to do so.

This reluctance of Russian Jews was, of course, condemned by their British enemies as unpatriotic – and in many cases that would have been true – but overall a slightly larger proportion of the total Jewish community served in the forces than the national average. Hertz knew that the numbers of objectors involved was small – the figure of 8 per cent was frequently quoted, though surely without statistical back-up – but as he said: 'Even a little wet straw can produce enough smoke to hide the stars.'

The persecution of Jews in Russia did not stop during the war. The Russians noted German efforts to recruit them and there was much international condemnation of Czarist anti-Semitic activities.[20] One of the most prominent Zionists, Nahum Sokolow, tried to persuade Hertz to support: 'a day for the suffering Jews of Russia'.[21] He wrote: 'The only point I am interested in is that an expression should be given to the most terrible martyrdom of our people, as a means to bring home to the Jews the fact of the unexampled sufferings of the defenceless and oppressed masses of our brethren and to stimulate the work of relief and help.'[22]

The problem for Hertz remained that an anti-Russian demonstration would not be welcomed by the government during wartime and could almost be considered treasonable. At the same time, Hertz was very supportive of Eastern European Jews. As he said, in introducing Sokolow at a meeting of the Union of Jewish Literary Societies in December 1915: 'Some of the most Jewish of Jewish life existed in the Eastern Jewries, where, during the last few generations, movements of rationalism, mysticism, moralism, all forms of spiritual endeavour had been active.'[23]

The stereotype of ghetto life, as primitive in Jewish terms, continued to have no greater opponent than the Chief Rabbi.

Solomon Schechter died in 1915. He had been a major influence in the development of the Jewish Theological Seminary in New York and its subsequent movement away from its Orthodox roots would not have had his approval. According to his obituary in the *Jewish Chronicle*: 'At no period of his life was he in sympathy with that tangential offshoot of the synagogue "German Reform". It was ... its antinomianism – the ruthless tearing up of immemorial Jewish culture, rites and institutions, that filled him with despair.'[24]

Hertz felt that Schechter was primarily motivated to keep worldwide Jewry together. He knew that Schechter was in favour of Hebrew, the traditional character of the liturgy, and of loyalty to the Torah.

On the home front, in September 1914, just a month after the outbreak of war, Rose gave birth to her fifth child and second daughter,

Josephine, at their temporary home in Gordon Square. It was a happy moment in the terrible war years. The casualties were horrendous and the Chief Rabbi worked to keep the community focused on the task at hand. In 1916 he was asked to give a ruling on whether *Cohanim* could fight. In Bible times they hadn't done so and there was some question about whether an exception could be made. Hertz laid it down firmly that where the safety of the country was threatened, *Cohanim* should fight like any other Jew.[25]

In making this decision he overruled the dayan he normally relied on for Beth Din halakhic decisions. Samuel Hillman had supported the din that *Cohanim* (priests) are not allowed to come into contact with a dead body. A proscription that makes it difficult to be on active service. Hertz also insisted that *yeshiva* students should enlist, counter to Rabbi Avraham Kook's view.

Kook was one of the most eminent Talmudic minds in the country, who would go on to be the first Ashkenazi Chief Rabbi in Palestine. He had been stranded in Switzerland at the outbreak of war and arrived in England in 1916. He preferred not to be involved with the local rabbinic authorities but, on this occasion, he made his views clear. Hertz gave an opposite ruling which should have been remembered when, in the future, Hertz was said to be unduly influenced by Talmudic authorities.

There was also the question of what attitude should be taken about Conscientious Objectors: those who refused to fight. Two ministers who felt that the objectors' point of view had merit were Joseph Hochman, now Hockman, and John Harris. They made their position clear in the pulpit, and when their lay leaders rejected their views, Hockman resigned and Harris was dismissed. Harris, who had served twenty-one years in Liverpool, had not bothered to ask Hertz's opinion before taking his stand and had little support in his congregation.

Hockman was a fine young speaker who, in 1915, had been appointed lecturer in Homiletics at Jews' College. He had, however, espoused other radical views and by this time was advocating mixed seating in synagogue, an end to *kashrut* and abandoning the law against riding to shul on Shabbat. Hertz grasped the nettle and threatened to withdraw his licence to be a United Synagogue minister, which was in the Chief Rabbi's remit. Hockman's resignation solved the problem.

As the views of ministers could have been seen by the outside world as representing the views of the community, it was reasonable to avoid giving anti-Semites such a gift. At the same time it raised again the question of whether a minister had the right to say whatever he liked from the pulpit. The *Jewish Chronicle* condemned one Honorary

Officer who had been heard to tell his minister: 'Never mind what we ought to know, that is our business and not yours, you preach what we like to hear and you will get on all right.'[26]

Nobody, of course, could stop Hertz preaching what he chose. He confined himself, primarily, to rallying the community to the Allied cause even as so many of their sons fell in battle. In June 1916 he went on a pastoral tour round the West Country, Wales and Manchester.

In Wales it was the first time they had been visited by their Chief Rabbi for eighteen years. In Swansea he gave a *drasha* (lecture) in Yiddish which was particularly appreciated. Hertz attracted large congregations, and vast audiences who packed the halls whenever he spoke to the general community. When he addressed a wider audience, he usually gave his lecture on 'The Bible as a Book', which was much admired by churchmen as well as Jewish audiences.

He supported local charities by making appeals from the pulpit. He attended civic receptions given in his honour and welcomed mayors to synagogue services at which he was preaching. He would have attended a civic reception in Cardiff, but had to hurry back to London to attend the memorial service in St Paul's Cathedral for Lord Kitchener, the British commander-in-chief, who had recently died when the ship he was travelling on was sunk. National events, calling on the president of the Local Government Board as a member of the National Council for Combating Venereal Disease, or the prize-giving for the Kilburn Talmud Torah (Sunday School), were all part of the Chief Rabbi's programme.

The war continued to take its terrible toll and civilians were suffering too. There was a mass meeting in February 1916 to raise money for the relief of Jewish victims of the war in Russia, and on that occasion all sectors of the Jewish community in Britain were well represented.

It was, however, the pastoral visits which contributed much to Hertz's popularity. He was a born leader and a fine orator and he made his audiences feel that they mattered to him. Not for a moment was the impression given that these were simply glad-handing exercises to gain more support from the locals. Hertz would deal with local issues more as a headmaster than a supplicant.

He would denounce quarrelsome congregations and call for greater decorum during services. When he spoke, crying young children would have to be removed. Throughout the provinces it was the Chief Rabbi who was the final court of appeal if there were disputes. He was certainly more of a firm father than a jolly uncle, but in a steadily more hedonistic age, he spoke out clearly for high moral and ethical standards.

Hertz made it a policy to visit Talmud Torahs on Sundays to see the children studying, and he also called on the Jewish boarding house at Cheltenham College, whose house master was Daniel Lipson. That academic would go on to be a headmaster and mayor of the town, before being turned down as a Conservative candidate for Parliament because he was Jewish. Standing as an Independent, he was returned by the electorate and served the constituency from 1937 to 1950.

As a Zionist, Hertz was always ready to come to the defence of the movement, which continued to be attacked as creating the impression of disloyalty to the country. It was also accused of reneging on a pledge of loyalty resulting from the emancipation of the Jews in the nineteenth century. In December 1916 Hertz responded to one such article, to the approval of the press: 'The ignoble and dishonouring theory that Jewish emancipation in Britain ... was the result of a bargain under which the Jews obtained justice in return for his renunciation of ancestral aspirations is blown sky high.'[27]

Of greater importance to the community at the time was the question of *shechita*. To ensure the meat was fit to eat, the supervision had to be impeccable, but there were hundreds of kosher butchers and, according to Rabbi Jung of the Federation, only sixty to eighty *shochetim*. The rabbi complained that the standards of supervision were inadequate and, as the Chief Rabbi appointed the *shochetim*, he held him, personally, responsible.

Hertz, for his part, was happy to be advised by the experts at the United Synagogue, even more than the members of the Board of *Shechita*. The arguments had gone on for years and it was a minefield. The perceived inadequacies had led to the court case in Liverpool and neither side was anxious to raise its heads above this parapet again.

Meetings between Hertz and Jung were inconclusive until Jung disclosed his hand. The Federation wanted to decentralize the supervision of *shechita* to their own rabbis, although the Chief Rabbi would have the final word. Had Hertz agreed, the power of his office would have been substantially reduced in this important area of communal activity; the Federation would undoubtedly have taken the change as the first step towards full independence from the Chief Rabbi's current role. There was disagreement on whether meat which had not been porged (deveined) was kosher. Hertz approved it but in later years non-porged meat would be declared *treif* (not kosher). At this time, however, Hertz decided to make no changes.

If the timetable of the Chief Rabbi was packed full of activity around community issues, it was also necessary to give guidance on more esoteric aspects of Judaism to those who sought it. Hertz had definite views, for example, on Jewish mysticism. He wrote an article in *Hibbert's Journal* on Cabalism: 'To ignore Cabalism ... is to leave unexplored large portions of the map of Jewish life and thought; that to remain ignorant of Jewish mysticism is largely to fail to grasp one of the distinctive sides of the Jewish genius and one of the greatest driving forces in Jewish history.'[28]

His daily round also took in government enquiries. In June 1916 he was giving evidence to the National Birth Rate Commission which was trying to establish the average size of a Jewish family. Hertz tried to explain to the commission, whose members included a number of Church dignitaries, the difference between a Jewish family in Whitechapel and one in Kensington. Although the former had between eight and twelve children and the latter about two and a half, the distinction between the cultures was not immediately obvious. Were they not all Jews? Yes, but ... Hertz did not feel disposed to go into the rulings of Maimonides or the intricacies of a Jewish sex life.

NOTES

1. Aubrey Newman, *The United Synagogue, 1870–1970* (London: Routledge and Kegan Paul, 1976). See statistics pp.215–20.
2. Editorial, *Jewish Chronicle*, 22 May 1914.
3. Robert Henriques, *Sir Robert Waley Cohen, 1877–1952* (London: Secker and Warburg, 1966), p.31.
4. Newman, *The United Synagogue 1870–1970*, p.131.
5. Editorial, *Jewish Chronicle*, 27 March 1914.
6. Editorial, *Jewish Chronicle*, 26 June 1914.
7. When Jews have disputes between themselves, they can go to the court of the Chief Rabbi, the Beth Din, for a ruling. It isn't binding as it would be in a British court, but if both parties agree in advance to abide by its conclusions, then its decisions are applied. In addition, in anything of a religious nature, the Beth Din determines what the Jewish law is and in areas like the synagogue, *kashrut*, marriage and divorce, the decision of the Beth Din is final. The Chief Rabbi was the chairman, the Av Beth Din.
8. Derek Taylor, *British Chief Rabbis, 1664–2006* (London and Portland, OR: Vallentine Mitchell, 2007), p.357.
9. Joseph Herman Hertz, *Sermons, Addresses and Studies*, Vol. 1 (London: Soncino Press, 1938), p.325.
10. Ibid.
11. Ibid.
12. Werner E. Mosse (ed.), *Second Chance: Two Centuries of German-speaking Jews in the United Kingdom* (Tubingen: J.C.B. Mohr, 1991), p.71.
13. Editorial, *Jewish Chronicle*, 12 June 1914.
14. Ibid., p.32.
15. *Jewish Chronicle*, 9 June 1914.
16. *Jewish Chronicle*, 2 January 1914.
17. *Jewish Chronicle*, 22 May 1914.
18. Walter Lacqueur, *A History of Zionism* (London: Weidenfeld and Nicolson, 1972), p.143.
19. Ibid.

20. *The Times*, 13 October 1916.
21. Letter from Nahum Sokolow to the Chief Rabbi, 22 July 1915, Jeremy Schonfield private family archive.
22. Ibid.
23. *Jewish Chronicle*, 17 December 1915.
24. *Jewish Chronicle*, 24 December 1915.
25. *Jewish Chronicle*, 17 March 1916.
26. *Jewish Chronicle*, 24 March 1916.
27. *Jewish Chronicle*, 1 December 1916.
28. *Jewish Chronicle*, 7 July 1916.

Chapter Six

A Pause for the Balfour Declaration, 1917

On 22 March 1915 Hertz became naturalized as a British subject. It was unusual for this to be approved so soon after arriving in the country, but Hertz was well trusted.

He then went to visit the Western Front. It was a journey specifically designed to give a positive demonstration of the allegiance of the community to the task of fighting the war. During his visit he went to major hospitals in the Boulogne area to talk to the Jewish wounded. He prayed at Jewish graves in the local military cemetery. He visited Sir John French, the British commander-in-chief. Over the course of more than a week he went down the line from Ypres in the north to Vermelles in the south. At one point he held a service with the roar of a heavy cannonade of guns as a backdrop. He visited field hospitals.[1] He told his audiences that he was reminded of visiting Jewish troops fifteen years before, during the Boer War, and he took the opportunity of pronouncing the British Empire: 'earth's nearest realization hitherto of might coupled with justice, of power joined to mercy'.[2]

In an official dispatch afterwards, French said that anyone who now chose to question Jewish loyalty and military ardour did so in defiance of the Declaration of the commander-in-chief of the British army. Hertz was perfectly sincere in his support for the war and it was a public relations triumph, serving as a contrast to the reluctance of some British-based Russian Jews to serve.

Hertz's public image grew again. Back home he had settled down to the more mundane tasks of his office. In November, for example, he presided at the annual meeting of the Hammersmith and West Kensington Religion classes. The following February, when the King opened the School of Oriental Studies at the London Institute, the Chief Rabbi was invited.

He was also starting to turn over in his mind the possibility of what would become his magnum opus. His translation of the book of Joshua for the Jewish Publication Society of America in 1896 had reinforced his belief that: 'A Jewish commentary on the Bible is one of the crying needs of Anglo-Jewry.'[3] Rose supported him in this but it would be some years before the work could start.

In spite of the demands of his office, Hertz still found time to teach Samuel and Leon some *Gemara*, the Aramaic text of the Talmud. He expected a high standard from the children. Leon complained to his mother after a series of corrections to his homework: 'Does father think I know anything?'[4]

When the war started, the Allied powers tried to resolve their differences over the Middle East. A secret agreement was drawn up by the French and British in 1916 to divide up the region after the end of hostilities, but in the Holy Land the British were only allocated the ports of Haifa and Acre. It was agreed that the rest of the country would be internationalized because of the world-wide interest in the holy sites. This settlement – the Sykes–Picot Agreement – was so-called because the British representative was Sir Mark Sykes and the French delegate François-Georges Picot. The Zionists were not consulted or involved in any way. France would later claim that Syria included the Holy Land and was, therefore, in the French part of the pickings, but that view would be rejected at the Versailles Peace Conference in 1919.

Keen as Hertz was on Zionism, it did not seem likely that Britain would support the idea of the Holy Land as a national home for the Jews. Herbert Asquith, the prime minister from 1908 to 1916, thought the idea fantastic and so it was. Setting out to regain and reoccupy a country that was lost 1,800 years ago is the stuff of dreams. In 1914 there were 85,000 Jews in the Holy Land but there were also 600,000 Arabs.

The majority of the core Jewish population in Palestine for most of the nineteenth century had been highly traditional and lived there to study the Torah in the country that had not been ruled by Jews since Biblical times. From the 1880s, however, about 35,000 Jews, mostly from Eastern Europe, had come to colonize the land. These founded a few agricultural settlements, developed vineyards with the help of Sir Moses Montefiore and the Rothschilds, and started to try to transform a desert into a land flowing with milk and honey.

In these endeavours they were helped by many rich Jews, even though the donors may have disapproved strongly of Zionism as a movement. The trouble with Zionism in their eyes continued to be that it suggested the Jews should have their own country and were, therefore, not happy to be citizens of the one in which they had been born or settled.

Hermann Adler had justly claimed that the Jews were persecuted around the world for having a different religion, rather than a different nationality. He insisted that, since the destruction of the Temple and the dispersion of the Jews, they no longer constituted a nation, but formed a religious community. The lay leader of the American Jews took the same view. In 1907, Jacob Schiff said: 'speaking as an American, I cannot for a moment consider that one can be at the same time a true American and an honest adherent of the Zionist movement'.[5]

Most Jewish leaders in Britain were anti-Zionist. The movement was seen as a self-inflicted hammer with which anti-Semites could hit Jews over the head. In 1914, in a community of over 300,000, only 8,000 were members of the Zionist Federation. Out of well over 10 million Jews, world-wide, there were only 130,000 members. The international Jewish community, as a whole, were not enthusiastic Zionists.

Edwin Montagu, secretary for India, led the opposition in the House of Commons. He was the son of Sir Samuel Montagu of the Federation of Synagogues, but this elegant aspirant to an honoured place in the British Establishment was not interested in Orthodoxy. He didn't want the government to support a National Home for the Jews, and the government found it difficult to ignore the views of a Jewish member of their own cabinet. Even when it was finally decided to issue the Declaration, it contained a sentence drafted by Montagu to reflect his concerns.

The Declaration, it said, should not affect: 'the rights and political status enjoyed in any other country by such Jews who are fully contented with their existing nationality and citizenship'.[6] When consulted on the final draft, Hertz asked for this to be amended to: 'the rights and political status enjoyed by Jews in any other country', eliminating the implied defence against an accusation of disloyalty.

That was what was finally agreed, but what were the other reasons for the government to entertain the idea of issuing the Declaration in the first place? Explanations have been suggested in plenty. Lloyd George, the prime minister in 1917, had been brought up on the Bible and favoured a Jewish return to their ancestral home as an end to their sufferings. Also he didn't want to see the Holy Land in the hands of what he considered to be agnostic and atheistic France.

Another reason advanced was the debt Lloyd George and the country owed Chaim Weizmann, the Zionist leader. It was Weizmann, senior lecturer in Biochemistry at Manchester University, who discovered how to make acetone with bacterial fermentation, using horse chestnuts, which made it easier to produce ammunition for the war. Lloyd George actually said: 'Acetate converted me to Zionism'[7] – but the Balfour Declaration couldn't surely have just been a way of saying 'thank you' to Weizmann; the war years were not a time for sentimental gestures and Weizmann was simply acting as a loyal citizen.

In fact Lloyd George was no stranger to the thinking of the Zionists. He had been introduced to Zionism as far back as 1903 when Balfour was the Conservative prime minister. Lloyd George was approached by Theodor Herzl to draw up a draft charter for an autonomous state for the Jews, which the Balfour government was considering offering them in East Africa. Lloyd George was only a lowly Liberal opposition MP at the time, but he was a partner in Lloyd George, Roberts & Co., solicitors, and a coming man. The Zionists became his clients and in lengthy discussions on the subject of the charter, he learned a great deal about Zionism.

Lloyd George was also being lobbied, after the Turks came into the war, by the first Jewish member of a British cabinet, Herbert Samuel. Samuel had been a politician from the time he left university and, although a member of the Cousinhood, took little part in Jewish affairs. Edwin Montagu was his cousin. Where Samuel stood on Zionism was unknown in 1914. What was also little known, however, was that his wife was a lifelong and intimate friend of Moses Gaster's wife, Leah. It was the Haham, a pillar of the Zionist movement, who first persuaded Samuel to take Zionism seriously.

Whatever Lloyd George's affinity with the ideals of Zionism might have been, as prime minister he was working on the agenda for which he had been appointed, which was to win the Great War. As with Cromwell's readmission of the Jews, the reason for the government's proposed policy in Palestine was that it was likely to be in the best interests of Britain.

The position of Arthur Balfour, the foreign secretary, was also a factor. Balfour was not a Liberal, unlike Lloyd George. He was brought into the coalition government during the war in order that a united country could confront its enemies. He had strong contacts in his Manchester constituency, though, with Charles Dreyfus, who was president of the Manchester Zionist Society. Dreyfus was a successful local businessman and chairman of the East Manchester Conservative Association. In 1906 he had managed Balfour's election campaign. The overall results had been disastrous for the Conservative party, but that wasn't the fault of Dreyfus.

Balfour was a great patriot and a great diplomat, but he had a guilt complex about the history of the Jews. As he said in 1916:

> Had Continental Europe followed the example set by this country for the last 250 years, its history would not be stained by many crimes and many injustices which now stand on record as a perpetual reproach to Christian civilisation. That in this country there is no Jewish question ... is due in no small measure to the fact that the Jews have shown themselves entirely worthy of the rights and privileges they enjoy as citizens of this country.[8]

If the interests of the United Kingdom and those of the Jews were the same, then Balfour liked the idea of doing something to balance the Judeo-Christian books. That opportunity came in the spring of 1916 when Britain and her Allies had a good chance of losing the war. Wherever you looked, Germany and her supporters were winning.

The Dardanelles campaign against the Turks had been a disaster and the battles on the Western Front were producing appalling casualties and little territorial gain. The Russians in the east were looking more and more like a beaten force. The cost of the war was ruining the country, the French were getting nowhere and the German blockade was biting.

The single event that could turn the tide was to enlist the Americans on the side of the Allies. Woodrow Wilson, the American president, was a Zionist supporter and the American ambassador in Constantinople was a Jew, Henry Morgenthau. The problem was that the vast majority of Americans were isolationist and not interested in, or very much against, going to war. Although there were plenty of Anglophiles or Francophiles, there were also large numbers of German and Austrian immigrants who supported the opposition. And why risk having a lot of your youngsters killed in a war between European powers 3,000 miles away? How would that benefit the United States?

In desperation, the Allied governments went over every option, no matter how remote, which might bring the Americans round. One thought was that American Jews might be able to influence President Wilson and his Congress. This influence was overestimated, but the British government were clutching at straws.

There was, as in Britain, a major difficulty with this train of thought; the American Jews also hated the Russians and with ample cause. Why then should they take the side of the Allies? An even wilder idea suggested itself. What about suggesting a National Home for the Jews in the Holy Land? Might not that tip the Jewish-American balance in favour of the Allies? It was a thought.

As time went by, the situation for the Allies worsened. In 1917 the Czar was overthrown. A few Jews took senior places in the new government. Now it was a question of could the Kerensky regime be persuaded not to make a separate peace with Germany? What might persuade the new Russian-Jewish politicians to vote to continue fighting for the Allies? Zionism? It wasn't likely. Most Jewish Communists would have favoured another organization: the Russian Jewish Bund. This was created about the same time as the First Zionist Congress in 1897. It was anti-Zionist because its founders felt that Zionism took the eyes of the Jewish workers off the Socialist Revolution.

The Declaration remained a possibility. Sykes, of the Sykes–Picot agreement, was given the job of advising the government on what to do. He talked to Samuel and Samuel put him on to Gaster. Not to an official spokesman for the Zionists, but to his wife's friend's husband. Moses Gaster, a dynamic communicator, went into overdrive to persuade Sykes that the impossible dream could come true.

Gaster made the position, as he saw it, crystal clear. 'The claim to be Englishmen of the Jewish persuasion – that is English by nationality and Jewish by faith – was an absolute self-delusion.'[9] Most Jews remained deluded, but Sykes was converted to Zionism. Balfour might get the credit for the Declaration, but it was Sykes who was its architect and, when he died in the influenza epidemic in 1919, he was sincerely mourned in Zionist ranks.

In Britain it was common knowledge that there was a minor pressure group called Zionists, who advocated that the Jews should go back to the Holy Land. There was also that considerable body of opinion who thought the Zionists were a front movement for the Germans. Haham Gaster had felt it necessary to say at the Eleventh Zionist congress in 1913 that Jews were fighting everywhere, to make it clear that they felt neither German, English, French nor Russian, but that their sentiments and thoughts were solely and exclusively Jewish.

That was in line with what Cromwell and Charles II had accepted 250 years before when it was agreed that Jews were not Spanish or Portuguese, even if they had been born in those countries and never naturalized as British. They were categorized instead simply as Jews. The position of the Mahamad in 1664 had changed as Jews became British citizens. Now the Haham's statement was the antithesis of the Sephardi leadership's current stance.

So what did British Jews, as a whole, think about the idea of a Declaration? Lucien Wolf was secretary of the Conjoint Foreign Committee. This was a joint grouping of the Board of Deputies and the Anglo-Jewish Association (AJA) which claimed to speak for

Anglo-Jewry on foreign affairs. Wolf would be the AJA's foreign policy spokesman at the 1919 peace conference, where he summed up the position of most British Jews at the time: that the Zionists were considered foreign Jews, with no authority to speak for native Jews of the United Kingdom and with whom, for the most part, they did not cooperate in the affairs of the community. The answer from those two major Jewish bodies had been made even clearer in a letter to *The Times*, published on 24 May 1917.

It was signed by David Alexander, KC, president of the Board of Deputies and Claude Montefiore, president of the Anglo-Jewish Association. Alexander was considered rigorously Orthodox and uncompromisingly integrationist. He was a senior barrister and the wording of the letter was carefully measured: 'the present claim is ... part and parcel of a wider Zionist theory, which regards all the Jewish communities of the world as constituting one homeless nationality, incapable of complete social and political identification with the nations among whom they dwell and it is argued for this homeless nationality a political centre and an always available homeland in Palestine are necessary'.

If this viewpoint were accepted: 'In the countries in which they [the Jews] are still struggling for equal rights they will find themselves hopelessly compromised, while in other countries where those rights have been secured, they would have great difficulty in defending them.'[10]

Alexander and Montefiore didn't want a declaration at any price, and felt, quite correctly, that they spoke for the majority of the community. The only risk they took in voicing these sentiments publicly was that neither president had a remit to present their personal views as those held by the body they led. There had been no prior consultations. Only the Conjoint had agreed to the initiative, by twelve votes to two, the previous week. Hertz was present but had no vote. He objected to the statement and walked out of the meeting. The members took no notice. They didn't consider it necessary to bother with the views of the Chief Rabbi.

At least Hertz knew enough about the proposal to write to *The Times*. The letter was not even on the agenda of a Board of Deputies meeting which had been held just four days before it appeared in the paper. This was typical of the treatment of Zionist motions over the past many years. Often they weren't debated, or policy was decided at the top, discussions guillotined, or a boycott applied to the topic.

The Conjoint members were delegates for their two organizations but, in like vein, the AJA members also did not report back for approval by their council, even on such a vital matter. They obviously expected their parent bodies to rubber-stamp their decision – particularly if they didn't know about it until too late. What they ignored was that there was a new Lord Rothschild to be considered and a comparatively new Chief Rabbi.

Natty Rothschild had died in 1915. His son, Walter, didn't like being upstaged any more than his father would have done, and he was about to put down his marker as the legitimate successor. He wrote to *The Times* on 28 May, in a dismissive statement towards his opponents: 'our opponents, although a mere fraction of the Jewish opinion of the world, seek to interfere in the wishes and aspirations of by far the larger mass of the Jewish people'.[11]

Hertz was happy to back up Rothschild, even though his lordship's contention was quite untrue. There was no way the Chief Rabbi was going to let Claude Montefiore, the founder of Liberal Judaism in Britain, have the last word on behalf of the Chief Rabbi's flock. The time was ripe for Hertz to speak out for the Zionist position. It gave him the opportunity to make his claim to be independent of the lay leaders and his view was also supported by the executive of the South African Zionists, who made public their disquiet. Jan Smuts was in Britain at the time and he met with Hertz in 1917 at the Savoy Hotel where he was staying. He diplomatically had another engagement, however, when Hertz invited him to a pro-Zionist rally.

Ignoring Hertz's views was an error that both Alexander and Montefiore were to regret. Hertz, after all, had been a vice-president of the South African Zionist Federation, and was well known to Lord Milner, who was now in the War Cabinet and helping to draft the Balfour Declaration. The arrogance of Alexander and Montefiore in thinking they could ride roughshod over Hertz illustrated their dismissal of the importance of both the man and his position.

They were now to learn that the views, courage and personality of their new Chief Rabbi were very different from his predecessors. On 24 May Hertz wrote to *The Times*:

> I cannot allow your readers to remain under the misconception that the said statements represent in the least the views held either by Anglo-Jewry as a whole, or by the Jewries of the Overseas Dominions ... It is indeed grievously painful to me to write this in your influential columns. But I am impelled to do so in the interests of truth, and in justice to the communities of which I have the honour and privilege of being the spiritual head.[12]

It was a slap in the face for the leaders of the two most prestigious Jewish organizations of the time, and highlighted the fact that the British communities of which Hertz was the spiritual head didn't want the declaration but had no voice. The battle, however, was by no means over.

On 29 May no fewer than eighteen of the lay Jewish leadership ranged themselves against their Chief Rabbi and backed up Alexander and Montefiore: 'we, being Jews of British birth and nationality [a dig at Hertz], actively engaged in public work in the Anglo-Jewish community, desire to state that we approve of, and associate ourselves with the statement ... published in *The Times* of the 24th inst'.[13]

Faced with such conflicting opinions, the government finally decided to consult eight Jews on the subject, including the Chief Rabbi. The Chief Rabbi replied:

> It is with feelings of the profoundest gratification that I learn of the intention of H.M. government to lend its powerful support to the re-establishment in Palestine of a National Home for the Jewish people. The proposed declaration of H.M. government that it 'will use its best endeavours to facilitate the achievement of this object' will mark an epoch in Jewish history. To millions of my brethren throughout the world, it will mean the realisation of Israel's undying hope of a Restoration – a hope that has been the spiritual lodestar of Israel's wanderings for the last 1800 years.
>
> The draft declaration is in spirit and substance everything that could be desired. I welcome the reference to the civil and religious rights of the non-Jewish communities in Palestine ... the overwhelming majority of Anglo-Jewry, as well as the Jewries of His Majesty's Overseas Dominions, will rejoice with me at this broad humanity and far-sighted statesmanship of the men who guide the destinies of the Empire.[14]

If there was no Jewish consensus, the government now had an even freer hand to make up its own mind in the best interests of the state. The Zionists would be a useful addition to the limited support they had in the Middle East. The fact that both Lord Rothschild and the Chief Rabbi, two of the most senior leaders of the British Jews – three if you count Haham Gaster – made it clear that they did want the Declaration, reassured the government that the religious voice of the community was in favour.

Important as the Board of Deputies and the Anglo-Jewish Association were, much as their members controlled the community's religious purse-strings and institutions, they were not icons or the spiritual leaders of the community.

Matters came to a head when the influential *Times* wrote on 26 October 1917 that: 'Germany has been quick to perceive the danger to her schemes that would be involved in the association of the Allies with Jewish National hopes and she has not been idle in attempting to forestall us.'[15] In fact, the Kaiser had been involved with Herzl long before the British became involved.

The Declaration came a few days later. Balfour made his famous, if fuzzy, statement of British support for a National Home:

> His Majesty's government view with favour the establishment in Palestine of a home for the Jewish people, and will use their best endeavours to facilitate the achievement of this object, it being clearly understood that nothing shall be done which may prejudice the civil and religious rights of existing non-Jewish communities in Palestine, or the rights and political status enjoyed by Jews in any other country.

The results for the British government were disappointing. The Russians still pulled out of the war, the American Jews didn't have the influence the government had hoped for and the Declaration was a serious embarrassment to British post-war Middle East policy, because it upset the Arabs who had not been consulted before it was issued. Years later Lloyd George dryly explained why there had been that omission: 'we could not get in touch with the Palestinian Arabs as they were fighting against us'.[16]

Events like the sinking of the RMS *Lusitania* in 1915, with important American casualties, probably had more effect on President Wilson's decision to enter the conflict than the Declaration. The likely consequences of the Balfour Declaration were not well thought out. The concept was based on the wildly overoptimistic hope that the Arabs and Jews would both be happy to allow Palestine to become a National Home for the Jews. That was never likely and it didn't happen.

To make matters worse for David Alexander, the wishes of influential Jews who were anti-Zionist had not been adopted. The Board of Deputies had met again and, astonishingly, voted by 56–51, with six abstentions, not to support their president's action. This substantially strengthened the view of the government. Was this support for the Chief Rabbi, though? Did it mean that the Board of Deputies had a Zionist majority? Many delegates specifically rejected any such idea.

As Deputy Simon Rowson, who voted for the Zionist position and against the views in the president's letter, said: 'I sincerely hope the decision will not be strained to represent support for the principles of the Zionist organisation.'[17] There were, in fact, probably no more than a dozen active Zionists on the Board.

The Board of Deputies did have a majority – that of members who felt they should have been consulted before the president acted. It was the lack of consultation which swung the vote in favour of the Zionists. The provincial deputies had been complaining about unilateral decisions in London for years; nobody had paid much attention. Now the provinces finally had the opportunity of getting their own back and they seized it with alacrity. An analysis of the voting shows the London/Provincial demarcation very clearly.[18] Of forty-five provincial delegates, only six supported the president. Five abstained and no fewer than thirty-four voted against him.

So probably the most crucial vote in the history of the Board of Deputies, disavowing the president's opposition to the proposal now known as the Balfour Declaration, was narrowly passed because a lot of deputies were piqued, yet again, at not having been asked their opinion. It was passed, not because of noble aspirations, because it was a farsighted strategy, or in support of the Chief Rabbi, but because of spite. Which is how a lot more history comes about than is generally acknowledged.

The president fell on his sword and resigned. The Conjoint Foreign Committee, formed from both the Board and the AJA, was dissolved. Among those who voted for the president – and, therefore, against Hertz's position – was Joseph Freedman, a member of the London Brondesbury Synagogue, representing the Chatham community, who would appear again more positively when the Hertz Chumash was published. The Declaration gave a terrific fillip to the movement, of course, because it created the possibility that this apparently totally unrealistic idea might, amazingly, come about.

Hertz's views had triumphed. Within five years of the start of his thirty-year rule as Chief Rabbi, he had shown that he was perfectly capable of taking on the Jewish Establishment, if necessary, single-handed. The independence of a Biblical prophet, the authority of a Ghetto rabbi and the devotion to free speech of an American citizen were alive and well and living in the Chief Rabbi's person.

If United Synagogue ministers found it difficult to 'challenge its masters', Hertz certainly proved he did not. He had taken on Kruger in South Africa before the Boer War and Max Langermann, his senior warden, widely considered the most powerful Jew in South Africa, in creating the South African Board of Deputies. If he believed in the cause, Hertz would fight anybody. The Honorary Officers, and particularly Waley Cohen, never learned that lesson.

General Allenby entered Jerusalem in December and Hertz wrote to the King offering his congratulation, saying that: 'The House of Israel ... fervently prays that ... [the allies would have] complete and lasting success.' While this was certainly true of the Jews fighting on the side of the Allies, a correspondent in the *Jewish Chronicle* rightly suggested that the Chief Rabbi might have misrepresented the situation, as Jews living in Germany, Austria and other enemy countries certainly hoped for nothing of the kind.[19]

The Jewish opponents of the concept of the Balfour Declaration regrouped and: 'established the League of British Jews which claimed to be non-Zionist rather than anti-Zionist, but which opposed with great vehemence the idea of a Jewish National Home'.[20] Waley Cohen explained its purpose as to enable: 'Jews of British nationality to voice their views independently of the Jews of foreign origin who are residing in this country but who feel no strong attachment to their British nationality.'[21]

The League went on to produce their own journal, the *Jewish Guardian* from 1919 to 1931. This set out to be in competition with the pro-Zionist *Jewish Chronicle*. The *Jewish Guardian* was influential in the next decade under the editorship of Sir Philip Magnus' son, Laurie Magnus, but ceased publication in 1931. Magnus died in 1933, by which time the Zionist cause was supported by a far larger proportion of the community.

It was necessary for Hertz to take whatever opportunities presented themselves to reiterate Jewish loyalty. In June there had been anti-Jewish riots in Leeds involving stone-throwing and some looting. The chief constable had taken firm action and the riots soon petered out, but they naturally concerned the community, which labelled the disturbances a pogrom. This illustrated their ignorance of the far more dreadful treatment of Jews in so many pogroms in Eastern Europe.

The national press condemned the outbreaks, but pointed out that the local cause for unrest was that a large number of Eastern European Jews had come to live in Leeds over a short period of time and had retained their traditional culture; shop signs in Yiddish, unusual dress, and a highly visible foreign presence disturbed many people in the town. Moreover, some of the local *Cohanim* had staged a protest meeting at having to serve in the armed forces and that hadn't gone down at all well with the general population. There was also a completely untrue rumour that the community's youth refused to enlist in the forces. In fact, 2,500 had already joined up out of a total Jewish population of 21,000.

Leeds was an isolated problem. The more typical attitude of the provinces was Hertz's pastoral visit to Sheffield in June. After the usual domestic programme, he gave his lecture on 'The Bible as a Book' and over 1,000 people turned out to listen to him, including the Lord Mayor.

By 1917 the First World War was continuing to claim vast numbers of casualties. In 1916, in the Battle of the Somme alone, there had been 420,000 British dead and wounded. At this point, prompted by Rose Hertz, the Chief Rabbi produced his *Book of Jewish Thoughts*, in a pocket edition designed for sailors and soldiers. It aimed to help alleviate the enormous challenge Hertz faced in bringing some comfort to the men facing death on the battlefield. It would go through twenty reprints, two world wars and hundreds of thousands of copies would be issued. The pocket edition was never designed to be put on sale.

The book tackles its objective brilliantly. It quotes famous writers, particularly on Jewish martyrdom over the centuries: Flavius Josephus on their suffering under the Romans, Ephraim of Bonn in 1180 on the effect of the Second Crusade, Isaac d'Israeli on the mass suicide in York in 1190, W.E.H. Lecky on the expulsion from Spain in 1492 and Ossip Dymov writing about pogroms in Russia in 1906.

The quotations are not just historical facts. They are personalized, so that each tells the story of an individual who died because he wouldn't be baptised, or suffered merely for being Jewish. Much of the material is moving because the experiences of an individual have far more impact than bare statistics. The serviceman faced with dying for his country was assured that he would join a long list of martyrs, who had achieved the survival of the Jews against all the odds over the centuries. It offered a purpose for the sacrifice.

The choice of quotations said much about Hertz. All his friends at the Jewish Theological Seminary in New York were represented: Morais, Kohut, Drachman and Schechter. Their thoughts are ennobled by being in the same company as Maimonides and Rashi. As he wanted to reach the widest possible audience, the Chief Rabbi also included the thoughts of Jewish religious leaders of whose theology he disapproved.

There are eleven quotations from Revd Morris Joseph, who had been forced out of the United Synagogue and gone to the Reform's Upper Berkeley Street. There were even two from Claude Montefiore, the creator of the Liberal Synagogue. A wide range of non-Jewish notables were brought in to bear witness, from President Theodore

Roosevelt and A.J. Balfour to Robert Louis Stevenson and Henry Wadsworth Longfellow.

Among the most telling was a quotation from a French historian, A Leroy Beaulieu, in 1893:

> They were here before us; they are our elders. Their children were taught to read from the scrolls of the Torah before our Latin alphabet had reached its final form ... before the Runic characters were known to the German of the North. As compared with the Jews, we are young, we are newcomers; in the matter of civilisation they are far ahead of us. It was in vain that we locked them up for several hundred years behind the walls of the ghetto. No sooner were their prison gates unbarred than they easily caught up with us, even on those paths which we had opened up without their aid.[22]

The book was designed to inspire both Jews and those who were interested in the ancient faith.

After the war, the British found they faced a major problem in the Middle East: they had to mediate between the Arabs and the Jews in Palestine, when they were given the mandate to run the country. It was soon obvious that the Arabs would be treated more favourably than the Jews by the administration. There were, for example, extensive riots over four days in April 1920. Some Jews had bought arms for self-defence.

One of their leaders, Vladimir Jabotinsky, who had helped create the Allied Zion Camel Corps, fought bravely at Gallipoli and helped form the Jewish Legion in the British army, was charged with possessing three rifles, two pistols and 250 rounds of ammunition. He was sentenced to fifteen years imprisonment. There had to be complaints in both *The Times* and the House of Commons at the severity of the sentence, before it was reduced to a year. By contrast Muhammad Amin-Al Hussein, one of the instigators of the riots, had fought in the Ottoman army during the war. He received a ten year sentence but was pardoned and made Grand Mufti of Jerusalem. He would support Hitler in the Second World War. It was never going to be a level playing field.

NOTES

1. *The Times*, 30 June 1915.
2. *Jewish Chronicle*, 2 July 1915.
3. Joseph Herman Hertz, *Sermons, Addresses and Studies* (London: Soncino Press, 1938), Vol.1, p.65.

4. File 60/1, J.H. Hertz Archive, Hartley Library, University of Southampton.
5. Leonard Stein, *The Balfour Declaration* (London: Vallentine Mitchell, 1961), p.70.
6. Samuel Landman (ed.), *Essays Presented to Dr J.H. Hertz, Chief Rabbi* (London: Edward Goldston, 1942), p.269.
7. Stein, *The Balfour Declaration*, p.120.
8. Ibid., p.149.
9. Landman (ed.), *Essays Presented to Dr J.H. Hertz*, p.269.
10. *The Times*, 24 May 1917.
11. *The Times*, 28 May 1917.
12. *The Times*, 24 May 1917.
13. The signatories were led by Lord Swaythling and included Edward Stern, Israel Abrahams, Leonard Cohen, Ernest Franklin, Michael Green, H.S.Q. Henriques, Joshua Levy, Laurie Magnus, Edmund Sebag-Montefiore, Arthur Moro, Philip Waley, Albert Woolf, Israel Gollancz, Charles Henry, Matthew Nathan, Lionel Abrahams and Isidore Spielmann.
14. Landman (ed.), *Essays Presented to Dr J.H. Hertz*, p.269.
15. Sean McMeekin, *The Berlin–Baghdad Express: The Ottoman Empire and Germany's Bid for World Power, 1898–1918* (Cambridge, MA: Harvard University Press, 2010), p.353.
16. Ibid., p.353.
17. Stein, *The Balfour Declaration*, p.120.
18. Stuart Cohen, 'The Zionists and the Board of Deputies in 1917', *Jewish Journal of Sociology*, 8 (1977/78). The attendance at the meeting was very high. 143 deputies were entitled to vote and 113 did. The numbers who voted was the highest turnout since the Board's formation 150 years before. Of the sixty-seven new members elected since 1913, most voted against the old guard; thirty-eight to sixteen with four abstentions and nine absentees. Geographically speaking, the split (figures *for* the president first) was: London congregation deputies and Sephardim: 22:4; London-based deputies representing provincial communities & overseas: 23:18 – one abstention; Provincial deputies: 6:34 – five abstentions; Total: 51:56 – six abstentions.
19. Editorial, *Jewish Chronicle*, 21 December 1917.
20. Chaim Bermant, *The Cousinhood: The Anglo-Jewish Gentry* (London: Eyre and Spottiswoode, 1971), p.372.
21. Niall Ferguson, *The World's Banker: The History of the House of Rothschild* (London: Weidenfeld and Nicolson, 1998), p.980.
22. Joseph Herman Hertz, *A Book of Jewish Thoughts* (London: Eyre and Spottiswoode, 1917), p.174.

Chapter Seven

The Grand Tour

Opposing the views of the president of the Board of Deputies and of the Anglo-Jewish Association (AJA) had been well within Hertz's compass. He was at home in august surroundings. At the banquet to celebrate the peace in January 1920, he found himself introducing the Lord Chief Justice, Lord Reading, a successful Jewish former cabinet minister. Hertz quipped: 'speaking as one Chief to another, some of us achieve chiefdom, others have it thrust upon them'.[1] As his good friend, Ephraim Levine, said of him: 'he appreciated a witticism and his own quickness in epigram was always a delight'.[2]

The challenges, however, were about to get greater. In February 1918, Robert Waley Cohen was elected a vice-president of the United Synagogue. As the president, Lionel de Rothschild, continued to be largely a figurehead, Waley Cohen inevitably came to have far more to do with the Chief Rabbi. This was a mixed blessing for both of them. In the words of Waley Cohen's cousin, admirer and biographer, Robert Henriques, the new vice-president was: 'brought into regular contact and inevitable conflict with a man who was every bit as stubborn as himself and whose powers of invective were almost the equal of his own'.[3]

The conclusions drawn by Henriques on the relationship between Hertz and Waley Cohen seem influenced by Henriques' own religious viewpoint as a member of the Reform Synagogue. In many ways Waley Cohen's approach was also the position of the Reform Synagogue and Henriques favoured his cousin's similar outlook. It was suggested later that: 'Orthodox leaders began to feel, with some justification, that Henriques was drawing young people away from traditional Judaism.'[4]

The word 'almost' in the quotation above might suggest that Waley Cohen's invective was stronger than Hertz but the key problem was a question of priorities. The root cause of the conflicts over the next twenty-five years was that Hertz was intent on upholding Jewish observance and Waley Cohen, even though he was at the top of the United Synagogue, had little time for this.

To take just one example, as a Cohen, he had the privilege of blessing a congregation during festival services. Waley Cohen regularly carried out this duty, but when he bought a farm in Somerset, he drove to London to perform it, even though Orthodox Jews are not allowed to drive on the Sabbath or festivals. For such a senior Honorary Officer of the United Synagogue to be well known for this behaviour, was to cock a snook at the law.

Far from appointment as an Honorary Officer, he would not even have been accepted as a *member* at the Orach Chaim synagogue. Waley Cohen preferred his spiritual approach to religion, rather than acting in accordance with Jewish law. This is defendable philosophically but it is totally inappropriate in a senior officer of an Orthodox synagogue organization. It is somewhat like William Webb Ellis playing football, picking up the ball and inventing rugby. He would not have remained captain of the football team.

Waley Cohen labelled his ideas a 'Spiritist' approach to Judaism. He emphasized the need for high moral and ethical standards. In fact all members of the Jewish community are supportive of such standards. In any religion there are, however, also important ritual elements: in Judaism, the *tsitsis* (fringed undergarment), *tefillin* (phylacteries), the separation of milk and meat, and *kashrut*, are just a few examples.

Jewish law has a special place in the survival of the Jewish people because it was the way the religion managed to survive for centuries. Without a country, always in a minority, subject to persecution, the Jews clung to the law as laid down in the Bible and interpreted in the sixth century Babylonian Talmud. The law was at the core of the religion, and Hertz was not going to let it be sidelined because it might suit an Honorary Officer with a different viewpoint.

The Spiritist approach differed from traditional Orthodoxy in its belief that the *mitzvot* should play a lesser role in Judaism. The Reform and Liberal movements agreed with this, but not the Orthodox Jews, for whom each *mitzvah* had to be seen as equally important as any other. Waley Cohen knew that he was not observing the Sabbath laws correctly among many others he chose equally to ignore. Waley Cohen's self-esteem would have made it necessary to justify this position to himself. Officially, he had to support such laws, but he constantly tried to move the United Synagogue closer to the Reform position, a strategy guaranteed to cause friction with Hertz.

Far from seeking compromise with a 'Spiritist' ideology, Hertz castigated it from the pulpit and in his writings throughout his ministry. Waley Cohen would be deeply embarrassed by the: 'Chief Rabbi's insistence on publicly and vehemently denouncing those congregations which contained many leaders of Anglo-Jewry who were not only Bob's relatives and friends, but also his colleagues on a variety of charitable committees.'[5]

From Hertz's point of view, he was not running a charity. If those who argued against the Orthodox approach were Waley Cohen's friends or leaders of the community, that was unfortunate, but it didn't alter anything. Hertz was there to uphold the *din*. If those who supported charities wanted to make it a condition of so doing that ignoring the *mitzvot* was officially acceptable, the Chief Rabbi would not succumb to blackmail either.

He was accustomed to dealing with lay leaders used to unqualified obedience from those around them. Max Langerman had been in that position at the Witwatersrand synagogue. As one of the earliest developers of gold mining on the Rand, Langerman had the same reputation for supporting the British cause as Hertz. He had been imprisoned after the Jameson Raid and banished from the country for two years afterwards. As the lay leader of the community after that war, he had been important enough to be made a member of the Transvaal Senate in 1907. Hertz had, nevertheless, stood his ground with Langerman on a number of issues and their relationship was often stormy.

Hertz was, nevertheless, fully prepared to maintain the courtesies with those with whom he disagreed. It was Hermann Adler who had prevented Morris Joseph from taking the Hampstead pulpit, leading him to move to the Reform's Upper Berkeley Street in 1893. Now he was celebrating his seventieth birthday and Hertz sent him warmest best wishes and congratulations on completing twenty-five years' service with the congregation.

One of the problems Hertz had with Waley Cohen was that his mother had often conducted the children's services at the Reform's Upper Berkeley Street synagogue. Hertz felt that she would hardly have failed to try to inculcate into her son her own religious views, though these were not those of the United Synagogue.

Admittedly, Waley Cohen had only agreed to accept the heavy responsibility of treasurer of the United Synagogue because he had a strong belief in public duty and because his father-in-law had held the same post. He was extremely diligent. It was often wondered whether he spent more of his working life at the headquarters of the United Synagogue or in his office as managing director of Shell Transport and Trading, a couple of miles away.

At first he thought that if he persevered in explaining his point of view to the Chief Rabbi, he would be able to bring Hertz round to his way of thinking. As early as 1919 he had written to him to suggest: 'an early accommodation of the differences that have arisen in the community on the Zionist question'.[6] There was, in fact, no way that these differences could be settled by an accommodation. Most Jewish leaders remained firmly anti-Zionist and Hertz was not going to alter his pro-Zionist stance.

The gap between them was clearly illustrated when Waley Cohen found himself in New York in the autumn of 1917. He spent Yom Kippur, the Fast, at the Liberal Synagogue, Temple Emanu-el and reported: 'I felt it more like an opera than a service ... most beautiful and impressive.'[7]

Waley Cohen might have learned from the history of Temple Emanu-el where initial minor changes in the ritual might lead. It had been founded in 1845 by thirty-three mostly German Jews as an Orthodox synagogue. In 1848 the congregation decided to use German rather than Hebrew for its prayers. An organ arrived in 1849 and calling up members to the reading of the law was abolished in 1853. Mixed seating was approved in 1854, when the New Year festival was reduced from two days to one. Barmitzvahs were abolished in the 1870s.

To the Orthodox accused of excessive rigidity, Temple Emanu-el was an example of the importance of inflexibility in maintaining the Orthodox position.

Waley Cohen earned his knighthood during the Great War by, among other things, helping to organize the immensely complicated oil and petrol supplies for the army and navy. He also advised an Inter-Allied Petroleum Council when the Americans came into the conflict. At the same time that he took on the vice-presidency of the United Synagogue, he was appointed petroleum adviser to the War Office. There is no question that Waley Cohen had many excellent qualities and was even a very fine amateur cellist.

Among his achievements was the development of the United Synagogue as an organization. He ran the business with the care and attention he devoted to Shell. He did support the Chief Rabbi on most occasions, and he would never allow anybody, other than himself, to criticize Hertz. When a Jewish newspaper (not the *Jewish Chronicle*) attacked Hertz in 1919, it was Waley Cohen who saw to it that they never did so again.

Hertz was always careful to choose his fights. At an early stage of his ministry as Chief Rabbi, he didn't want to score points for the sake of it. So when Waley Cohen's mother, Sissy (Julia) Cohen died in 1917, Hertz went out of his way to heap praise on the deceased.

He referred to her: 'conspicuous ability and zeal which have left their mark strongly upon our communal organisations'. He went on:

> Everywhere she looked for the unity underlying the diversity in our religious life, and refusing to admit that the various movements at present agitating Jewry were irreconcilable ... a fine mind that endowed her with remarkable clarity of vision in regard to all the larger social problems of the day; a wise heart vibrating with sympathy for every good cause within and without the Jewish community; and a Jewish soul – such would be my summing up of this rare flower of Anglo-Jewish culture. [8]

Hertz's encomium wasn't just a question of not speaking ill of the dead. At the time, of course, the differences between the United Synagogue and the British Reform positions were not irreconcilable.

A lot of the opposition to Hertz's leadership also came from leaders of the Right Wing. Their popular spokesman, Victor Schonfeld, was the rabbi of the very Orthodox Adath Yisroel synagogue in North London. Although both Hertz and Schonfeld came from the *Torah im Derech Eretz* school, Schonfeld could create his own levels of observance for his one small congregation. Hertz had inherited a system and, if he wanted to alter it, he would need time to do so.

Almost as soon as he had been elected, Hertz was asked by Schonfeld to confirm that the Adath Yisroel synagogue was 'a body of Jews' for the purpose of having a marriage secretary. As the synagogue didn't recognize the authority of the Chief Rabbi, Hertz withheld his confirmation for six years in the hope that the congregation would change its mind. It didn't do so and as it was perfectly obvious that it was indeed a community of Jews, Hertz was using the Marriage Act incorrectly for purposes for which it had not been designed. At the same time it was true that Schonfeld was making life very difficult. Herman Adler had used the same tactics with the Sunderland Beth Hamedresh community in his time.

Schonfeld was insistent on sanctioning divorces and arranging *chalitza* ceremonies[9] on his own authority as well. If remarriage became an issue in the future, however, it would be Hertz, as the British Chief Rabbi, who most ministers around the world would ask to confirm that the *din* had been followed and the woman in question could celebrate another wedding. Obviously Hertz would find this difficult if he didn't know anything about the cases handled by Schonfeld.

If a congregation wasn't recognized by the Chief Rabbi, those who wanted to get married had to have a Registry Office wedding with a

Synagogue ceremony some while after. Outside the Jewish community it was the civil ceremony that made the marriage legal. The situation created complications. For example, to make the synagogue ceremony halakhically acceptable, it was necessary to ensure that the witnesses at the civil ceremony were ineligible to act in that capacity in the synagogue. Close female relatives were, therefore, a popular choice for the civil ceremony.

Normally, Hertz was anxious to improve relations between the various Orthodox communities. The Sephardim had been the major force in British Jewry when Sir Moses Montefiore was alive and they guarded their independence. Now Hertz was beginning to outshine their own highly intellectual religious leader, Moses Gaster, who had lost the confidence of the Sephardi ruling body, the Mahamad. They were still sensitive, however, to any suggestion that the Ashkenazi Chief Rabbi had any influence in their world. As a peace offering, Hertz gave them a portrait of their greatest Haham, David Nietto, and a fulsome letter of personal warm regards. The Sephardim were suitably flattered.

Schonfeld and Hertz had worked together during the war to help the Belgian refugees and those Austro-Hungarian Jews who had been interned. Now that the danger had passed, Schonfeld turned to domestic considerations and announced that he objected strongly to the standards set by the dayanim of the London Beth Din. He wrote to Hertz to complain:

> There is a far-felt and manifold dissatisfaction. There are matters of religious principle which make it impossible for observant Jews to entrust their ritual instructions to the London Beth Din. There are thousands who feel that although the Beth Din may think it necessary to compromise on religious matters for the sake of the unity of the community, they cannot expect of observant Jews, who in their private lives know not of religious compromise, to submit to a state of affairs thus created.[10]

The United Synagogue rejected the generalized accusations out of hand but invited Schonfeld – if he came by himself – to meet with the Chief Rabbi and the Honorary Officers. Hertz always considered Schonfeld as his most severe critic on the Right Wing, though in 1919 he provided the confirmation that was needed for the *Adath* community to have a marriage secretary after Schonfeld agreed to a compromise. In future Schonfeld would continue to act on his own volition but would inform Hertz after the event of the facts in each case. That would include marriages as well. Hertz agreed with this and even offered Schonfeld a seat on the Beth Din, but the negotiations broke down.

Schonfeld would make it known that: 'I do not regard it [The United Synagogue] as a strictly Orthodox institution.'[11] He thought it was prepared to make too many concessions concerning the *din*. This was one of the reasons he wanted to change the existing set-up by which the United Synagogue alone appointed the dayanim on the Beth Din.

Other problems remained for the strictly Orthodox. If they were members of a United Synagogue congregation, the United Synagogue rule was that no burial could take place within forty-eight hours of death. This provided sufficient time for the decorous organization of the obsequies. It wasn't, however, according to the Halacha. This laid down that the body had to be interred as soon as possible, normally within twenty-four hours. In later years, with better organization, the correct rule was applied, but at this period the very Orthodox were unable to apply the Halacha correctly.

One particular subject to which Schonfeld also objected continued to be *shechita* – the humane slaughter of animals. The rules covering the subject are very extensive and the Chief Rabbi had the responsibility for licensing the slaughterers and seeing that they were properly supervised. Normally the financial aspects were dealt with by the Board of *Shechita* and the Chief Rabbi left them to make the necessary arrangements. In the summer of 1918, however, the Board was faced with an ultimatum: the *shochetim* would go on strike if they didn't get a 30 per cent increase in their wages. Furthermore, they wanted permanent contracts of employment when they had worked for the Board for eight years.

The Board couldn't afford the increase. They had a £2,500 overdraft and were losing £100 a week. They had approached the government's food controller for permission to raise the prices of kosher meat but they had been turned down. The government didn't want the cost of food to go up during the war. At the same time, a *shochet* could earn as little as £1.50 a week and, with inflation, it was no longer a living wage. It looked as if there was an impasse and the Orthodox community might very soon be going vegetarian.

Hertz stepped into the breach. He announced that he would go to see the Minister of Food and ask the government to make an exception. An agreement was reached with the ministry and it was also agreed that the master butchers would pay more for their licences. The *shochetim* received a rise and the Chief Rabbi the plaudits: 'A Chief Rabbi, a business man, and a benevolent autocrat, all united in a single personality, we imagine a striking evolution in a great office.'[12]

Hertz was, however, not universally admired. Waley Cohen's biographer, Robert Henriques, probably summed up the view of a lot of the Cousinhood when he wrote:

> The position of Chief Rabbi in Britain has always been very difficult to maintain, except by a high minded, broad-minded man of great personality able by his quality to win respect from all sections of the Community. In the century or so since the Chief Rabbinate was instituted only the first one or two occupants of this office have risen to these demanding heights, and Dr Hertz was not one of them.[13]

Henriques went on: 'Unfortunately the Chief Rabbi was unable to distinguish between the respect due to his office and the deference which he felt was due to him personally. He tended to seek publicity for himself on all occasions and to discover a denigration of his office in almost any incident or encounter which did not feed his vanity.'

Henriques was writing in 1966, twenty years after Hertz died, and he must have been well aware that the Chief Rabbi had eventually been given one of the highest decorations in the Honours List. If Hertz was vain, he had a lot to be vain about.

The sour tone of these comments and the superior attitude adopted by the author, apart from his obvious lack of knowledge of the Chief Rabbi's predecessors, illustrates, however, the poisoned atmosphere that so often existed when Hertz and Waley Cohen met. There should have been no contest. On the one hand you had the physically impressive Waley Cohen, fully capable of running an organization like the United Synagogue, which was minute compared to his own company, Shell Petroleum.

On the other hand you had Hertz, small, American, living on a modest salary, initially unconnected with the broad spectrum of the Jewish leadership in Britain, and with no deep understanding of business. When Waley Cohen first met him, it would have seemed an easy task to make Hertz into just another acolyte. Waley Cohen believed he could intimidate Hertz and he used every weapon in a senior executive's armoury to do so. All to no avail.

Hertz was attacked from other sides as well. At the end of the war, there was a witch-hunt to identify anybody who had cooperated with Germany during the conflict. The investigations were conducted by members of the Naturalisation Revocation Commission and it was only necessary to be found to have lacked patriotism, for naturalized immigrants to be made stateless.

This happened to a number of Jews, often on suspect evidence, and Hertz himself was challenged on his record in May 1918. When he appeared before the Commission, however, the only paper produced was a letter from Lord Milner, giving the Chief Rabbi his full support. Nothing further was heard of the proceedings. Denunciations could come from many sources and, in view of the Chief Rabbi's known activities, the likelihood of an anti-Semitic attack could not be discounted.

Hertz had worked hard during the war on behalf of the community. Many of his efforts were not in the public eye. For example, after the meeting of Jewish Chaplains to the Armed Forces in 1918, the Senior Jewish Chaplain, Solomon Lipson, had written to the *Jewish Chronicle* that: 'I would like it to go beyond the conference how helpful Dr Hertz has been and his deep interest in any proposal for the increased comfort of those serving in the forces.'[14] Lipson, himself, had served as a Chaplain since 1905 and had been Mentioned in Dispatches.

Hertz was deeply involved in educational matters, ensuring that a series of readers were published for the use of children at Hebrew classes, one of which he found time to write himself. He encouraged the community to do more about promoting Jewish education. As he said, in his usual challenging manner, at the Union of Hebrew and Religion Classes at the time: 'The Jewish community was notorious for its neglect of the spiritual requirements of its poor and its rich ... neglect was rampant.'[15]

The very Orthodox bodies felt the same way and, at a communal conference arranged in 1919, they went to a lot of trouble to draw up a memorandum on extending the scope of the Hebrew educational curriculum. This, however, was dismissed out of hand by the conference organizers as irrelevant. The apparent aim of the conference was to improve the status of Jewish higher education rather than its contents.

There were small pockets of excellence in Talmudic studies in various parts of the country. There was a small *yeshiva* in Leeds and another in Liverpool. The most notable was the *yeshiva* Etz Haim, which had been set up by a devout group in the East End of London at the beginning of the century. They did not, however, choose to come under the aegis of the Chief Rabbinate.

Among their finest teachers was Rabbi Nachman Shlomo Greenspan who had arrived from Belgium in 1914. Greenspan was a towering Talmudic scholar who had received his rabbinic diploma at the age of 18 and had studied under some of the greatest names in European scholarship. His family was Polish and in 1918, after spells as the head of both the Liverpool and Leeds *yeshivot*, he took over as head of

Etz Haim. He would die in office forty-three years later. His students during those years included the future Chief Rabbi Lord Jakobovits and many other distinguished *rabbanim.*

It might have appeared sensible to adopt a *yeshiva*, rather than Jews' College, as the nub of the effort to improve Jewish education in Britain, but neither side had any interest in such a move. It would have been impossible for either of them to reach agreement on issues of authority and Etz Haim would have wanted to remain completely independent. When Victor Schonfeld started to put together his own right-wing organization, this was the natural home for the *yeshiva*. Greenspan's core focus anyway was entirely on the *yeshiva*, rather than on Jewish education within the whole community.

There were situations where Hertz couldn't turn back the tide but he still tried to use his influence. As the High Holydays approached, he asked synagogue ministers throughout the Empire to take the opportunity at Yom Kippur to preach against the dangers of intermarriage.

Rose Hertz, for her part, appealed at public meetings for a whole range of causes, from more Jewish nurses for Jewish troops in Egypt, to help for Jewish Lady Workers involved in the war effort at home.

The war ended in November 1918 and the following January Hertz was made a Commandeur de l'Ordre de Leopold II of Belgium: 'in recognition of the constant and generous help given to my country in the course of the war'.[16] He also received a signed licence from George V, giving him permission to wear the insignia. In March 1919 he was also officially thanked by the Queen of Romania for his help for the Romanian Red Cross during the war. There was more good news in May when Rose gave birth to their third daughter, Ruth, who would be their last child.

The United Synagogue had to face a number of post-war challenges. When British Jews had abandoned their faith in the past, there had often been influxes of overseas co-religionists to Britain to replenish the ranks. After the First World War, legislation to prevent immigrants coming to Britain was strengthened and the Jewish community would now have to be self-perpetuating. With increasing affluence, however, the average size of families was reducing. If the United Synagogue's membership fell, its financial position would be affected, and the urgent question was how to retain the loyalty of new generations when they moved out of the East End.

It was fortuitous that, at this crucial moment, the finances of the United Synagogue were suddenly markedly improved. The New Synagogue, which had been opened in the City in the eighteenth century, was running out of members, so it was agreed to sell the building, the accepted figure being £135,000. Today that would be about £20 million. Preservation Orders were not involved as they would probably be now. Waley Cohen sensibly created the St Helens Court Fund and used the proceeds of the synagogue sale to help support groups of Jews who wanted to build synagogues in areas to which they had recently moved. It was possible to loan them money at low rates of interest provided the synagogues agreed to owe allegiance to the United Synagogue when they opened.

In return Hertz ensured that traditional synagogue services would remain in place. In 1919 he told the independent Western Synagogue in London, who recognized his authority, that they couldn't have an organ for Shabbat services, even if it was played by a non-Jew. He did, however, allow them to say the traditional prayer for the community in English.

Another request for change came in 1920. Three senior United Synagogue ministers asked the Chief Rabbi to agree to change from reading the whole Pentateuch in synagogue in the course of the year, to doing so over a period of three years. This had been raised before, but Hermann Gollancz at the Bayswater Synagogue, Aaron Asher Green at Hampstead and Michael Adler at the Central occupied three of the most important pulpits in the capital.

Gollancz had been independent enough to go to Europe to get his *semicha* in 1897 against Hermann Adler's wishes. He would be knighted in 1923, the first rabbi to be so honoured. Hertz still refused to give his consent. The United Synagogue Act 1870 stated that the organization would follow the Polish and German ritual which excluded the Triennial cycle. As a consequence, if the cycle had been adopted, many congregants would have had an unassailable case for objecting.

Another problem had been how to deal with the different kinds of United Synagogue communities in everybody's interest. There were congregations with diminishing membership, notably in the East End, whose finances needed support from the centre. There were also new congregations which needed help to get started and substantial communities which would make a profit every year.

A solution in 1899 had been to set up a parallel organization for new communities called the Associated Synagogue scheme, whose participants wouldn't contribute to the central United Synagogue budget. The only exception would be a small contribution to the Chief Rabbi's office.

A few congregations joined the scheme before Hertz took office, but the cost of subsequently becoming a full constituent member of the

United Synagogue was too great, and the idea was dropped in 1927. It was replaced by a District Synagogue scheme and later by an Affiliated Synagogue scheme. However, the wealthier London communities and benefactors continued to carry the large majority of the financial burden.

The immediate post-war period found the Russian Jews suffering massacres again during the Civil War. Between 1919 and 1920 tens of thousands died in the Ukraine in nearly 900 pogroms. When Hertz spoke of such horrors, he reported that he had met with surprised incredulity from ecclesiastics, statesmen, philanthropists and even the leaders of his own community. In twenty-five years' time there would be more incredulity and at a vastly higher cost.

The results of the Great War were far reaching. Hertz needed to take a position on changing situations in many countries. In Turkey, for example, a secular government had replaced the old regime. The Turkish Chief Rabbi: 'introducing far reaching reforms in the Jewish laws of divorce. These have, however, not found recognition with the rabbinic authorities of other lands'.[17]

Even a minor development which was not accepted throughout the Orthodox world could produce a schism, and those who practised it would find themselves outside the pale.

After the war the Prince of Wales went to Canada on an official visit and Hertz had the idea of following suit. When he had been in South Africa he had known of the difficulties that the small Jewish congregations had in maintaining their faith in isolated regions, far from the family feeling of larger communities. Hertz knew how welcome he had always been when he undertook to visit the outposts, and it struck him that this would apply in even greater measure if the Chief Rabbi from London visited them, to show they were not forgotten.

He suggested to the Honorary Officers of the United Synagogue that he undertake such a tour and a Council meeting on 23 March 1920 issued the invitation for him to do so. It was what Hertz wanted but it was not the most opportune moment. Returning home from promoting the Jewish Memorial Fund in Cardiff, on 26 March Hertz was suddenly taken ill and needed an operation to remove his appendix. This was a more serious process than it is today and Hertz was still in the nursing home three weeks later after surgery. He was determined, however, to be at Leon's barmitzvah on 24 April and just managed it.

In preparing for the journey Hertz suggested to Waley Cohen that he would like to take a message from the King with him. Waley Cohen probably discounted or didn't know about Hertz's dealings with important personages in his earlier career. He replied:

> I cannot quite agree with you that it is of the utmost importance that you should be received by the King before you go. If His Majesty's interest in his Jewish subjects is sufficient to make him desire to have from you on your return an account of our Communities throughout his Dominions, that I think would be a compliment to the Community that would be greatly appreciated, but I cannot feel that any use of such an audience should be made for the purpose of impressing the Dominions.[18]

Waley Cohen presumably felt that Hertz had ideas above his station, but the Chief Rabbi was only drawing on his South African experience. In the colony he had no difficulty in reaching Lord Milner if he wanted to do so, and he was also very much persona grata with the governors of the provinces. What was more, he had met the King when he was the heir apparent and Hertz had been chosen to make a speech welcoming him. It wasn't for personal aggrandizement that Hertz wanted the tour to be a success.

After all, he would be leaving his wife and family for nearly a year. Ruth Hertz had only been born in 1919, and Hertz was devoted to his wife and offspring. At the same time, Hertz was extremely conscientious and prepared to carry out the most onerous programme to help encourage the Empire communities. Looking at his speaking schedule, it is surprising that he was able to carry it out without injuring his health.

Hertz couldn't arrange an appointment with the King without the support of the United Synagogue. Waley Cohen withheld this, but at the same time he was very sensitive to the Chief Rabbi's position.

> It seemed to Bob that the expenses of preparing for the tour coming on top of those of a long illness from which the Chief Rabbi had just recovered would be too great a financial strain: consequently he wrote round to half a dozen friends to raise a sum of several hundred pounds, an unsolicited grant which was privately handed to the Chief Rabbi.[19]

(The sum was £500, the equivalent of about £48,500 today in terms of average earnings.)

If the true importance of Hertz's pastoral tour of the Empire was recognized at the time, it was apparently not mentioned. Indeed the *Jewish Chronicle* said that the whole idea of an Empire-Chief Rabbi was a ridiculous illusion.[20] The fact was, however, that in future the Jews in America would become, primarily, Conservative or Reform.

The British would largely remain Orthodox. What would be the theological position of congregations in the Empire, including South Africa, Canada, Australia and New Zealand? Hertz was determined to defend the Orthodox approach.

The Jewish communities in those countries did indeed remain largely Orthodox. A factor in determining this must have been their spiritual leader, a spellbinding Orthodox orator, who would take the trouble to travel round the world to visit their often very small communities and give them encouragement. What is more, he would be welcomed by non-Jewish leaders and treated with great respect. By association, he enhanced the status of all the communities he visited.

The only comparable international Jewish figure had been Sir Moses Montefiore in the nineteenth century, a Jewish hero all over the world. Now a second emerged, strong, confident and fully capable of leading. In achieving the objective for which he had been entrusted. Hertz should take a good deal of credit, even after this passage of time, for the continuing Orthodoxy of the Commonwealth congregations.

This was not, however, Waley Cohen's objective in supporting the tour. He had another agenda. The aftermath of the First World War saw the creation of memorials of all kinds to those who had fallen in the conflict. Few families had been totally unaffected by the slaughter. The Cenotaph, the War Graves Commission, the Armistice Day ceremonies, the Royal Masonic Hospital and the countrywide building of monuments in remembrance, were the fruit of a national effort to ensure that those who had sacrificed their lives were not forgotten. In May 1919 Hertz attended a memorial service to commemorate the death of Edith Cavell, the nurse executed as a spy.

Waley Cohen wanted a Jewish version of the same idea: 'as a monument to the Jews of the British Empire who had fallen in the war and as a thanksgiving to those who had been spared'.[21] He conceived of a Jewish college of learning at Oxford or Cambridge. It would be to establish: 'a permanent centre of Jewish learning – a college for the training of Rabbis, Ministers and Teachers and for the teaching of Jewish children, ensuring that every child shall be brought up in the full knowledge of Judaism and the faith of his forefathers'.[22]

The hidden agenda was that it was believed such a college could also help to solve another of Waley Cohen's bugbears; the attempt to make immigrant Jews fully English was not helped by the fact that so many of the available recruits for the ministry came from the Continent. They were foreign, they were often more religious than their prospective communities, they didn't speak English well and they didn't understand the British way of life. For Waley Cohen, the ideal ministerial candidate would be a public-school boy, Oxbridge educated, and able to speak nicely. Revd Alfred Bender in Cape Town was a shining example.

If more thought had been given to the problem, it would have become evident that such a college would not have appealed to the kind of Orthodox youngster who was considering the ministry as a career. Neither Oxford nor Cambridge could provide kosher food or a Jewish environment. Bernard Homa, a stalwart of the *Machzike Adath*, turned down an Exhibition at Cambridge for this reason, though the Perse School in the town did have a Jewish boarding house.

At Central Hall, Westminster, on 11 June 1919 the War Memorial project was launched and it had Hertz's warm support. The aim was to raise £1 million, and all the various elements of the community were present at the meeting and agreed to the objectives. It was hoped that, as Hertz visited the international congregations, he would be able to gather support from them as well.

At the outset, however, Hertz was warned by many overseas communities that they were not prepared to give donations as they had their own memorials to finance. Indeed all the Empire communities together only gave a total of £70 a year to the maintenance of the Chief Rabbi's office in London. In the event, however, Hertz obtained promises of more than £50,000 during his travels.

Although the idea of raising £1 million for Jewish education, as a memorial for those who had died in the war, was dear to the heart of both Hertz and Waley Cohen, it did not arouse a great deal of enthusiasm in the community as a whole. Over a number of years, even a powerful committee could raise only about 25 per cent of the amount needed. Waley Cohen would eventually have to settle for nurturing Jews' College students.

Of course, Hertz knew that he was an unknown quantity in many of the countries he visited and he was very concerned that his visit might be a damp squib. He now suggested that his record should be sent on in advance, but Waley Cohen opposed this as well, saying that there was a likelihood that it might be misinterpreted:

> All such things tend to enhance the complete misunderstanding of your motives which already exist in certain quarters … these people mistake for personal ambition your anxiety that your tour should achieve great things for the future of Anglo-Jewry … I feel … that you can never achieve that success which your great qualities entitle you to expect unless you succeed in sinking

> personal pride, personal convenience and comfort, and in fact every personal consideration.[23]

Not surprisingly, Hertz found Waley Cohen's comments offensive. He had spent a good deal of his time in South Africa on arduous journeys to small communities to conduct a marriage or celebrate a local barmitzvah. As he told Waley Cohen: 'You were recently with me at Cardiff. I do not think there was much personal pride there to be sunk, and had you accompanied me to Scotland you would have noticed very little personal convenience or comfort.'[24]

Time and again, Waley Cohen adopted for himself the role of headmaster, guru and father-figure, consumed with self-importance and certain that his advice to the Chief Rabbi was always impeccably correct. When he was in one of these moods, Hertz found him insufferable.

Hertz was to be accompanied on the tour by Albert Woolf, whose official title was vice-president but whose field of activity was, effectively, to be in charge of fundraising for the United Synagogue. He had undertaken to try to raise the money for the War Memorial project. They travelled together for eleven months to South Africa, Australia, New Zealand and Canada without the benefit of air-travel, and visited forty-two communities in a 40,000 mile journey.[25] Hertz's concerns that his visits would arouse no interest proved to be triumphantly mistaken. The warmth of the receptions he received was remarkable. Typical of the effect he had was a report in the *Sydney Daily Telegraph*:

> The Chief Rabbi is a small man with a broad and mobile face, but with kind, shrewd eyes, a face that puffs and crinkles with every passing phase of emotion … Of the mere tricks of oratory there are none at all … he speaks as simply and as naturally as if he were talking to a few chosen friends by his own fireside … To hear the Chief Rabbi is to understand how much Christianity had adopted and adapted from the Jews.[26]

Wherever he landed, the Chief Rabbi was greeted by the greatest in the land: Prince Arthur of Connaught welcomed him to Pretoria with Field Marshall Smuts, Lord Forster was on hand in Sydney, Lord Jellicoe at Auckland. Governors, archbishops and cabinet ministers were pleased to shake his hand. There was an illuminated sign outside the Winnipeg Town Hall in Canada which for three days read 'Welcome to Dr Hertz'.

The beneficial effect of the visit for the local Jewish communities was summed up by the *Johannesburg Sunday Times*: 'There can be no doubt of the warmth of his welcome from his old congregation. He comes not only as the High Priest of English Jewry, but as an old friend who through long years of unselfish work among us, endeared himself equally to Jew and Gentile. His influence spread very much further than his sectarian labours.'[27]

Passover in Sydney was particularly memorable. The community hired the Sydney Town Hall for Hertz's talk on 'The Bible as a Book': 'Half the Christian clergymen of Sydney appeared to be present … sparkling epigrams, admirable literary style, real eloquence and scholarship … uplifts the Jewish community, Judaism and Jewish literature in the eyes of non-Jews.'[28]

Altogether Hertz spoke to the general public in twenty cities and estimated that his audiences reached 30,000 in total. It wasn't just the Chief Rabbi, however, who was highly regarded as a result of his tour. The *New Zealand Herald* sent a reporter to hear him: 'I have been listening to a sermon and the Chief Rabbi has confirmed me in my opinion that to be a Jew is a thing in which a man may well take pride.'[29]

The effect of Hertz's addresses to non-Jewish audiences both on his tour and at home were highly beneficial to the current image of the Jewish people. It had only been in August 1921 that *The Times* had produced irrefutable proof that a notorious anti-Semitic book, *The Protocols of the Elders of Zion*, reporting a spurious international Jewish plot for world dominance, was a clumsy forgery. At the time, popular writers like Hilaire Belloc, G.K. Chesterton and H.G. Wells were warning of a Jewish threat to the British way of life. Hertz's lectures gave out a far more positive message, and his growing personal reputation helped considerably to improve the general public's view of the community.

Albert Woolf was a success as well. His 'geniality, courtesy and desire to assist the various congregations made him genuinely popular'.[30] It was, naturally, hard for both men to be away from their families for so long. Hertz sent postcards home regularly. One to Josephine from Perth read 'Daddy had dinner with the Governor in the terrible castle in the picture. He was called Pommy. Mama could tell you why. Kisses, Daddy.'[31] 'Pommy' was Josephine's pet name as a child. Rose and the children wrote him letters. Samuel even wrote them in Hebrew in which he was becoming proficient.

Hertz's time in South Africa enabled him to commend a higher status for the ministers than that enjoyed by many of his colleagues in Britain. He referred to Alfred Bender in Cape Town:

> who is a most popular and respected figure ... In this his position is typical of that occupied by a number of Jewish ministers in the Dominions where congregational leadership is often in the hands of the minister; with a consequent enlargement of his sphere of public service and a deeper respect for his office within the community than is the case in some older Kehillah.[32]

Hertz didn't spare himself. In three weeks in Western Canada he gave eleven sermons and attended thirteen meetings. He spoke to six Canadian Clubs, gave four Bible lectures, to which both Jews and non-Jews came, visited seven Talmud Torahs, and had four receptions. He was also entertained by four lieutenant governors, received by seven mayors and visited three premiers. In the three weeks he covered 2,000 miles.

The large attendances at his public lectures were a tribute to him. Jews would come from hundreds of miles away and Hertz was particularly gratified by: 'a gift of £2,000 he received in Sydney to enable him to start his work on translating the Pentateuch'.[33] He sent loyal greetings to George V in June 1921 and was told that the King 'received with much gratification' his good wishes.

Overall, the tour was a resounding success and when the Chief Rabbi finally arrived back in Southampton on 30 August 1921, it was to a great deal of applause from the community and a personal audience with George V. Lionel de Rothschild, as president of the United Synagogue, offered the community's heartfelt thanks and said that Hertz had performed an incalculable service by his epoch-making tour. Hertz had achieved this with de Rothschild's full approval. The president would be less enthusiastic about Hertz when the Chief Rabbi's views and his own did not coincide.

NOTES

1. Joseph Herman Hertz, *Transactions of the Jewish Historical Society of England*, Vol. 9 (London: JHSE, 1918/20), p.33.
2. Revd Ephraim Levine in Isidore Epstein (ed.), *Joseph Herman Hertz, In Memoriam* (London: Soncino Press, 1947), p.30.
3. Robert Henriques, *Sir Robert Waley Cohen, 1877–1952* (London: Secker and Warburg, 1966), p.231.
4. Chaim Bermant, *The Cousinhood: The Anglo-Jewish Gentry* (London: Eyre and Spottiswoode, 1971), p.381.
5. Henriques, *Sir Robert Waley Cohen*, p.339.
6. Ibid.
7. Ibid., p.340.
8. *Jewish Chronicle*, 12 January 1918.

9. When a childless woman is widowed, the deceased's brother is obliged to marry her in order that the brother's line is perpetuated. A *chalitza* ceremony is required if the woman releases the brother from that obligation.
10. Letter, 6 May 1918, in J.H. Hertz Archive, Hartley Library, University of Southampton, File 86/9.
11. Derek Taylor, *British Chief Rabbis, 1664–2006* (London and Portland, OR: Vallentine Mitchell, 2006), p.353.
12. *Jewish Chronicle*, 25 October 1918.
13. Henriques, *Sir Robert Waley Cohen*, p.339.
14. *Jewish Chronicle*, 8 March 1918.
15. *Jewish Chronicle*, 4 January 1918.
16. Letter from the Belgian ambassador in London, Jeremy Schonfield private family archive.
17. Joseph Herman Hertz, *Sermons, Addresses and Studies*, Vol. 3 (London: Soncino Press, 1938), p.369.
18. Henriques, *Sir Robert Waley Cohen*, p.341.
19. Ibid., p.341.
20. *Jewish Chronicle*, 1 October 1920.
21. Bermant, *The Cousinhood*, p.371.
22. *Jewish Chronicle*, 3 September 1918.
23. Henriques, *Sir Robert Waley Cohen*, p.342.
24. Ibid.
25. J.H. Hertz, *Transactions of the Jewish Historical Society of England*, Vol.10 (London: JHSE, 1921/23), p.149.
26. *Sydney Daily Telegraph*, cutting in Jeremy Schonfield private family archive.
27. Hertz, *Transactions of the Jewish Historical Society of England*, Vol.10, p.149.
28. *Jewish Chronicle*, 1 July 1921.
29. *New Zealand Herald*, cutting in Jeremy Schonfield private family archive.
30. *Jewish Chronicle*, 1 July 1921.
31. Jeremy Schonfield private family archive.
32. Hertz, *Transactions of the Jewish Historical Society of England*, Vol.10, p.149.
33. Ibid.

1. Esther Moshkowitz, Joseph Hertz's mother.

2. Hertz's father Simon: plum-farmer, Hebrew poet and teacher.

3. Joseph Hertz in 1891, beardless, while at the Jewish Theological Seminary.

4. Rose Freed graduating in New York, 1904.

5. Hertz in Johannesburg, probably in the 1890s.

6. The Hertz family arriving in at Liverpool from New York, 1913. Leon, the second son, is to the left, close to his mother whose pregnancy (with Judith) is concealed by flowers. JHH holds the hands of Daniel and Samuel.

7. Hertz's induction at the Great Synagogue, London, in 1913. A previously unpublished sketch.

8. Hertz touring the Western Front during the Great War.

9. Hertz on his Pastoral Tour, 1921 in Rotorua, New Zealand, with, lef to right, Revd Goldstein, Mr Ezra o Bombay and a Maori guide, Bela, whc also met the Prince of Wales.

10. Rose Hertz with her children in 1925: closest to her is Ruth, and then clockwise, Josephine, Daniel, Leon, Samuel and Judith.

11. Rose Hertz being presented at Court in 1929. She was unwell and died later that year.

12. Armistice Day at the Cenotaph, probably between 1925 and 1929. To the left of Hertz are Winston Churchill and, behind him, Stanley Baldwin. To the right are Neville Chamberlain and Lord Balfour.

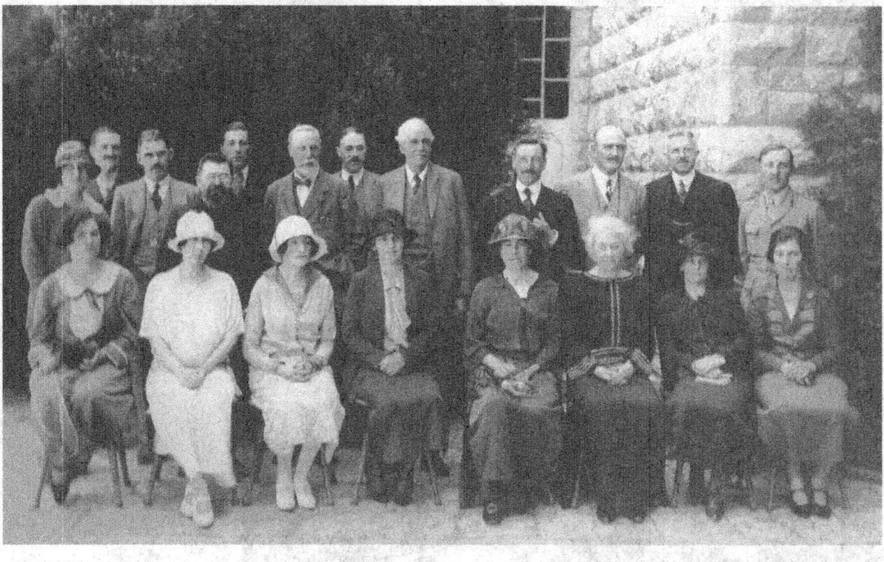

13. The inauguration of the Hebrew University in April 1925 was attended by British dignitaries, including, to the right of Hertz in the back row, Lord Ullswater, Lord Balfour, the High Commissioner Sir Herbert Samuel and Lord Allenby. Lady Allenby is fourth from the left in the front row, followed by Lady Samuel, Lady Ullswater, Rose Hertz and a Miss Castello. The photograph was taken at Government House, Jerusalem (now Augusta Victoria Hospital).

14. Rabbi Hertz (second from right) with Robert Waley-Cohen (second from left) at a dinner in 1934. There are few pictures of them together.

15. A commemorative medal struck in honour of Hertz's silver jubilee as Chief Rabbi in 1938.

16. Hertz delivering a sermon, probably in the late 1930s or early 1940s.

17. Hertz conducting a commemorative service in the ruins of the Great Synagogue, Dukes Place, London, burned in the Blitz, 1941.

18. Hertz with the Archbishop of Canterbury, Cosmo Lang, at a meeting organized by the Board of Deputies to protest against Nazi atrocities, 1942.

19. Hertz with Church leaders at a Chamber of Commerce luncheon at the Connaught Rooms, 10 February 1944. With Hertz, left to right, are The Archbishop of Canterbury William Temple, the Protestant theologian Revd Leslie Weatherhead, and the Roman Catholic Archbishop of Westminster Edward Myers.

20. A pencil sketch by Joseph Oppenheimer, dated 1938, later used for the posthumous portrait now in the London School of Jewish Studies.

21. Hertz in his library at 103 Hamilton Terrace during the 1930s.

Chapter Eight

Defending the Office

The Chief Rabbi had covered 40,000 miles and came home after nearly a year in much need of a rest. The Pastoral Tour had achieved a great deal: 'the personal touch which he has been able to establish with those to whom he was but a tradition … will serve him in good stead for many a long day'.[1] He returned to London, however, to find that Waley Cohen had been plotting behind his back to change the organization of Jews' College, the seminary in London that the United Synagogue supported to train ministers.

When Waley Cohen set about raising the £1 million (at least £40 million in today's money) for the Jewish Memorial Fund, the early reaction had shown that it wasn't going to come from the Orthodox. One possible additional source was the members of the Reform movement, but they would need to be offered a benefit in return.

Waley Cohen came up with the idea of an entirely new organization: an Academy, part of which would be Jews' College, while the other part would be devoted to providing courses for other religious denominations within the community. The two bodies would have a common council and Waley Cohen might well have expected to be invited to take the chair himself. The Chief Rabbi's Jews' College would then be in a subordinate position to the Academy.

Without telling Hertz, Waley Cohen had opened negotiations with Claude Montefiore, the leader of the Liberal movement, about obtaining more pupils and funds by introducing a course for Progressive students for the rabbinate. From Waley Cohen's public point of view, it would help the finances of Jews' College and achieve his objective of bringing the opposing parties closer together. Shell would have admired the commercial logic, but it was astonishing that Waley Cohen could ever imagine that he could undermine the Chief Rabbi's position as the head of Jews' College, by presenting him with a fait accompli of this kind.

The ex-minister of Upper Berkeley Street, Sir Philip Magnus, had been elected a vice-president of Jews' College in 1915 and was much in favour of the discussions. He would die holding the office in 1933, but the gap between Orthodoxy and Reform would still be there. Jews' College was an Orthodox institution. Claude Montefiore, of course, wanted to achieve an improved status for his movement, which would have come from religious cooperation with the Orthodox United Synagogue. Depending on your viewpoint, the gap would narrow or the wedge become thicker.

When Hertz found out what was happening he went to work to have the idea rejected. He knew that Jews' College would have become a laughing stock in Orthodox circles around the world if it became part of an organization which also trained Progressive students. When he returned to London, however, negotiations were already at an advanced stage. His first line of defence was to insist that the two organizations should be separate and distinct. Waley Cohen, the man whose word was law in Shell, now found himself with a fight on his hands. Hertz also found himself under attack from the Right Wing for having anything to do with the Academy idea at all.

Waley Cohen pleaded for the Academy. He promised Hertz that considerable segments of the United Synagogue congregations had contacted him to register their approval and that the Right Wing had also given him their support. He argued that if the Memorial Council didn't achieve its objectives, Hertz would always rue the day he had opposed the Academy. He insisted that it would be enough to trust to the loyalty and wisdom of the Anglo-Jewish community to protect the future of the college. None of these arguments carried much weight and they undermined what was left of Waley Cohen's credibility with the Chief Rabbi.

As the future of Jews' College had been threatened by underfunding almost since its inception, the new concept seemed wildly overoptimistic. The Reform movement still represented only a small percentage of the Jewish community and Waley Cohen was attempting to make the tail wag the dog. Long acrimonious discussions ensued.

For his part, Hertz could see that the two proposed Academy divisions, with opposing theologies, would be at each other's throats from the start. He also found any willingness to compromise opposed by a new body formed to defend the status quo. The Organisation of Observant Traditional Jews of Great Britain soon had a membership which included five dayanim and the Chief Rabbi of Ireland, Isaac Herzog. When it convened Hertz wasn't there, but he recognized the strength of feeling among Orthodox *rabbanim* and saw that compromise was impossible. He did point out that when he returned from the Pastoral Tour he had been faced with a plan for an Academy which would be one joint organization. He had argued for it to be split into two totally separate organizations, but he now set his face totally against that idea as well.

It remains difficult to understand Waley Cohen's belief that he could take over the Chief Rabbi's religious authority in the area of education. If the rabbinical seminary wasn't Hertz's responsibility, then the United Synagogue Act was a dead letter. It should have been obvious that if he didn't have Hertz on his side initially, his objective was going to be much more difficult to attain. In the oil business at the time, however, a great many agreements were valid only as long as it wasn't advantageous to break them. That was the world in which Waley Cohen laboured for many years, and obstructive juniors could usually be brushed aside.

Waley Cohen could never accept that, in working with the Chief Rabbi, it was at best a meeting of near-equals and, if it came to the crunch, he was going to finish up the junior partner. Hertz retained his ultimate weapon: his possible threat of resignation on religious grounds. The risk that he might do this simply wasn't worth taking.

Although the War Memorial Council approved the idea of the Academy by ten votes to seven, the opposition soon swelled, the necessary money wasn't forthcoming and the idea had to be dropped. Waley Cohen still wanted greater control and now saw another possible way of improving the quality of ministers. This time it involved the Council successfully taking over the Chief Rabbi's role in approving ministerial appointments. This had always been the Chief Rabbi's final responsibility, but Waley Cohen had done a great deal of work identifying potential ministers and persuading them to enter the profession.

It was because Waley Cohen spent so much time ensuring that there was a good choice of candidates to fill ministerial vacancies that he had dreamed of a new university college. This would train candidates for both Orthodox and Progressive congregations before a period of study at Jew's College. He went to a great deal of trouble to, personally, identify suitable candidates for training for the ministry and was highly regarded by those young men he took under his wing. Now, with Waley Cohen in the chair, the War Memorial Council passed a resolution that: 'As a result of its enquiry into methods of improving the status of the Jewish Ministry will, in consultation with the ecclesiastical authorities, weigh the various needs throughout the Empire and give the advice accordingly to ministers and to those who are making appointments in the Jewish Ministry.'[2]

It was, of course, an outrageous suggestion. Pausing only to offer the sop of 'consultation with the ecclesiastical authorities', the aim was clearly to seize powers for which the Council had no authority or mandate, and thereby to undermine the Chief Rabbi. Hertz was furious at the use of the plural in 'authorities'. He insisted, correctly, that he was the only authority, according to the United Synagogue's constitution, and that he intended to remain the sole holder of that responsibility.

The Council's statement was dismissed in the *Jewish Chronicle* as another example of: 'a growing disposition in the Chairman, Waley Cohen, to indulge in a high handed and imperious manner in the position he takes in public affairs'.[3] There was certainly always a need to recruit able ministers, but their main qualification should have been their halakhic expertise. How Waley Cohen or his Council were to be the final arbiters on that subject was unclear and the proposal was obviously a political manoeuvre. The idea came to nothing, but Waley Cohen survived unbowed, as he always had. There were many other areas where he could seek to undermine the Chief Rabbi.

One opportunity came up in December 1925 when the Council decided to convene a conference on Jewish education. It was noticeable that Hertz did not attend and the community wondered whether he had decided not to do so or hadn't been invited. All was made clear in the *Jewish Chronicle*:

> The War Memorial Council insist that any speech, address or sermon in connection with the Memorial delivered by the Chief Rabbi shall, before it is published, be submitted to the censorship of the Council. That body claims the right to omit anything Dr Hertz may have said and to send it out to the public in the form of which they approve.[4]

Hertz paid no attention and refused to attend or speak at the conference. The *Jewish Chronicle* denounced the Council's diktat as outrageous and blamed Waley Cohen for it: 'Does Sir Robert realise the enormity of the position he has assumed? ... It surprises me that you should associate yourself with anything so mean and unworthy as the vendetta you are carrying on against Dr Hertz.'[5]

In fairness, Waley Cohen was the chair of a body which Hertz supported, but had not created. Because the subject was religious education, any comments he made could be automatically assumed to have the approval of the War Memorial Council, but this was not always the case. Hence Waley Cohen's attempt to muzzle the Chief

Rabbi. As neither man had any intention of giving way, the likelihood was that the situation would later deteriorate even further. This danger had no effect on Waley Cohen.

It was obvious that Waley Cohen's concept of the ideal United Synagogue minister was some considerable distance from a *yeshiva*-trained Talmudic scholar. Most *yeshivot* considered they didn't have the time to cover modern and scientific thought in their curricula; attempts to do so by Hildesheimer, Simon Hertz's teacher, had limited success. Hertz's own training had been along these lines but he was a rarity. Hertz, too, wanted more candidates for the ministry. He had worked hard to collect donations for the War Memorial Fund: 'From our first landing ... I made the vital necessity of providing efficient teachers and interpreters of Judaism for the congregations of the Empire, the burden of practically every sermon, address, or public appeal I delivered.'[6]

At the time, the policy of the United Synagogue's lay leadership towards even cornerstones of Orthodoxy could be dismissive. Asked on one occasion for financial assistance for a congregation's *mikveh* (a ritual immersion bath), Head Office replied that it was not inclined: 'to depart from the principle hitherto guiding the United Synagogue, viz: that it is no part of its function to provide or manage *mikvehs* for the London community'.[7]

In fact, a *mikveh* is an important part of an Orthodox community's infrastructure. The *din* states that if Jews are setting up a congregation, they should try to create a school, obtain land for a cemetery, build a *mikveh* and buy a Sefer Torah. Only then, on the list of priorities, comes a synagogue building. The United Synagogue would have taken the view that few would use the *mikveh* and that the money could be better spent in other ways. This did not excuse a blanket dismissal of *mikveot*.

The rows rumbled on but at the same time it was Hertz's national and international status that was growing. He paid a triumphant pastoral visit to Ireland, speaking in Dublin, Cork and Belfast. The Irish Free State had recently been created and when the Chief Rabbi compared the experiences of the Irish and the Jews, he struck the perfect chord with his hosts.

By the end of his first ten years in office, Hertz had become very popular. As far as the Jewish East End man-in-the-street was concerned, Hertz had shown he cared for them. He would regularly preach on Yom Kippur to their overflow services, which were needed as so many Jews only came to synagogue on that one day of the year. The services were, primarily, for the poorer members of the community who could not afford a synagogue seat, and were held in local cinemas. The Chief

Rabbi was a welcome presence on those occasions and his inspiring sermons in Yiddish were much appreciated.

He was also quite prepared to use humour, if the occasion was appropriate, and this went down well too. Opening a new synagogue Council Hall, he said: 'Mark Twain has explained that a dog, when you feed and house him, would never bite you, thus showing the principal difference between a man and a dog.'[8]

In 1923 another potential crisis appeared. A new Slaughter of Animals Bill was introduced into the Commons and, once again, the question was raised whether *shechita*, the Jewish method of slaughter, should be permitted. The existing law was that animals had to be pre-stunned before being killed, but animals killed by *shechita*, the cutting of the throat, were excluded from this provision.

The extremely detailed laws of *shechita* were first documented in the Babylonian Talmud in the sixth century but no more humane method of slaughter has ever been scientifically proven to be an improvement. Hertz wrote to *The Times*:[9] 'According to the testimony of a host of experts, including Lord Lister, Sir Michael Foster, Dr Leonard Hill and Dr T.P. Openshaw', *shechita* was humane. Lister had been the world expert on antiseptics, Sir Michael Foster held the Chair of Physiology at Cambridge and Dr Hill was a famous Zoologist who had been awarded the prestigious Harben Gold Medal. Hill wrote and supported the Chief Rabbi's contention.

Hertz went on: 'In their commendable zeal towards the brute, the enemies of the Jewish method of slaughter should not forget to deal justly with their fellow men.' The Duchess of Hamilton wrote to ask if at least the Chief Rabbi would agree that those parts of the animal killed by *shechita* which weren't kosher, could be prevented from being sold by non-kosher butchers. Hertz replied in *The Times*:[10] 'I certainly could not be a party to withholding the privilege of eating the best and healthiest meat from any of His Majesty's subjects.' Hertz had Waley Cohen's full support on matters of *shechita* and a general election, which was called at the end of the year, killed the bill.

As Hertz pondered the problems of the community after the war, his main concern was its lack of Jewish knowledge. Throughout his career the Chief Rabbi had seen the effect on members of the community of the contrary arguments put forward by both the ultra-Orthodox and the Reform and Liberal movements. Jews unable to see the flaws in the philosophies emanating from what Hertz saw as distortions of Judaism, could be lost to the community he led.

To prevent this happening he believed Jews needed to acquire four skills. They needed to know the laws of Judaism, the Hebrew language, the history of the Bible and Jewish history over the centuries. Armed with that knowledge, they could then make an informed decision on where they wanted to stand. On those firm foundations Hertz was satisfied they would be most likely to decide to remain within the Orthodox fold. If they didn't have that knowledge, he knew they could easily become divorced from the community, persuaded by arguments in which they could not see the shortcomings.

He called his concept 'Positive Historical Judaism', but such expressions can easily be claimed to have other meanings, particularly as the years go by. The expression 'Conservative Judaism', for example, has meant very different things at different times.

Hertz understood Jewish history in depth. He wanted to encourage the study of the subject and, in 1922, he agreed to become President of the Jewish Historical Society of England, which had supported research into Jewish history since its foundation in 1893. It focused on British Jewish history and had helped many of its members have their work published. Hertz would have recalled that when the Jewish Historical Society of America was formed in 1892, he had been at its inaugural meeting.

The problems facing Hertz were immense. To succeed, individuals had to want to learn, they should have both learning resources and the time to learn, with competition coming from the cinema, the radio and the need to earn a living. Despite all his efforts, convincingly as he spoke, plus the contribution he made with his own books and his strenuous efforts to raise the necessary funds, Hertz met with only limited success – but there would have been even less if he hadn't tried so hard.

Orthodox communities read their prayers in Hebrew, but few congregants could translate them into English. The Sefer Torah, the parchment scroll of the Chumash or Pentateuch, containing the first five books of the Bible, would be produced each Sabbath to read the weekly portion. The congregation might be able to follow the recital, but would not have understood the words or much about the Bible studies which commented on the text.

It was to the immense credit of every congregation that Hebrew had managed to survive the centuries without being spoken as an everyday language, but Hertz knew he needed to set a higher standard than that. He had few good Talmudic brains among his ministers; very few of the quality that taught and inspired the communities of Eastern Europe.

The only Daily and Sabbath Service prayer book that had taken root in the United Synagogues was Singer's Prayer Book, first published in

1890 and destined to continue in use, with some modifications to the present day.

The Singer Prayer Book had no commentary and the Chumash had similar problems of comprehension. It had been neglected for years, although Schechter had called for a popular version as far back as 1899. The problem with the existing version was that: 'Kalisch's (Marcus Kalisch 1828–85) on Genesis, Exodus and Leviticus were not written for the synagogue or for the Jewish Home. All other Jewish Scriptural publications in England and America, either omitted the Hebrew text or were without a Commentary for general use.'[11]

If Hertz was concerned about the standards of Jewish education, it was significant to the ultra-Orthodox that, at that conference on the subject in 1919, he was seen walking among the delegates without his head covered. As a critic at the time commented: 'He had not yet asserted himself against the prevailing laxity',[12] but this merely illustrates the variety of practice even within Orthodox circles. Covering the head under most circumstances was then rather a *minhag* (custom) than a *din*.

A monograph by a distinguished Orthodox Talmudic expert, Rabbi Professor Dr Samuel Kraus of the Vienna Theological Seminary, questioned the obligatory nature of the practice, except at prayer and when eating. A *minhag* that is followed for centuries can become the equivalent of a *din*, or it may not, and the influential Samson Raphael Hirsch in Germany tended to take a relaxed view. At Victor Schonfeld's future school, the boys would not cover their heads for lessons on secular subjects.

Hertz recognized the problems he would face over education almost as soon as he returned from the Pastoral Tour. He was, personally, prepared to study any text which might throw additional light on Jewish studies. Others disagreed and preferred to disregard non-Jewish sources. What might have been a storm in a teacup grew to be a substantial problem, when some youngsters at the Hampstead Synagogue Hebrew classes asked the minister, Revd Aaron Green, whether they could be told something about the New Testament. The Christian view on the Hebrew Bible differed markedly from the Jewish position and the youngsters wanted to know how to react.

Green consulted with Hertz and it was agreed that there would be no harm in a few talks being given, after the end of the classes, to those who were interested. The speakers would be experts in the field and would see the arguments from the Jewish point of view. Hertz knew that his predecessor, Hermann Adler, had given twelve sermons at the

Bayswater Synagogue in 1868 of an ecumenical nature, and relied on the rabbinic saying: 'Know what answer to give to the unbeliever.'

When the idea of discussing the New Testament after classes became known, there was a positive cavalry charge of Jews on hobby horses. The Orthodox rejected the very idea of the New Testament being discussed on synagogue premises. Rabbi Herzog, the Chief Rabbi of Ireland, declared himself 'horrified and amazed',[13] but Herzog was more Right Wing than the United Synagogue. He had been awarded his *semicha* in England by two distinguished *rabbanim* in Adler's time. This was very unusual.

Other opponents of the Chief Rabbi's authority said that he had the right to lay down the law on United Synagogue services but that classes were not services. The Left Wing supported the idea of wider study, but apologists said that it could be seen as a Jewish attack on Christian theology.

Waley Cohen was in favour of the ecumenical approach and, on behalf of the United Synagogue, said that the whole question was entirely a matter for the Chief Rabbi. The *Jewish Chronicle* was not happy with this. It suggested that Waley Cohen demonstrated: 'testiness towards anything like dissent from views upon which his mind is made up'.[14]

Hertz believed that Orthodox Judaism could defend itself perfectly well without putting up barriers against the study of other religions. He often clashed with, rather than ignored, Montefiore and the Liberals and the supporters of Biblical Higher Criticism. This latter group said they were motivated by the result of archaeological studies which were said to throw new light on the origin of the Bible. Schechter had been the first to label this approach 'Higher Anti-Semitism'. In the forthcoming Hertz Chumash the Chief Rabbi would call on a wide selection of non-Jewish academic and philosophical sources to support his own views.

The row over the Hampstead Synagogue classes was not, however, worth a major battle and Hertz said it wouldn't happen again. There were lines to be drawn, though. He took the opportunity to make it clear that he did not want his ministers preaching in the Reform Upper Berkeley Street Synagogue. While he was away on his Pastoral Tour, both the Birmingham minister, Abraham Cohen, and Liverpool's Samuel Frampton, had done so without his knowledge or approval. He felt that if the community approved of clear divisions, then it should be consistent. He banned pulpit exchanges.

The Hertz Chumash would be an important initiative to make synagogue services more attractive to congregants. The overall objective, however, remained to retain the families of nineteenth-century refugees within the Orthodox community and to make them more English.

The choice of synagogue was wide. First, the *shtiebels*, the small synagogues where refugees from the same areas of Eastern Europe could stick together. Then there was the Federation of Synagogues to which many belonged and which still had slightly more members than the United Synagogue. There was also the United itself, and then the smaller numbers belonging to the Reform and the Liberals plus, of course, the ancient community of Sephardim.

If those were the options, what was the major benefit the majority of the refugees needed from the United Synagogue? Where the United scored heavily was its continuing ability to come up with the financial backing new groupings needed to start a synagogue, through the St Helens Fund.

Refugee Jews did not want to continue to live in the poverty of the East End. Most were upwardly mobile and, with the expansion of the underground system, transport to the London suburbs became much easier. When they could afford it, large numbers moved home. Between 1913 and 1920 new synagogues opened in Brixton, Richmond, Chelsea, Hornsey and Wood Green, and Walthamstow and Leyton, all admitted to the United Synagogue, even before the full benefit of the sale of the New could be realized. Whatever their disagreements, Hertz and Waley Cohen were both making the United Synagogue an increasingly attractive option.

In their new synagogues – and there would be another twenty-nine before Hertz died – the immigrants and their children achieved a measure of the respectability they craved; comfortable in their new blue silk *tallesim*, led by top-hatted wardens and with ministers wearing Church of England clerical collars.

Not for nothing would the Revd Saul Amias become known as the 'Bishop of Edgware' and the Revd Isaac Livingstone of the Dunstan Road synagogue as the 'Vicar of Golders Green'. What was on offer was the chance for the community to renounce its foreign origins. It was the opportunity to belong in those surroundings that they wanted and, by joining the United Synagogue, they would have two other benefits: a famous Chief Rabbi and a parent organization which could boast, among its Honorary Officers, some of the most prestigious names in Anglo-Jewry.

Many of the immigrants also became Freemasons, which gave them additional gratification and Hertz, on occasions, joined them at Masonic meetings. A past grand chaplain of the Grand Lodge in South

Africa was very welcome. He was present in 1923 at a meeting of the Lodge of Tranquillity.

It didn't matter to most members that their ministers were often treated without due deference by the elected lay leaders. They didn't listen when Hertz protested against the ruling lay cliques or described democracy in the United Synagogue as a convenient method for Honorary Officers to get their own way. Everybody would pay deference to the Chief Rabbi but Hertz was aware that his actual power within the community was limited; as he said, his chief weapon was the word.

The increasing effort to be seen as more British was also designed to counter the bad publicity emerging from the fact that several major Communists were Jewish. An understandable hatred of the Czar and the horrors of the pogroms after the war, were ample explanation for Jews supporting the Communist opposition. It was not sufficient to prevent the view growing that the victory of Communism in Russia was supported by what came to be known as 'international Jewry'.

In addition, as the Communists became the chief opponents of Fascism in the years to come, the impression that they and the Jews were allies gained strength, on the basis that the enemy of my enemy is my friend. The Kibbutz movement in Palestine owed much to the ideals of Communism, and Jewish candidates were always more welcome in Labour than in Conservative constituencies.

Hertz spoke out against the perceived Jewish–Russian alliance at the Central Synagogue in 1922: 'To London belongs the melancholy glory of having in recent years been the centre of a particularly noisy and noisome school ... journalistic, aristocratic, reactionary – who with one voice declare the Jew to have ever been the leaders of revolution in the modern world, as well as the authors of all the ills that the present day is heir to.'[15]

In speaking in these terms the Chief Rabbi was, of course, being thoroughly political and this produced protests from many of the Honorary Officers of the United Synagogue. This, as usual, did not deter Hertz, who would continue to defend the community whenever he felt it necessary.

Hertz was highly critical of efforts by the Liberal Jewish movement to draw closer to the Church of England. In 1924 a Jewish–Christian conference was arranged by the Liberals and Hertz felt that it was not only a retrograde step but that the Jewish delegates were pusillanimous in their defence of their religion. No one objected when the senior Christian delegate said that the objection to the Jew as a neighbour was not racial but sanitary!

By the 1920s, the number of British Jews who were seriously interested in Jewish theology was small. They were less observant than their parents and grandparents. One effect of poverty had been that people lived in close proximity, spotlighting those who rode on the Sabbath or ate in a non-kosher restaurant.

In the London suburbs, however, the second generation could live private lives. As a consequence, very few found it necessary to switch their allegiance from Orthodoxy. It was true that the creed of the Reform and Liberal movements did not denounce non-observance of the *mitzvot*, but that was no longer an essential benefit, as it would have been in the more observant world of the East End. The second generation might attend a United Synagogue only on rare occasions, but they remained members in good standing.

What was most generally observed was the Seder Night and eating matza at Passover, circumcision for their male children, barmitzvahs for their sons, fasting on Yom Kippur, periods of mourning for the dead, attending synagogue on the anniversaries of the deaths of their parents, visiting the cemetery and using a smattering of Yiddish for old-times sake.

Above all though they wanted to see their children marry partners who were halakhically Jewish. If a Jewish-Orthodox child married out of the religion, it was felt to shame the family and often created enormous heartbreak. Jews had remained faithful to the religion for 2,000 years at a tremendous cost, and it hurt when their privileged descendants were ready to abandon it all. Children who were the products of a marriage where the wife was not, halakhically, Jewish, would not be accepted as such.

One ambition for the parents was to give their children a better start in life than they had enjoyed. Having had only a rudimentary education themselves, they saw going to a public school as a way of achieving this. The option of a Jewish school hardly arose because there were so few of them. A Jewish boarding house at a public school had existed briefly at Harrow under a Breslau graduate, Dr Chotzman in the 1880s, and small boarding houses still existed at Clifton, Bristol, Perse, Cambridge, and soon-to-be-closed Cheltenham. In all, though, they wouldn't have had more than 150 boarders.

Public schools were mostly Christian foundations and set great store by their Christian philosophy. If they accepted Jewish pupils, it would be on a quota and they made few allowances for the practice of Judaism. As late as the 1980s some schools were praised for allowing their Jewish pupils to attend synagogue on *either* of the two holiest days of the Jewish year, Yom Kippur or Rosh Hashanah, but not both.

In most public schools Jewish pupils had to attend chapel prayers, be taught the New Testament in religion classes and, of course, the food at the boarding house wouldn't be kosher.

The public schools were fully entitled to set down their own rules, though some decisions might have been tinged with anti-Semitism or hypocrisy. For example, Mill Hill School in London was insisting on attendance at Saturday morning classes for its Jewish pupils in the 1960s even though its prospectus boasted of its religious tolerance. The brochures pointed out that it was established on the outskirts of London in 1807 because non-conformist schools, by law at the time, were only allowed many miles from the city centre.

What the parents who sent their children to such establishments were, effectively, showing their children, was that a good education, gained at the expense of their Judaism, was a bargain. If the children eventually had to choose between marrying out and remaining within the fold, the example their parents had given them implied they should drop the religion. When, as so often happened, that was the result, many parents felt betrayed by their children even though it was they who had given the initial example.

Hertz knew that a public school education led, on many occasions, to the children of senior members of the community being lost to it. Families so affected were not the topic of polite Jewish society, but that would not deter the Chief Rabbi.

In 1924 he paid a pastoral visit to Liverpool and tackled the problem head on at a public meeting:

> Unfortunately there was now growing up a class of so-called better Jews who seemed to be marching to suicide. They sent their children to Public Schools where they got New Testament instruction without any Jewish education whatever. He would class these people as 'undesirables' not only to the Jews but also for the non-Jews; a disgrace to the Jewish name and a danger to non-Jews because religious conviction was the rock on which character was built.[16]

Hertz said it again at a dinner the same evening. He would have known that, in calling the parents a disgrace, he was attacking a wide range of the most senior members of the community, who would have squirmed with embarrassment and been furious at what they would have considered his temerity. The *Jewish Chronicle*, however, commented:

> Dr Hertz occasionally is compelled to say some very ugly truths and, when he does, they well forth from him with incontinence of zeal, directness, and courage which are his sure characteristics ... It is interesting to observe how it is precisely that class that has been wont to look down upon and despise our poorer brethren ... and who call them 'undesirables' ... Thus has the bird come home to roost.[17]

At the same time, Hertz never tried to exclude those whose standards of Orthodoxy would not have enabled them to join a community like Orach Chaim. He defined the Anglo-Jewish brand of Orthodoxy as: 'The synthesis of the best citizenship and the broadest humanitarianism, with the warmth and colour, the depth and discipline of the olden Jewish life.'[18]

It was a carefully worded policy. Nobody would object to striving to be a good citizen or a humanitarian. Everybody would vote for retaining the warmth and colour of Judaism, if they were allowed to define what that involved for themselves. It was the: 'depth and discipline of the olden Jewish life' which was the medicine, and when Hertz had to define the contents of such Judaism, he would cite the *din* and the belief that Moses had been given this at Sinai.

It was the strict laws concerning conversion that created the most problems for non-observant Jews, who had little awareness of the traditional law observed by Hertz and the Beth Din.

The process involved in Orthodox conversion was searching and, as the years went by, it became more lengthy. The purpose was to place religious belief ahead of convenience, and set the law on a pedestal which neither riches nor position could countermand.

There were new ways of communicating and one of these was the radio. The first station, 2MT, broadcast for half an hour every Tuesday from February 1922 and developed into the British Broadcasting Company that November. Only two years later, Hertz was invited to broadcast on 5 October 1924. His subject was the High Holydays, and he memorably described the New Year and the Day of Atonement as: 'The lighthouses on the shores of eternity'.[19] He would be invited to appear again on many future occasions and his broadcasts during the Second World War were truly inspiring.

With Rose's encouragement Hertz put a tremendous amount of work into the new Chumash. He had already dipped his toe in the water when Benjamin Szold, a member of the Bible Revision Committee of the Jewish Publication Society in America, enlisted the young rabbi to do the necessary work on the book of Joshua in 1898.

The new Chumash, if it was done well, could help solve two major concerns. First, it would prove that rabbinical law, the Oral law, was still entirely valid. Second, it would repel the attacks on the origins of the Pentateuch by critics who insisted that it was written by a number of authors over a long period of time: the 'Higher Criticism' of the Bible undermined this fundamental of Jewish Orthodox belief and Hertz wanted to prove it wrong. He said: 'My conviction is that the criticism of the Pentateuch associated with the name of Wellhausen [Julius Wellhausen 1844–1918] is a perversion of history and a desecration of religion.'[20]

In addition Hertz argued that: 'To the rabbis the real Torah was not merely the written text of the Jewish books of Moses; it also included the memory enshrined in that text as expounded and unfolded by the interpretation of successive generations of Sages, who made its implicit Divine teachings explicit.'[21]

In preparing the new Chumash Hertz realized that he would never have the time to study the multitude of commentaries written over the centuries, covering every word in the five books. Nothing less would be acceptable, however. So he decided to recruit a team of ministers, each of whom would do part of the groundwork. He would then edit the results.

His colleagues were paid very little and put in differing amounts of work – although some substantial. They do not appear as joint authors, which aggravated a number of them. On the other hand they were warmly acknowledged in the Preface. On the title page Hertz merely describes himself as the 'Editor of the Commentaries'. He received all the royalties from the publications, however, which would be substantial for the rest of the century, but then he had, of course, paid for the contributions of his colleagues. The longer notes on special themes at the end of major sections were entirely his work.

The initial research on the project started in 1920 and continued with the benefit of the £2,000 donation Hertz had received in Australia on his Pastoral Tour. He announced the initiative at the Conference of Anglo-Jewish preachers in 1923 but the work would only be completed several years later.

Hertz's treatment of the scholars who worked on the Chumash with him was typical of his approach. They knew that, in principle, he was in favour of working with them, supporting them and improving their lot. At the same time he was not a team player.

Few authors like having their work changed and Hertz, commenting on the contribution of his collaborators in the Preface, said: 'they allowed me the widest editorial discretion. I have condensed or enlarged, recast or rewritten at will'. It must often have been irritating for the co-authors. What would emerge at the finish, though, was a volume which continued to be one of the two standard books in the English-speaking synagogue for sixty years. It was widely used in America as well; it was both academically informed and designed for easy reading and understanding by the layman.

The eventual result would be one volume covering the whole Pentateuch and Haftarot [Prophetic readings] with commentaries designed to be understood by the man in the street. The commentaries were drawn from a wide range of sources: contemporary Jewish, ancient Jewish, Christians, academics and even non-believers. He said it was a rabbinic principle to: 'accept the true from whatever source it come'. His aim was to: 'place a Chumash in every English-speaking home' and for years after his death communities all over the world used his magnum opus in their synagogues almost exclusively.

In spite of this laudable objective, the United Synagogue Honorary Officers refused to promote the book to their members. Hertz wanted it advertised on the back of synagogue invoices but the idea was turned down.

Perhaps any attempt at marketing was considered demeaning by the Honorary Officers; selling was not respectable in polite circles in those days. They may have considered the idea an attempt to increase the Chief Rabbi's royalties. Certainly to interpret his intentions in that way would have been quite consistent with their attitude on other subjects. The royalties did augment the Chief Rabbi's income, but he remained seriously concerned about the financial position of his family after his death. He was now 50 years old and knew he had no pension, although he was not expected to retire.

The work eventually covered the first five books of the Bible read annually in synagogue. Its commentaries assembled positive remarks from many sources. This aroused the ire of the Right Wing who felt that no endorsement was needed from non-Orthodox sources, but Hertz was merely remaining true to the research for a paper he had produced when he served in Syracuse thirty years before.

It was on Bachya Ibn Pakudah, a great eleventh-century philosopher, and was delivered to the Mikve Israel Association of Philadelphia in December 1897. In it he reiterated Bachya's views on how to assess sources:

> Know that neither the teachings nor the explanations which I propound ... are altogether original to me. They are thoughts gathered by me from the works of sages in the Midrash and the

> Talmud and from other Jewish writings; furthermore, from the utterances of philosophers of antiquity and our own days, and from the works of various and divers authors. I am willing to learn from anybody and everybody.[22]

Hertz wrote: 'This trait on the part of Bachya (and Maimonides) must not be construed as lack of originality.'[23]

The right-wing critics also questioned some of Hertz's views and the arguments continue. What Hertz achieved, however, was a clearer and more inspiring explanation of what was in the Torah than had ever been written before. The project was begun in the autumn of 1920 and the first volume, that of Genesis, came out in the spring of 1929.

The five individual volumes were published by the Oxford University Press initially, but they were combined by the Soncino Press in 1938. The powerful message of the book was to be that without the rabbinical commentators referred to in its notes, the religion could not have continued to be a meaningful way of life. Without them, its teachings would have been permanently anchored in Biblical times. However, Hertz's insistence on the importance of Bible instruction and Bible distribution aroused scorn in parts of the community. Hertz said that he deliberately faced ridicule and misrepresentation. Being Hertz, he stuck to his guns, and in this at least he had the support of Victor Schonfeld.

One problem with the Chumash was the immense amount of time that was needed to edit the contributions. Hertz burned the midnight oil year after year. Rose Hertz must have been very supportive but the children would have been deprived of a great deal of their father's time. It was said that Hertz only occasionally went to the cinema, seldom to the theatre and that his greatest hobby was reading: 'He could roam through his library and lay his hand immediately upon any work that bore upon the conversation and exhibit a quite uncanny knowledge of its contents.'[24] He had the interests of a scholarly cleric of his time and the Chumash must have given him great pleasure. His visual memory was remarkable.

A major problem with the Chumash was its cost. Generous as the community was in looking after its poor, disabled and old people, it didn't have much interest in rabbinics. Jews' College had to survive on a pittance and efforts to raise money for Jewish education regularly fell well below their targets, with generous donors being few and far between. Eventually, he would find the necessary benefactor in Joseph Freedman, who had a chain of furniture shops and had voted for the president of the Board of Deputies in 1917 against Hertz's own views. As a consequence of Freedman's generosity the one volume edition could be sold for a third less than would otherwise have been necessary.[25]

NOTES

1. Joseph Herman Hertz, *Early and Late: Addresses, Messages, and Papers* (Hindhead: Soncino Press, 1943), p.237.
2. *Jewish Chronicle*, 27 January 1922.
3. Ibid.
4. *Jewish Chronicle*, 11 December 1925.
5. *Jewish Chronicle*, 15 July 1921.
6. Joseph Herman Hertz, 'Opening Address in 1923 at the Conference of Anglo-Jewish Preachers' (London: Oxford University Press, 1923), p.19.
7. Derek Taylor, *British Chief Rabbis, 1664–2006* (London and Portland, OR: Vallentine Mitchell, 2007), p.356.
8. The opening of the Borough Synagogue Council Hall in 1927.
9. *The Times*, 30 April 1923.
10. *The Times*, 12 May 1923.
11. Joseph Herman Hertz, 'Preface to first edition', *Pentateuch and Haftorahs. Deuteronomy 1936* (London: Oxford University Press, 1929–1936), p.vii.
12. Bernard Homa, *Footprints in the Sands of Time* (Privately printed, 1990), p.47.
13. *Jewish Chronicle*, 18 November 1921.
14. *Jewish Chronicle*, 27 January 1922.
15. Sermon in the London Metropolitan Archives.
16. *Jewish Chronicle*, 4 January 1924.
17. Ibid., p.8.
18. Hertz, 'Opening Address in 1923 at the Conference of Anglo-Jewish Preachers', p.19.
19. Joseph Herman Hertz, *Sermons, Addresses and Studies* (London: Soncino Press, 1938), Vol.1, p.165.
20. *Jewish Chronicle*, 27 January 1922.
21. Benjamin J. Elton, *Britain's Chief Rabbis and the Religious Character of Anglo-Jewry, 1880–1970* (Manchester: Manchester University Press. 2009), p.168.
22. Joseph Herman Hertz, *Bachya, The Jewish Thomas a Kempis* (New York: Jewish Theological Seminary, 1898).
23. Ibid.
24. Aubrey Newman, 'Chief Rabbi Dr Joseph Herman Hertz, CH' (London: United Synagogue, 1972), p.13.
25. Joseph Freedman was also chairman of the United Synagogue Building Committee from 1933–35.

Chapter Nine

Home and Away, 1924–25

The Chief Rabbi's reputation had been much enhanced by the Pastoral Tour in 1921, even if Waley Cohen was now considering making an attempt to get rid of him, much as if he were a difficult junior at Shell.

In 1923, when Hertz was celebrating his tenth year in office, Waley Cohen wrote to him:

> I have felt in recent months that the path that you have followed has often not been the wisest one and I often hoped that you might be willing to accept advice from your lay friends and that in that way you might achieve better ends for our Community which I know you dearly cherish, whilst at the same time avoiding the controversy which must seriously hamper your activities.[1]

In fact, although Hertz's attitude might, on occasions, hamper his achievement of his objectives, it never affected the effort he was prepared to put in. Not surprisingly, the letter resulted in further exchanges of letters of an increasingly acrimonious nature. Waley Cohen continued to see himself as far more than Hertz's 'commercial manager' of the United Synagogue.

In 1924 he had written to a friend, Redcliffe Salaman, that: 'I am afraid that nothing can be done for our Community so long as the present Chief Rabbi is there.'[2] Salaman, a distinguished scientist from Cambridge, prominent in many of the community's charities, told Waley Cohen:

> Frankly I do not agree with you, and in any case you have to remember that he is here and his life is a good one. Therefore it is up to the leaders to arrive at a modus vivendi, and with all the good intentions in the world, I do not think you have done that. You have tried to push him further than he wanted to go … and you have unnecessarily hurt his feelings.[3]

It wasn't the best of times to try to be rid of the Chief Rabbi anyway. That year he would be found as an honoured guest on the royal dais at the opening of the Wembley Exhibition. Hertz viewed Waley Cohen as not that different from the laymen in other synagogues he had known, who had tended to be a continuous irritation. In 1927 he would tell the Conference of Anglo-Jewish preachers that: 'Leadership has almost everywhere today been wrested from the Jewish minister by the lay element ... who ... desire the clergy to surrender their independence and perform the functions delegated to them as the controlled servants of the lay element and as the paid interpreters of the aspirations or prejudices of that lay element.'[4]

Those sentiments wouldn't have gone down well in the United Synagogue boardroom. Whereas Waley Cohen criticized the Chief Rabbi in private correspondence and at one-to-one meetings, Hertz often criticized the lay officials in public. It was not surprising that Hertz was not very popular with them on those occasions.

Hertz's *Book of Jewish Thoughts* had now been expanded from a pocket edition for free distribution to the troops, to a library edition published by the Oxford University Press. He took the opportunity of sending a magnificently bound copy to the Duke of York (later George VI) as a wedding present. The Duke sent him a hand-written reply from Buckingham Palace: 'I am writing to thank you and Mrs Hertz so very much for your kindness in thinking of giving me the *Book of Jewish Thoughts* for a wedding present. I am very glad to accept it and to have it.'[5] At least the Chief Rabbi was correctly treated in court circles, whatever Waley Cohen thought about his being the centre of controversy.

In 1924 the Liberals bought the site on which they would build their splendid synagogue, seating 1,350, in St John's Wood opposite Lord's cricket ground. It was dominated by vast classical pillars and, when it opened in 1925, aimed to represent architecturally a growth in the importance of the small Liberal section of the community. In the East End: 'Progressive services initiated jointly by the Liberals and Reformers ... were attracting up to 1,000 worshippers on Sabbaths.'[6] Nonetheless there were about 400,000 Jews in Britain at the time and the Liberals were, to a large extent, only a London movement. To describe such a tiny percentage as: 'this seemingly unstoppable Liberal bandwagon',[7] as Persoff argues, is a considerable exaggeration.

The United Synagogue Council was worried at the time at the number of discharged men from the forces who had failed to return to worshipping in the synagogue. Their faith in the Almighty might well have been shaken by the appalling scenes of war they had witnessed and endured. So the Council asked Hertz to deliver a series of sermons to try to correct the situation. He agreed to do this, and decided that one of the reasons for the drift from synagogue attendance was the way the left wing had denigrated so many traditional Orthodox practices.

So Hertz gave three sermons in different London pulpits in December and January 1925–26, devoted to an attack on Liberal theology. He called the sermons 'The New Paths – Whither do they Lead?' It was, in fact, far from clear that ex-servicemen had indeed flocked to left-wing shuls. A caustic Revd Ephraim Levine told a congregant, who had announced his transfer from the Orthodox New West End synagogue to the Reform Upper Berkeley Street synagogue, that he didn't mind which synagogue his congregant chose not to attend!

The sermons were not what the United Synagogue Honorary Officers had wanted. Many had friends within the Liberal community. Waley Cohen attempted to reprimand the Chief Rabbi for changing their agreed brief:

> Many of us had felt that the destructive criticism of Liberal Judaism would not serve to strengthen genuine doubting waverers in their allegiance to Traditional Judaism; we respected your feeling that the task of criticizing Liberal Judaism was necessary, but we understood that you were satisfied for that to be carried out in your first series of sermons. If the press reports are correct, you have in your second series done little more that continue your criticism of Liberal Jews, some of which they do not even admit to be theirs.[8]

What neither man was discussing was the hidden agenda; the attack Hertz actually made was on the Cousinhood which Waley Cohen represented, as was clear from the first of the New Paths sermons, which described the Greeks in the times of the Maccabees and Chanukah:

> These ancient books tell us of the eagerness displayed by the upper classes in Jerusalem 2,000 years ago, to abandon Torah, Sabbath and Covenant in their desire to be ... Hellenized, not only in outward things, but in thought and life as well ... the utter lack of sympathy of some Jews today with things Jewish, and their exaggerated deference ... to the superficial customs of their non-Jewish neighbours, is thus no new phenomenon.[9]

If the cap fitted, the Cousinhood were invited to wear it. The Liberals had indeed been destructively criticizing Orthodox Judaism for many years and nobody was telling Claude Montefiore, Lily Montagu or Israel Mattuck that there should only be a specific number of occasions when Orthodoxy could be castigated. There was also no statute of limitations on a response, but Hertz was never defensive in justifying Orthodox Judaism if it was attacked. He responded as strongly as he felt necessary. He took offence at the criticism and called on Waley Cohen to stop slandering him, and to pay him the respect that an English gentleman should show the Chief Rabbi.

The three New Paths sermons caused a furore because Hertz was attacking the theology of Claude Montefiore. One letter writer commented that it was: 'as if it were the blasphemy of the Holy Ghost'.[10] The reputation of Montefiore started with his name, which was linked to the greatness of Sir Moses Montefiore.

Montefiore was a serious academic with a first in Classics from Balliol, Oxford, who had founded the influential *Jewish Quarterly Review*, a journal which published the writings of many fine scholars. His published works included *Aspects of Judaism* in 1894 and *The Bible for Home Reading* in 1896, among many others. He was wealthy and in his younger days had helped Simeon Singer write his prayer book. His mother had financed it. His scholarly help was acknowledged in every edition from 1890 until 1964 when his name was replaced by a vague reference to 'a noted scholar'. It is unlikely that Hertz would have approved such an excision, especially in view of his attitude to quotations in his Chumash commentary.

Montefiore was also, however, an admirer of the teaching of Jesus and St Paul. His Liberal Judaism abandoned much of the Orthodox tradition and, consequently, conflict with the views of Hertz was inevitable. There was also a hidden agenda: one major attraction of Liberal Judaism was that it made conversion to Judaism easier than in the Reform synagogue, and far easier than in the Orthodox world.

A considerable number of the Jewish rich and famous were able to have their partners, or their children's partners, converted more easily when they married out of the faith, even if this wish for conversion was often a strategy for communal acceptance, rather than the acquirement of new and deeply felt religious beliefs.

The left-wing movement had been far more successful in gaining adherents in the United States than in Britain. Hertz knew exactly which left-wing theologians had attacked which traditional practices. So in his three sermons his criticisms spread far and wide, even if not all modernisers adopted identical programmes.

Montefiore chose to dismiss Hertz's examples by saying that: 'the follies or vagaries or idiosyncrasies of two or three individuals are used to discredit Liberal Judaism'.[11] In fact, Hertz gave twenty-eight separate instances of named Liberal rabbis who, by their speeches or actions, had attacked core Orthodox beliefs and practices. Everything from advocating the abolition of circumcision, Yom Kippur or various festivals to promoting the prohibition of *shechita* in Switzerland. He even named a number who had eventually converted to Christianity.

In constructing his arguments, Hertz was meticulous in his phrasing. As Ephraim Levine recalled years later: 'He often confessed that the gravity of his message and the burden of care under which he laboured, demanded verbal precision.'[12] Added to detailed efforts he made to formulate his arguments, Hertz could now bring to bear: 'a sort of encyclopaedic mind that ranged over the whole field of learning, theological and secular'.[13]

Montefiore fought back. Hertz had said that Liberal synagogues were holding services on Sundays rather than Saturday. Montefiore pointed out that such Sunday services were for weekdays, not a replacement for Saturday. He didn't point out that there were no other weekday services, as there were in Orthodox synagogues. Far from wanting to abolish circumcision, Montefiore said there was a prayer for it in the Liberal prayer book. It was still true, however, that converts to Liberal Judaism were not required to be circumcised.

Oddly enough, the question of circumcising adults had come up at the very beginning of the Jewish return to Britain. A number of the new Sephardi congregation in Stuart times had not been circumcised. If the Inquisition found someone who had, they knew he was a Jew and, if his father had been forcibly converted, then the son could be labelled a heretic. He could then be executed in any country which acknowledged the authority of the Inquisition, such as Spain, the Spanish Netherlands or Portugal. Once they were in London, however, this reason disappeared, making it necessary to look more closely at the failure to carry out the procedure.

It was also the case that circumcision for adults was very painful before the invention of anaesthetics, increasing the reluctance to undergo the operation. In spite of all this, Haham Jacob Sasportas, the first English Haham, insisted that anybody who wanted to belong to the Sephardi congregation had to be circumcised.

There was much argument and counter-argument between Montefiore and Hertz and neither was averse to bringing into the argument the minutest detail to support their case. Far from modifying his criticism, as his Honorary Officers were asking, Hertz gave a series of sermons in the course of 1926 which were again designed to attack the philosophies of the non-Orthodox. These, put together with the

New Paths sermons, were published by the Oxford University Press as *Affirmations of Judaism* in 1927.

Relations with the Reform movement remained correct throughout this time. Upper Berkeley Street appointed a new American rabbi in 1926, Joel Blau, who unfortunately died after a year in office when he was only 40 years old. He was cremated, which is not permitted in Orthodox circles, but Hertz and Dayan Lazarus both attended the memorial service at his synagogue.[14] In future years, as the Reform movement moved further away from Orthodox practices, the religious courtesies would be increasingly difficult to maintain.

In spite of all his efforts, the numbers joining the new Liberal movement were never a significant percentage of the community: 'He [Montefiore] died [in 1938] disappointed and embittered by the limited success of Liberal Judaism which he blamed on the rise of Zionism.'[15] The denunciations of his theology by Hertz were doubtless another important factor.

It would be wrong to believe that Waley Cohen was consistently not cooperative at this time. For example, when Hertz brought up problems with *shechita* and *kashrut*, Waley Cohen would note what Hertz wanted and set out to achieve the objectives for him. It was, primarily, on the importance of the observance of the *mitzvot* and the question of ultimate authority that they differed.

Waley Cohen would also, on occasions, disagree with the views of the United Synagogue council. In 1926 it voted to collect money for Keren Hayesod, the Zionist fund-raising organization. Waley Cohen was against this and delayed the implementation of the decision for two years with legal quibbles.

Hertz had his own relationship problems. Those with the Right Wing remained outstanding. Basically, Hertz considered that the ultra-Orthodox congregations who refused to accept his authority were weakening the community.

It wasn't all confrontation, though. On 1 April 1925 the Hebrew University in Jerusalem was opened on Mount Scopus, by Lord Balfour. The foundation stone had been laid by Chaim Weizmann in July 1918, just seven months after General Allenby had captured the city from the Turks.

The Chief Rabbi received an invitation to help consecrate the building and to stay with Rose at the high commissioner's residence in the Augusta Victoria Hospital. Hertz's contribution to the passing of the Balfour Declaration had not been forgotten and, if he criticized the secularity of the Zionists, he always strongly supported their religious wing. He was honorary president of the British branch of the Mizrachi Organisation, the religious Zionists, for many years.

Sir Herbert Samuel, the high commissioner, was expecting luminaries from all over the world to come to the opening, as the trustees of the university included Albert Einstein and Sigmund Freud. Lord Allenby was returning to the scene of his military triumph, and there were also the architect of the Balfour Declaration, Lord Balfour, Chaim Weizmann and senior academics, as well as Rabbi Kook, Chief Rabbi of Palestine. The Hertzs were in excellent company.

Rose Hertz was far from overwhelmed though. She wrote home: 'Lady Clayton, wife of the Chief Secretary, is a beautiful woman, gorgeously dressed, and she knows it!'[16] Rose Hertz didn't like her. She showed: 'a lack of sympathy with Jewish aspirations in Palestine'. When it came to ceremonies, however, the Chief Rabbi's wife struggled a little: 'I shall wear my black (American) dress – a large summerish hat would have been useful. I should have brought my black satin shoes also.'

They decided to make a holiday of their visit and Rose Hertz faithfully recorded the events of the six weeks they were away from home.[17] They arrived in Palestine on 25 March, travelling via France and Switzerland, and enjoyed a trip on a gondola in Venice before taking ship via Milan. Palestine was underdeveloped compared to those European countries through which they passed. On arriving at Government House in Jerusalem they discovered that there was a serious water shortage: 'so we are rationed to one paraffin tin a day per person'.[18] They also decided to become vegetarians for the period of their stay, as the high commissioner hadn't been able to find a Jewish cook.

Rose Hertz found the poverty in which so many lived in Jerusalem hard to bear: 'In the Old City, low filthy roads, full of dirt and animal refuse, indescribable smells.'[19] The effects of poverty were distressing: 'Oh! The sandals one saw being resurrected – uppers with a thin bit stuck on in place of a sole.'[20]

She did find that the Wailing Wall had been cleared of beggars:

> A careful list was being made of those old and decrepit people who would never have any means of support, and they would be given a regular weekly allowance on condition that they would not go to the Wailing Wall and beg ... In time it is hoped that Jews will no longer feel ashamed at the sight of half-starved, half-naked, maimed mendicants appealing to tourists for help.[21]

The poverty left a lasting impression: 'The rat holes people live in (in the Old City) have made me very unhappy.'[22] A lot of make-do-and-mend was necessary. At the Blind Institution: 'the tiny tables and chairs were made of old packing cases'.[23] In the countryside there was progress: 'The Jewish bits of land were green and beautifully kept and the contrast with that of the Arabs was most marked.'[24] Relations between the Arab and Jewish communities were fragile though. In the Old City in Jerusalem: 'We came to one spot where he [the guide] told us that Jews were not allowed to walk, so I promptly walked across the road ... I felt it was my business to decide where Jews were to walk and not he or anyone else.'[25]

The missing ingredient in Rose Hertz's lengthy account is any report of personal security. It was provided for Balfour, but the Hertzs wandered round the towns and went on long journeys through the country, to both Jewish and Arab sites, without any minders beyond the taxi driver and any friends who might join them. Rose Hertz even went on foot to the Bazaar in the Old City with the high commissioner's wife.

On 1 April the University was declared open in a giant amphitheatre seating 2,000 with another 10,000 lining the nearby hillside. The consecration ceremony dragged on with some interminable speeches. Rabbi Abraham Kook, the first Ashkenazi Chief Rabbi during the British mandate, had said he wouldn't take part in the consecration ceremony. When he changed his mind, Hertz happily agreed to only give the concluding prayer. Rabbi Kook spoke for three quarters of an hour, about half an hour longer than expected.

Hertz kept his contribution short to try to recover some time and was well received: 'When the people heard "King George", applause broke out, which Father stopped at once.'[26] By now, dictating the behaviour he wanted from a crowd presented no challenge to the Chief Rabbi. He was also capable of making his addresses in Hebrew, English or Yiddish according to his audience. This time he spoke in Hebrew.

Balfour made a particularly good impression: 'That handsome man, tall, and with a benign face – grey hair, red robe, etc., speaking to so vast an assembly'.[27] The gala dinner to celebrate the opening of the university saw sixteen speeches: 'We broke up at 11.30 o'clock.' The Samuels had invited the Hertzs to stay at Government House for Pesach, but they reluctantly decided that the standard of *kashrut* would not be sufficiently high, somewhat to the embarrassment of Lady Samuel. It was also too far to walk to shul and the Chief Rabbi wanted to observe a second Seder service which was not the custom in Palestine. So, at the risk of seeming ungracious, they moved on to more Orthodox friends.

In the days after the ceremony, they visited Haifa, Tiberias and Safed before leaving by boat for Alexandria. On the way home they stopped off in Naples to see Pompeii and went on to Rome and Berlin.

Hertz returned to London to face the friction with the Right Wing, which he took very seriously. He was hurt that: 'the ultra-pious tolerate us'[28] but he understood their thinking. It was true that the majority of the United Synagogue members obeyed few *mitzvot*, but there were limits to what behavioural patterns he could change. Hertz knew his members had Jewish mothers and, therefore, were halakhically Jewish. The right wing had no option but to accept this.

A year later one of the most powerful right wing voices, Rabbi Dr Victor Schonfeld, died. Schonfeld had created the Union of Orthodox Hebrew Congregations. His son, Solomon, would marry Hertz's daughter, Judith, and become a powerful ally of the Chief Rabbi, but that was long in the future. Hertz regarded Victor Schonfeld as 'the leader of the opposition to the rabbinate as long as he lived'.[29]

He also resented the title Schonfeld had taken for the Union of Orthodox Hebrew Congregations. It suggested to the uninformed that, while the member congregations of the UOHC were Orthodox, any synagogue not affiliated to it was not. Hertz called the appellation a fake name.

Such comments only exacerbated the problem of getting the Right Wing and the United Synagogue to work in harmony. There were also a few pockets of ultra-Orthodox Jews outside London. One was the Beth Hamedresh in Sunderland whose practices reflected the very Orthodox community they had mostly come from in Lithuania. In competition with the original Sunderland synagogue, they were known colloquially as the Greeners and the less Orthodox community was referred to as the Englisher shul.

Up the road from Sunderland was Gateshead and here, too, a deeply Orthodox community had emerged. Neither Gateshead nor the Sunderland Beth Hamedresh acknowledged the authority of the Chief Rabbi, though Sunderland had promised to do so when Hermann Adler held the post, as a quid pro quo for his approval of their request to appoint a marriage secretary. They reneged. This did not mean that Hertz was unpopular in the North East – he had only recently been made very welcome on a visit to the Gateshead community – but the Greeners wanted to retain their independence, as would have been the case on the Continent.

In 1926 a few pioneers in Gateshead started a *yeshiva* and invited Rabbi Abraham Sacharov to come to England and accept the post of *Rosh Yeshiva*. They did not consult with the rest of the community who already had a synagogue rabbi. A letter to the *Jewish Chronicle* from a Gateshead member even suggested that starting a *yeshiva* was a 'harebrained idea'.

From Hertz's point of view, having struggled for years to raise sufficient money to keep Jews' College going, the last thing he wanted was a competitor. Furthermore, it was perfectly possible that Gateshead would prove more fertile ground for such a foundation than London. The first *yeshiva* in the country, Etz Haim in the East End of London was still hard at work. One of Hertz's first engagements as Chief Rabbi had been to consecrate its new building in 1913. He would do the same when it moved to larger premises in 1937.

Hertz had good relations with the London *Yeshiva* but the one in Gateshead was very likely to be less prepared to be influenced by his views. Etz Haim had been underpinned financially in its early days by Lord Swaythling and members of the Federation who acknowledged the Chief Rabbi's authority. This was very unlikely to be true of Gateshead, whose original founders were a breakaway congregation from Newcastle, formed because they did not consider the level of Orthodoxy there to be acceptable by their standards.

With unemployment high, work permits were hard to come by, and when the Home Office investigated the application for an entry permit for Rabbi Sacharov, Hertz persuaded the Home Secretary, the anti-Semitic William Joynson-Hicks, not to grant a work permit.

When news of this came to light, Hertz explained his behaviour by saying that there were already plenty of equally qualified rabbanim in Britain who could fill the post and who needed the job. In view of the difficulty he found in recruiting Talmudic experts for his own needs, this was somewhat unlikely.

When a question was asked in the House of Commons in February, Joynson-Hicks replied: 'The application for the admission of this Polish Rabbi has not been supported by any argument beyond the fact that the Gateshead congregation have elected him, and though I have made enquiries, I have been unable to ascertain any special grounds for acceding to the application.'[30]

Although Rabbi Sacharov's application was refused, the Gateshead pioneers were not discouraged. In 1929 the27-year-old Rabbi Nachman Landynski was chosen and this time a visa was granted. Nonetheless, for some further years, Hertz would not acknowledge the Gateshead community as suitable to have a marriage secretary.

As Chief Rabbi he was required by law to confirm that a community applying for permission to conduct weddings consisted of Jews, and to deny this in the case of Gateshead was nonsense. The sticking point remained that they still wouldn't recognize his religious authority over the congregation. Gateshead were not giving in. The alternative, for the time being, remained for a member of the local Registrar's Office to be present to legalize any nuptials.

Eventually the Gateshead *Yeshiva* was created with the help of financial support from members of the Sunderland Beth Hamedresh, and Hertz gave his permission for them to have a marriage secretary. The community still doesn't recognize the Chief Rabbi's authority but, today, the Gateshead *Yeshiva* is famous throughout the Jewish world, and its authority in religious decisions is highly regarded.

NOTES

1. Robert Henriques, *Sir Robert Waley Cohen, 1877–1952* (London: Secker and Warburg, 1966), p.342.
2. Ibid., p.343.
3. Ibid.
4. Joseph Herman Hertz, 'Opening Address of the Chief Rabbi at the 1927 Conference of Anglo-Jewish Preachers' (London: Oxford University Press, 1927), p.2.
5. Jeremy Schonfield private family archive.
6. Anne Kershen and Jonathan Romain, *Tradition and Change: A History of Reform Judaism in Britain, 1940–1995* (London and Portland, OR: Vallentine Mitchell, 1995), p.97.
7. Meir Persoff, *Faith Against Reason: Religious Reform and the British Chief Rabbinate, 1840–1990* (London and Portland, OR: Vallentine Mitchell, 2008), p.224.
8. Aubrey Newman, 'Chief Rabbi Dr Joseph Herman Hertz, CH' (London: United Synagogue, 1972), p.16.
9. Joseph Herman Hertz, *Affirmations of Judaism* (Oxford: Oxford University Press/ Humphrey Milford, 1927), p.149.
10. *Jewish Chronicle*, 30 April 1926.
11. Hertz, *Affirmations of Judaism*, p.179.
12. Revd Ephraim Levine in Isidore Epstein (ed.), *Joseph Herman Hertz. In Memoriam* (London: Soncino Press, 1947), p.30.
13. Ibid.
14. *Jewish Chronicle*, 28 October 1927.
15. See http://www.historytoday.com/dunia-garcia-ontiveros/treasures-london-library-claude-montefiore-cautious-revolutionary. Duna Garcia-Ontiveros is the head of bibliographical services at the London Library, which benefited greatly from Montefiore's philanthropy.
16. Jeremy Schonfield private family archive. Rose Hertz wrote home a great deal and in great detail. Her account of the journey covers thirty-five double-spaced foolscap sheets. The account of her trip is taken from the letters.
17. Ibid.
18. Ibid.
19. Ibid.
20. Ibid.
21. Ibid.
22. Ibid.
23. Ibid.
24. Ibid.
25. Ibid.

26. Ibid.
27. Ibid.
28. Jeremy Schonfield private family archive.
29. Ibid.
30. *Hansard*, 8 February 1926. Vol. 191. CC671-2W.

Chapter Ten

A Pause for Calendar Reform, 1924–31

In 1923 there occurred an opportunity for the Chief Rabbi to act on the world stage. It was to be the only time in his life when he occupied a truly international spotlight and it made his reputation for the rest of his career. It was Hertz who led the battle to prevent the calendar being changed by the League of Nations, and Jewish communities throughout the world played a part in the struggle to keep the existing system.

The advantages of a common and accurate calendar are easy to recognize. When working out train timetables, for example, it is awkward to have a 365-day year. There were powerful arguments, however, against changing the format. The struggle started in November 1923 when the League of Nations communications and transit section decided to set up a Special Committee to enquire into the reform of the calendar. It was odd timing because the Gregorian calendar had only just been adopted by the last country to come into line: Greece. Of the laggards, China had endorsed it in 1912, Turkey in 1917 and Russia in 1918. It was now agreed by everybody.

The Gregorian calendar had been introduced by Pope Gregory II in 1582 because its predecessor, the Julian calendar, was eleven minutes a year too long. It took 350 years for everybody to accept the alternative. The Jews kept to their own calendar for their Sabbaths and festivals, which hadn't been changed after almost 2,000 years.

One of those who wanted to correct the situation was an English-born accountant working in the Canadian railways company, Moses Cotsworth. He had presented a paper on the subject to the Royal Society of Canada as far back as 1908, and had written a proposal for a fixed calendar in 1922 when he founded the International Fixed Calendar League.

In addition, George Eastman, the creator of Kodak, also decided that business administration would be easier if the year were divided into four quarters of ninety-one days, thirteen months of twenty-eight days each, with a blank day to complete the 365. This might have helped with business bureaucracy, but it would have meant breaking with a sequence of weeks comprising seven days that went back to antiquity. Saturday one year would become Sunday the next and Monday the year after. It was an American initiative, powered by commercial and financial interests, financed by Eastman and Cotsworth and led by Willis Booth, the American president of the International Chamber of Commerce.

The members of the committee were Booth himself, a Dutch academic, a French astronomer, and quasi-official representatives of the Vatican, the Greek Catholic Church and the Archbishop of Canterbury. The divines announced from the beginning that they were not representing their churches officially. There was no Jew on the Committee; the League of Nations had responded to objections to this by promising to appoint one, but they never did. Moses Cotsworth was clear about Jewish objections. He said that as the Jews formed less than 1 per cent of humanity, they couldn't stand in the way of 'progress'.

Eastman was not accustomed to taking 'no' for an answer and could finance the calendar reform project for as long as it took to be agreed. As he saw it, the League of Nations committee was just the first step. Now it was agreed to ask governments if they approved of a change. It was also announced that the committee would consider any other suggestions for calendar reform. No fewer than 183 different schemes were received from all over the world. Cotsworth was asked to advise on their feasibility.

When Hertz heard of the proposal, he was seriously alarmed. To have a movable Sabbath day would be disastrous for Jewish practice. As in South Africa when, as a newly arrived rabbi, he argued with Kruger about disabilities suffered by foreigners, Hertz was not overawed by powerful men or organizations; not even the League of Nations. It was the British Chief Rabbi who started to organize world-wide Jewish opposition to calendar reform.

Soon the Conference of American Liberal Synagogues, the Central Conference of American Rabbis and the Rabbinical Authorities of Conservative and Orthodox communities in America wanted him to add their protests to the proposal. The problem for the Jews in America was that their country had rejected the opportunity to join the League of Nations and so they had no official standing in the organization. Involvement by Americans would only be by invitation.

It wasn't until January 1925 that Hertz managed to secure a hearing at a Calendar Reform Committee meeting. He was given just twelve-days notice to put his delegation and arguments together. Afterwards, at its February gathering, countries like Britain, India, Germany and Belgium pronounced themselves against reform and the agitation seemed to be at an end.

This was, however, far from the case. Eastman financed a major press campaign in America, and attempted to persuade the American House of Representatives to endorse the proposal in 1928. The House referred it to the Committee on Foreign Affairs, which was chaired by the congressman who had introduced the initial resolution. Fortunately for the opposition to the idea, there was one member of the committee, Solomon Bloom, who was not going to let the recommendation be approved without argument, and the House took the idea no further.

The committee in Geneva now asked governments to appoint National Committees of Enquiry to see if anybody was disadvantaged by the Gregorian calendar, which its opponents now referred to as the Jewish calendar, and which, it was now absurdly asserted, was partly responsible for the financial crisis. As the Gregory in question was a Pope, this Jewish appellation did suggest a hope that the case for a new calendar might be strengthened by allying it to anti-Semitism. The committee was supposed to be investigating the topic impersonally, but they had obviously moved towards being totally partisan to their cause.

In June 1929 Hertz set up a Standing Vigilance Committee to create a massive petition against the reform. He wanted it to be signed by every adult Jew and Jewess in the world. When it became clear that this was too ambitious, the emphasis moved to encouraging Jewish communities to sign a protest. Support for Hertz had by now come from the World Organisation for the Defence of the Sabbath, based in Berlin, and rabbinical authorities in Central and Eastern Europe.

It did not come from Waley Cohen, however, who told him in 1927 that he should confine himself to purely ecclesiastical matters and leave the lay leaders of the community to deal with the rest. If the alteration of the Sabbath day was not an ecclesiastical matter, however, it would be difficult to find a subject where it was. Hertz replied by quoting Lord Rothschild who had said that his responsibilities touched on every point which concerned the religious, moral and general welfare of the community.

Hertz joined with other opponents of the scheme, including Cecil Roth, the Jewish historian, who agreed to act as Secretary of the opposition. Memos on the subject between them were 'From CR to

CR, re: CR'. The Press covered the story and called it 'The Battle of the Sabbath at Geneva'. This gave a further boost to Hertz's international reputation. In organizing the opposition, Hertz managed to deliver a protest at the League of Nations, signed by hundreds of thousands of Jews from all over the world. Direct mail to all the Jewish communities elicited this response, including no fewer than 55,000 signatures from Holland.

A decision was due to be made by the League of Nations in October 1931. At a Frankfurt meeting in the May of that year Hertz was made chair of the effort to ensure that communities sent in protests. The money to finance the campaign had to be raised and the United Synagogue, the Sephardim and particularly the Federation, sent cheques. Money also came from Empire communities and from Warsaw and the Preussischer Landesverband and Jüdischer Gemeinden in Germany. Hertz campaigned against the reform in many parts of Britain. He talked on the subject in Manchester in March 1931 and was gratified when the Lord Bishop of Manchester created a precedent by calling on him to pay his respects.

Meanwhile the League of Nations committee had doubled in size. Room had been found for the vice-president of the Society for the Simplification of the Calendar, but there was still no Jewish representative. The Committee had written to sixty governments to ask them to set up committees of enquiry. Only twenty-eight had done so and just fourteen sent in a reply. Of these, six said 'no', six favoured change and two were neutral.

The committee report, which was supposed to be impartial, still recommended change, calling Jewish arguments exaggerated. They said that the discomfort of a religious minority should not stand in the way of the economic advantage of the majority. Of course the powerful Lord's Day Observance Society existed in England to ensure that economic advantage was not the only criterion to be taken into consideration. The Emperor Constantine had passed his National Sunday Law in 321CE and the society continued to protect its observance.

Hertz now moved to persuading prominent Jews around the world to write objecting to the idea, but he was concerned that the British government might not recognize the inherent danger of the situation until it was too late. So he contacted his own MP, Sir Rennell Rodd, and arranged for him to ask a question in the House: 'Will the Secretary of State take precautions that this country should not be committed to a prejudicial decision by the appointment to the Conference for the Reform of the Calendar, which will meet in Geneva on the 12th

October, of a representative who has already definitely pronounced himself in favour of an eight day week.'[1]

This was agreed, but the timing was tight. It was at the end of September that the Federal Council of Evangelical Free Churches of England passed a resolution that there should be a change only if all religious bodies agreed to it. The Lord's Day Observance Society joined soon after. The mood was gloomy though. In June the *Jewish Chronicle* had summed up the position: 'According to all accounts, the League of Nations is likely to reject the plea which has been made by Jews against the proposals for what is termed Calendar Reform. We should hence have no small difficulty in adjusting to the new conditions the due observance of the Sabbath.'[2]

Hertz and Roth set off for Geneva, convinced that the odds were stacked against them. Objectors were to be allowed only fifteen minutes to make a brief address. Reformers were categorized as members of government bodies and allowed to speak for as long as they liked. On 12 October, 111 representatives of forty-two nations met to reach a decision.

Few delegates understood the implications, and the speeches of the reformers took up half the time of the conference. The delegates of Argentina, Belgium, Canada, China, France, Germany, Greece, Hungary, Japan, Portugal, Spain, Switzerland and Yugoslavia agreed that the calendar should be altered. The situation continued to look bleak. As one proponent put it: 'If any hardship is to accrue to a minority from the new Calendar, it would be self-imposed because of continual refusal to conform to the determination of the majority'.[3]

At which point the conference heard a rousing speech from the Chief Rabbi who quoted Lincoln to support the position of the minorities: 'It is as if a highwayman [said] "stand and deliver" or I shoot, and then you will be the murderer.'[4]

The conference was then addressed by Sir John Baldwin of the British Foreign Office. Baldwin suggested that the word 'reform' implied improvement and stated that, in his government's opinion, changing the calendar would do nothing of the sort. As *The Times* said on 13 October: 'Their [The Jews] religious scruples on a matter so fundamental to them deserve respect and there will be a large number of Christians sharing those scruples ... The question really resolves itself into the balancing of simplified book keeping against religious scruples and looking for variety, and in such a balancing, human interests are bound to weigh the more heavily.' The mood of the conference began to change.[5]

The contribution of one delegate was particularly unhelpful to Hertz. The Czechoslovakian representative said that there had been no complaints from that country's Jewish communities. Over lunch, Hertz gave him 129 official resolutions from Jewish communities in Slovakia and in the afternoon, the delegate told the conference he had been mistaken.

The crunch came the next day when the French asked whether the delegates present represented their governments or their own opinions. Germany seconded the enquiry. The delegates admitted that their governments had not advised them to seek change. The Swiss delegate then moved that the views of a minority could not succeed against the majority. Only three out of forty-two countries supported him.

Eventually it was agreed that it was an inopportune time to consider reforming the calendar. The reformers said that this meant that another conference on the subject would be called for 1935 although they had no authority to do so. It was actually convened in 1937, and with the same result. The idea would be turned down yet again by the United Nations in 1956.

At the League of Nations almost everybody now agreed that it had been a stupid idea from the beginning. *The Christian* magazine said: 'Whereas a short time ago it seemed certain that an eight day week would be established, now, at length, in the words of Dr Hertz ... "the delegates of 40 nations have rung down the curtain on the Calendar Reform movement and the curtain will remain down for at least a generation".'[6] This proved rather optimistic since there is a magazine and an association dedicated to calendar reform even now.

When it was all over Hertz was hailed as a hero, and other religions, which would have been adversely affected had the calendar been changed, were also indebted to him. At this point Hertz became known all over the world and rose above the provincial squabbles of his own community.

His opposition within the United Synagogue was also finding the going tougher. There was growing disagreement between the Honorary Officers and the Council. The Honorary Officers still came from the Cousinhood, but the Council was elected from small businessmen, second-generation immigrants, Talmudic scholars, the old, the middle-aged and even some young people. Where the Honorary Officers had been accustomed to the Council rubber-stamping their decisions, they now found the natives becoming restless.

Hertz, himself, came from European stock and was an immigrant to Britain. He could fairly claim to be one of them. He was also persona grata in Establishment circles and even in the provinces where the United Synagogue flag hadn't yet been planted. It was generally agreed that: 'of all things that can be said about Dr Hertz detrimentally, the least true would be that he is apt to "put on side" [behave in a superior manner] as it is called.'[7] The Chief Rabbi had the support of the majority.

NOTES

1. *Hansard*, 15 September 1931.
2. *Jewish Chronicle*, 5 June 1931.
3. Ibid. There is a full account of the calendar reform negotiations by Chief Rabbi Hertz in the *Transactions of the Jewish Historical Society of England*, Vol.13 (London: JHSE, 1932/35), pp.189–246.
4. Ibid.
5. *The Times*, 13 October 1931.
6. *The Christian*, 19 October 1931, in Hertz, *Transactions of the Jewish Historical Society of England*, Vol.13, p.189.
7. *Jewish Chronicle*, 15 July 1921.

Chapter Eleven

The Unkindest Blow

The leadership of the entire British Jewish community was still a much sought after ambition, though the power politics involved were disruptive. One of the objectives of many members of the council of the United Synagogue was to extend the coverage of the organization to encompass communities outside the capital. This would certainly have strengthened a number of the smaller congregations and a committee had been set up in 1920 to examine the possibilities. It had reported in 1923 but the Honorary Officers never seemed to get around to the subject until all the other items on the agendas had been completed, and it was usually put back to the next meeting when it again re-emerged after 10.00 p.m.

One of the committee members was a lawyer who pointed out that the Charities Commission, who had approved the original 1870 deed, would have to support an Amending Act if the United Synagogue was to extend itself to 'Ireland and the Empire'. In 1926, without consulting the Council, Waley Cohen asked the Charities Commission to approve such a change. The Commission refused to do so, pointing out, as the United Synagogue Committee had known it would, that such an alteration would be a diversion from the main objective for which the organization had been created.

It was another Waley Cohen bid for more power, and this time there was fury among the Council delegates. So many members were on their feet shouting that the business of the Council could not proceed. At one point a vote of 'no confidence' in the Honorary Officers was proposed and Waley Cohen decided to vacate the chair for another officer. Eventually things quietened down, but the hard work the committee had put in went for nothing.

By contrast, a few months afterwards, the Chief Rabbi addressed a large congregation at the Whitefields Tabernacle in London. In the 200 years of its existence at least three prime ministers had spoken there and the Wesleyan tradition favoured inspiring speakers and enthusiastic audiences. The Chief Rabbi maintained the standards. A largely working-class Christian audience was 'kept spellbound':[1] Hertz could hold an audience better than most preachers in the country. He used humour, a vast variety of sources, quoting those who were against his views as well as those who agreed with him. As he said: 'I always like to quote the sceptics.'[2] He got a standing ovation and was well reported. (In later years, the Tabernacle would be totally destroyed by the last rocket to hit London in 1945 but was rebuilt in 1957.)

In 1928 a Slaughter of Animals Act for Scotland was introduced in Parliament. The humanity of *shechita*, as a way of killing animals, was always a contentious subject outside the Jewish community. It seemed implausible that the provisions of the Babylonian Talmud in the sixth century could not have been improved on in modern times. Hertz was able to quote Dr W.M. Haffkine, of the Pasteur Institute, who had said that the Jewish method not only guaranteed that the animal suffered no pain but prevented the spreading of microbes, and so was a benefit to the human race.

It was agreed in the Scotland bill that only the Chief Rabbi should be allowed to licence *shochetim*, as had been the case for many years. This angered Victor Schonfeld who complained of the perceived anomaly that: 'No rabbi in Scotland should have the right to grant Kabbalah [a licence] to Shochetim except through the Chief Rabbinate of the United Synagogue.'[3] In 1930 the Federation would call a conference at which they said this system should be altered to enable them to be included, and the Sephardi Mahamad added its supporting voice to the proposal.

The former Haham, Moses Gaster, even gave a presentation to twenty MPs in the House of Commons on the subject. Gaster remained in his old age a most impressive speaker and one MP said it was a pity he wasn't in the House. For a former Haham to question the authority of the Chief Rabbi, though, was hardly helpful to the community's public image, but Gaster still resented having lost his office and, with it, his power base. The religious authorities were, in general, seriously aggrieved. The Federation and the UOHC said a single authority was 'inimical to Judaism and contrary to Jewish law'.[4] It was yet another chapter in a battle over *shechita* which had been going on for very many years.

In 1933 the Slaughter of Animals Bill for England and Wales would include a provision for a Rabbinical Council to be set up to licence *shochetim*. The Chief Rabbi would chair it, the Sephardim would provide the Deputy Chair, and there would also be two representatives from the Federation, one from the UOHC and two more rabbis nominated by the Board of Deputies to represent provincial communities. It was agreed that Orthodox communities could opt out of the whole system and have their own *shochet*, but only if 40 per cent of the congregation voted in favour of the action.

Amid all the responsibilities of his office, Hertz was also devoted to his family. At home, the children were proving the value of having two academic parents. Samuel had got into Cambridge and read Hebrew. Leon and Daniel had gone to Oxford where Daniel at New College was proving an exceptional medical student, and Leon was settled down at Wadham. Judith would follow them to Somerville College, Oxford. Far from academia, Hertz was busy opening new synagogues. The Jewish movement to the leafy suburbs was continuing to lead to the need for new shuls and in one month in September 1927 the Chief Rabbi consecrated or laid foundation stones for six new buildings.

As the decade drew to a close the poor relationship between Hertz and Waley Cohen continued to be a source of concern. Both men were even more determined to get their own way. Hertz made a joke of his approach and said that he: 'never neglected the peaceful solution; when all other means had failed'.[5] Perhaps as a consequence the impression has come down over the years that he was more given to verbal aggression than Waley Cohen.

The facts disprove this. Waley Cohen's biography, written by his cousin, is hagiographic. Yet Henriques wrote about events in 1928: 'the tension between them was often intolerable, and outbursts of temper when both men shouted and raved their recriminations at each other were not uncommon'.[6] The point is, though, that the protagonists on those occasions to which Henriques refers were not Waley Cohen and Hertz. They were Waley Cohen and his chairman at Shell Petroleum, Sir Henri Deterding. Within a few months after their relations had reached that low, Waley Cohen resigned from Shell.

Waley Cohen almost immediately took on a mountainous problem, becoming chairman of the African and Eastern Trading Corporation in January 1929. He had many friends in the City who recognized his ability. Together with the Niger Company, the African and Eastern dominated the Palm Oil industry in Nigeria, and there was a sound case for amalgamating the two companies, as trading conditions were difficult for each. During those negotiations, Waley Cohen had to work with Niger Company executives and, eventually, with their owners, who later became Unilever. He was put in charge of the amalgamated company and his individual management style was welcomed by the acolytes he favoured and terrified those he did not.

As far as his Board colleagues were concerned: 'They found his domineering determination and quick, volcanic rages, intolerable.'[7] It was finally agreed that the new joint company would be run by committee decisions of the Board rather than by Waley Cohen pretty well on his own. When he ignored the agreement he had signed up to, the Board fired him in February 1931. He never recovered his eminence in the world of big business.

In spite of Waley Cohen's unsuccessful attempts to achieve total control by bullying at Shell and United Africa, he claimed that any adverse result was the fault of those who didn't agree with him. When he considered the Chief Rabbi's undoubted authority in matters affecting the community, he took a very different view. As he wrote to Hertz in 1928:

> I do not think you will ever find the Anglo Jewish community willing to submit to the unquestioned authority of anyone in any matter other than questions of pure 'din'. I certainly am not. I count it as a great blessing that it has always been the practice in our Community for the leaders – lay and clerical – to take counsel together and to reach a common agreement and work together in the interests of the Community, and we should all be only too delighted if you would do that with us.
>
> I do not think pontifical authority could be justified, and I should very much regret it if you finally decided that it is essential to your self-respect.[8]

The tradition was certainly for the leaders to take counsel together, but Waley Cohen knew very well that the Chief Rabbi had the authority to make final decisions on a wide range of subjects affecting the community. To compare this to 'pontifical authority' was to try to enlist anti-Catholic sentiment, and this was mischievous or worse. Furthermore, to attribute the Chief Rabbi's determination to make decisions to a desire to bolster his self-respect was demeaning of his official role. Hertz responded by quoting the constitutions of the United Synagogue, the Board of Deputies and Rothschild's brief at his installation. He was doing what he had been appointed to do.

Just as Henriques would see faults in his cousin when he wrote his biography, so Ephraim Levine, one of the Chief Rabbi's foremost friends and supporters, recognized Hertz's shortcomings. He wrote: 'He was not an easy member of a committee when any controversial subject was under discussion, for once he had made up his mind, it was difficult, if not impossible, to move him.'[9] After another massive row at a committee meeting, Waley Cohen wrote to Hertz: 'The last time we met I am afraid your – as it seemed to me – inexhaustible powers of destruction exceeded my far too limited patience.'[10]

It would be difficult to be more patronizing. Waley Cohen was graciously admitting to the minor fault of not having sufficient patience, while accusing the Chief Rabbi of the major shortcoming of having inexhaustible powers of destruction.

In response, Hertz was more direct, if less elegant, on this occasion. He spelt out the position, as he saw it, very clearly:

> I miss in your letter an apology for the wild abuse which you shrieked at me on October 27th last ... one of your favourite defamatory phrases is 'the Chief Rabbi is a destructive force in the Community' – because I baulked your attempt to undermine traditional Judaism ... [the situation would not improve] unless and until you understand that the Chief Rabbi is the moral teacher and guide of the Community, and not the bondsman of any one individual of the community. Threats and invective are to no avail to divert me from any course of action which I deem is dictated to me by conscience, self-respect or considerations for the welfare of Judaism and Jewish people.[11]

The discussions had degenerated into bare-knuckle verbal brawls but Waley Cohen's capacity for self-delusion never deserted him. At the end of his own life, Waley Cohen wrote to a friend about his relations with Hertz: 'I am sure you would be the last person to agree that my mild and patient method of argument is any way rightly described as "pressure"'.[12]

As far as Hertz was concerned, little had changed since his time in Syracuse and South Africa. The lay leaders of those communities had also tried to get him to accept a subordinate role, and he had resigned from Syracuse and still created the Board of Deputies in South Africa. His 1900 letter to the *Jewish Chronicle* had laid down his views on the role of lay leaders in a Jewish community and he hadn't altered his opinion: Honorary Officers should be his commercial managers and not the keepers of his conscience.

The Chief Rabbi remained under fire from Waley Cohen and his supporters for many more years. They felt that he should try to win the respect of all sections of the community but this was impossible if 'respect' involved accepting views Hertz felt were antipathetic to Jewish law.

Hertz was broad-minded in accepting secular input, he had a spellbinding personality, as was commented on throughout his life, and he successfully won the respect of large sections of the community who didn't agree with him. By this point in his ministry he had indeed achieved prestige over a greater international and theological range of bodies than any previous Chief Rabbi. But he refused to preside over the watering down of Orthodoxy in Britain.

The 1930s would present new and more serious challenges. He would try hard to bind the community together in the face of the Nazi threat, but felt it was no part of his ministry to win respect from Jews who disagreed with the tenets of Orthodox Judaism. He couldn't change the Jewish law to please those who found it inconvenient or spiritually questionable. Such action would have led to Jewish Orthodox communities abroad rejecting his authority, which would have isolated and potentially delegitimized his own members internationally.

In 1928 he had wanted to set up an international conference on the divorce problems which women faced in Judaism, but there was little enthusiasm for it among the clergy. He managed to secure agreement that women members should be allowed to vote in synagogue elections, but even that was achieved only with difficulty. The Suffragette movement had made an unanswerable case for emancipating women, but the Beth Din only grudgingly admitted that the act of women voting in synagogue elections was not against Jewish law while they still disapproved of it; the fight for equal rights for women in society as a whole had a long way to go.

When it became clear that Hertz wouldn't buckle under Waley Cohen's pressure, Lionel de Rothschild, president of the United Synagogue, was brought into the argument. The subject that caused de Rothschild to intervene was ministers' pensions, which Hertz wanted to be augmented from the funds in the War Memorial to relieve the poverty many elderly ministers faced at the time. It was a battle the Chief Rabbi had fought on behalf of colleagues for many years and there was no one else to represent them.

De Rothschild wrote a letter to Hertz which Waley Cohen made even more condemnatory. The result received by the Chief Rabbi contained an attempt to change the constitution of the United Synagogue without the approval of their Council. De Rothschild wrote:

> Hitherto our affairs have been governed by the duly constituted Councils and the duly elected Executives of our various communal bodies. You appear to repudiate their authority altogether and to desire to exercise overriding powers in the governing of our communal affairs. I think it is right that I should say to you quite clearly that I can be no party to any such arrangement. I feel it to be essential that our Community should be governed in the future, as it has in the past, by the duly constituted bodies … and whilst it

> is in every way proper that you should always proffer your advice and guidance ... the decisions must rest with those duly elected bodies and not with you ... and must be loyally accepted by you.[13]

De Rothschild went on that the disagreements couldn't continue and that, if necessary, he would call a full meeting of the United Synagogue Council to consider the attitude of the Chief Rabbi. He must have known, though, that he was bluffing. In the end he didn't call the Council meeting and Hertz didn't agree to change his style. Indeed, that autumn he had been consulted by the BBC on whether they should broadcast a *Kol Nidre* service from the Liberal Synagogue. Hertz said that it would give much offence. He didn't seek general approval for his stance, but the idea was still dropped. Hertz's authority, set down in the United Synagogue constitution, remained unaltered though the constant sniping at it was wearying.

It was, in any case, unlikely that the non-Jewish media would pay as much attention to a lay leader as to the Chief Rabbi. This would be particularly true in international matters before the rise of Hitler. In the 1920s the main opponent of organized religion was the Communist regime in Russia, where even the teaching of prayers to children could result in heavy terms of imprisonment. A long letter from the Chief Rabbi on this topic appeared in *The Times* on 14 February 1930. This time he knew that all religious leaders would support his viewpoint but he added that:

> The world now confidently looks forward to the leaders of opinion outside the Churches for a pronouncement on these happenings. There are in England both scientists and men of letters of international renown, whose words carry weight in Russia, and whose protest could not be dismissed by militant atheists as being the benighted opinion of 'clericals' and 'reactionaries'. Let them voice their indignation and horror at this spiritual pogrom.

Hertz went to war on many fronts. He had attacked the Liberal viewpoint in his sermons 'The New Paths', but the Reform movement had remained closer to the Orthodox, at least until a new rabbi was appointed to Upper Berkeley Street: Harold Reinhart. He was American, more attuned to a modernist outlook and a man of determined views. As a confirmed pacifist he refused to have the Stars and Stripes flag in his synagogue when America entered the war in 1917. He said he considered it an emblem of war, although the flag is central to American patriotism. In London he wanted to extend the buildings of the Reform congregation but he met resistance. This led him to label the Synagogue Council: 'feeble and futile'[14] and the synagogue 'handsome but hollow'.[15]

Eventually he persuaded the Reform Council that the effort to find common ground with the Chief Rabbi was also futile. At the Annual Meeting of Upper Berkeley Street in April 1930 the Council recommended to the attendees that Upper Berkeley Street should join the World Union of Progressive Judaism. This organization had Claude Montefiore of the Liberals as its president and Lily Montagu as a supporter. Of the 1,266 members of the synagogue, only sixty attended and the recommendation was passed by thirty-nine votes to six. By this small number of votes the Reform movement in Britain decided to move further away from the Orthodox position.

What also concerned Hertz was Britain's faltering efforts to create a National Home in Palestine. He said as early as 1929 that the Mandatory Government had not only failed to try to implement the Balfour Declaration, but had tried to fail.

Certainly Hertz could at least rely on the *Jewish Chronicle* to give him support. Economics came to the fore with the Wall Street Crash in October 1929, and the *Jewish Chronicle* decided to look at the finances of the Chief Rabbi. They came to the conclusion that his salary was 'grossly inadequate'.

They chose to criticize the fact that he didn't have a car, though senior clerics didn't drive at the time. Solomon Schonfeld was the first rabbi to have a car in 1933 and was considered daring. As the years went by Hertz was more concerned by the fact that there was no pension provision in his contract if he became seriously ill and that his daughters were not provided for in any way, should they not marry.

The United Synagogue had its own financial problems which would be exacerbated by the effects of the Slump. Waley Cohen and his colleagues were struggling with the declining membership of synagogues in the East End, as the younger generation headed for the suburban hills. The East End had an increasing number of synagogues with a financial deficit and the suburban synagogues needed building funds. There were also other organizations which looked to the United Synagogue for their main financial support. In 1931 the total cost of the Visiting Department, Discharged Prisoners Fund, Welfare, Beth Hamedresh, Beth Din and the Chief Rabbi's Fund were over £16,000. Of that the United Synagogue provided over £11,000.

Support from the other main synagogue organization, the Federation, was poor. There had been an agreement that part of the profits from the sale of kosher meat and tombstones would be used to underpin the costs of Jewish religious education, but the Federation failed to do this and even reneged on the £1,000 it normally provided from its own funds.

The Slump also brought a reduction in offerings by members who received an honour in the Sabbath service. In addition two synagogues being built under the aegis of the Federation ran out of money. As a consequence, Willesden (1931) and Dollis Hill (1932) became part of the United Synagogue. The Federation accused the United Synagogue of poaching its members, but Waley Cohen courteously protested that they were simply helping out when asked. He rightly pointed out that the United Synagogue had rescued the finances of the Willesden Synagogue which had cost £12,000 to build; in today's money, about half a million pounds.

It was in keeping the United Synagogue afloat financially that Waley Cohen made a tremendously valuable contribution in terms of his own time and organizing abilities. It was precisely in these areas that there was little cause for conflict with Hertz. Under Waley Cohen the United Synagogue was particularly effective in building new synagogues and no fewer than thirty-four joined the organization between 1912 and 1945.

The Chief Rabbi continued to be a respected public figure. In July 1929 the Hertzs were invited to be 'received at court' at Buckingham Palace, which was a signal honour. Rose wrote home giving full details of her dress and accessories. Where some particularly Orthodox Jewish wives would cover their heads with a *sheitel* (wig), Rose Hertz never did. She said, though, that they found the event boring and left early.

At the end of August the Chief Rabbi and his wife celebrated their silver wedding. Among the many congratulations they received was a charming letter from the Sephardi Mahamad. From his earliest days under the tutelage of Sabato Morais, Hertz had a soft spot for the Sephardim and his first sermon had been at a Sephardi synagogue. Now the Mahamad took the opportunity to record that: 'You have given proof of the most friendly sentiments by which you are animated towards the congregation.'[16]

Sadly, the celebrations were to be short-lived. In the autumn Rose fell seriously ill. There was a history of heart trouble in the family and at the time there was little that could be done. She was suffering from arteriosclerosis, or hardening of the arteries. She rallied at the end of the year and was even able to return home to Hamilton Terrace to join the family for a Sabbath dinner. Unhappily, in January she succumbed to a cerebral haemorrhage, which led to a coma and her death on 18 January. It was Leon who took on the melancholy role of registering her death.

Rose Hertz was only 49 and her typically spirited letters home in recent months made her passing all the more poignant. The community grieved for the Chief Rabbi but nothing could assuage his heartbreak. It is customary for rabbis to marry again if they are widowed, but Hertz never seems to have considered such an option. Rose Hertz was very popular in the community, charming and helpful, intelligent and supportive of a wide range of charities. For a woman as vital as she had always been, it was a great sadness to see her cut down so young: 'He never really recovered from it. There was a maiming sense of loss, ever fresh, that remained with him to the end.'[17]

Few wives of Chief Rabbis receive the credit they deserve for the support they provide so unstintingly. The organizations for whom Rose Hertz had worked were determined that this would not be true in her case. They all came together to promote a Shilling fund for a suitable testimonial – the First Women's Lodge of B'nai B'rith, the Bayswater Jewish Schools, the Butler Street Girls Club, the Club and Hostel for Deaf Girls, the Deborah Wenter Jewish Girls Club, the Grocery Relief Fund, the Jews Free Reading Room, the Jewish Maternity Home, the Jewish Schools Boot Fund, the Ladies Aid at the London Jewish Hospital, the Ladies Auxiliary at Jews' College, the Union of Jewish Women and the Women's International Zionist Organisation.

Lord Rothschild offered a considerable sum, but was rather obtusely told that he could contribute only a shilling. The family regretted a decision that limited what could be done with the memorial fund. In 1932 the Chief Rabbi consecrated the Rose Hertz Memorial Hall in Woburn House, the home of the United Synagogue. It later housed the Jewish Museum. It had cost £75,000. Hertz unveiled a portrait of his wife and, naturally, spoke with great emotion on that sad day. It remained a tribute to her until the building was sold towards the end of the century.

NOTES

1. Aubrey Newman, 'Chief Rabbi Dr Joseph Herman Hertz, CH' (London: United Synagogue, 1972), p.24.
2. *Jewish Chronicle*, 25 March 1938.
3. Ibid.
4. Ibid.
5. Derek Taylor, *Solomon Schonfeld: A Purpose in Life* (London and Portland, OR: Vallentine Mitchell, 2009), p.48.
6. Pamela Shatzkes, *Holocaust and Rescue: Impotent or Indifferent? Anglo-Jewry 1938–1945* (Basingstoke: Palgrave, 2002), p.38.
7. Ibid., p.38.
8. Ibid., p.241.

9. CRREC Minute Book, J.H. Hertz Archive, Hartley Library, Southampton University Archives.
10. Harry Rabinowicz, *A World Apart: The History of Chasidism in England* (London and Portland, OR: Vallentine Mitchell, 1996), p.158.
11. The author in conversation with Jacob Schonfeld in 2006.
12. Louise London, *Whitehall and the Jews, 1933–1948: British Immigration Policy, Jewish Refugees and the Holocaust* (London: Oxford University Press, 2000), p.100.
13. Joseph Herman Hertz, *Early and Late: Addresses, Messages, and Papers* (Hindhead: Soncino Press, 1943), p.58.
14. United Synagogue Archive, File 2132, London Metropolitan Archives.
15. Letter 17 June 1942, London Metropolitan Archives.
16. Paula Hill, B'nai B'rith Albert Einstein Lodge, Jerusalem, paper, 15 January 2003, Jeremy Schonfield private family archive.
17. Ibid.

Chapter Twelve

Difficult Times

Life had to go on and Hertz went back to work. As early as February he was writing to *The Times* to protest at the new Russian regulation that children could not have any religious instruction.[1] Just before Rose died, the first book of the Pentateuch commentary was published in December. As Hertz wrote in the preface:

> Jewish and non-Jewish commentators – ancient, mediaeval and modern – have been freely drawn upon. 'Accept the truth from whatever source it come' is sound rabbinic doctrine – even if it be from the pages of a devout Christian expositor or of an iconoclastic Bible scholar, Jewish or non-Jewish. This does not affect the Jewish Traditional character of the work ... likewise, my refusal to eliminate the Divine either from history or from human life.

This was the viewpoint of Bachya and Maimonides and Hertz considered that was ample precedent. Furthermore he believed that rabbinic teaching had benefited from the changing world over the centuries, and that this did not have to mean abandoning its core principles. Furthermore, where there had been innovations over many centuries, they had acquired the force of Jewish law:

> He read prodigiously and even to the end had a retentive memory ... his commentaries on the Pentateuch and Siddur pay tribute to the notes and glosses of others, while a multitude of minor studies ... show the many sources on which he drew. His manuscripts and proof pages ... demonstrate the care he took to select exactly the right word or phrase to suit the meaning he had in mind ... Cecil Roth wrote appreciatively 'there would not be a word too much; there would not be a word too little; the phrasing was

> so perfect that it appeared easy and inevitable ... Unfortunately many of these drafts were already in printed proof stage so that the printers complained that he was their most expensive author, and that his Bible was the only book to make them use swear words ... he was in the truest and greatest sense of the word a 'populariser', intent on bringing [explanations] home to the public which was ... unconscious of the wide stream of knowledge and information that was available.[2]

Hertz's theological position remained concentrated on defending the traditional assertion that the: 'whole of the Pentateuch is the unmediated word of God, handed directly to Moses or (in the case of the last few verses of Deuteronomy which describe the death of Moses) to Joshua'.[3]

The book was well received, though it had its critics. Gaster, who was a major scholar in his own right, was particularly scathing. The former Haham, who had produced a translation of the Sephardi prayer book, excused his objections to the Chumash by quoting inaccurately the rabbinic instruction: 'Whenever the Divine Name is being profaned, honour must not be paid to one's teacher', which was more than a bit harsh on Hertz.

Specifically, Gaster labelled the Chumash 'dilettantism' and 'thoughtless sycophantism' and Hertz rightly considered the criticism a personal attack. As Gaster by then had been out of office for many years, the condemnation had little effect. It was, nevertheless, a shame to see a falling out of two such senior rabbis, who had stood side by side to support Zionism against the bulk of the Jewish lay leadership during the war.

While he was working on the Chumash, Hertz did not neglect the needs of the younger generation. He was involved in producing another new children's prayer book, which Claude Montefiore generously supported financially. Even with something that elementary, there was still some carping; it was suggested that the book had elements which were not according to the German and Polish rite, to which the United Synagogue was committed by its constitution. The Reform prayer book used Sephardi elements and that was the objection here. Hertz took it in his stride.

A prayer for barmitzvah boys was included that had been written by the nineteenth-century Sephardi Haham, Benjamin Artom, and Hertz had approved the introduction of batmitvahs for girls. With Hertz, improvements could come from any Orthodox source. He was particularly pleased when the Mocatta Library was relocated to

University College, London and later augmented with the collections of Judaica of Rabbi Sir Hermann Gollancz and Lucien Wolf. If he considered the level of Talmudic expertise to be unsatisfactory within the community, at least it now had two excellent libraries at Jews' College and in the Mocatta Collection.

Despite his terrible loss, the Chief Rabbi still presented very well in public. As the *Manchester News* reported at the time:

> Though 60 years of age, he is as virile and energetic as a man of half that age. He has amazing power as an author … it is not merely that he has an inspired flow of smooth knit phrases, but that he has a masterly ability to marshal his arguments in a logical progression, which is overwhelming in effect … with … an almost impeccable list of public offices, ranging from governorship of the University at Jerusalem to Vice Presidency of the League of Nations Union.[4]

The latter organization was the most influential in the British Peace Movement with 407,000 members in 1931.

Hertz's brilliance in the pulpit was illustrated in many ways. In 1934 he went on a pastoral visit to Wales and addressed the local non-Jewish dignitaries. Here was a Hungarian American, naturalized British, in a small Welsh town, trying to win over people who had, most probably, never met a Chief Rabbi, or knew much about his religion. Where could the common ground be?

Hertz found a perfect answer. He congratulated the Welsh on their love of the Bible and went on: 'There is sympathy between little nations like the Welsh and the Jews.' The Jews had a few hills and valleys in Biblical Palestine: 'yet they had changed the face of the world and created those principles of Justice, Freedom and Democracy which had found no more hearty followers and adherents than those in the Welsh hills and valleys'.[5] A senior politician might well have been proud to have thought up such an approach.

By now the Chief Rabbi fitted in well with the wider community. He had a ready wit and a gift for the apt phrase. Hertz knew precisely where he stood on the individual elements of Judaism, but his definition of the United Synagogue's overall position was vaguer. He now described it as: 'religious advance without loss of traditional Jewish values and without estrangement from the collective consciousness of the House of Israel, is the Anglo Jewish position in theology'.[6] Almost anybody could describe their version of Judaism in the same way. In practice, though, Hertz's decisions were far less inclusive.

Faced with surviving the Slump and the twelve years of the Third Reich, with its anti-Semitic attack of horrific brutality, Hertz sought to keep the community together in the face of political and economic menaces. If this had proved impossible in the past, it would not make matters easier now if he proclaimed the Orthodox position too stridently.

Recent commentators on Hertz's description of Anglo-Jewish theology are still grappling with exactly what he meant. It may not have occurred to them that Hertz didn't want to be clear on the subject. A lack of clarity had held the United Synagogue together very well over the years. As Israel Finestein has pointed out, the wording: 'has no meaning when it comes to application, save for the expedient "umbrella" connotation often attached to it ... Hertz made a virtue of necessity. The necessity was to retain, as far as he could, the unifying factors in the community. His memorable phrasing has little to do with theology'.[7]

There were limits to how far Hertz would take cooperation. The Oxford Ministers Fund was a charity supporting the Oxford University community and the distinguished scholar, Herbert Loewe, had been selected by the trustees to run the organization of which Hertz was a trustee. He and Loewe had been acquaintances for years, but in 1931 Loewe decided to make changes in some of the services for which he was responsible. Hertz wrote to him that he would never have supported the fund if the services were, as he contended, as un-Orthodox as he had found them on his last visit. He considered that the service was, as he put it, being turned into a mockery.

The Federation of Synagogues was in difficulty as well. In 1930 Morry Davis was elected president and began a reign that lasted till 1944. During that period there were no elections for the Honorary Officers of the Federation and, as the official historian of the Federation wrote years later: 'Under Davis the Federation dispensed with Council elections and transformed the Federation presidency into an unelected dictatorship.'[8] Hertz, as Chief Rabbi, was responsible for sanctioning the marriages and divorces within the Federation and approving the appointment of rabbis, *chazanim* (cantors) and *shochetim*. If the Federation acted in accordance with Jewish law, which Davis ensured was the case, the process of approval was little more than a rubber-stamping exercise.

Davis was a powerful local politician who was elected Mayor of Stepney. He was able to rule the Federation with his supporters, but the image of the organization suffered badly by comparison with the United Synagogue and the new, even more traditional, Union of Orthodox Hebrew Congregations.

No breath of scandal ever emerged while Hertz and Waley Cohen were in office, though Waley Cohen's hold on the United Synagogue's Honorary Officers was as firm as the Davis regime. The difference was that Waley Cohen did indeed hold elections and won them. Even though the relationship between Hertz and Waley Cohen was often fraught, they were still able to cooperate on many fronts: synagogue education classes, *kashrut* and helping the Jews in Germany were only three of them.

Victor Schonfeld had died on 1 January 1930, two weeks before Rose Hertz and, like her, also aged 49; he too, was deeply mourned. It is indicative of the relationship between the United Synagogue and the Union of Orthodox Hebrew Congregations at that time that Gaster was invited to deliver a eulogy at the funeral but the Chief Rabbi was not.[9] Gaster at least had been the Sephardi Haham, but Rabbi Moshe Rabbinowitz, who also gave a eulogy, was only the rabbi of the Sunderland Beth Hamedresh, which didn't recognize the authority of the Chief Rabbi. It was a clear snub.

During the periods of mourning, floods of well-wishers called at both the Schonfeld and Hertz family homes. Judith Hertz recorded how impressed she was when she met Solomon Schonfeld, Victor Schonfeld's son, with what she later described as his laughing blue eyes. It was Solomon Schonfeld who succeeded to his father's post in 1933. Whatever attraction there might have been between them, however, a Chief Rabbi's daughter was far above a *yeshiva* student and former articled clerk in those class-conscious days.

When he returned from Europe with *semicha* and a doctorate, the younger Schonfeld worked very hard to win the leadership of the Right Wing. He drew large numbers of small congregations under the UOHC banner, particularly when German refugees started to arrive after Hitler took power. The Federation's position as the major rival to the United Synagogue was further undermined.

Schonfeld's other main concern was the development of his father's school. His mother, Rachel Leah Schonfeld, had undertaken to keep it going while he was studying abroad, but it was extremely difficult to do so financially. She appealed to the Chief Rabbi for help in 1931 when the school's overdraft was increasing by £1,000 a year. Hertz, who was trying to sort out the £12,000 owed by the Bayswater Jewish schools, was not able to help.

Hertz did agree, however, in 1933, to be a patron of Schonfeld's Jewish Secondary School. He would try to help any Jewish educational initiative to flourish. He particularly admired the Sarah Schenirer girls' schools in Poland. Schenirer sent an emissary, Dr Judith Rosenbaum, to

London to try to raise money for the schools. She would later marry a German refugee, Isidor Grunfeld, who became a dayan in the London Beth Din.

Judith Grunfeld, who grew to be of the most respected voices in Jewish education, was new to fund-raising when she first arrived in London. She had been welcomed by the Chief Rabbi and thrown in at the deep end when he arranged a small dinner for her with some appropriate Jewish donors.

When the time came for her to speak, Grunfeld started by painting the picture of the spiritual deprivation of the girls in Europe and her projected solution. She came from a wordy and sentimental school of oratory. To her surprise, at this very early point in her address, she was interrupted by Hertz, who thanked her for her quarter-finished contribution and started to talk of the necessary budgets and outgoings with which Schenirer had to deal. As he explained to Grunfeld in private later, the 'aesthetic and moral approach' was not the best way to reach the pockets of the senior members of the United Synagogue!

A major figure in the ultra-Orthodox rabbinic opposition to Reform in the 1930s was Rabbi Yechezkel Abramsky, whom Hertz persuaded to accept the position of senior dayan at the Beth Din in 1935. The Chief Rabbi wanted to strengthen the Talmudic expertise on the Beth Din after Dayan Hillman had left for Palestine in 1934. His first choice, Rabbi Yechiel Yaakov Weinberg, from the Hildesheimer Seminary in Berlin, had decided he didn't want to leave his institution; German Jews were suffering and Weinberg wasn't going to jump ship. He would be a prominent leader in the Warsaw Ghetto during the war to come, but survived and lived on until 1966.

It is commonly assumed that rabbis live sheltered lives, spending most of their time dealing with the minutiae of the law, and out of touch with the challenges of the present day. Like Weinberg, Abramsky's experiences were very different.

Abramsky was a rabbi by the time he was 17 and ministering in Russia when the revolution came. He actively opposed the Communist attacks on religion and was prevented by them from taking up rabbinic posts in Palestine in 1926 and 1928. When he produced an anti-Communist magazine, he was arrested and sentenced to five years hard labour in Siberia. Only the intervention of Chancellor Brüning of Germany secured his release in exchange for six Communists.

Stalin allowed Abramsky and his wife to emigrate but would agree to him taking only two of his four sons with him. The condition for allowing the others, Moshe and Jacob, to leave was that Abramsky should invent a fifth. That man would be a Russian agent who could work as a spy in Britain under his new alias. Abramsky refused to agree to this.

In 1932 he came to London on a Nansen passport – issued by the League of Nations to stateless refugees – to take the pulpit of the very Orthodox Machzike Adath synagogue in London, which had been vacant since Rabbi Kook had left for Palestine years before. Hertz arranged for the ministry to be offered to him so that he could legitimately obtain a work permit.

It was then arranged by Bernard Homa, a Labour member of the London County Council and son of a founder of the Machzike Adath, that the leader of the Labour Party, George Lansbury, would intervene on his behalf with the Russians, together with a minister at the Foreign Office, the future prime minister, Anthony Eden. Their efforts were successful and the other two sons were granted permits to emigrate as well. Abramsky knew the real world.

One of Hertz's objectives was, as always, to improve the reputation of the London Beth Din. In the rabbinic world, the greater the Talmudic experts who serve on a Beth Din, the higher its regard internationally. The supply of the best brains is always limited, but with the Communist oppression of all religions, together with the excesses of Hitler's Germany and growing Polish anti-Semitism, there was a better reason for the finest minds to move away from the centres of Jewish religious life in Europe. Abramsky was, however, not initially impressed with the offer of a seat on the London Beth Din, which he considered insufficiently Orthodox.

Eventually, in June 1935, he was persuaded to accept the post of senior dayan on condition – it was written into his contract – that he would never be asked to give a decision which was contrary to the Shulchan Aruch, the sixteenth-century codification of the rules of Judaism. Criticism of the appointment centred on his lack of English and his perceived extreme Orthodoxy. Waley Cohen was in favour of his appointment, considering him a probable Talmudic counterbalance to the Chief Rabbi. The Union of Hebrew Congregations were also happy to welcome Abramsky, but they campaigned for more dayanim of a similar quality to be appointed by the United Synagogue.

It was significant that at the time there was discussion about including a clause in Abramsky's contract obliging him to do anything the Chief Rabbi considered applied to the post of a dayan. Waley Cohen opposed this, writing to his fellow vice-president, Sir Isidore Salmon of Lyons, that this would negate: 'what has always been a vital principle of the United Synagogue not to do, namely, vest in the

Chief Rabbi the allocation of duties instead of finally in the Honorary Officers of the United Synagogue'.[10]

It remained Waley Cohen's view that even in dealing with the structure of a Beth Din, the Chief Rabbi should not have the final say. Waley Cohen occasionally seemed to have lost touch with reality, as the Honorary Officers completely lacked the expertise to take on such a responsibility.

It was noteworthy, however, that Ewen Montagu, the future president of the United Synagogue, said of Abramsky that he was not inflexible. He said he always tried to find a way to say 'yes' when faced with a problem concerning an individual and the law.[11] For example, a woman can officially be declared a widow only if there is a witness to the death of her husband. In war there may not be such witnesses, so Abramsky would later provide soldiers with a Conditional Get [divorce] that they could give their wives before they went overseas. This would have the same effect that such women would be legally permitted to remarry.

Abramsky also allowed non-kosher wine to be served at functions under the supervision of the Beth Din, although he made it clear that they would take no responsibility for it. In future years he would serve on the Beth Din with Dayan Gollop, even though his Hampstead synagogue still had a mixed choir.

The legal decisions which dayanim are called on to make must be tempered with good sense. The constant objective is to create peace and harmony, so long as the law isn't broken. In 1932, for example, as head of the Beth Din, Hertz was involved in a request by the Ashkenazi Great Synagogue in Sydney to use the Sephardi, rather than the Ashkenazi, form of prayers for the *Kol Nidre* service. This was to avoid saying an Ashkenazi prayer for a return of animal slaughter which was not in the Sephardi service. Hertz agreed to this.

Whatever the evidence, Abramsky was accused by Hertz's detractors of making Hertz more rigid in his outlook. Criticism centred on forbidding the porging of hindquarters of animals (removing the veins) to make them kosher. If they weren't porged, they should have been passed on to the non-kosher butchers, which would have involved the kosher butcher in a financial loss. As Jewish butchers were a substantial source of charitable funds, they had agreed to porge the meat if asked to do so by their customers, but to sell the meat unporged otherwise. As if the customers would porge it for themselves. This was, in fact, the practice in Sephardi communities but less likely in Ashkenazi families.

Abramsky had been anxious to end this attempt to avoid the *din*, as had Victor Schonfeld, in an argument that went back to the nineteenth century. This is the example most often quoted today of Hertz becoming over-influenced by his new Beth Din.

It needs, however, to be seen in a larger context. The dayanim had a duty to administer the *din* and that was what they did. Abramsky was never a Zionist and he didn't approve of Hertz's pragmatic theology. Overall, however, he was a highly respected authority and, when he died in 1976 at the age of 90, it was reported that 40,000 people came to the funeral.

Blaming Abramsky did, however, give Hertz's detractors a new weapon. They had tried to undermine Hertz by attacking his theological decisions and had got nowhere. The Chief Rabbi knew the *din* and had the authority to apply it. If, however, it could be shown that he was using that authority incorrectly because he had been brainwashed by Abramsky, then the attack could be renewed. A case could be made that he needed some form of lay advisory committee to defend him from the Right Wing. It was an insidious argument and it received a lot of coverage, but Hertz and the Beth Din hadn't changed; they were there simply to interpret the law.

Hertz was also able to strengthen the Beth Din in later years by the appointment of the German lawyer, Isidor Grunfeld who studied for *semicha* and was such a powerful intellect that Hertz appointed him a dayan in 1939.

The election of Hitler was immediately followed by a first wave of anti-Jewish legislation and the need was for an effective response. In November the Federation's Morry Davis masterminded a Jewish Representative Council for the Boycott of German Goods and Services. The aim was for an economic boycott of Germany but Hertz: 'declined "officially and openly" to have anything to do with it, citing the views of the German Orthodox that its implementation was likely to be counterproductive.'[12]

The threat of Nazism drew the various Jewish communities together to try to work in mutual defence. Fascism did have some support in Britain initially and the effect of the snobbishness in certain British circles easily translated into mildly anti-Semitic acts. As the *Caterer* magazine said in an article on the application of a colour bar in a five-star hotel in 1925: 'After all, we have known both American and English people to leave moderate size hotels because of the acceptance of Jews, and the latter being given tables in the dining room in the immediate vicinity.'[13]

The right of a Jew to take his seat in the House of Commons didn't mean that he could also be seen in a smart restaurant or in the boardroom of some companies. Even a Rothschild was refused on occasion and there were many firms which would never have dreamt of appointing a Jew as a Director.

The professions were hardly better. Many law and accountancy firms wouldn't offer Jews Articles and many golf clubs and tennis clubs had quotas or bans. British anti-Semitism was a hydra with many heads, even if none of them was particularly venomous. Faced with relatively minor discriminatory practices and barriers, British Jews still knew they were well-off compared to their coreligionists elsewhere.

There were elements within the community who wanted to take to the streets in order to fight the Fascists when they held provocative marches. Neville Laski, on behalf of the Board of Deputies, and Hertz, as the Chief Rabbi, wrote to the *Jewish Chronicle* to oppose any such action: 'The participation of Jews in disturbances with Fascists, whatever the provocation, brings discredit upon the Anglo-Jewish community and can only be harmful to the general cause we all have at heart.'[14]

Typical of the anti-Semitic propaganda sweeping Germany was an accusation that ritual murder was a part of Judaism. When this appeared in a newspaper controlled by Julius Streicher, Hertz wrote to *The Times* again in 1934 to counteract this calumny: 'Permit me to recall to your readers the protest signed by the Archbishops of Canterbury and York, the Cardinal Archbishop of Westminster and others that appeared in your columns on May 6th 1912. (Ritual murder was described as) a relic of the days of witchcraft and black magic, a cruel and utterly baseless libel on Judaism.'[15]

The Archbishop of Canterbury followed up with a letter of support. The Chief Rabbi's relations with the church remained not only cordial but rested firmly on the high regard the Bishops had for him. When he wrote a special prayer for the Jubilee of George V in 1935, the Bishop of Liverpool was so impressed that he asked permission to repeat it from the pulpit of Liverpool Cathedral.

Hertz was a firm supporter of the World Congress of Faiths and presided at some of their meetings. In 1936 he found himself introducing a Hindu clergyman and in his opening address he quoted Epictetus, Isaiah and Marius, the Epicurean. Nobody could accuse Hertz of restricting his reading to Jewish sources.

Anti-Semitism may have been in evidence but, even at its peak, the British Union of Fascists never won a single seat in the House of Commons. In the election of 1931 they polled 36,000 votes, the Communists 75,000 and the National Government 14.5 million. The BUF's largest meeting was at Olympia in 1934 but the brutality with which the stewards manhandled hecklers seriously alarmed the government. Stanley Baldwin, the deputy prime minister, sent one of his MPs to the rally as an observer of the two-year-old movement. He received an anguished report: 'I could not help shuddering at the thought of this vile bitterness, copied from foreign lands, being brought into the centre of England. I came to the conclusion that Mosley [the Fascist leader] was a political maniac and that all decent people must combine to kill this movement.'[16]

In 1937 the government set about crippling the activities of the British Union of Fascists. It passed the Public Order Act which banned the wearing of unofficial uniforms and gave the police powers to ban marches. Of even more importance, the government quietly agreed with the BBC that Sir Oswald Mosley should never be allowed to broadcast on the radio again. When Margaret Thatcher, the prime minister in the 1980s, had legislation passed to make the broadcasting of the voices of the Irish IRA leaders illegal, there was righteous indignation about state censorship. Baldwin avoided this by simply coming to a private and confidential gentleman's agreement with Lord Reith. By 1939 membership of the movement had halved. The ban would last till 1968. Shorn of their publicity, the BUF was effectively destroyed as a political movement.

Bernard Levin, the *Times* journalist, summed up the situation in the 1930s, many years later when he wrote that: 'decent society in those days was filled with people who had forgotten what anti-Semitism *had* led to, and who could not guess what it *would* lead to'.[17]

Dean William Inge, the Dean of St Paul's, was one of those who could glimpse the future. In 1933 he spoke in the pulpit about the new anti-Semitic measures which Hitler, since his election as chancellor of Germany, had introduced: 'Why the German government should behave in that strange manner he could not even guess. It was foolish as well as wrong, for the Jews had stood by the graves of all their oppressors in turn.'[18]

One side-effect of the influx of German refugees was a substantial strengthening of the Talmudic expertise available to the Progressives. A considerable number of the immigrants were able Reform rabbis and Reform Jews were prominent among those arriving. This was because Reform had taken a greater hold in Germany than in Britain, simply because it had started in Germany in the early nineteenth century.

This was balanced by the arrival of similar numbers of the very Orthodox from Germany and eventually from Austria and Czechoslovakia. Unlike the British Jewish community, which had been able to survive in a spirit of middle-of-the-road English compromise, the two sides in Germany had been at each other's spiritual throats for nearly a century, although the Left Wing was in the majority. The

Anglo-Jewish approach was now under threat from both America and Europe. Whereas in 1934, 82 per cent of Orthodox marriages involved at least one native-born partner, the newcomers would add a new strand to the composition of Anglo-Jewry.

Hertz recognized the threat of the Nazis very early on and knew that the most comprehensive effort would be needed by the entire British-Jewish community to ameliorate the plight of their coreligionists. He took every opportunity on his pastoral visits to plead for funds for them. Now it was agreed that efforts by Keren Hayesod on behalf of Zionist projects would in future also cover attempts to help the German refugees. Waley Cohen thought this arrangement would be too advantageous to the Zionists who might well receive a larger share of any funds raised, but the collaboration between the Keren Hayesod and the appeal for money for the German refugees grew still closer.

Hertz considered that uniting the community to rescue refugees from the Nazis was even more important than rejecting their spiritual views. It was this approach which led him to accept an invitation to speak at the opening of the Reform Synagogue's new social hall in 1934.

In his address he said:

> I feel that my presence here today requires some explanation. It is certainly not due to the fact that I dismiss the religious issues that led to the formation of this synagogue ninety-four years ago as of trifling importance. I am the last person in the world to minimise the significance of religious difference in Jewry. If I have nevertheless decided to be with you this morning, it is because of my conviction that far more calamitous than religious difference in Jewry is religious indifference in Jewry.[19]

Hertz even agreed to participate in the occasional religious service with Progressives. A few years later, together with senior rabbis from the Reform and Sephardi synagogues, he consecrated the new Cambridge University synagogue in October 1937. Each conducted an element of the service, sat together and prayed together. When Rabbi Leslie Edgar for the Liberals had completed his part of the proceedings he returned to his seat next to Hertz. The Chief Rabbi shook his hand, as is the custom, and joked: 'I didn't know you could speak Hebrew!'[20]

On yet another occasion in 1937 the branches of British Judaism held a joint service. This was at the Great Synagogue in the East End to mark the coronation of George VI. Hertz represented the United Synagogue, Bueno de Mesquita the Sephardim, Simmonds the Reform and Mattuck the Liberals, all of whom conducted parts of the service while their lay leaders sat together in the warden's box.

As the 1930s wore on, arguments about religious differences continued to pale into insignificance compared to the threat posed by the anti-Semitism of Adolf Hitler. In 1933 Hitler could attack only German Jews and this, at least, gave the British community the chance to concentrate on that single problem. Initially, only a few realists appreciated the need to persuade all the German Jews to emigrate before it was too late. The majority, eventually, did leave before the war, but the task of finding them somewhere else to live was difficult in the extreme.

Jewish organizations around the world tried to create havens for refugees. Not for the first time, one of these would be Britain and Hertz joined the Board of Deputies when they called on the government soon after Hitler came to power, to discuss what could be done. Both sides realized the gravity of the situation, but diplomacy was vital in arriving at a satisfactory approach.

From the government's point of view, immigration was a contentious issue in a country striving to emerge from the Slump, and with millions of its own citizens unemployed. It was feared that simply to allow unfettered Jewish immigration would be politically unpopular, and would not cast the Jewish community in a good light. In the 1890s Jewish immigrants had been accused of undercutting the wages of the British-born, in industries like tailoring. It could happen again.

Furthermore, the country was in a difficult financial position. With large numbers unemployed, tax revenues had suffered and outgoings on dole payments had increased. Exports had been badly affected by the Slump and yet there were demands for more spending for rearmament. Accepting the financial burdens of unlimited immigration – even if the newcomers were refugees – was not an option.

The Americans, like many others, refused to alter their immigration quota, and the British would block another possible escape route by eventually limiting Jewish immigration into Palestine. This was to avoid alienating the Arab states, whose oil and neutrality would be needed if war broke out.

The Jewish leadership in Britain recognized the justice of the government's economic arguments and came up with a noble solution: they would guarantee that if immigrant visas were granted, they would, themselves, ensure that the state wasn't called on for any financial support – now or in the future.

For 150 years the representative body discussing Jewish concerns with the government of the day had been the Board of Deputies.

Its current head, Neville Laski, was a highly regarded barrister and a member of the delegation to the government. There was also the chairman of the newly formed German-Jewish Aid Committee, Otto Schiff, who had been instrumental in getting the Jewish community out of Belgium in the First World War. The Home Office were happy to accept his word for the massive commitment involved. In the end it was agreed that visas would be provided for the total of 1,000–5,000 refugees, that both sides considered would be in need of them. The final figure, however, would be 50,000.

The years that followed saw vastly increased demands on the charitable efforts of the Jewish community. From 1933 to 1939 an astonishing £3 million pounds was raised to help the German-Jewish refugees. That means that about 400,000 people – men, women and children – produced £144 million in today's money (about £350 a head).[21]

When Hertz reviewed what he was doing for Jewry world-wide to raise the money needed, he was particularly aggravated at individuals spending too much on ostentatious functions. In Manchester he vented his criticism: 'The prophet, Malachi, held that good manners – walking humbly with thy God – constituted one third of religion and morality.'[22]

As the recognition of the danger posed by Hitler to the Jews in Germany sank in, Waley Cohen too wanted to produce a comprehensive and coordinated response throughout the community. This, he believed, had to include every division of British Jewry and it soon did. This cooperation, however, developed in many minds into a desire for Ecumenicalism.

Many favoured what Hertz called a 'fraternization' of all religious communities, designed to create a better environment for collaboration. Hertz pointed out that: 'a veritable mania for religious "fraternization" is about, that can only bring down the contempt of clear-thinking men on Anglo-Jewry'.[23] As a result: 'A cry commonly heard was that the Chief Rabbi and the Beth Din had fallen into the hands of the "Ultras" who were exerting in consequence an influence that their numbers alone did not warrant.'[24]

It reached a point when an Anglican bishop was being installed and a representative was invited from among the Jewish clergy. The minister later said to the canon of the cathedral that it had been a wonderful discourse by the bishop and he could have preached the same sermon, word for word. The canon commented dryly: 'Then either you have lapsed into heresy or we have'.[25]

Hertz recognized the need for cooperation, but felt that the price was too high if it involved sacrificing Jewish observance. He would then be betraying his office and the Right Wing would become the only flag bearers for the Orthodox approach.

Very few great scholars had yet to emerge from the ranks of Jewish ministers or from the graduates of Jews' College. There were no *poskim* (halakhic decision-makers) to compare with Abramsky, who did set out to tighten up rulings in certain areas. The view took hold, for example, that there should be stricter conditions for 'matrimonial' conversions to be permitted. Orthodoxy acknowledges conversion on religious grounds but not if it is merely to facilitate marriage to a Jew, which is regarded as a conversion of convenience.

To many people one of the attractions of Progressive congregations was the ease of conversion they offered. About 2 per cent of the marriages in the Orthodox Great Synagogue in the late eighteenth and early nineteenth centuries had involved converted partners but, for later Orthodox authorities, the question remained whether it was a matter of faith or matrimonial felicity.

The Liberal Synagogue, who asked for the least commitment of converts to the *mitzvot*, did not have the right to certify marriages in its synagogue in the North of England. The Chief Rabbi who had, by law, to confirm that it was a community of Jews, hadn't done so. The alternative was for the Liberals to go to parliament for the certificate, which the Reform Secessionists had done successfully in 1852. To keep the peace at this difficult time, Hertz agreed to confirm the Liberal congregation as qualified, recognizing that as they sent delegates to the meetings of the Board of Deputies, it could hardly be denied that they were Jewish. This did not go down well in the Orthodox ranks and Hertz later regretted that he had not left the Liberals to go to parliament.

Despite the theological disputations, relationships between the Jewish communities between the wars were more cordial than they would later become. Violently as Hertz attacked the views of Claude Montefiore in public, the two remained on good terms. When visiting Montefiore for tea with his daughter, Judith, the Liberal leader warned him: 'Tell it not in Gath, Dr Hertz, but the milk is not supervised!'[26] Hertz would have been amused.

There were, however, hidden agendas. The increasingly powerful Zionist lobby wanted to link the danger facing German Jews to their own aim to obtain larger quotas for Jews wanting to emigrate to Palestine. To such Zionists the fate of continental Jews had to be incidental; they simply regarded them as potential casualties in the war to make the future Jewish state a reality.

Chaim Weizmann, who became the first president of Israel, would make the Zionist position clear at the twentieth Zionist conference in 1937, when he said: 'I want to save two million of youth ... the old ones will pass, they will bear their fate or they will not. They were dust, economic and moral dust in a cruel world ... only a remnant shall survive ... we have to accept it.'[27] As he pointed out 'the world is divided into places where the Jews cannot live and places they may not enter'.[28]

This drastic forecast would be endorsed in December 1938 by David Ben Gurion, who would later be the first prime minister of Israel. He went on record on the same subject: 'If I knew it would be possible to save all the children in Germany by bringing them over to England and only half of them by transporting them to Eretz Israel, then I would opt for the second alternative. For we must weigh not only the life of the children, but also the history of the people of Israel.'[29]

Building a Western industrial nation in the Holy Land was a long-term project, and even former opponents were joining the effort. Although Waley Cohen was originally no Zionist, he did much to help in the development of Palestine between the wars. He was responsible for the creation of the Palestine Corporation which made many projects possible. These included the Nesher Cement Company, the diamond industry, the Palestine Salt Company, the Union Bank, the Levant Bonded Warehouses and the Ihud Insurance Agencies, among others.

It was also his idea to have an ocean installation for Shell on the Mediterranean. From this came the massive Haifa Refinery and the Kirkuk-Haifa pipeline which was 628 miles in length and opened in 1935. Waley Cohen and his wife were there as the representatives of Shell but then disaster struck. Their car was in a crash soon afterwards; Waley Cohen was badly injured and his wife tragically killed. There was widespread sympathy for the man who never stopped working for the Jewish community.

The viewpoint of die-hard Zionists could have had catastrophic consequences. For example, the Swedish government also became concerned about the threat to German Jews. They passed a law in their parliament to suspend their immigration policies in favour of German-Jewish refugees. The religious head of Swedish Jews, however, Rabbi Marcus Ehrenpreisz, a fanatical Zionist, grotesquely postulated that to save German Jews would reduce the pressure on the British government's Palestine quota system. He, therefore, persuaded the Swedish government to withdraw the law. Many Jews died in gas chambers who could otherwise have been saved.

To Hertz, this Zionist attitude was unacceptable. Jewish law clearly laid down that saving life was one of the greatest *mitzvot*, if not *the* greatest. For Zionists, the most welcome refugees would be those able-bodied enough to go on to Palestine and help build the country. Talmudic sages and physically inactive *yeshiva* students were not on their priority list. As the Zionists were well-organized and often dominated committees dealing with government authorities on the subject of visas, the odds were against Orthodox refugees. For Hertz this distinction was against Jewish law. The Talmud makes no distinction between victims, on the principle that 'who can say whose blood is the more red'. The Zionists were not, however, going to allow their aims and objectives to be undermined by ancient Jewish laws.

Hertz's position was that he had supported the Zionist movement from its inception, but not unquestioningly. In 1936 religious Zionists formed the Mizrachi Federation of Great Britain and Ireland, and Hertz agreed to become its honorary president. In 1937 there was a thirty-fifth anniversary dinner of the World Mizrachi Organisation in London at which Hertz called for a change in the Zionist approach. He deplored the public desecration of the Sabbath in Palestine: 'They drained mediaeval swamps, but they must prevent the formation of moral swamps.'[30]

The Jewish community in Britain was keen to rescue its brethren, although they weren't as keen on keeping them in the country. Most native-born Jews would have preferred Britain to be a transit-camp refuge before the migrants moved on. So would the government. The problem here was not just that the migrants were foreign, but that they were often poor and some were considered an embarrassment; society was far more class conscious in those days than it is today.

Worse, some refugees, once in Britain, remained staunchly patriotic about their homeland. They were quite prepared to criticize anything in England which failed to measure up to the standards of German efficiency at home. This did not go down well with the indigenous population, and the Jewish Refugee committees felt it necessary to provide newcomers with leaflets in German asking them to stop forthwith. Which they didn't. British Jews thought the German refugees were biting the hand that fed them, and were concerned that the refugees' appearance and behaviour would let the side down.

German Jewish refugees tended not to be sympathetic to the British Jews' concern about image. They did not appreciate that, for mainstream Jewry, the right image was the ultimate prize. The policy of accepting refugees, nevertheless, had some very positive results for the government. There were many parts of the country where the Slump had inflicted almost irreparable damage to employment figures as firms went bankrupt in considerable numbers.

The government tried to get new firms to open businesses in the worst-hit parts of the country which were designated 'development areas'. In spite of considerable publicity and urging, very few British companies were prepared to do so. The government decided to provide a special incentive. It made it known informally that if German-Jewish businessmen applied for visas, they were more likely to get them quickly if they agreed to start a business in a development area. This proved a very successful spur and well over a hundred companies were created as a result.

Rabbi Dr Victor Schonfeld's successor as the leader of the Union of Orthodox Hebrew Congregations, his son, Solomon, set out to improve the relationship between the right-wing communities and the Chief Rabbi's United Synagogue. This was prickly, to say the least. For example, Hertz had come to the consecration of Rabbi Eli Munk's right-wing Golders Green Beth Hamedrash in 1935 and had taken the opportunity to attack ultra-Orthodox Jews, who he said: 'Hadn't sufficient Judaism to love their fellow Jews and to cooperate with them.'[31]

The Union of Orthodox Hebrew Congregations, for its part, had been pressing since 1929 for an improvement in the expertise of the dayanim of the London Beth Din. The UOHC's position was still that some dayanim weren't sufficiently knowledgeable in the Talmud to carry out their functions. This criticism of the United Synagogue by a tiny community on the Right Wing was widely resented, and matters weren't improved when Schonfeld created his own Kedassia kosher label.

The idea was that manufacturers making products acceptable to the UOHC would be able to use the label, and that the organization would set an even higher standard of *kashrut* than that approved by the Beth Din. The *Adath* had always nominated approved shops but this now became a new cause of conflict. It was considered *lèse-majesté* by the United Synagogue for the Union of Orthodox Hebrew Congregations to suggest that the United Synagogue weren't setting the proper standards.

A concrete instance arose in the summer of 1936. The Home Office gave a visa to a German butcher, to whom the Beth Din then gave a licence to run his business. When he tried to use the UOHC Kedassia label, he was told by the United Synagogue Beth Din that he couldn't do so and that his licence was solely for products approved by them.

Schonfeld wrote to complain to Hertz: 'I shall try and ascertain from you *personally*'.[32] Hertz wasn't intimidated and wrote back tersely to reiterate the position of his Beth Din. That was the end of it. There were justifiable arguments on both sides, but if there had been a basic accord between them the problems could have been settled amicably.

Leon, the Chief Rabbi's second son, was 28 by this time and decided to emigrate to Palestine. He obtained a job with the Palestine Corporation, which had been created by Waley Cohen, and settled down in Haifa. There he found a cosmopolitan Jewish community with refugees fleeing Europe and a British administration including staff like him. On 16 November 1935 he met Irene Majerczik, a German refugee graduate of Imperial College in London and he proposed to her on 1 December.

Neither family were happy. Irene's family didn't want her to marry an Englishman she hardly knew, and the son of a rabbi didn't appeal to them either. The Hertz family were concerned about her being culturally so unfamiliar and about whether he could support her. In January 1936 the Chief Rabbi's mother died, adding further grief to his loss of Rose. Leon and Irene's marriage would be a welcome relief. Eventually, when the Chief Rabbi and Irene's father met, they happily discussed a renowned Spanish-Jewish philosopher, Hasdai Crescas, and Benedict Spinoza, and decided they were content for their children to marry. The Hertz contingent came to the wedding in March 1936.

Irene was not particularly Orthodox and did not keep a kosher home. Hertz pointed out that he wouldn't be able to eat with his grandchildren under those circumstances. They agreed that Irene would be able to make the kitchen kosher if she was given a month's notice. Early in 1940 she received a telegram from London: 'This is one month's notice. Father.' They got on very well.[33] Leon went on to work for Barclays Bank for many years.

NOTES

1. *The Times*, 14 February 1930.
2. Aubrey Newman, 'Chief Rabbi Dr Joseph Herman Hertz, CH' (London: United Synagogue, 1972), p.13
3. Revd Ephraim Levine in Isidore Epstein (ed.), *Joseph Herman Hertz, In Memoriam* (London: Soncino Press, 1947), p.30.
4. *Manchester News*, 20 March 1931.
5. *Jewish Chronicle*, 8 June 1934.
6. Benjamin J. Elton, *Britain's Chief Rabbis and the Religious Character of Anglo-Jewry, 1880–1970* (Manchester: Manchester University Press, 2009), p.165.
7. Israel Finestein, *Scenes and Personalities in Anglo-Jewry, 1800–2000* (London and Portland, OR: Vallentine Mitchell, 2002), p.10.

8. Geoffrey Alderman, *Jewish Chronicle*, 10 February 2012.
9. Bernard Homa, *Footprints in the Sands of Time* (Privately printed, 1990), p.85.
10. Letter, 12 June 1935, Acc 2712/15/0053, London Metropolitan Archives.
11. *Jewish Chronicle*, 25 February 1966.
12. Geoffrey Alderman, 'The Holocaust: Why Did Anglo-Jewry Stand Idly By?' (New York: Touro College, 2001).
13. Derek Taylor, *British Chief Rabbis, 1664–2006* (London and Portland, OR: Vallentine Mitchell, 2007), p.360.
14. Raphael Langham, *250 Years of Convention and Contention: A History of the Board of Deputies of British Jews, 1760–2010* (London and Portland, OR: Vallentine Mitchell, 2010), p.152.
15. Letters, *The Times*, 1 June 1934.
16. Taylor, *British Chief Rabbis*, p.361.
17. Greville Janner and Derek Taylor, *Jewish Parliamentarians* (London and Portland, OR: Vallentine Mitchell, 2008), p.63.
18. *Jewish Chronicle*, 5 May 1933.
19. *West London Synagogue Bulletin*, London, June 1934.
20. Rabbi Edgar in conversation with the author.
21. Pamela Shatzkes, *Holocaust and Rescue: Impotent or Indifferent? Anglo-Jewry 1938–1945* (Basingstoke: Palgrave, 2002), p.26.
22. *Jewish Chronicle*, 18 May 1934.
23. Joseph Herman Hertz, *Sermons, Addresses and Studies*, Vol.2 (London: Soncino Press, 1938), p.203.
24. Aubrey Newman, *The United Synagogue 1870–1970* (London: Routledge and Kegan Paul, 1976), p.107.
25. Taylor, *British Chief Rabbis*, p.362.
26. Jeremy Schonfield private family archive.
27. Derek Taylor, *Solomon Schonfeld: A Purpose in Life* (London and Portland, OR: Vallentine Mitchell, 2009), p.38.
28. Michael Marcus, *The Unwanted: European Refugees in the Twentieth Century* (London: Oxford University Press, 1985), p.185.
29. Benny Morris, *Righteous Victims: A History of the Zionist-Arab Conflict, 1881–2001* (London: Random House, 2001).
30. Jeremy Schonfield private family archive.
31. Epstein (ed.), *Joseph Herman Hertz*, p.30.
32. Taylor, *Solomon Schonfeld*, p.43 (emphasis in original).
33. Irene Hertz-Majerczik, *Through Life My Way* (Ra'anana: Docostory, 2003), p.70.

Chapter Thirteen

The Road to Disaster

Legislation against Jews by Hitler was foremost in the minds of the Jewish community in Britain, but anti-Semitic attacks on Jews were not restricted to Germany. There was also growing anti-Semitism in Poland in the 1930s and the conditions under which the three million Jews in that country lived deteriorated every year.

Poland's economic problems in the 1930s were catastrophic. Unemployment was at a high level, but there was no excuse for the government specifically to exclude Jews from welfare payments. Jews owned over 70 per cent of the small shops in the country, so the Polish government passed a law in 1936 to oblige shopkeepers to put the name of the owner on the fascia. Jewish shops were thereby identified and suffered many attacks, besides suffering attempts to get the Poles to boycott them. In 1937 the Polish Medical Association added to their constitution a ban on Jewish membership and the Polish Bar followed suit. In 1938 Jews were forbidden to belong to the Union of Journalists. Jewish students had to sit in a segregated area of lecture halls at university and their numbers dwindled from 25 per cent of the total in 1921 to 8 per cent in 1938.

The objective of the Polish government was to encourage Jews to emigrate, and between 1919 and 1942 over 140,000 did go to Palestine. Hertz agonized over this discrimination, as well as another blow, the banning of *shechita* in Sweden and Finland. The Nazis would still eventually try to blame the Jews for the Second World War, but as the trigger for the declaration of war by the Chamberlain government would be the invasion of Poland, it would seem unlikely that 'international Jewry' would be so keen to rescue a country with such an anti-Semitic record.

The mood in Britain in the 1930s was strongly in favour of appeasement. No British political party that advocated rearmament and an involvement in overseas wars would have won the 1935 election. The vast majority of the country wished the Jews no harm, but what went on in Europe they considered of little importance, and they wanted to keep out of it. The essential outcome for them was never again to find their sons and fathers dying in the slaughter of trench warfare. In addition they had enough economic problems of their own without bothering about other people in foreign lands.

While the proposed solution to European conflict, as illustrated by the actions of the British government at the time, was the appeasement of Hitler and Mussolini, Hertz would never take a similar line about discrimination against Jews. His Yom Kippur message in 1936 was aimed at the widest possible international audience. He wrote as the Chief Rabbi of the British Empire:

> The Rabbis of the principal Jewries of the world, in special messages for the Day of Atonement, solemnly appeal to civilized opinion everywhere against the vilification of Judaism and the Jewish people at the recent Nazi gathering in Nuremberg.
>
> Herr Hitler in his insatiable hatred of the Jew, is not content with robbing the German Jew alone of his human rights. He has now in addition launched a campaign of fanatical defamation against the whole of Jewry throughout the world. He seeks to identify Judaism, the mother of religions, with Bolshevism, a system which has showed itself subversive of all religions. He would penalise seventeen million Jews ... for the deeds of a handful of men in Russia, who have completely cut themselves off from the Jewish people and their ancestral Faith.
>
> His charge that '98% of the heads of the Soviet ... Republics are Jews', is false: of the Presidents of the separate Soviet Republics and the People's commissars there are, in a total of nineteen, only two men of Jewish birth. Be it remembered that the rise of Bolshevism to power in 1917 was made possible by Herr Hitler's former colleague, General Ludendorff, who arranged Lenin's passage through Germany, with the declared purpose of inoculating the Russian masses with the Communist idea. For this result of German political sagacity, Herr Hitler now blames the Jews. Not content with this he makes fantastic allegations as to the responsibility of Jewry for the ghastly massacres on both sides in the tragic conflict in Spain! These monstrous accusations are patently designed to rouse the passions of the mob against the Jew, and are an example of the very method of propaganda denounced by Herr Hitler himself in 'Mein Kampf' ... 'The very enormity of a lie' he indignantly writes 'contributes to its success ... the masses of the people easily succumb to it, as they cannot

> believe it possible than anyone would have the shameless audacity to invent such things … even if the clearest proof of its falsehood is forthcoming, something of the lie will nevertheless stick'.
>
> Israel has often been downtrodden and helpless, but has never been without the hope and courage born of Faith. Israel's strong armour against Nazi calumny is trust in the God of Righteousness, Who alone can bring to naught the designs of hatred, purify the hearts of those blinded by malice, and open their eyes to the sacredness of Justice and Brotherhood among the children of men.[1]

Meanwhile Waley Cohen was giving his support to Winston Churchill as one of the few opponents of appeasement. Churchill had lost a fortune in the Wall Street Crash and his finances were in a sorry state. Waley Cohen in 1936 organized a £50,000 fund to give him the wherewithal to carry on his work. The money was raised by a number of eminent people who called themselves the Focus Group. Funding also came from the Czech government. Without Waley Cohen's efforts, Churchill's work would have been difficult to sustain.[2]

Churchill was, however, a voice crying in the wilderness. The people wanted to believe he was wrong in warning against the Fascists. They would continue to support Chamberlain in his attempts to reach a peaceful end to Nazi aggression until the bitter end. The leaders of the Jewish community knew that the Chief Rabbi's message would be an irritant to those who just wanted peace. They saw a danger that the community would be labelled warmongers, for wanting to defend their foreign coreligionists. It was a sensitive situation.

In August 1936 Hertz was to sustain another tragic loss. His son, Daniel, committed suicide at the age of 26. The coroner at the inquest[3] made it clear that the cause of death was an overdose of Nembutal. Daniel had left a note and the coroner commented: 'From a note he left behind it is quite clear that his state of mind was such that he had apparently lost faith in himself.'[4]

After St Paul's and New College, Oxford, where he won the University Gotch Memorial Prize and Medal in Physiology and was Rowden Scholar, Daniel went on to be a house physician at University College Hospital. He was described as quiet, charming and brilliant, but one of his lecturers said: 'He set himself appallingly high standards.'[5] Jewish law ordains that a suicide cannot be buried in a Jewish cemetery unless, at the time of his death, he was mentally ill. It was agreed that this ruling applied to Daniel. A fine art deco tombstone with a bronze relief plaque by Benno Elkan marked his grave in Willesden cemetery for many years. The coroner's verdict was that he had 'killed himself while of unsound mind'.[6]

With the right degree of sensitivity the coroner disclosed no further information and why Daniel took his own life remains unknown. It was a shocking blow to his father, who had helped those in trouble throughout his rabbinate. His inability to prevent his son from taking his own life must have been terribly galling. He was perhaps aware that the demands of his public life made it difficult for him to maintain as close a relationship with all his children as he would have wished.

Hertz was now over 60 and Daniel's death was a further reminder of mortality. The Chief Rabbi continued to worry about what would happen to his unmarried daughters after his passing. They had shouldered the burden of trying to replace their mother and looked after him devotedly. Invitations would read 'Chief Rabbi Hertz and Miss Hertz at home', or Judith would accompany him to Synagogue Hebrew Classes and hand out the prizes. Judith didn't enjoy these occasions and Josephine did more of them when she grew up.

It was still the case that no arrangements had been agreed with the United Synagogue about his pension if he had to retire through ill health, or about dowries for the girls. He had asked the Honorary Officers to make such arrangements which, had they raised the subject themselves, would have spared him the humiliation. Not to do so was small-minded and demeaning to a man who had raised the image of the community by his continuous efforts. As Hertz wrote to a colleague: 'Need I stress the fact that nothing but stern duty to my unprovided children would have overcome my reluctance to put the above in writing.'[7]

The respect in which Hertz was held stretched across the country. In June 1936 he had been on a pastoral visit to the Plymouth community, an ancient congregation with a fine synagogue, but always with small numbers. Hertz gave a sermon on the Sabbath and talked to the children at the Hebrew classes on the Sunday morning. On the Sunday evening he gave a talk at the Guildhall to both Jews and non-Jews on his familiar topic, 'The Bible as a Book'. It was attended by an audience of more than 1,000.

Afterwards the Bishop of Plymouth said that they had listened to a most remarkable address on the greatest book in the world by one of the greatest leaders of one of the greatest races. It may have been fulsome, but any lay leader trying to undermine the authority of the Chief Rabbi was competing with a public relations icon. There were, of course, still occasions when Waley Cohen's image was the better choice with sections of the general public. In November 1936 he was invited by the Cambridge Union to debate a motion 'That the government's use of force in Palestine is a confession of its failure to grasp and solve the country's problems'. Waley Cohen persuaded 149 to vote for the motion but 163 voted against it. In the current climate it was a good effort.

Even in his relations with the ultra-Orthodox, Hertz's reputation had risen. Bernard Homa reported that a meeting in 1937 was supposed to resolve an argument between the Union of Orthodox Hebrew Congregations and Hertz, but Harry Goodman, who was representing the Union of Orthodox Hebrew Congregations, supported Hertz rather than his own organization. When Homa criticized him for this after the meeting, Goodman pointed out that he had invited Hertz to attend the Silver Jubilee of the Aguda movement, and didn't want to upset him. Solomon Schonfeld had been told to support the Aguda representative's side as well, and Homa resigned the presidency of the Union of Orthodox Hebrew Congregations in disgust.[8]

Where the Chief Rabbi and Schonfeld were fully in agreement was on the subject of Jewish education. Hertz wanted Jewish children to have intensified Jewish studies and Schonfeld was one of the few equally anxious to set aside far more time in his school than was available in Sunday morning classes.

In 1938, with the forthcoming celebration of the Chief Rabbi's Silver Jubilee in office, it was agreed to mark the occasion by raising a fund devoted to Jewish educational causes. One beneficiary would be the Stepney Jewish schools, to which Hertz had given preference when the Schonfelds had asked for financial support for their operation a few years before. The other would be Schonfeld's Jewish Secondary School Movement.

One of the advisers influencing Hertz could well have been Isidor Grunfeld, the husband of Judith, who was a great supporter of Schonfeld. The refugee lawyer had been appointed registrar to the United Synagogue Beth Din and would undoubtedly have spoken up for Schonfeld if his wife had asked him to. The foundation for a more harmonious relationship between the Chief Rabbi and the religious head of the Union of Orthodox Hebrew Congregations was first laid on that common educational ground.

Over 2,000 donors supported the fund, which raised £1,500. At the Grosvenor House dinner to mark the milestone in the Chief Rabbi's ministry, with all the Jewish luminaries available present, it was the 26-year-old Schonfeld who presented him with a scroll of honour containing the names of the donors. Schonfeld's feel for photo opportunities was already exceptional.

The problem for Schonfeld, though, was that the community in the 1930s did not see Jewish schools as a priority. The vast majority felt that Sunday School would suffice. Schonfeld had only the one small school in North London but he had a firm objective for it. He recognized that the community saw public and grammar schools as their yardstick of quality. So he decided he would run his school accordingly, with prefects, academic gowns for the teachers, sports days and, in the future, even a chess match against Harrow. Where the oldest Jewish school, the Jews' Free School, had been created to teach poor children how to earn a living, Schonfeld sought their admittance to the middle class.

Waley Cohen presided at the dinner and even on this celebratory occasion couldn't resist the opportunity to snipe. He described the event as: 'one of those rare occasions when they were gathered together as a united religious community'.[9] Once again the fact was ignored that Hertz was responsible for the maintenance of Orthodox Judaism, rather than a sheepdog gathering the flock together.

Claude Montefiore, for the Liberals, was more diplomatic: 'Though I differ deeply from the Chief Rabbi in matters biblical and theological, we have stood, and still stand, side by side, where Jewish honour and the Jewish good name are concerned.'[10]

The occasion was a happy one, but Hertz took a leaf out of Waley Cohen's book. He, too, would use the platform to give vent to one of his continuing frustrations, the difference being that he was the guest of honour: 'There is not yet an end in Anglo-Jewry to the short-sighted and disastrous starving of higher theological teaching.'[11] Gateshead and Schonfeld's work on developing his school were the only new stars in the Jewish educational firmament.

Hertz also used the occasion of the Jubilee dinner to reiterate his philosophy as Chief Rabbi. He would: 'not be known as a stammering witness to his faith and a half hearted defender of his people'.[12]

In the wider world, senior politicians were becoming more concerned at the way the Jews were being treated in Germany. Stanley Baldwin, the former prime minister, set up the Lord Baldwin Fund for Refugees and made an appeal for the Jews on 8 December 1937 to which the public contributed more than £500,000; a truly heart-warming result. It wasn't just Germany though. The virus of anti-Semitism was still spreading. In Poland, an anti-*shechita* law had now been passed. Just as discriminatory, if a Jew said publicly that he thought a sentence in a Polish court was unjust, he could be imprisoned for up to two years. The Romanian government was also increasingly anti-Semitic and the situation in many parts of the Continent was deteriorating.

By 1938 the Chief Rabbi was 66 years old. His wife had died and he sadly missed her support. Judith would get married in 1940 after which Josephine would accept the responsibility of taking her mother's place. As a friend wrote of her when she died in 1994: 'Josephine sacrificed marriage and career to act as hostess, companion and housekeeper for her father ... in their gracious home in Hamilton Terrace, London, of a size requiring more staff than could be afforded. [After his death] the drawing room was converted to become a one-room flat for the rest of her life.'[13]

She lived nearly fifty years more until she was 80, and the contrast between the public life of the Chief Rabbi's hostess and the obscurity of those latter years could not have been easy for her. She retained many friends and Lady Jacobovits, the future Chief Rabbi's wife, added: 'from the day I came to England, I valued her advice'.[14]

Hertz was now at an age when most men retired, but he was still undertaking a full programme of activities as Chief Rabbi, and he was still at loggerheads with Waley Cohen. One pleasant event in 1937 saw his election to membership of the Athenaeum Club, the most prestigious in the capital. He had also enjoyed the events marking the completion of his twenty-five years in office.

Before the spring of 1938 brought the celebration of that milestone, he wrote to one of the Honorary Officers to say what he expected to be done to mark the occasions: a public function, some kind of illuminated address, a religious rally to include deputations from the provinces and the Empire and: 'the function must be made an occasion to remind the outer world that far more than a commercial or professional body, Anglo-Jewry is a spiritual community'.[15]

Hertz received more than an illuminated address. Eminent scholars often receive a volume of essays, a Festschrift, to recognize such an anniversary. A volume of this kind was duly presented to Hertz who knew he deserved it, but was flattered by its quality.

If Hertz reviewed what he had achieved or failed to achieve in twenty-five years, the positives must have outweighed the negatives. Even if the new generation was not as observant as its ancestors, it was still clear that the United Synagogue, the Federation and the Union of Orthodox Hebrew Congregations, under Schonfeld, had grown considerably in membership. The Beth Din was stronger under Dayan Abramsky and Dayan Grunfeld. The status of the Chief Rabbi had been enhanced by his work over the years, the Pastoral Tour had been a great success and he had successfully resisted efforts to reduce the authority of his position.

The Chumash was completed and his *Book of Jewish Thoughts*

had sold in vast numbers. Attempts to change the calendar had been successfully resisted. On the negative side there still wasn't a United Synagogue for the whole of Britain, and he had not been able to improve the conditions for his ministers very much.

Hertz's other problems were far more serious: war was looming in the immediate future. In 1938 Hitler was still content to be rid of the Jewish segment of the German population. Forbidden to take most of their possessions with them, the way was clear for officially approved looting of their assets. The government gorged itself on Jewish bank balances.

The man in charge of bringing German Jews to Britain was Otto Schiff, chairman of the renamed Jewish Refugee Committee. Schonfeld was also making heroic efforts. By comparison with Schiff's overall achievement in rescuing so many of the German Jewish population, Solomon Schonfeld's personal contribution would not be all that large, though it involved many acts of personal courage. It is ironic that Schiff, responsible for most of the 50,000 rescued, is either forgotten or denigrated, while Schonfeld has correctly received the plaudits he so richly deserved. Schiff is accused of not doing enough, while Schonfeld is praised for doing anything at all.

In 1938, Michoel ber Weissmandl, the son-in-law of the head of the Nitra *Yeshiva* where Schonfeld had studied, wrote to Schonfeld to demand action as the danger facing the Austrian Jews worsened. He accused Schonfeld – and if the cap fitted, anybody else around him – of indifference to the developing calamity. He wrote in capital letters: 'ARE YOU MADE OF STONE THAT YOU DON'T MELT?'[16] The situation was indeed desperate and this was the only possible approach; not supplicatory, not coaxing, not appealing. Weissmandl demanded and Schonfeld learned the lesson. His fund-raising took on another dimension.

Schonfeld added a forceful approach to his armoury of persuasive tactics. In non-financial negotiation with authority, however, the young Schonfeld was more flexible than the Jewish leadership as a whole. Schonfeld recognized better than the Jewish leaders that politics is the art of the possible. The leadership would meet in conferences and resolve to ask the government for major policy changes to help with the refugee problem. Conference speakers have a habit of trying to outdo each other in the extravagance of their demands.

Schonfeld, unrestricted by conference resolutions, could be more pragmatic. He knew he had no lever when dealing with government departments, other than the force of persuasion. By contrast, the Jewish leadership tried to act as a pressure group on the national stage in order to impress their community that they were doing their best. Unfortunately, they were trying to achieve unrealistic objectives when the whole country was facing potential disaster.

The British government were confronted with overwhelming dilemmas. At the time Lloyd George's government issued the Balfour Declaration it had made conflicting promises to the Arabs in order to persuade them not to support Britain's enemies in the First World War. These promises naturally led to both sides crying 'foul' in the 1920s and 1930s. British interests now had to come first though; no other approach made any sense.

So the truth was that the Jews had very little influence. The British government, seeking to neutralize the Arab nations, would introduce a White Paper in May 1939 which reduced Jewish immigration into Palestine to a tiny fraction of what was – and would be even more – needed by Jewish communities contemplating flight from Europe. The situation was complicated further by the need to reduce support for Hitler within Britain.

There was already a degree of anti-Semitism, still based on supposed world-wide international conspiracies, described in the discredited *The Protocols of the Elders of Zion*. For those who hated Jews, no accusation was too far-fetched and the government worried that the public might be gullible and believe such rubbish. They, therefore, chose to be very careful in how they dealt with Hitler's fanatical hatred of the Jews and with the worsening anti-Semitic legislation within Germany.

The purpose of British diplomacy was to try to stave off war. Interference with the internal affairs of another major European country would very likely have the opposite effect, leading to an aggravation of the ongoing crisis, without necessarily helping the German Jews. Moreover, interference was not accepted practice in diplomatic circles at that time.

To avoid adverse publicity about renewed immigration, it was impossible, officially, to obtain sufficient visas for refugees. The Jewish authorities in Britain had to go through meandering authorized channels to help those who wanted to leave Germany, and later Austria, Czechoslovakia and Poland. In addition, many German Jews overoptimistically hoped that the Nazi excesses would be a passing phase and stayed put. Pragmatism and optimism were uneasy bedfellows.

Hertz was desperate to help any Jew threatened by Hitler, but he didn't have the support he needed. His two able dayanim were both refugees and it wasn't their role to take the lead in the purely secular area of public relations. Neither was it their responsibility to help

Hertz in negotiations with a Britain which, to them, had recently been a foreign country.

It would have been helpful had Hertz had some powerful clergy to back him up, but United Synagogue ministers continued to be firmly under the thumb of the lay leaders of their congregations. They were pointed in the direction of synagogue administration. They could comfort mourners, lecture barmitzvah boys and visit the sick. They weren't appointed to give their communities leadership. With a few exceptions, that role was strictly reserved for synagogue Honorary Officers.

Even in those perilous times, the heads of different Jewish bodies, attempting to help refugees, continued quarrelling among themselves and jockeying for advantage. In July 1938 the Orthodox Agudas Yisroel had opened an Emigration Advisory Service in London to deal with emigration enquiries. It was immediately criticized by Otto Schiff, chair of the Jewish Refugee Committee who said he was: 'heartily sick of Agudas Israel and their machinations'.[17] He told the Hilfsverein, the Jewish organization in Germany dealing with emigration: 'its committee is absolutely condemned by all the leading organizations'.[18]

Agudas Yisroel, the Zionists and the German Refugee Committee were only three of the organizations involved. There were also others, including a new branch of the World Jewish Congress, the Board of Deputies, the United Synagogue, the Beth Din, the Federation, the Union of Orthodox Hebrew Congregations and Hertz himself. That didn't complete the list, but it indicates how difficult it was for so many independent bodies to agree on a common approach. Typically, Harry Goodman ridiculed the: 'fantastic claim to "speak for world Jewry"' of the World Jewish Congress in his publication, *Jewish Weekly*.[19]

Gradually the Board of Deputies was becoming dominated by Zionist delegates, but this wasn't true of all the main leaders. Neville Laski, the president of the Board, was anti-Zionist and, together with Waley Cohen, disagreed with the Board's Council when it resolved to complain to the government that the Balfour Declaration was not being honoured. Without authority from their organizations, Laski and Waley Cohen told Whitehall officials in private to take no notice of the protests, as they were not representative of the community as a whole.

Jewish organizations fiddled while many central European countries burned with anti-Semitic oppression.

A few months before, in March 1938, the Germans had marched into Austria and annexed the country. Jacob Rosenheim, the international president of Agudas Yisroel, turned to Hertz for support.

They both agreed that a special fund was needed to provide additional help for German Jewry, and to raise the funds to help Jews in countries threatened by the Nazis. Hertz agreed to serve as chairman. It was Schonfeld, as a well-known fund raiser, who was suggested for the role of director of the Chief Rabbi's Religious Emergency Fund, which, in November, became the Chief Rabbi's Religious Emergency Council (CRREC). Hertz and Schonfeld may have clashed in the past, but in the present emergency they found it easy to set aside their differences.

In building their relationship there was another consideration for the Chief Rabbi of an intensely personal nature. When Daniel had committed suicide in 1936 the Chief Rabbi and his children had been bereft. Daniel had been the brightest of Hertz's offspring and if anyone appeared in the future to fill the yawning gap, it might relieve the pain.

Less than two years later, Hertz enthusiastically greeted the 26-year-old Schonfeld as Rosenheim's nominee and Weissmandl's spokesman. Here was a real rabbi, not an Anglo-Jewish reverend. Here was the young man Daniel might have been and one who not only approved of Hertz's orthodoxy but who, by his own behaviour, suggested that a little more stringency could be added even to the Chief Rabbi's approach.

The first meeting of the CRREC was held on 21 July 1938 and the only people present were Hertz, Harry Goodman, another supporter, Jacob Rosenheim and Schonfeld. Others would join later, but it was from that nucleus that the volunteer body started. Thirteen thousand appeal letters were sent out.

There were five meetings of the CRREC in 1938, but only three in 1939 and one in 1940, according to the Minute Book.[20] Once Schonfeld got his feet under the table, he was happier to work without interference, in line with his normal approach in the future. He shared a dislike for committees with the Chief Rabbi and Waley Cohen.

For the Jewish establishment, the most aggravating thing about Rabbi Dr Schonfeld was that he couldn't be controlled by the United Synagogue lay leaders. He wasn't their employee and his organization was totally independent of them. Nor, disastrously for the Board of Deputies, was he bound by any community agreement on how to approach the government. For 150 years that had been the role of the Jewish Board of Deputies. They were democratically elected, represented the majority of the community and were full of Jewish leaders.

By contrast with this august assembly, Schonfeld seemed a loose cannon, and was regarded with deep suspicion by the lay leadership.

If Waley Cohen's aim for years had been to gain total religious control by wearing down the Chief Rabbi, the last thing he wanted was to see him now provided with a new burst of energy by a young, vigorous, independent, charismatic assistant with the same views as his chairman – or even more extreme.

From the point of view of the lay leadership, even more outrageous was the fact that the young rabbi was prepared to stand his ground with them. If they wanted a battle, Schonfeld was prepared to give as good as he got. Neville Laski, the son-in-law of Moses Gaster, knew the power of the lay authorities, but also that it was the rabbi who often ruled in very Orthodox communities. He had seen the arrival of the Rabbi of Ger at a railway station on the Continent: 'Hundreds of thousands of, to me, Mediaeval looking Jews wearing strange hats and kaftans crowded on to the platform ... Excitement reigned supreme. I stood on a railway truck against a fence to obtain a better view, but soon repented, as a surging crowd, marching step by step with the Rabbi, nearly turned me and the truck into the roadway.'[21]

Schonfeld came from a community which could, in the future, have the same regard for its own rabbinic leader, although Schonfeld would never have gone along with this level of devotion. He was not in favour of such hero worship, but who could see into the future?[22]

Otto Schiff, now heading the German Jewish Aid Committee (GJAC), was concerned to keep within the parameters agreed with the government. He was not prepared to endanger the trust they had in him, based on his reliability in dealing with refugees in the First World War. His core problem was to make sufficient funds available to make good on the promise that the state wouldn't have to support any of the refugees. Schiff told the government that the GJAC did not believe that Hertz's CRREC had the money to back up the requests they were making for visas.

Hertz told the Foreign Office emphatically that he did not rely on funds from the GJAC to maintain the ecclesiastics he was representing. Schonfeld angered Schiff by promising he had sufficient guarantors even when he was several short and was busy forging the signatures of some others. Schiff played by the rules while the CRREC would do anything to save a life.

The Council for German Jews also favoured refugees who might want to go on to Palestine. Orthodox children were less likely to have that wish than those from Zionist families. Hertz and Schonfeld put Orthodoxy first and Zionism second in their list of priorities.

The horrors of Kristallnacht in Germany in November 1938 shocked the non-Fascist world. Thirty thousand Jews were sent to concentration camps, hundreds of synagogues burned and thousands of Jewish businesses destroyed or damaged. The Council for German Jewry sent another high-powered delegation to call on Neville Chamberlain, the prime minister. The need to admit more refugees was somewhat reluctantly recognized.

Hertz went with Neville Laski, Viscounts Bearsted and Samuel, Lionel de Rothschild and Chaim Weizmann. Chamberlain evinced: 'deep concern and sympathy, but made no firm promises'.[23] In fact, the granting of visas did become easier, particularly for children under 17 who wouldn't affect the labour market. Large numbers of families in Britain – Jewish and non-Jewish – agreed, effectively, to foster the children and a large number did so until they grew up.

On 21 November in the House of Commons it was agreed that any Jewish child who had a guarantor for their maintenance could come to England with just a document to prove their identity. In July 1939 the government agreed to take over their maintenance when the Jewish relief organizations had to admit that they could simply no longer cope financially.

When it came to Orthodox and Liberal rabbis and their families, compiling the lists was in the hands of the *Kultusgemeinde*, which was the body of Jews who were designated to work with the Nazi Central Office of Jewish Emigration. The *Kultusgemeinde* often rejected Orthodox applicants and Julius Steinfeld, the Agudas Yisroel leader in Vienna, asked Schonfeld for help, particularly with Orthodox children. In Britain, the Movement for the Care of Children from Germany told the *Kultusgemeinde* that Schonfeld wasn't authorized to deal with them, but they eventually agreed to overlook this.

Entry visas from the Home Office remained the critical factor. When the *Adath* considered the problem, they cautiously agreed to take care of just ten refugees. Schonfeld thought this number derisory by comparison with the size of the problem. He had in mind 500, and the problem remained obtaining the necessary visas. Hertz had no difficulty in arranging another appointment with the Home Office, which he attended with Schonfeld, but the pressure on the job market had to be uppermost in that ministry's mind. How could they square the circle?

Although Schonfeld's role as director of the CRREC could be portrayed as administrative, both Hertz and the young rabbi knew that Schonfeld would not be satisfied to watch situations develop. The problem to which Schonfeld gave top priority was the danger facing rabbinic leaders and synagogue officials in Germany.

So the request was for those 500 visas, and the Home Office asked Hertz and Schonfeld why Britain needed these extra 500 ultra-Orthodox officials? What special skills did they possess which were unavailable in a country with millions unemployed? Among other suggestions, Schonfeld provided an answer the Home Office were generously prepared to accept. Orthodox Jewish men wear an undergarment called a *tsitsit*, with knotted fringes at the four corners. Schonfeld told the Home Office that all the proposed refugees knew how to make these fringes. The country was, in fact, as short of *tsitsit* knotters as it was of flint knappers! Nevertheless, the Home Office nodded gravely and provided the visas. Schonfeld also managed to persuade the Dutch to accept forty-three rabbis, the French twenty-eight and the Belgians seven.

Schonfeld's explanation would never have occurred to Otto Schiff and, if it had, he would have rejected it as ludicrously far-fetched. Schonfeld knew better: the Home Office just wanted an excuse to accept refugees because they were decent men. Schonfeld provided the fig leaf and it covered the nakedness of the argument. The Home Office, in the end, provided: '800 permits for Orthodox and Liberal rabbis and their families, as well as various functionaries and Talmudic students. The permits granted (other than those made available for communal positions in Britain) were temporary, pending emigration overseas'.[24]

There were other specific problems: 'Hertz had no end of trouble from both the government and the refugee organizations over their rescue of Rabbi Schneider and his (ultra-Orthodox) students who did not make sufficient attempt to become acculturalized to British society. Zionism never entered the equation.'[25]

The Board of Deputies was anxious to gather as much non-Jewish support as possible. As a consequence when they arranged a mass meeting of protest at the Royal Albert Hall in December 1938 the Chief Rabbi was the only Jewish speaker and the non-Jewish, Viscount Cranborne, presided.

In Austria, the Agudas Yisroel discovered that Orthodox children were still not being included in the lists and alerted Hertz and Schonfeld that this was the case. The Home Office was persuaded to issue them with permits anyway which marked the beginning of the Kindertransport movement to Britain.

The children all needed guarantors and, where these were unavailable, Schonfeld fell back on his old solution of forging the signatures of one of his friends, relatives or members of his community. Or he would tell them that he had discovered a long lost relative of theirs with the same name and the relation only needed their guarantee to get a visa. If that didn't work and the numbers needing authorization still exceeded the number of permits, Schonfeld would simply add them to the list and trust that the immigration officials at the ports would not count them too carefully and send them back. In later decades, when his local council set limits to the number of pupils he could accept at his schools, he would ignore the restrictions in a similar way.

Throughout, he was careful to observe Jewish law. One Friday night he was making up the papers for the Home Office with young members of the community. Writing on the Sabbath is normally prohibited but is halakhically permissible if it is done to save human life. One of his friends asked if he could smoke, which is also forbidden on Shabbat. Schonfeld said certainly not. The papers were then taken by Schonfeld to the Home Office by car, which is again normally prohibited on Shabbat. After which, once the job was done, he walked miles home, leaving the car to be picked up after Sabbath, when driving was allowed again.

Finding homes for thousands of children involved both Jewish and non-Jewish families. Hertz was naturally concerned that they be brought up in Jewish surroundings and stepped in when a group of fifty children were about to be sent to a vicar in north-east England by a Mrs Bentwich. Waley Cohen had no objections and pointed out that Mrs Bentwich had been appointed to arrange for their housing. Hertz pronounced this baseless, claiming that he himself had been the authoritative officer since 1913!

The children did end up in Jewish homes but a large number were fostered by kindly Christian families, which led to a considerable percentage of the children being lost to the community in later life. The Reform authorities also complained that Reform children weren't being fostered in Reform homes. The CRREC did their best for all the children, setting up a Refugee Children's Department and a Children's Relief Fund.

The problems were piling up. So many Jewish refugees had arrived that it was clear that a transit camp was needed to house up to 3,000 who would otherwise be homeless. It was a useful fiction that the refugees coming to Britain were merely in transit for other countries. Permanent immigrants were still not popular, but although a considerable number of the refugees did move on, it was fortunate for the cultural and economic life of the nation that many did not. These stayed to enrich the country, as had so many other refugees in the centuries before them.

At this point architect Ernest Joseph remembered that there was a derelict camp at Richborough, near Sandwich in Kent which dated from the First World War. The owners agreed to lease it to the Council for German Jewry. It contained two adjacent camps called Kitchener and Haig.

Frank Samuel, a United Synagogue vice-president, persuaded Unilever to provide the food and supplies at cost price as maintenance was restricted to 10 shillings (50p) a week. In January 1939, Hertz, Waley Cohen and Sir Alexander Maxwell, a senior civil servant, met at the Home Office and agreed that if the refugees didn't have a passport they could still be given a certificate to enter the country by British offices in Berlin and Vienna. Inmates at the camps could do internal repairs but no other work, although their wives could be employed as domestic servants for families in Kent.

In December 1938 permission was given for a total of 300 children, and about 10,000 followed them in 1939. Many were temporarily housed in another camp and their upkeep paid for by the United Synagogue. Ministers were sent to the camp to look after the children. One difficulty was that many of the children who arrived wouldn't eat the food because they were afraid it was non-kosher.

Bereft of parents, confused by their surroundings, they were often in a pitiable mental condition. Even so, when Hertz wanted to speak at the Passover service at the camp, Waley Cohen initially refused to make arrangements for him to do so. It was only when Hertz approached the Marquis of Reading that Waley Cohen was told to comply with the Chief Rabbi's wishes.

By the end of 1938 the Jewish relief organizations had been augmented by similar non-Jewish organizations. They were set up by the TUC, the Quakers, Save the Children Fund, the International Student Service, the Society for the Protection of Science and Literature, the Church of Scotland and the International Hebrew Christian Alliance. Fund-raising was undertaken by the Christian Council for Refugees from Germany, whose executive body included representatives from the Church of England, the Roman Catholic Church, the Free Churches and the Church of Scotland.

Hertz spoke for the whole community when he said:

> I feel it my duty to express the profound appreciation of Anglo-Jewry for the wonderful, nation-wide sympathy with the victims of religious and racial persecution; to voice officially my community's gratitude for the stand for decency and right made by Parliament, in the Press, and in every avenue of British life and thought … I am happy to be the spokesman of my Faith and People in the matter of such appreciation and gratitude.[26]

Even as the Jewish community faced the coming catastrophe of the Polish Jews, the horrors of Kristallnacht and the efforts to include refugee children on Kindertransport, there was still time for the battle for religious authority within the United Synagogue to flare up again. This time a convert to Judaism applied to the Hampstead synagogue for membership. The synagogue wanted to accept him even though he had chosen not to be circumcised. The Honorary Officers at the United Synagogue said that admissions were their responsibility. Hertz said that if the convert wasn't circumcised, he couldn't join the synagogue. The Honorary Officers told Hampstead that if he applied, he couldn't be turned down. The two sides clashed head on, with the Hampstead synagogue in the middle.

The membership of the Hampstead Synagogue included many personal friends of the United Synagogue Honorary Officers. The congregation had sought to go its own way before. Hermann Adler had refused to accept Revd Morris Joseph as their minister, they had a mixed choir which was not according to some views of the traditional law, and their minister during the 1913 election had been involved in the internal politicking. There was precedent for them chafing under the Chief Rabbi's position of ultimate authority in religious matters.

Even though it is absolutely fundamental in Orthodox Judaism that a male be circumcised, the Honorary Officers wanted to ignore the age-old ruling. They wrote to Hertz: 'The Honorary Officers cannot be a party to the United Synagogue entering upon a policy of inquisition in regard to its members which would be entirely contrary to its whole spirit.'[27]

The language was as inflammatory as ever. To designate a fundamental of the religion as an 'inquisition' was ludicrous. Furthermore, 'the whole spirit' of the United Synagogue was supposed to be to maintain Orthodox practice. Hertz insisted his decision be approved and wrote to them again to spell out the position: 'The Honorary Officers do not seem to realize that when they put in writing that they "cannot share my views" as expressed in a religious ruling, they are arrogating to themselves religious powers that they do not possess.'[28]

The Honorary Officers had no alternative but to back down. The episode showed how much the relationship between Hertz and the Honorary Officers in day-to-day matters continued to deteriorate, even in those most difficult of times.

When war came, only two members of the refugee camp were interned. Half volunteered for the army. They served in the Pioneer Corps although they were not allowed to carry weapons. When a wireless station was built they did, however, listen into and record German transmissions. Five companies of refugees were eventually at Dunkirk, although when they got back, they had to give up their arms again.

The high regard in which Hertz was now held outside the community was further illustrated when he was awarded an Honorary LLD by London University in 1938 and made a Doctor of Hebrew. Wishing to help his old collaborator in the war against calendar reform, Cecil Roth, Hertz had also persuaded the Bearsted family, the founders of Shell Petroleum, to endow a Readership at Oxford University in post-biblical Jewish history. He then persuaded the university to agree to accept Roth as the first incumbent.[29]

Keeping the authorities friendly was a constant requirement. For example, Hertz took Schonfeld with him when he went to see representatives of the Home Office in Glasgow to thank them for their help with refugees. It was considered ironic in some Jewish circles that Hertz was accompanied by a Rabbi whose organization didn't recognize his authority, but Schonfeld was the director of the CRREC.

The administrative load in processing the children was enormous. Judith Hertz had volunteered to help in the CRREC office and, as she and Schonfeld worked long hours together when he was in London, it was easy for a friendship to develop. Schonfeld asked Judith to marry him and Judith accepted his proposal, which was announced in *The Times* on 5 October 1939. Even this happy event was used by Schonfeld's critics to attack him. Some would suggest he had married Judith as a career move.

There was greater warmth in Judith's letters to Schonfeld than those he sent her. This is easily explained. First, Judith Hertz had more time for correspondence and was able to express herself at greater length. Second, she was literary, had learned a great deal of poetry by heart and was well acquainted with the correspondence of Keats.

Schonfeld was always going to be a difficult husband and controlling so powerful a personality was a challenge for even as intelligent and devoted a wife as Judith Hertz. She knew what to expect, though. She had written to him in October 1939, when they got engaged: 'to the most impossible person I know – and the only one I want to know'.[30] Judith needed his warm and strong personality.

Years later he was talking to the adolescent daughter of a friend as they walked home from her house after a Sabbath lunch. The young woman said that she hoped she would grow up to be a genius. She recalls that Schonfeld told her to wish for no such thing. He said that Hertz was a genius but, as a result, Judith was a deeply unhappy woman. Genius often comes at a high price for those who have to live with it.[31]

There were other reasons for this sad state of affairs. The Hertz household had been without its mother since 1930. The Chief Rabbi was in great public demand while his children grew up, and their needs could well have been one burden too many. One relative recalls that in those years there was little warmth in the Hertz household.

It would be generally agreed among their closest friends that Judith was the only one who could handle her husband. Lady Hazel Sternberg, whose husband, Sir Sigmund, was a Schonfeld cousin, said that Judith was: 'clever and nice. She was calm and accepting'.[32] She had always known that it wouldn't be a normal married life, because she was going to be married to a public figure, who would constantly have other demands on his time. Nevertheless, the pair had the theatre and the cinema in common and Judith would provide the home and harbour for when Schonfeld had finished being buffeted by the gales of his many responsibilities.

It was suggested by some that Schonfeld saw his marriage as a way to improve his chances of becoming Chief Rabbi. The position had gone from father to son on three occasions in the past – David and Isaac Nietto, Hart Lyon and his son Solomon Hirschell, and Nathan Marcus Adler and his son Hermann, but never from father to son-in-law. A pragmatist like Schonfeld was, however, unlikely to have harboured such hopes. He belonged to the *Adath,* and the power in the land when it came to voting for a new Chief Rabbi lay with the United Synagogue. He must have known his chances were, at best, negligible. He later said to one of his sons that he never wanted the role since he could never have done what he wanted and, to judge by Hertz's difficulties, he may have been right.

This was, in fact, Schonfeld's second marriage. A few years before, when he had met a young Jewish woman in Vienna who had needed a passport to leave the country, he married her. They were divorced six months later. The fact that Hertz knew the young rabbi had been divorced proved no obstacle in those perilous days. Marrying a Jewish woman in order to provide her with a lifesaving passport was heroic rather than questionable behaviour. Even when the second marriage was to a Chief Rabbi's daughter, the first could be easily explained.

Just before the war Irene, Leon's wife, was able to bring her children, Gilly and Jonny, to London to see their grandfather, who even provided them with a nanny. Unfortunately the visit had to be curtailed so that Irene could get back to Palestine which she only managed after some unpleasant clashes with various continental security forces on the way.

For many German refugees in Britain, it was not just the customs and mores of the locals that were strange to them. They were used to different forms of synagogue service. One group of refugees set up their own synagogue in London and briefly allied themselves to the Liberal movement, since in Germany that was the description of their neo-Orthodox congregation. When they discovered that they were with the wrong grouping, they were very unhappy. It wasn't until 1952, however, that this particular synagogue stopped their religion classes for the children being conducted in German.

Refugees often wanted to follow their own ritual and customs and, in particular, to hear sermons in German. They were often connected with the United Synagogue by this time and appealed to them for help. The subject was discussed at a heated Council Meeting in July 1939 which, after three hours, reached an impasse. The Council wouldn't accept the recommendation of the Honorary Officers that permission be given. Speakers felt that the sooner the refugees removed anything German from their lives in Britain, the better.

They also felt that many refugees were joining the United Synagogue even though they were really Liberal or Reform. Members of the Council were afraid that Progressives were going to infiltrate the United Synagogue. Hertz made his own position clear: 'not only are these services permissible but I can conceive of few undertakings more urgent, wise and beneficent than this religious enterprise which the Honorary Officers at my earnest request are placing before the Council.'[33]

The Council voted to delay a decision for six months, after which all the Honorary Officers promptly resigned. It didn't augur well for the running of the organization as war loomed.

NOTES

1. Jeremy Schonfield private family archive.
2. Institute for Historical Review, http://www.ihr.org/jhr/v07/v07p498_Okeefe.html.
3. *The Times*, 1 September 1936.
4. Ibid.
5. Daniel Henry Hertz, In Memoriam, Jeremy Schonfield private family archive. Written by Dr P. D'Arcy Hart, lecturer, University College Hospital, London.
6. *The Times*, 1 September 1936
7. Hertz to Dr M. Epstein, 26 April 1937, United Synagogue Archive, London Metropolitan Archives.
8. Bernard Homa, *Footprints in the Sands of Time* (Privately printed, 1990), p.89.
9. *Jewish Chronicle*, 25 March 1938.
10. *Jewish Chronicle*, 25 March 1938.
11. *Jewish Chronicle*, 29 April 1994.
12. *Jewish Chronicle*, 18 January 1946.

13. Obituary, Muriel Emanuel, *Jewish Chronicle*, 24 April 1994.
14. Ibid.
15. Aubrey Newman, 'Chief Rabbi Dr Joseph Herman Hertz, CH' (London: United Synagogue, 1972), p.24.
16. Derek Taylor, *Solomon Schonfeld. A Purpose in Life* (London and Portland, OR: Vallentine Mitchell, 2009), p.48.
17. Pamela Shatzkes, *Holocaust and Rescue: Impotent or Indifferent? Anglo-Jewry 1938–1945* (Basingstoke: Palgrave, 2002), p.38.
18. Ibid.
19. Ibid., p.241.
20. CRREC Minute Book, J.H. Hertz archive, Hartley Library, Southampton University Archives.
21. Taylor, *Solomon Schonfeld*, p.53.
22. The author in conversation with Jacob Schonfeld in 2006.
23. Louise London, *Whitehall and the Jews, 1933–1948: British Immigration Policy, Jewish Refugees and the Holocaust* (London: Oxford University Press, 2000), p.100.
24. Ibid.
25. Geoffrey Alderman, *Controversy and Crisis: Studies in the History of the Jews in Modern Britain* (Boston, MA: Academic Press, 2008), p.360.
26. Joseph Herman Hertz, *Early and Late: Addresses, Messages, and Papers* (Hindhead: Soncino Press, 1943), p.58.
27. United Synagogue Archive, File 2132, London Metropolitan Archives.
28. Letter, 17 June 1942, London Metropolitan Archives.
29. Paula Hill paper, 15 January 2003, B'nai B'rith Albert Einstein Lodge, Jerusalem. Jeremy Schonfield private family archive.
30. Jeremy Schonfield private family archive.
31. Author's private conversation with the lady.
32. Lady Sternberg in conversation with the author.
33. *Jewish Chronicle*, 21 July 1939.

Chapter Fourteen

An Even Worse War

Running an organization like the United Synagogue in wartime was fraught with problems from that first fatal day in September 1939. Key personnel enlisted in the forces and communities were evacuated to escape the expected aerial bombing. Destruction caused to towns in Spain during the recent civil war had been a grim warning of what would be likely to befall British cities. Children were sent to safer parts of the country and the headquarters of the United Synagogue moved from central London to Edgware.

It did not help that the Honorary Officers of the United Synagogue had all resigned the previous July. A meeting of the Council in September, however, soon after the outbreak of war, saw them withdraw their resignations, and Waley Cohen was ideally placed to impose his will still further on the organization. He was unencumbered by family considerations, was rich enough to spare the time, and dedicated enough to want the job, even though it was even more laborious than before. He was competent to run a large organization, had no larger responsibility and quickly took steps to make his control even more complete.

The council meeting in September recognized that members had their own wartime problems to resolve, and agreed to suspend all Standing Orders and to schedule no further Council meetings. All power was placed in the hands of the Honorary Officers, except the right of twenty or more members to call for a Council meeting. There would be no further meetings until 1942. Waley Cohen was given full power in all administrative matters.

The main task was to hold together an organization which, inevitably, found itself with many uncompleted programmes. Building projects unfinished at the beginning of the war had to be mothballed. Income sank as a result of members moving away and many synagogues would be destroyed or damaged in the bombing. It was necessary to cut costs, so it was agreed that the salaries of ministers and administrators would be reduced. Waley Cohen made every effort to solve a host of financial problems in the most difficult of circumstances and was, primarily, responsible for the United Synagogue continuing to balance its books.

The Second World War lasted for nearly six years. For the first two of those years Britain was losing. The first great victory, at El Alamein, would not come until the war was two and a half years old. In Britain, between July and December 1940, more than 70,000 people were killed in the Blitz. The observance of Jewish laws became more and more difficult, and also peripheral to daily life for a great many members of the community.

What was needed to keep the community together was strong and united leadership. In the United Synagogue that wasn't on offer. Waley Cohen still wished to decide the religious approach of the community according to his own lights, but resisting him remained the indomitable figure of the Chief Rabbi. The two were now hardly on speaking terms. A historian of the United Synagogue recorded: 'the allegation [was] that the Honorary Officers of the United Synagogue were doing all they could to sabotage any attempt made by the Chief Rabbi to induce a religious revival and that instead they were trying to sweep away all distinction among Orthodox, Reform and Liberal Jews.'[1]

Such a judgement is, however, an exaggeration. It is true that Waley Cohen was still concentrating on a Spiritist approach and was able to persuade other Honorary Officers to follow his lead. It is equally true that in the field of Jewish education he would try to sideline the Chief Rabbi. Examples of a non-Orthodox approach to problems, like the opposition to the provision of kosher food for Pesach for evacuee children, could also be identified.

Overall, however, all this was a long way from an attempt to sweep away all distinctions. The lay leaders of the individual United Synagogues and of Orthodox provincial and Empire synagogues would never have allowed this to happen, as the Honorary Officers would have known.

Nevertheless, Waley Cohen still craved untrammelled authority. He had it in administrative matters and he still wished to compete with the Chief Rabbi in spiritual areas, if he was so inclined. The organization's problems in surviving supported the argument for reducing the emphasis on observing the *mitzvot*, but Hertz did not see it that way. There might have to be failures in observance but, as far as he was concerned, the *mitzvot* had to remain the cornerstone of Judaism.

Waley Cohen could control the Honorary Officers and, in the dark days of the war, Hertz saw their antagonism to his insistence on the importance of *mitzvot* as a serious threat. One Honorary Officer asked him if he seriously thought anybody would be keeping kosher after the war.

In 1940, as communities fragmented, it was agreed that there would be a campaign for 'A Recall to the Synagogue'. It was more of a public relations exercise than anything else. Families were still fleeing towns likely to be bombed, although there were some notable exceptions, some pockets of Orthodoxy, which grew when newcomers arrived from the cities.

Hertz wanted to help those new communities as much as he could, but his Honorary Officers aimed to reduce his areas of responsibility rather than increase them. So when Hertz asked for a list of the new communities, the secretary of the United Synagogue, Philip Goldberg, refused to give it to him. It was only after Hertz threatened Lionel de Rothschild with legal action if the list wasn't forthcoming that it was reluctantly provided. It might seem inconceivable that the United Synagogue would be threatened with legal action by its own Chief Rabbi, but that is what happened.

Schonfeld's school children had been evacuated to Shefford in Bedfordshire and, under the inspiring Judith Grunfeld, formed an Orthodox enclave in five villages. The Jewish community in Cambridge was enhanced by a number of world-famous Jewish Talmudic scholars and Hertz moved there temporarily himself. In general, though, Orthodox Jewish life was very difficult.

Hertz never doubted eventual victory, but he retained a sense of humour. According to the parliamentary diarist, 'Chips' Channon, when the Chief Rabbi was asked his views when he met George VI in 1940, he was alleged to have assured the king that the Allies would eventually prevail, but added 'all the same, sir, I would put some of the colonies in your wife's name'![2]

One indication of the near-breakdown of relations between Hertz and the United Synagogue Honorary Officers was their conflicting approaches to the 'A Recall to the Synagogue' campaign. Waley Cohen introduced it by emphasizing the Spiritist approach. When Hertz addressed a United Synagogue conference on the subject in 1940, he condemned the concept in no uncertain terms:

> We at once see that the financial side of synagogue administration is not all-important; and that we can have nothing but contempt for those zealots of business efficiency in religion who would tear

> down the two Tables of the Law from the front of our houses of worship and replace them with the balance sheet. Besides, deification of business management, coupled as it so often is with colour-blindness to Jewish spiritual and cultural values is unwise even from the purely business point of view.[3]

There could be no doubt who Hertz was talking about: it was his own Honorary Officers, and he was criticizing them in public. He made his views even clearer a month later in a sermon at the Hampstead synagogue: 'This is not a Recall to Religion but a Recall to the Synagogue. The difference is profound … our recall is not to some nebulous something, allegedly spiritual, that opposes itself to nothing in particular … it is a Recall to the Synagogue with its Thou Shalts and Thou Shalt Nots.'[4]

There was no way back from such a denunciation. Where Waley Cohen and Hertz had been able to patch up their differences in the past, there was now open warfare. Waley Cohen showed he would go to extremes to have his own way. Having been rejected by Shell and United Africa, Waley Cohen's self-esteem rested to an extent on his position and authority within the United Synagogue. The Chief Rabbi remained an obstruction, even after Lionel de Rothschild died in 1942 and Waley Cohen succeeded him as president.

There should have been a way for Hertz and Waley Cohen to bury the hatchet, at least for the duration of the war. If there was to be a return to the synagogue and prayer, it was more likely to emerge from the constant threat of death which hung over everyone in Britain during the Blitz. Lose the war and the concentration camps loomed for all Jews. The difficulties of rationing, the night-time blackout, the unknown whereabouts of loved ones in the forces and the constant stream of bad news about the progress of the war, made prayer a more attractive activity to the normally uncommitted.

In the early days of the war a recall to the synagogue was hampered by the destruction of synagogues like the Great and the Central in London and the exhaustion of thousands of civilians who would be up all night fire-watching, checking that no light was visible to guide bombers to their targets or dealing with unexploded bombs and air raid casualties.

In London thousands tried to snatch a night's sleep away from the bombing, on the platforms of underground stations. The general view was that there would be time enough to return to the synagogue or to improve moral and ethical behaviour if and when the war was won. Hertz seemed to be trying to hold the fort on religious observance at an impossible time.

Because of the overwhelming importance of the blackout, special rulings for services had to be made by Hertz and the Beth Din. These were announced in the *Jewish Chronicle* on 15 September 1939, two weeks after the war began. From now on every evening service would have to finish half an hour before the blackout started. Services for Rosh Hashanah would start at 8.30 in the morning and finish by 10.30. In this way casualties would be minimized if the building was bombed, as the gatherings would last a minimum amount of time. The length of the service would be reduced by excluding *piyutim* (liturgical poems) and replacing *chazanut* (cantorial art) with plain reading. Yom Kippur services would last from 11.30am till 1.00pm and from 5.15pm to 6.30pm. As the *shofar*, the ram's horn, may only be blown at nightfall on Yom Kippur, this part of the service was also cancelled.

What took up an immense amount of time was the mass of administrative detail which Waley Cohen and the Chief Rabbi assiduously dealt with at the United Synagogue, and which Schonfeld carried out on behalf of refugees and internees through the aegis of the Chief Rabbi's Religious Emergency Council.

The work load was heavy but Schonfeld was willing and supportive. It was no surprise that, during the war, Hertz told Dayan Lazarus, who had become a full-time dayan in 1938, that he felt his sole reliable support was his son-in-law. The accusation was then made that Hertz was unduly influenced by Schonfeld. This he rejected in a letter to Waley Cohen in 1942: 'The idea that I am "giving ear" to unwise counsel or that I am guided by anyone in my dealings and correspondence ... is quite illusory.'[5]

When the war broke out, several refugee initiatives had to be abandoned. For example, there had been a last-minute effort in April 1939 by Weissmandl and Schonfeld to bring out 200 Jews from Nitra, where the Union of Orthodox Hebrew Congregations' rabbi had first studied for his *semicha*. The idea was to move them to Canada and America, but visas and transport were needed. Negotiations dragged on and they were still unresolved when the war started and time ran out. Most of the 200 died in the Auschwitz concentration camp and their rabbi died of typhus in the woods with the partisans.

In 1939 Hertz immediately turned his attention to the problems of looking after the Jewish members of the armed forces. He would build on his First World War experiences and set up the Jewish War-Services Committee under the chairmanship of Lionel de Rothschild. Waley Cohen was the vice-chairman and Jewish notables, such as the Marquis of Reading and Neville Laski, agreed to serve. Hertz invited the Progressives as well as the Orthodox to participate. The single unifying factor for the community was the Chief Rabbi.

Dr Bernard Homa was also asked to take part: a senior member of the Right Wing who would prove a valuable ally to the Chief Rabbi in the future, even if they had disagreed on halakhic matters in the past. The heads of the armed forces accepted Hertz's decision that the Committee would represent the Anglo-Jewish community, and that their recommendations would be accepted, unless the Chief Rabbi wished to make a personal decision. Waley Cohen became chairman after Rothschild.

Meanwhile, the Chief Rabbi's Religious Emergency Council concerned itself with religious observance. For the troops in the field it was often the performance of Jewish rituals which helped those fighting fearsome odds to keep up their spirits. It was assumed that a Jew going into battle was helped by having a set of *tefillin* in order to pray in the correct manner in the morning, even if it wasn't his normal practice. These were duly provided.

From March 1941 every observant Jew in the forces received a fortnightly kosher food parcel with the help of the Ministry of Food. The Chief Rabbi's Religious Emergency Council (CRREC) also arranged supplies for Passover for the troops: in 1944 they would send out 25,000 lbs of matzo, 500 lbs of meat, 15,000 pints of wine and 5,000 *Haggadot* (text for the Passover *seder*). They also sent out thousands of prayer books, as well as an enlarged edition of *The Book of Jewish Thoughts* which was reprinted many times.

In 1939 there was only one Jewish chaplain, Dayan Mark Gollop, who had held the post since 1926, in succession to Revd Michael Adler DSO who had been appointed as long ago as 1908. Gollop, originally from Russia, had served with distinction as a chaplain in the First World War and was mentioned in dispatches during the Greek campaign. Gollop recruited more Jewish chaplains, with the approval of the Chief Rabbi, and rubber-stamped by the Ministry of Defence. Hertz decided to leave the paperwork for the appointments to a subcommittee headed by Waley Cohen, but this would provoke a major disagreement in 1943.

As Hertz set out to lead the community through the Second World War, he had three important domestic concerns: keeping in touch with evacuee children, taking care of their religious education far from the centres of Jewish communities and providing them with kosher food. Schonfeld did much of the leg work. As he wrote to Hertz in March 1940:

> Pesach arrangements for the children billeted in the country are being made, if only on a limited scale. Money for this purpose has been given by the Federation. I had to protest again with regard to kashrus at the Richborough Camp [where many of the refugees were housed]. In the end Waley C agreed that I go down and make suitable arrangements ... On Thursday I attended the meeting of the Council for German Jewry on your behalf and settled various items favourably. The grant for our rabbis is being continued and we can just manage with our present numbers.[6]

There was an early contretemps over the Jewish education of evacuated children. Waley Cohen saw this as an opportunity to move the Liberal synagogue into a leading position and ingenuously suggested that a new committee was needed to tackle the problem, as the United Synagogue and the Board of Deputies were too busy on other matters. Such a body was proposed to consider 'The future of institutional Judaism'.

When it first met the Chief Rabbi wasn't asked to attend, perhaps because it was known that he rejected the Spiritist approach. As a consequence, the conclusions reached by the conference delegates would be more likely to be accepted if he wasn't there. The United Synagogue vice-president, Frank Samuel, even said that the Chief Rabbi's attitude was 'un-Jewish'. Again the Honorary Officers' behaviour was almost unbelievable. Not only did they treat the Chief Rabbi dismissively, but they seemed to believe, even after having been forced to give way so many times in the past, that they had a chance of any unorthodox decisions being accepted.

The Committee nominated Lily Montagu, a founder of the Liberal Synagogue, as chair even though 75 per cent of the community was Orthodox. Waley Cohen clearly wanted the education of Jewish children to be decided by a committee headed by a Liberal, who, admittedly, had the distinctions of being both a CBE and a Justice of the Peace. These were hardly pertinent, however, when the subject was, primarily, the education of Orthodox Jewish children. As head of the Union of Orthodox Hebrew Congregations, Schonfeld hadn't joined the discussions, not wanting to risk being committed to decisions of which he didn't approve. He condemned it roundly as: 'intended to throw all Jewish education into the hands of these people, excluding all Orthodox Jews'.[7] Hertz publicly vetoed the committee: 'There is a serious danger of Jewish religious education being deprived of its Jewish and religious character ... it is clearly my duty as Chief Rabbi ... to rescue our educational machinery from the hands of men who are inimical to Traditional Judaism and its fundamental institutions.'[8]

Those in charge of religious education in their sections of the community were wary of working together, due to their different theological approaches. For example, since there weren't enough Jewish teachers in the country to educate the widely scattered evacuated children, Schonfeld offered thirty refugee rabbis known to the Union of Orthodox Hebrew Congregations. He was told that their English wasn't good enough, which may or may not have been relevant, but their contribution would have been much better than nothing.

There was little goodwill among the leaders. When the question of cooperation between the Union of Orthodox Hebrew Congregations and the Committee was raised at the Union's AGM in the summer, Schonfeld told the meeting that it was farcical that they had to face a situation in which questions of *kashrut*, the law and *chinuch* (education) were administered by people who were not only indifferent, but opposed to the traditional laws.

There was evidence to prove his point. Waley Cohen had been antagonistic towards a move to try to provide matzo for evacuee children on Passover, on the grounds that, in times of rationing, it was wrong for the Jewish community to ask for special treatment. In fact, bread was only rationed after the war, when flour cost too much in precious foreign exchange. During the war the government decided that rationing bread would be too unpopular to sustain but Waley Cohen didn't want to exploit the situation.

Hertz defended *kashrut* at a United Synagogue conference in July 1940:

> As to the Orthodox Jewish child, his whole religion stands or falls with the dietary laws. For Judaism is to him not a matter of words; it is the readiness to do what he does not like to do, simply because it is right; and not to do what he would very much like to do, simply because it would be wrong to do it: it is character-training through observance, discipline, self-restraint.[9]

Waley Cohen should have foreseen that it was highly unlikely that Hertz would relinquish overall responsibility for the education of Jewish children. With Selig Brodetzky and Neville Laski from the Board of Deputies trying to pour oil on troubled waters, the Chief Rabbi arranged with the government to set up his own Joint Emergency Council for Jewish Religious Education. In retaliation for their own behaviour, he didn't invite any Honorary Officers of the United Synagogue to participate, but only the religious authorities of the Sephardim, Federation, Union of Orthodox Hebrew Congregations, provincial and Zionist organizations.

The Reform and Liberal movements hoped to have their own alternative Council, but found their differences too great. Rabbi Reinhart summed up the problem: 'an association in which the parties concerned agree only on this; that they won't agree to anything'.[10]

When, in May 1941, Frank Samuel asked why the Honorary Officers had been left out of the committee, Hertz told him frankly that, in his view, none of them would have replied to an invitation without Waley Cohen's permission: 'the self-appointed dictator in Jewish religious education. I could not invite him because he is inimical to Traditional Judaism ... far more so, for example, than the late C.G. Montefiore, who was open and above board in his attacks on Orthodox Judaism'.[11]

The Chief Rabbi went on to make additional comments on the president of the United Synagogue's style of leadership, even though Waley Cohen was now the head of the Orthodox organization: 'He is incurably wedded to the Hitler technique, with outbursts of shouting and abuse, whenever he does not get his own totalitarian ways ... No-one who was present will ever forget the fury with which Sir Robert greeted ... my proposal to make Kosher provisions for evacuee children.'[12]

There were powerful and able men among the Honorary Officers of the United Synagogue, and it seems unlikely that they would simply approve without argument anything that Waley Cohen wanted to do. On the other hand, Waley Cohen was the only official who was prepared and able to carry the burden of the work involved in running the United Synagogue. If his colleagues were less aggressive in their opinions, they were of a similar mind and bore some of the responsibility for the dysfunctional nature of the organization.

It was a disgraceful way for the community to be led in wartime. A compromise was eventually reached on the organization of Jewish schooling by the creation of the London Board of Jewish Religious Education, which combined both Hertz and Waley Cohen's committees, but under Hertz's chairmanship. The strain, however, had begun to tell on the Chief Rabbi. He became ill from overwork early in 1940 and was instructed by his doctors to recuperate. He chose Haifa, where his views on Solomon Schonfeld, who had become his new son-in-law, were summed up in a letter he wrote to his sister, Sadie, that March:

> I have been decidedly unwell for some time. Finally, after the high Festivals, I was ordered a complete rest in bed to be followed by two or three months in Egypt or Palestine. I chose the latter and have lived since February 9th within hailing distance of my grandchildren. [Leon and Irene's children, Gilly and Jonathan.]

The day after Yom Kippur, Judith announced to me 'Father, I promised to marry Dr Schonfeld.' My reply was 'If you have promised, you must keep your promise.' And she did. They were married on January 16th at 103 Hamilton Terrace, the undersigned officiating. They flew to Palestine for their honeymoon and by accident I ran across them in Rome on their return journey.

Dr Schonfeld is a Hungarian, by descent that is, for he was born in London. His father led the opposition against the Rabbinate as long as he lived. The son then took up the parable. The crisis came some two and a half years ago, in connection with the German refugee children and the problems that followed in their wake. I found that of all the clergy, he possessed the most personality, common sense and fearlessness towards the assimilated aristocrats. His help proved invaluable. I could never have ventured to rescue 250 German rabbis and families without him as my Shammas [synagogue master of ceremonies], representative and 'Cossack'. Add to this he is an exceptionally handsome man, six foot high, blue eyed, a renowned shnorrer [fund raiser], persuasive and affable; it is understandable that he could have won Judith. They are very happy.

My visit here was strictly private. I kept out of all trouble.

Your loving, Joe.[13]

The marriage between Solomon and Judith, intelligent people working together for a common cause, lasted for over forty years until Solomon's death, and they remained devoted to each other.

Schonfeld wrote to Hertz as 'Dear Father' and signed himself 'Shlomo'. He gave a clue to the underlying cause of Hertz's ill health when he wrote: 'You seem to have made wonderful progress towards recuperation – but please do keep in hiding from the public eye, the mere hearing of communal troubles will cause you so much worry and undo all the good that has so far been achieved.'[14] Hertz was being weakened by the assimilated aristocrats and was also now beyond the usual retiring age.

Hertz clearly liked Schonfeld. As he had said at the wedding: 'Nothing fills me with greater joy than such a sole resolve on the part of the man into whose hands I now place an infinite trust – the happiness of my child.'[15]

As time passed, while they disagreed on occasions, his admiration for the young rabbi grew. As he said to Schonfeld's brother, Jacob, on his barmitzvah: 'You're going to be a great man – just like your brother.'[16] For his part, Schonfeld ensured that the Union of Orthodox Hebrew Congregations accepted the: 'Chief Rabbi's position of central religious authority for the Anglo-Jewish community'.[17]

Because of his support for Schonfeld, Hertz was again accused of being over-influenced by the Right Wing. He responded: 'As Chief Rabbi, I am supposed to care for religious teachers, Rabbis, scholars and clergy. Rabbi Schonfeld's activities come under this heading. This is not a communal matter, but a religious matter, and when it comes to religious matters, no communal organization has the right to dictate to the Chief Rabbi.'[18]

In Haifa he was able to stay with Leon and Irene and their children. He took the opportunity to call on the high commissioner to protest about the White Paper which restricted Jewish immigration into Palestine. There was no progress and he left the meeting, as Irene reported, silent and furious. He got more pleasure from taking his grandchildren every week to the shopping centre. To keep them quiet while he looked at the books, he agreed to a programme with the toddlers that would take in the book shop, followed by the toy shop, followed by the sweet shop. After he left, Irene took the children to live with Hertz's sister, Sadie, in South Africa, where eventually Leon was able to join them.

Waley Cohen was keen to offer his services to the government, but Churchill did not take him up on the offer. This was in spite of Waley Cohen's support of the Focus Group. It was possible that Churchill thought that to give a role to an Honorary Officer of the United Synagogue would be grist to Joseph Goebbel's Nazi propaganda mill, constantly trying to blame the Jews for the war. It was pointed out that there were still international neutrals to be won over to the side of the Allies if this could be achieved.

This explanation doesn't hold water: the government were quite prepared to use Jewish contributions if they helped the war effort. Chamberlain had asked Sir Isidore Salmon, a vice-president of the United Synagogue and head of Lyons, the food company, to create the Royal Catering Corps. Ewen Montagu, who became a vice-president of the United Synagogue in the same year, would lead the team which successfully created 'The Man Who Never Was'. This stratagem persuaded the Nazis that Sicily would not be the location for an attack on Italy after the North Africa campaign. In May 1940 Churchill asked Manny Shinwell to take up a position at the Ministry of Food, only to be rejected by the future Labour minister and chairman of the party in 1942. Shinwell was no friend of the premier.

Ironically, the only wartime job Waley Cohen was given by the government was in 1942 when he was appointed to advise them on *kashrut*. Both Hertz and the Board of Deputies wrote to him protesting that they should have been consulted, probably concerned that someone who didn't himself observe those rules was now in charge of their maintenance. At this point, a development ended an argument which had frequently occurred since 1891: the question of whether unporged meat was kosher. The Beth Din now stated that there were not enough porgers left in the country because of wartime enlistment. They were, therefore, going to prohibit unporged meat. It had taken some years but Abramsky had finally had the regulation approved.

The government's rejection of Waley Cohen's offer of help must have been a bitter blow. He was seven years younger than the prime minister and had performed well in the First World War, but his dominant personality and fierce temper would have been well known, raising questions about his ability to lead a team. Since nobody was prepared to take the risk, Waley Cohen was sidelined.

In September 1940 Lionel de Rothschild and Hertz were staying in Harrogate, a Yorkshire town, considered safe from attack, when a stray German bomber dropped three bombs, one of which flattened Hertz as he was walking in the hotel gardens, and killed another guest. The *Jewish Chronicle* reported that he was only bruised and shaken, though that could have been to avoid the community knowing how serious his injuries were. The explosion did affect his hearing for the rest of his life.[19]

Physically, it seems likely that, had it existed at the time, Hertz would certainly have benefited from heart surgery. As far as his mental state at the time is concerned, an unbiased account of his mental health is available, a long report that Neville Laski sent to Waley Cohen in June 1941. Laski had asked for a meeting with Hertz to see if he could soothe relations between the Honorary Officers of the United Synagogue and their Chief Rabbi. Laski wrote: 'I am unable to do other than praise the relevance, lucidity, forcefulness and I might almost say objectivity of his remarks.'[20]

Laski was a King's Counsel (KC) and his judgement could be trusted. Hertz, for his part, accused Waley Cohen of telling ministers that: 'ever since his bombing experiences at Harrogate, the Chief Rabbi was not responsible for his actions'.[21] Waley Cohen must have known that this would get back to Hertz, and if it wasn't medically true, it was defamatory, spiteful, underhand and outrageous. Indeed, in 1942, Hertz was mentally alert enough to publish the *Authorised Daily Prayer Book*, his own extensive commentary on Singer's prayer book, a classic which still remains in print. He continued to make well-received and self-confident speeches. Typical was his oration at the Jubilee meeting of the Etz Haim Yeshiva in 1943.[22]

Hertz knew of the rumours and responded: 'Should strength of expression and insistence on a point of view by myself be construed as ill health and not be construed in the same way when it is utilized by others to oppose me?'[23] It was a good point but it didn't stop the opposition. His doctors warned him not to become overexcited.

There was also the continuing problem of the internees. At the outbreak of war, one of the most serious domestic issues the government faced was the possibility of sabotage and the creation of a Fifth Column of spies and fellow-travellers, keen to undermine the war effort. The expression 'Fifth Column' had emerged from a similar situation in the recent Spanish Civil War and was much in the public mind. The government had a responsibility to keep the nation safe from treasonable activities and correctly thought it safer to overreact rather than risk leaving enemy agents at large.

Internment was, therefore, introduced for senior members of the British Union of Fascists and for any immigrants over the past fifty years who might also be suspect. These ranged from Italian hoteliers to nineteenth-century Jewish refugees.[24] It was difficult to decide quickly which Jewish immigrants might pose a threat and it seemed better to intern too many rather than too few. So thousands were arrested and sent to the Isle of Man. They were not ill-treated, although their families lost their bread winners, businesses foundered and children were deprived of parents.

Many recent refugees found themselves in a country about which they were totally ignorant, especially the small proportion that had come from *yeshivot*. They still had to be approved by an Aliens Tribunal if they were not to be interned when the war came. One group had been particularly criticized by their tribunal and Neville Laski asked Hertz whether something could be done to educate them in British ways. Hertz replied that he thought a mountain was being made out of a molehill. He went on to say he did not:

> regret, and certainly need not apologize for my having rescued these Yeshivah students from Nazi concentration camps. Nor was it my first duty to teach them either British geography or English games, but to enable them to live. And I have yet to learn that ignorance of British geography or of English games on the part of a poor hounded human being is sufficient reason for him being interned.[25]

Laski faced a real problem and Hertz was occasionally more aggressive in his reactions than was strictly necessary. Both he and Laski had the interests of the refugees at heart, but Hertz could be overprotective, cutting down opposition to his views with stinging prose. He was primarily concerned to have the Jewish internees released as soon as possible. He also wanted their conditions improved, and since he wanted that done quickly, he gave the responsibility for visiting the camps to Schonfeld, as the director of the Chief Rabbi's Religious Emergency Council.

For Schonfeld at the CRREC, the first task in connection with internees was to feed the family of the breadwinner who had been imprisoned. That meant more fund-raising. It was then necessary to reassure the internees' partners that their other half was safe and well, since it was easy to confuse the concept of an internment camp with that of a concentration camp. After all, the first concentration camps had been created by the British in South Africa, as Hertz well knew. Then it was necessary to ensure that conditions in the camps were as good as possible, and to have released any internees who were ill.

Schonfeld persuaded the War Office to give him a pass to visit every camp. In the first few months after they were set up, he completed four tours to each of them. Schonfeld was able to explain the situation to the camp commandants in impeccable English, and to outline the necessary Talmudic observances which the Orthodox internees would wish to obey. He did this with sufficient charm to ensure that kosher kitchens and synagogues were established in the camps, paid for by the CRREC, and that rabbis were selected to minister to the internees.

As Schonfeld reported later: 'overcrowding was rectified, occupations and entertainment schemes were organized, unsuitable camps were replaced with better ones and there were arrangements for services and the instruction of children. Kosher food purchased by the Council was sent to improve diet. The Council was responsible for the release of about 1,000 internees'.[26]

There were some extraordinary situations in the camps. In Port Erin on the Isle of Man a New Year service was held in the local cinema. There were 200 in the congregation, but no *minyan* of ten male Jews to form a quorum for full public prayer. The 200 were all women who had been separated from their menfolk. This Schonfeld could do nothing about.

There has been much criticism of internment, on the grounds that innocent people were imprisoned, but in war action often has to be taken in a rush. In the early days of the war, the country was fighting for its existence against an overwhelmingly more powerful military force and it was no time for half measures.

Hertz's problems with the United Synagogue Honorary Officers were not his only wartime communal clash. The Board of Deputies had been expanded to be more inclusive, but this had led to increasing friction between the pro-Zionists and the anti-Zionists. This would eventually lead to a victory for the pro-Zionists in 1943 and a diminution of the influence of the old Cousinhood families. It was those delegates who Hertz had found it necessary to take to task in 1941 when, on 28 July, his secretary wrote to the president of the Board:

> Sir, Certain statements with regard to the activities of the Chief Rabbi that were made at the recent meeting of the Board of Deputies at Manchester must have left a false impression on the mind of the general public; namely, that the Chief Rabbi is under the Board, and that all approach to the government, touching Jewish matters is exclusively through the Board. The Chief Rabbi feels that such misconceptions cannot be allowed to pass without correction.
>
> 1. Some members of the Board do not appear to realize that the Chief Rabbinate is older than the Board of Deputies and is quite independent of it. [This was accurate; Aaron Hart (1705–56) was, effectively, Chief Rabbi but the Board of Deputies was only formed in 1761.] On the contrary, it is the Board of Deputies that is, in one vital respect of its activities, subject to the guidance of the Chief Rabbinate. Paragraph 42 of your constitution reads: 'The guidance of the Board on religious matters (inclusive of matters relating to marriages and matters involving questions affecting the religious customs and usages of the Jews) shall remain as heretofore with the Ecclesiastical Authorities, to whom all such matters shall be referred.'
> 2. Equally mistaken is the view that communication on Jewish questions with any Ministry is confined to the Board. Since the Chief Rabbi's election in 1913 he has on various occasions approached the different Ministries, and has hundreds of times received communications from them ... and it could not be otherwise. Viewing the Jewish community as primarily a religious body, all these government departments turn direct to the Ecclesiastical Head of that denomination, whenever a religious problem arises.
>
>   Thus, at the outbreak of hostilities, the Government requested the Chief Rabbi to take charge of all religious matters affecting

> members of the Jewish Faith in H.M's Forces ... as a general rule, the Chief Rabbi co-operates with the Board; but he has not hesitated to take an independent course when in his opinion the higher interests of Judaism and Jewry so demand. Two instances will make his position clear.
>
> a. In 1913 at the International Congress for the Protection of Girls and Women, the Chief Rabbi denounced the detestable 'Yellow ticket' policy of the Tzarist tyranny. He roused the conscience of the world against this unspeakable infamy, and was overwhelmed by congratulations from the European communities. He did not consult the Board, as he knew full well that it would not have consented to his course.
> b. In 1917, the Board was guilty of what Zionists call 'A great betrayal of Jewry'. It attempted to prevent the issuing of the Balfour Declaration, and officially informed the Government that Zionist aspirations were repugnant to Jewry. The Chief Rabbi publicly denounced their action, and helped to secure the support of Britain for the promulgation of the Jewish National Home ...
>
> Under your leadership, the Board is rendering excellent service ... In no sense, however, does this mean that the reins of Jewish religious education have been handed over by the Chief Rabbinate to the Board; and nothing that has been said will deflect him from taking any step which he deems essential for the religious welfare of Anglo-Jewry, and from fulfilling the sacred tasks of the High Office entrusted to him by the United Hebrew Congregations of the British Empire.[27]

If the Board of Deputies thought the Chief Rabbi was a spent force, they were disabused. His clear statement that he led, primarily, a religious body, reminded them that he was qualified to lead because he had the greater knowledge of Judaism.

On 10 May 1941 the Great Synagogue was destroyed in the Blitz. After more than 200 years the centre of Ashkenazi Judaism in Britain was no more. Admittedly a large proportion of the Jews in the East End had left for the more attractive suburbs, so that the Great had become isolated from the mainstream, but it was still held in great affection.

Hundreds attended a service in the ruins of the synagogue in September and 2,000–3,000 thronged nearby Creechurch Lane, where the first British synagogue of modern times had been established: 'The Chief Rabbi delivered his sermon vigorously and forcefully, and his powerful voice could be heard over the drone of the aeroplanes that occasionally passed over.'[28] His sermons continued to inspire. At Passover in 1942 he: 'spoke with insight, courage and vigour on the timely subject of civilian morale'.[29] Whatever Waley Cohen might have said, to Hertz's audience the Harrogate incident appeared to have had no long-term effects.

In 1941 Hertz broadcast over the BBC to the Jews in Europe,[30] and during the war he would broadcast at Passover and Rosh Hashanah. The recording of his broadcast at Pesach in 1942 is still extant.[31]

The scale and horror of the Final Solution had become known by then and Hertz talked about it in the broadcast. His view on German responsibility for the atrocities would be rejected by his community for many years thereafter, but the Chief Rabbi was, as usual, uninfluenced by other opinions. He said that he was prepared to excuse the fact that: 'millions of German nationals have all along approved of Nazi policies' and insisted that: 'punishment must be confined to the blood stained leaders'.[32] He insisted that only the Nazi leaders should be blamed for the horrors of the war and not the German people: 'Men and women who speak the language of Edmund Burke, do not draw up an indictment against a whole people'. (Burke, the brilliant eighteenth-century Irish politician warned about government tyrannizing minorities.)

He was addressing a community who knew that hundreds of thousands of Jews were being murdered in concentration camps, who had lost friends and relatives in the Blitz and who had every reason to hate Germans with an intense passion. Nevertheless Hertz told them that a crime committed by Nazis: 'does not justify vengeance on the whole German nation ... wholesale condemnation would be irrational'.[33] Hertz took the opinion of Jewish sages as a lodestone:

> Hillel's selection of 'Thou shalt love thy neighbour as thyself' ... as the 'whole of the Torah' is well known. Akiba, likewise, looked upon that Golden Rule as the Great Commandment. His companion, Ben Azzai ... selected for that pre-eminence the truth contained in Genesis v.1. 'This is the book of the generations of man' – not black, not white, not heathen, not Hebrew, but MAN.[34]

Everybody in his time acknowledged the power of Hertz as a speaker but it is more helpful in assessing his impact if the original material is available. Hertz had just four minutes in 1942 to pass on his message to his listeners; a message which the vast majority would not have wanted to hear.

Listening to the broadcast today, a number of conclusions can be drawn. Hertz did not coax, suggest or theorize. His is the voice of a strong leader, enunciating each word with clarity and switching his speed and emphasis, so that the listener is always wondering what will come next, rather than being turned off by an academic drone.

It is a powerful voice, giving instructions, and the delivery makes nonsense of Waley Cohen's suggestion that the Harrogate bomb had affected Hertz's mental capacity. There is no hint of an American accent, but just the faintest trace of Yiddish, for those who can recognize it. Hertz ends his sentences on the upbeat and he extends the words he wants to emphasize: 'immemorrrrrial'.

Even with only four minutes available, he manages a touch of humour. He talks about the length of time it will take to rebuild European culture after the Fascists: 'Remedies being proverbially slower than diseases.' He was near the end of his life but that could never be deduced from the broadcast. It was the voice of a prophet, not a follower.

Hertz was now leaving much of his pastoral work to Schonfeld. When he called for a week of Jewish Rededication in aid of his Jewish War Fund, it was Schonfeld who signed the letter to the British congregations as honorary secretary of the fund.

There continued to be a serious need for more money. Over the years half a million pounds was raised and spent by the CRREC on: 'rescue, relief and rehabilitation, on welfare among children, Servicemen, internees and others in need'.[35] (This amounts to some £20 million today.) Many methods were adopted but Schonfeld preferred to call on possible donors in person rather than write, a method that worked because he was very persuasive.

Only the Chief Rabbi could call for support from the whole community as so many congregations were not affiliated to the United Synagogue. The larger role of Schonfeld, however, appeared to the United's Honorary Officers to be a step towards undermining their authority. The recognition that Schonfeld was increasingly prepared to challenge the Jewish establishment provided additional fuel to their anger at his position.

They were soon to have a chance to fight back when Hertz and Schonfeld visited the Home Office on behalf of the North London *Yeshiva*. The Home Office sent a copy of the minutes of the meeting to Hertz at the United Synagogue. This wasn't his personal office and when the letter was opened by the officials, they found that the Home Office had referred to Schonfeld as the Deputy Chief Rabbi.

The United Synagogue immediately wrote back to say there was no Deputy Chief Rabbi: 'We think it important that you should be made aware that Dr Schonfeld holds no office under the United Synagogue and is not connected with any synagogal organization which participates in the maintenance of the Chief Rabbi or recognizes its authority.'[36]

A copy of the letter was sent to the Jewish Chronicle who commented that someone in the organization clearly wished to undermine Schonfeld. This was almost certainly Waley Cohen since nobody else would have had the authority to authorize such a letter. The *Jewish Chronicle* was equally heavy-handed in rebuttal, saying that if every official mistake was demolished with such a barrage of contradiction and with such absence of tact, good feeling and savoir faire, it wasn't going to help the cause.

With Hertz's support, Schonfeld threatened to sue the Honorary Officers for slander, as he had never suggested he was Deputy Chief Rabbi. For their part, the Honorary Officers considered relieving Hertz of his office, but came to no decision.[37] Waley Cohen cuttingly suggested on a number of occasions that Schonfeld take his place among the chaplains to the Forces, implying that he lacked the courage to do so. It would also, of course, have been a demotion. The truth was that Schonfeld risked his life on a number of occasions on forays to Europe to help rescue refugees before the war, and would do so again in the future.

In May 1941, in pursuit of his desire to concentrate on his Spiritist approach rather than the observance of the *mitzvot*, Waley Cohen arranged a meeting with a religious agenda at which all sections of the community were represented. In addition to Honorary Officers and officials of the United Synagogue, he invited Sephardim, Leonard Montefiore from the Reform and Rabbi Mattuck from the Liberals. Opposition to Waley Cohen's action came from Hertz and the Beth Din, and from the Board of Deputies who were now strongly Zionist and concerned that their political aims would now be watered down.

Robert Henriques represented Waley Cohen's views in his posthumous biography, describing the opposition as: 'an alliance of alien dogma, custom and superstition which had never before been any part of Judaism except in dark corners inside the ghettos of Eastern Europe'.[38]

Even as Hertz's ministry was drawing to a close, Waley Cohen's party simply couldn't appreciate that they were describing normative teachings of the Babylonian Talmud as: 'alien dogma, custom and superstition'. They were, of course, the *din*, and attempting to demonize it didn't alter that fact.

The less observant way of life of much of the British-Jewish community has occasionally been described as '*Minhag* Anglia', a nomenclature that seems to lend it legitimacy but which doesn't alter the rules. Hertz knew that abandoning any part of the *din* was a precedent for abandoning more of it, as had been proved on many occasions in the past by assimilationist movements.

As Aubrey Newman said in his commemorative lecture to mark the centenary of Hertz's birth in 1972: 'Dr Hertz is nowadays frequently presented as a paragon of mellowness and leniency in matters of Jewish law. This must be a case of wishful thinking.'[39]

Hertz had, in fact, said in 1942: 'Refusal to listen to that word of command on the part of the administration of the Orthodox community meant ... religious anarchy.'[40] He had repeated the message in a sermon at the Hampstead Synagogue, which had it printed. Behind the scenes, however, Waley Cohen persuaded the Hampstead Honorary Officers to destroy all the copies. Opposition to the Chief Rabbi had never before reached such a level.

NOTES

1. Aubrey Newman, *The United Synagogue, 1870–1970* (London: Routledge and Kegan Paul, 1976), p.156.
2. Chips Channon diary, 3 June 1943, in Ned Sherrin (ed.), *The Oxford Book of Humorous Quotations* (Oxford: Oxford University Press, 2009), p.344.
3. Joseph Herman Hertz, *Early and Late: Addresses, Messages, and Papers* (Hindhead: Soncino Press, 1943), p.156.
4. Sermon preached at the Hampstead Synagogue on 17 August 1940.
5. File 2805/4/5/54, London Metropolitan Archives.
6. Jeremy Schonfield private family archive.
7. Solomon Schonfeld, *Jewish Religious Education* (London: Jewish Secondary School Movement, 1943).
8. Derek Taylor, *Solomon Schonfeld: A Purpose in Life* (London and Portland, OR: Vallentine Mitchell, 2009), p.99.
9. Hertz, *Early and Late*, p.158.
10. Meir Persoff, *Faith Against Reason: Religious reform and the British Chief Rabbinate, 1840–1990* (London and Portland, OR: Vallentine Mitchell, 2008), p.247.
11. Letter from Chief Rabbi Hertz, File 2132, United Synagogue Archives, London Metropolitan Archives.
12. Ibid.
13. Jeremy Schonfield private family archive.
14. Ibid.
15. Taylor, *Solomon Schonfeld*, p.71.
16. The author in conversation with Jacob Schonfeld.
17. *Jewish Chronicle*, 18 January 1941.
18. Ibid.
19. *Jewish Chronicle*, 20 September 1940.

20. File 2132, United Synagogue Archive, London Metropolitan Archives.
21. Letter from Hertz to Waley Cohen, 5 April 1943, File 2132, United Synagogue Archive, London Metropolitan Archives.
22. Joseph Herman Hertz, *Transactions of the Jewish Historical Society of England*, Vol.15 (London: JHSE, 1939/45), p.179.
23. File 2132, London Metropolitan Archives.
24. Many famous Italian hoteliers and restaurateurs who had been in Britain for up to thirty years were interned. The author's uncle, who had arrived in 1895, had never bothered to get naturalized. He was arrested, and it required a policeman friend to vouch for him in order to avoid internment.
25. David Cesarani and Tony Kushner (eds), *The Internment of Aliens in the Twentieth Century* (London: Frank Cass, 1993), p.86.
26. Solomon Schonfeld, *Message to Jewry* (London: Jewish Secondary School Movement, 1958).
27. Hertz, *Early and Late*, p.233.
28. *Jewish Chronicle*, 26 September 1941.
29. *Jewish Chronicle*, 10 April 1942.
30. *Jewish Telegraphic Agency*, 11 April 1941.
31. Chief Rabbi's broadcast, 6 April 1942, British Library Sound Archives.
32. Ibid.
33. Ibid.
34. Ibid.
35. Pamela Shatzkes, *Holocaust and Rescue: Impotent or Indifferent? Anglo-Jewry 1938–1945* (Basingstoke: Palgrave, 2002), p.84.
36. Taylor, *Solomon Schonfeld*, p.86.
37. Benjamin J. Elton, *Britain's Chief Rabbis and the Religious Character of Anglo-Jewry, 1880–1970* (Manchester: Manchester University Press, 2009), p.224.
38. Robert Henriques, *Sir Robert Waley Cohen, 1877–1952* (London: Secker and Warburg, 1966), p.386.
39. *Jewish Chronicle*, 29 September 1972.
40. *Jewish Chronicle*, 18 January 1946.

Chapter Fifteen

The Final Years

When Germany invaded Russia, Hertz's long-standing criticism of the Communist regime had to be abandoned for the sake of the war effort. At a public meeting in September 1943, Hertz recognised the Russian contribution to defeating Hitler: 'If Russia had not made her immortal stand, Jews in this country would by now have been led off in death trains.'[1] By contrast, he said that in the past: 'the silence of large sections in the country had been taken by the Nazis as an encouragement to continue their techniques of annihilation'.[2]

All of a sudden prominent Russian Jews appeared in London. Shloime Mikhoels, the director of the Yiddish State Theatre, had a long meeting with Hertz, Barnett Janner MP and Dr Selig Brodetzky. Hertz reported that Mikhoels had 'expressed sentiments to which no Jew, no matter how pious, could take exception'.[3] He also noted: 'that anti-Semitism was a crime in the USSR'.[4] Even if everybody knew how much the Russians had been doing to eliminate religion as a whole throughout their territories, the official picture had now changed.

Faced with the horror of Nazi exterminations, the Jewish efforts in Britain, on behalf of their continental brethren, remained fragmented. The Zionists still wanted to link the plight of the Jews with the restrictions on Jewish immigration into Palestine. That not-so-hidden agenda took precedence over everything else. The elections for the Board of Deputies in 1943 had returned a Zionist majority and Laski had been replaced by Selig Brodetzky as president. Meanwhile, the official Jewish bodies muddied the water with large, impractical ideas.

For example, Brodetsky wanted all the Jews in Europe to be designated British-protected, a decision which would have been ignored by the Nazis and might have prejudiced the safety of those on the Continent who were genuinely British subjects. Another proposal in early 1943 asked that: 'The German government should be told, through some appropriate channel, that Jews, especially women and children, should be allowed to leave all countries under German control.'[5]

Exactly which channel to use for conveying such demands was conveniently left open for the government to decide, as well as how to ensure that Hitler paid any attention to such instructions. It was also considered the government's responsibility to work out how to provide the vast tonnage of shipping the Jewish pressure groups would need if they were able to move the Jews to safety.

In 1942 the Board of Deputies created a Consultative Committee to try to coordinate the interested parties and to make a common approach to the government. It met regularly for six months, but as everybody continued to try to influence the authorities individually as well, it fell apart in recriminations.

Everybody's intentions were admirable. It was just that the recommendations were grandiose and unrealistic. The Jewish academics, scientists and businessmen in authority were dealing with situations for which nothing could have prepared them. It is easy with hindsight to come up with ideas that might have been more practical than those adopted. Even as early as the end of 1940, nothing could have stopped the Nazis perpetrating the Holocaust.

Throughout the war, efforts were made to enable Jews to reach countries where they would not be persecuted. Most of these initiatives came to nothing. Only Jewish refugees in such far-flung havens as South America or Shanghai could be readily supported. Over 400 rabbis and theological students in Shanghai were legitimised by Hertz by describing them as the greatest theological college in World Jewry. After the war 500 exit permits were issued for Sweden by their authorities to a group that eventually reached America. Hertz also tried to persuade the Irish government to issue visas and had a meeting with the Irish commissioner in London for that purpose. Unfortunately it didn't produce any results.

Schonfeld tried to obtain visas for Mauritius for any Jews who could reach neutral countries in Europe, such as Spain or Switzerland. Every Jewish refugee body in Britain harangued the government on behalf of their brethren. There were only small successes, but each was highly significant to the people who benefited. Some neutral diplomats on the Continent had issued visas for Jews which their countries refused to honour. The Chief Rabbi's Religious Emergency Council (CRREC) took up the cases with the South American and other governments concerned and many hundreds were successfully rescued as a consequence.

The British Foreign Office promised that everything would be done that was 'compatible with the requirements of military operations',[6] which enabled them to avoid doing anything at all. In its defence, it was, however, asked to consider a number of impractical and naive solutions. The World Jewish Congress and the Jewish Agency, for example, asked it to extract two million Jews from Europe and the JA invited it to 'forget legalities and make Palestine into a Jewish sanctuary'.[7]

Even so, as Richard Law, the civil servant at the Foreign Office handling the response, remarked: 'We would be in an appalling position if these stories should prove to have been true and we have done nothing whatever about them.'[8] That was precisely what happened but the Allies needed to stall and had little difficulty in dragging out discussions until public interest waned.

The government was, admittedly, embarrassed by the United Nations condemnation of the massacres. That was read out in the House of Commons. Sir Henry (Chips) Channon MP recorded the moment in his diaries:

> Jimmy de Rothschild (Liberal MP for the Isle of Ely) rose and with immense dignity, and with his voice vibrating with emotion, spoke for five minutes in moving tones on the plight of these peoples. There were tears in his eyes and I feared that he might break down; the House caught his mood and was deeply moved. Somebody suggested that we stand in silence to pay our respects to those suffering peoples, and the House as a whole rose and stood for a few frozen seconds. It was a fine moment.[9]

Schonfeld was realistic. He understood the government's position and tried to circumvent the problem. If no declaration would pass if it included offering refuge in Palestine, then perhaps Britain should promise, 'temporary refuge in its own territories or in territories under its control'?[10] There was support from no fewer than 277 MPs for a motion to that effect in the House, but the Board of Deputies would have none of it. Brodetsky, as a Zionist, would not support a motion which left out Palestine, and had been asked by the American Zionist organization to have the measure stifled.

Brodetsky had another reason for opposing the motion. He continued to dislike any attempt to influence the government except through the medium of the Board of Deputies. They were the official conduit between British Jews and parliament, and Brodetsky felt he had to hold the line.

As Schonfeld supporters worked for the motion, the Board of Deputies lobbied against it. Supporters were now, naturally, confused and started to withdraw their support. The motion failed and Schonfeld, correctly, blamed the Board of Deputies, saying that the sabotage by Jews of his efforts to help Jews had met with success. Indeed, for the Board to put its own personal prestige ahead of the remotest chance of rescuing Jews on the Continent was inexcusable.

This internal squabbling made it easier for the government to reject approaches it didn't like, since it was not clear whether they represented the views of a majority of the Jewish community. In fact the House of Commons motion would probably have failed anyway, because the government felt that a statement on the subject by Clement Attlee in January 1943 covered the ground more fully than Schonfeld's draft.

In truth, the British could do little. They were fighting for survival and the oppressed Jews were not even British citizens. They also wanted to deprive the Axis powers of foreign currency to fight the war, rather than bribe them to let Jews escape the concentration camps. They had military targets for bombing raids, rather than railway lines leading to concentration camps. Moreover, it remained the case that if they made special efforts for Jews, they would be providing the Nazis with propaganda that the war was merely a Jewish international conspiracy.

The British authorities were committed to surviving the Nazi onslaught and they had few resources to devote to anything else. Even if the Nazis had been prepared to release prisoners in exchange for their own nationals in captivity, the British would have wanted their own citizens back rather than non-British Jews. Hertz knew this, but worn down with grief, he found it difficult to accept that he could only attack the enemy from the pulpit and by continuing to support the war effort.

In Christian as well as in Jewish circles in Britain, there was frustration that so little could be done. From this desire to show support for the victims came the formation of the Council of Christians and Jews in March 1942.

Another reason the organization was proposed was the high regard in which the Chief Rabbi was held in Church circles. One Archbishop of Canterbury, Randall Davidson, had said of Hertz's *Book of Jewish Thoughts* that he couldn't lay it down without reading it from end to end. Revd W.W. (Bill) Simpson, who became the general secretary of the Council, was particularly impressed by the Chief Rabbi and said of Hertz: 'His *Affirmations*, as an exponent of Orthodox Jewry was as superb as his criticism of those who trod the "New Paths" of Reform and Liberal Judaism were trenchant. He was neither a respecter of persons nor a puller of punches.'[11]

Hertz was not sure he wanted to be a part of the new body. It reminded him of attempts by the Liberal Synagogue to find common ground with the Church in creating the London Society of Jews and Christians. He made it clear that he disliked arranging 'Jewish-Christian conferences'. He had set out his views before a distinguished audience at the Lucien Wolf Memorial Lecture in 1938: 'we should never forget that fraternization is neither desired nor desirable'. He repeated his position at the World Congress of Faiths in London in 1943:

> A noted historian of Hellenism reminds us that ancient Rome would have been quite prepared to give the God of Israel a place in her pantheon. It was Israel, he said, that refused such religious annexation. The One God taught by Judaism is alone the living God, was Israel's reply. And Israel has, throughout the ages, steadfastly refused all 'entangling alliances' with other faiths.[12]

Hertz was even ambivalent about the idea of a United Synagogue for Britain, to create a more inclusive national Orthodox body. He was totally even-handed, however, with regard to other religions. A congregant in London had once written to him to ask for his support in complaining about the ringing of church bells in his neighbourhood, which he found irritating. In his reply, Hertz rejected any attempt to interfere in the way any religion practised its faith.

A prime mover of the Council was William Temple, Archbishop of York and, from 1942, Archbishop of Canterbury. Temple was prepared to accept the Chief Rabbi's position and, over lunch with Hertz in November 1941, persuaded him to become one of the four joint presidents of the Council, with himself, the moderator of the General Assembly of the Church of Scotland and the moderator of the Free Church Federal Council.

Cardinal Hinsley, the head of the Catholic Church in Britain, also had reservations. He was very willing to condemn anti-Semitism, but was unsure how Rome would feel about an association with a body like the Council. He declined initially to become a joint president, but was eventually persuaded to do so.

A central point on which Hertz and Temple agreed was that the Council's suggestion that schools should in future give a fair presentation of Judaism was completely unacceptable. Hertz felt that this might be considered an unwarranted intrusion by Jews into Christian religious instruction. Both clerics took the view that 'definiteness and distinctiveness' were necessary between the faiths. Hertz made sure that there would be no hint of missionary work in the Council's proceedings.

There was, however, a degree of distaste in 1941 when the Bishop of Oxford publicly baptised a Jewish refugee and his family of four at

Easter, appearing to follow a tradition of baptising Jews at that time of the year. Such triumphalism was not appreciated in Jewish circles.

Waley Cohen was particularly helpful in creating the Council, raising the funds for it, and acting as its honorary treasurer until his death, but he now suggested that United Synagogue ministers should speak in church if invited to do so. He didn't tell Hertz that he was going to raise the issue. When Hertz learned of it, he made it very clear that he objected strongly, seeing it as another step towards an ecumenical approach to religion.

Knowing Hertz's views, the United Synagogue Honorary Officers tried to avoid his becoming involved. When the Dollis Hill minister was invited by the BBC to broadcast with Bill Simpson on the principles common to Judaism and Christianity, Frank Samuels ordered a draft of the proposed discussion to be prepared, so that he and Waley Cohen could decide whether the Chief Rabbi should be consulted. The attempted side-lining of Hertz was becoming quite blatant.

Hertz was also concerned that no representatives of Orthodox Jewry had been proposed for the Council of Christians and Jews Executive committee. He considered Waley Cohen didn't fall into that category. It took the chairman of the Council to reach agreement with him on a solution, although the financial side of the Council remained in the care of Waley Cohen. The Council was launched to general approval in October 1942, the year that Hertz celebrated his 70th birthday.

The community marked the occasion by planting the Hertz Forest, the largest in the Western Galilee, on a hillside near Kibbutz Hanita, where his daughter-in-law, Irene, had family. A memorial stone bench was dedicated to Rose Hertz by Rebecca Sieff, the first president of the Women's International Zionist Organization.

With the creation of a Council of Christians and Jews, occasions for disagreement between religious leaders might have been expected to disappear, but it took only a few months for Hertz to take the Archbishop of Canterbury to task in the columns of *The Times*. His Grace had told the Bank Officers Guild that 'Mosaic law forbade Israelites to lend at interest to a brother Israelite, but those ethics did not extend beyond the tribal community'.[13]

Calling the address 'admirable', Hertz suggested that His Grace would: 'welcome the following clarification of the meaning of the scriptural words' which showed that if a foreign merchant passing through Palestine in Biblical times charged interest, then the Israelite could also charge him interest. Otherwise: 'And if thy brother be waxen poor … then thou shalt relieve him; yea, though he be a stranger or a sojourner; ... take thou no usury of him or increase. (Lev. XXV, 35, 36)'.[14]

Hertz was equally concerned about the shortcomings emerging in his own community. Accusations that Jews were engaging in black market activities were accurate, if often very exaggerated. The black market had sprung up to make profits from scarce and rationed goods. The community did not want to discuss the subject in public but Hertz did. He made it the theme of a sermon at the St John's Wood Synagogue in May 1942. His condemnation was published in *The Times*: 'Twenty-seven centuries ago the prophet, Amos, indignantly denounced cornering the market in foods, rebuking the rapacious merchants for their greed, their dishonesty and their meanness.'[15]

There was a need to improve the image of the community at the time. Such anti-Semites as there were still tried to present the war as a Jewish conspiracy. Hertz would criticize Jewish black-marketeers but he would deal firmly with the anti-Semites' suggestion that they were the main transgressors in the black market. Hertz defended the community against this, saying in another sermon at the St John's Wood synagogue: 'Jews form but a relatively small portion of the 47,000 offenders prosecuted under this head [the black market] and yet some enterprising journalists seem to speak of this transgression of the law as an exclusively Jewish crime.'[16]

The fate of Jewish children not under his care also continued to worry Hertz throughout the war, and he fought for the Guardianship Act which was finally passed in 1944. This established that Lord Gorell would chair a committee who would have guardianship rights over all refugee children in Britain, reducing the danger of their being baptised, but too late for a considerable number of them. Gorell was chair of the Movement for the Care of Children from Germany and was an admirable individual, but Hertz was the natural choice of the Association of Jewish Refugees. He had asked for the responsibility in 1943 but the task fell to Gorell.

In the King's New Years' honours list in January 1943, Hertz was made a Companion of Honour (CH). The Order had an original membership of 17 in 1917 when it was founded. Now its membership was increased to 65, but it remained an extremely select group of notables, whose qualification for the award was that they had performed services of national importance. The CH is ranked just below the Order of Merit, but the membership in 1943 still included Winston Churchill and General Smuts of South Africa, two statesman who had first met Hertz forty years before.

The honour is recommended by the prime minister, and Churchill might well have remembered the young rabbi with whom he shared a train carriage on his way from capture by the Boers to Lourenço Marques in 1899. George V had created the Order in 1917 and Queen Mary might also have remembered the rabbi who welcomed her to Natal when she was Princess May.

For Hertz and the community it was hugely significant. The Royal family had shown friendship towards Hermann Adler by making him a Companion of the Victorian Order in 1909, but Hertz was the first Jewish Companion of Honour, and was now recognised nationally as well as by his own community. The badge of the Order has the inscription: 'In action faithful and in honour clear.' Hertz could reflect that he had lived up to that description when he received the award from George VI in February in a private audience. The King offered Hertz dinner, and it is reported that they sat down in the royal quarters for a companionable meal of fresh vegetables eaten uncooked, and discussed the world.[17]

The *Manchester Guardian* added a relevant note: 'It is not only a personal tribute to Rabbi Hertz but a timely expression of sympathy for the afflictions of the Jews.'[18] The enormity of the Holocaust was being finally exposed and the *Jewish Chronicle* pointed out that, whereas Judaism was being denigrated by the Nazis, its leader in Britain had now been honoured by the government.

That leader's health was, however, failing. The pressure of work had undermined his resistance: 'He was an old man before his time and when sickness began to pursue him he had little power of resistance.'[19]

An immense volume of work was undertaken by the CRREC and Schonfeld's report for 1942 included representations to nine government departments and four overseas embassies. The Jewish Servicemen's Kosher Food Service provided a regular fortnightly delivery to Jews in the armed forces, and also now to American forces based in England. At Passover the Service sent *matzot*, Haggadot and food to thousands, and for the New Year the CRREC sent out the necessary *shofarim*, the ram's horn. Hertz also set up a Literary Fund to provide prayer books and the Ministry of Food asked the CRREC to supervise the distribution of *lulavim* and *etrogim* (four symbolic species) for Succot.

Regular monthly grants were provided for a number of European religious leaders, although there were always insufficient funds to maintain the desired standard of support. For those still stranded in Europe little could be done, though Hertz and Schonfeld went to see the Russian ambassador to plead for Polish rabbis and students who had fled to Russia. The ambassador agreed, on behalf of his government, to allow them to go to Palestine.

Hertz could plead in the residences of ambassadors, but his relations with his own Honorary Officers were now extremely bad. He wrote to say that, on doctor's orders, he would no longer attend meetings and would see them only individually. He told them it would be many months before this situation would change. In the attempt to wear him down, their criticism had now reached a level of such pettiness that he was accused of using United Synagogue envelopes improperly for his personal correspondence.

Hertz had declared 13 December 1942 a Day of Mourning and Fasting and had discussed it with the foreign secretary, but with little result. In Britain the community's finances were always close to being overwhelmed. The CRREC alone had to maintain 985 individuals, to find refugees jobs, provide accommodation and arrange hospitality. For instance, as far as the needs of the internees were concerned, in 1940 the first Jewish cemetery on the Isle of Man was consecrated.

The CRREC negotiated for the release of internees in Canada and Australia as well as in Britain. Children remained of particular importance and the Joint Committee for the Religious Education and Welfare of Refugee Children was formed as part of Hertz's Central Committee for Jewish Refugees.

There would never be sufficient funds so, when he lacked resources, Schonfeld had to fall back on bluff. Reference was made in the CRREC Annual Report to the activities of the American and Canadian Chapters of the Council. The American Chapter started with only one member, Schonfeld's brother, Moses, who had emigrated before the war. Schonfeld covered over the cracks which were inevitable if a mammoth series of problems were to be effectively tackled by a small organization. Under the circumstances Schonfeld performed miracles. The total annual budget for the year was about £20,000, of which half came from the government. The other £10,000 had to be raised from the *community* which wasn't easy in wartime.

In 1943 Dayan Gollop, the senior chaplain to the Forces, had a heart attack. Waley Cohen and Donald Cohen, the secretary of the Jewish War Services Committee, went to see him and reported back that he had asked for Revd Leslie Edgar to act for him in his absence. Edgar had been acting as his assistant and knew the bureaucratic demands. There is a major difference, however, between 'Assistant to' and 'Assistant'. The attempt was made by Waley Cohen to effect the transition and Edgar started to sign his letters: 'Acting for the Senior Jewish Chaplain.'

There were, however, eighteen Orthodox chaplains at the time and just one Liberal – Edgar. It was another attempt to side-track Hertz, who had not been consulted, and said that: 'as Orthodox Jewry furnished 97 per cent of the Jews in HM Forces, the Senior Chaplain in control of army religious activities should be Orthodox'.[20] Even if that percentage was on the high side, he was right about a substantial majority being Orthodox.

The title gave Edgar an apparently senior role, and implied that the Chief Rabbi considered him a suitable, if temporary, replacement for the senior Jewish chaplain. The religious legitimacy which Hertz would appear to give the Liberal movement by this move was precisely what he had been fighting against for thirty years. Waley Cohen never gave up trying.

The Committee responded that Edgar had in no way replaced Gollop, although the *Jewish Chronicle* did refer to him as the: 'Temporary Senior Chaplain to the British Forces'.[21] Given the opportunity, he would have doubtless moved slowly into that role. Edgar, as a Liberal minister, was later reported to have said that 'Traditional Judaism is unable to face the realities of our times'[22] and was unlikely to support the Orthodox party line.

Hertz wrote to the Army Council, appointing Revd Arthur Barnett to be *locum tenens* for Gollop, which decision the Committee attempted to overturn. Waley Cohen, Neville Laski and a number of other senior figures were invited to a meeting of the Committee in late November 1943 at which only Bernard Homa supported Hertz. Nevertheless, the Chief Rabbi had his own way. He had already threatened to dissolve the Committee if they didn't do what he wanted, and nobody doubted that he would keep his word. Everybody knew that the Ministry of Defence would support the Chief Rabbi over the opinions of lay members of a Committee appointed by him.

The eventual replacement for Gollop was Israel Brodie, who had been a chaplain in both world wars and would become Chief Rabbi after Hertz. Waley Cohen had been overruled again in his battle to bring the Progressives into the mainstream of the community. When Hertz died, one of the first things Waley Cohen did was replace the Committee with one on which the Progressives did have representation.

Solomon Schonfeld wrote to Homa after the bruising meeting:

> Dr Hertz, who, as you will understand, is rather knocked out after Wednesday's drawn-out meeting, asks me to write to you to express his personal thanks for your co-operation. The staunch and statesmanlike manner in which you defended the Orthodox point of view was the saving feature of the whole proceedings. Dr Hertz tells me that he could not have done anything without your co-operation.[23]

It was in 1944 that the Butler Education Act appeared, including a promise to help religious schools, which included Jewish ones, as a result of Hertz's negotiations. To take advantage of this, the Chief Rabbi arranged a Communal Conference on the Reconstruction of Jewish Education in Great Britain. He was, unfortunately, too ill to take part in it.

The Chief Rabbi's health was not strong and opponents within the United Synagogue sought to take advantage of this. It was not surprising that Hertz felt that: 'he had no one to fall back on at all, and he had, therefore, made Dr Schonfeld his right hand man in everything'.[24] The religious and administrative parts of the United Synagogue were headed by an increasingly dysfunctional leadership and relations between Hertz and Waley Cohen had so deteriorated that delegations of friends of each used to meet, rather than the two principals. Sometimes this worked but often the deadlock remained. A further meeting was requested but Hertz had eventually had enough and replied:

> These meetings have in the past been singularly barren of results. You have rarely granted any request of mine, no matter how urgent its need for Judaism or Jewry at large … Notwithstanding all this, I assured the Honorary Officers of my readiness, as soon as my health permitted, to resume personal meetings, provided there was preliminary rectification of crying injustices towards me.[25]

Waley Cohen's was positively bellicose. He wrote: 'The spirit of your letter is so defamatory and hostile that the Honorary Officers cannot but regard it as a refusal of any intention of friendly consultation.'[26]

Hertz and Waley Cohen had now been working in the same organization for thirty years, but the United Synagogue president still hadn't accepted Hertz's understanding of his role. In another letter to Hertz, Waley Cohen insisted: 'The Chief Rabbi is charged by the very nature and terms of his appointment so to carry on his duties as to promote peace and concord within the whole community.'[27]

In fact, Hertz's main duty was to ensure that the United Synagogue continued to be an Orthodox community, accepting Jewish law. So far apart were the two sides that one United Synagogue treasurer described the community as 'rabbi ridden'.[28]

Hertz was still, occasionally, prepared to overrule his Beth Din and Dayan Abramsky. In 1943, when they had instructed a couple to wait ninety days before getting married, the youngsters appealed to Hertz who told them to go ahead whenever they wished. The Beth Din were displeased and Hertz said diplomatically that he had been unable to contact them at the time, which was a pretty lame excuse.

On other occasions he supported the Beth Din against the Honorary Officers. A case in point concerned the Finchley Synagogue in 1945, and was a blatant attempt by the United Synagogue Honorary Officers to undermine the authority of the Beth Din. A warden at Finchley had slandered the *chazzan* (cantor), who went to court and won. The warden wanted the synagogue to pay the damages and another warden asked the Beth Din to settle the argument. The Beth Din asked the wardens to attend the court to give their points of view but they refused and the Honorary Officers of the United Synagogue supported them.

The dayanim wrote to them that: 'we should not have joined the Beth Din and we do not consider it an honour to be associated with such a body'.[29] Waley Cohen and Frank Samuel held that as it was the synagogue's finances which were under consideration, it was not a religious matter in which the Beth Din should be involved. This showed their ignorance of the role of a Beth Din; *Batei Din* over the centuries had always been called on to settle commercial disputes between Jews as rabbinic writings show.

The United Synagogue Council met to discuss the situation and the Beth Din, chaired by Hertz, issued a ruling that: 'we deem it our duty to state that in Jewish law it is the bounden religious duty of any Jew or Jewish organization to obey a summons of the Beth Din of his community, whatever be the subject at issue'.[30] The National courts were the only ones with enforceable authority to make such demands, but a religious organization like the United Synagogue could surely be expected to support its own court.

In a stormy meeting of the United Synagogue Council, Frank Samuel said that: 'either the secular power of the community were in the hands of the laity or of the Rabbinate. It seems that the Chief Rabbi was under influence that hadn't previously applied'.[31] Hertz, it was hinted again, was a tool of the dayanim. Waley Cohen said he had 'evil forebodings' if it was agreed that, as the Chief Rabbi had laid down, the Finchley issue was a religious matter.[32] The meeting broke up in acrimony without a decision being made.

When it reassembled later in the month, the Honorary Officers who had been stoutly defending the Finchley Synagogue, announced that they had noted a new factor. As Waley Cohen said: 'they had been much impressed by the suggestion that had not occurred to them before, that the Finchley Synagogue's Honorary Officers' unwillingness to go before the Beth Din might be construed as a discourtesy to, or lack of respect for, the Beth Din. The last thing that the Honorary Officers or Finchley would wish'.[33] The Honorary Officers had taken soundings and knew that the mood of the Council was not to support them against the Chief Rabbi. They withdrew to fight another day. It was agreed unanimously that Finchley would call on the Beth Din.

The authority of the dayanim had been maintained but it had been a battle. Hertz's view of the ideal rabbi was summed up in his address at the Jews' College Speech Day in 1943. He said: 'The primal demand upon the students who seek instruction within its walls is loyalty in life and in death, to the Torah and Tradition of Israel, and unconditional obedience to its commandments.' He went on to quote Solomon Schechter who had said: 'It permeates the whole of your life. It demands control over all your actions, and interferes even with your menu.'[34]

In November the president of the Federation of Synagogues was sentenced to six months imprisonment for forging an identity card, using a false name and attempting to bribe a police officer. It was the end of an era for Morry Davis, who had dominated the Federation for fifteen years.

The state of the Federation, according to its critics at a meeting held after the court case, was lamentable. One member said: 'Their ministers, badly paid before the war, were many of them without a home now. The same applied to readers. Synagogues were locked because they had no membership. The older generation was dying out and the young had drifted away. And the reason was sheer neglect by those responsible for their 60,000 members.'[35]

Another lamented: 'They could have made a place of honour for the Federation within the community. Instead of which they had caused the Federation to become a byword for incompetence and incongruity.'[36]

The public image of the United Synagogue as an embodiment of rectitude, led by a famous and respected Chief Rabbi, cemented the leadership of the organization within the British Jewish community. Hertz still found the energy to canvas for his own choice of president for the Federation and Aaron Wright was duly elected. He even retained the strength to inspire an audience. In May 1944 at a service of mourning and prayer at Bevis Marks synagogue for the victims of the Warsaw Ghetto, Hertz's account was heart-rendering. He spoke of the Polish Jews: 'They were given only one-fifth of the quantity of food required to maintain life. It was a diet for death; so much so that in 1940, of Warsaw's 500,000 Jews, no less than 60,000 died of starvation. Moreover tens of thousands were being deported to labour camps. Of these deportees, not one ever returned alive.'[37]

The Warsaw Ghetto, the 'largest Jewish Kehillah in Europe had been reduced to 40,000 souls',[38] yet:

> The Nazi troopers who came on Passover eve for the usual number of victims for deportation were met by a fusillade on all sides and died in the flames of their own exploded tanks ... the surviving defenders barricaded themselves in factories, houses and streets; and desperately contested every inch of ground – till food and weapons failed them. They killed one thousand of the enemy during the six weeks that they had held their grounds, and they fought and died to the last man.[39]

The sermon had the vitality of a war correspondent and its content could move any audience. So much for rumours about the Chief Rabbi's failing physical and mental health. Hertz hadn't finished though:

> Thus, although the Nazi killing of thousands daily began early in 1941, it was October 29th 1942, before the lay leaders of Anglo-Jewry arranged a public protest meeting. Some of these leaders were quite distressed even over the Day of Mourning and Prayer I proclaimed in the December following. I need not now comment on such Olympic calm, strange reticence and heathen indifference. Suffice it to say, that they were not calculated to stir the men at the helm of the political universe to speedy action in human salvage.[40]

The leaders in question, who would have been in the congregation, should have been extremely embarrassed.

The eventual liberation of the concentration camps revealed the special needs of some of the surviving remnant. Those of the ultra-Orthodox weren't the same as those who were less Orthodox or not Orthodox at all. Rabbi Eli Munk, a distinguished leader in the strictly Orthodox world, was just one who tried to help the very Orthodox to follow the *mitzvot* again: the CRREC sent kosher food, *tefillin*, prayer books, *taleisim* and *Sifrei Torah*. One of the rabbis attached to the British forces, Rabbi Baumgarten, listened to the appeals of the ultra-Orthodox and obtained permission from the army authorities to build a *mikveh*.

A *mikveh* is an essential element of an Orthodox marriage and even in the appalling world of the camps, some couples had fallen in love and survived. The commitment of the Orthodox was such that, lacking warm clothing, medicines, suitable buildings and innumerable other necessities of life, what they asked for was a *mikveh*.

When the camps started to be liberated, Schonfeld organised over a dozen mobile synagogue ambulances, lorries fitted out with kosher food, medical supplies, prayer books, a Torah scroll and a kitchen. The first was consecrated by Hertz in November 1944 at the Egerton Road Synagogue in London. The Chief Rabbi quoted, as pertinently as usual: 'and when he (Jacob) saw the wagons that Joseph had sent to carry him, the spirit of Jacob, their father, revived' (Genesis 45.27). In February 1945 20,000 tons of kosher food was sent to France.

In January 1945, Hertz finally got it all off his chest. He wrote to tell the Honorary Officers of the United Synagogue exactly what he thought of them. If physically he was by now frail, he retained his command of devastating prose:

> Having disposed of those portions of your letter which deal, or evade dealing with the Finchley Synagogue case, I must not neglect answering the other charges you level against me.
>
> You stigmatise my letter as 'the culminating effort to exercise a dictatorship in disregard of the constitution of the United Synagogue.' This is odd; it attributes to me the bearing and manner of 'dictatorship' which is notoriously characteristic of one of your own body.
>
> You wisely give no details; but, as it is a libellous charge, I must request you to furnish me with a list of those dictatorial efforts. And I assume you will accompany each item in that list with concrete details, and some evidence for the allegations made.
>
> In the meantime you assure me that the authority of the Chief Rabbi 'has always been recognised and maintained by the Honorary Officers'. This assurance that you give me sounds like mockery. In confirmation, I need but bring a few memories which will clearly point out on which side real, and not imaginary, dictatorship is to be found.
>
> (a) You may still remember the abortive attempt made to destroy Jews' College by the introduction of an unorthodox 'Academy'. I fought that proposal with all my might because I deemed it fatal to Judaism; and the overwhelming majority of British Jews, whether within or without the United Synagogue, fervently applauded my stand. Not so the Honorary Officers of the United Synagogue. In that historic conflict, all the then Honorary Officers publicly voted against me.
>
> (b) But to come to more recent cases of 'dictatorship'.
>
> 1. In October 1943 Sir Robert appointed, without my

knowledge, a minister of the Liberal synagogue as temporary senior chaplain in circumstances that made it probable that he would become the permanent head of the Jewish chaplaincy department, at any rate 'to the end of the war'. As my protest was disregarded, I appealed to the Army Council, with the result that Rabbi Brodie is now the occupant of that responsible office.

2. When, three years ago, the Hampstead synagogue printed a sermon of mine in which I urged the duties of kashrut and obedience to authority in Judaism, Sir Robert ordered the destruction of the whole edition of that printed sermon. I have never found out how it was destroyed, whether by fire or otherwise. 'Please don't press me' piteously pleaded the *parnass* [warden] when I asked him for details. At any rate, never before has a British Chief Rabbi's sermon been suppressed by the lay administrators of the community.

3. In 1939, Sir Robert would not consent to my giving a Passover address to thousands of German refugees at Richborough Camp. I placed the matter before the Marquis of Reading, the Chairman of the Central Council. Sir Robert was *ordered* to invite me to give the address. This is further evidence of the loyalty to the Rabbinate on the part of the President of the United Synagogue!

4. Even stranger is the following act of all the honorary officers. When, as a result of the dispersion from the blitzed metropolis, United Synagogue groups sprang up in central and southern England, I asked to be furnished with a list of those associate synagogues for the purpose of pastoral visitation. I received an official refusal. This was an astounding reply to have sent, and I called attention to it at the next meeting with you, in vain. So I went to Mr. Lionel de Rothschild ... and asked him point-blank whether he really wished me to take legal action. The list duly arrived.

This ardent desire to shut the doors of United Synagogue houses of worship in the face of the Chief Rabbi was accompanied by an attempt to eliminate me from the executive of the educational organizations. This was undertaken by several of the honorary officers, who decided against requiring the approval of the Chief Rabbi for syllabuses of instruction, and also against his certification of teachers. As I could not consent to such monstrous proposals, the whole matter had to be placed before the public, and the President of the Board of Deputies had to intervene before you came to see that Jewish religious education was one of those 'subsidiary charities' of the United Synagogue which are 'under the supervision and control of the Chief Rabbi.' (Deed of Foundation 1871).

All the above instances – and they could be multiplied tenfold – show but too plainly how little the eight signatories of the last letter to me respect the rights and office of the Chief Rabbi. It seems that when you complain of the Chief Rabbi's 'dictatorship' you are adopting the all-too-human device of ascribing *our* failings to those whom we desire to discredit.

(c) You never tire of reiterating that 'the authority over financial and secular matters is vested solely in the council.' Everyone agrees, but you are not satisfied with this. You maintain, in effect, that whenever in any human situation a financial factor enters – and where does it not enter? – there the religious guidance of the Chief Rabbi is 'impertinent interference'.

Thus, in September 1938, I ruled that a male proselyte who had not undergone *milah* [circumcision] could not become a member of the United Synagogue.

I am informed on high authority that when Sir Robert heard of this ruling, he fairly fumed over 'priestly dictatorship'.

I soon received a curt communication from him, telling me that admission to synagogue membership was a 'financial matter' and was no concern of the Chief Rabbi, and that the secretary of the synagogue in question had been instructed to disregard the interference of the Chief Rabbi, and to proceed with the membership admission. Though eventually, after I had met you, Sir Robert retreated from the untenable position taken up, there were the usual table bangings.

This *milah* incident left an unpleasant memory behind it - namely the readiness on the part of the honorary officers to abolish even the Abrahamic covenant for a membership fee. Such definition of the financial came as a complete surprise to me, and fully justified me in my lament that there are leaders in Anglo-Jewry who, so to speak, are ready to tear down the Tables of the Law from the portals of our synagogues and replace them by the balance sheet.

Your personal hostility to me leads you to defame me even to Government departments. I need not recall your Home Office denunciation. Though you proudly refer to it even in yours of 14 March, it was something distinctly damaging to the Jewish name, and against all ethical teaching. 'Thou shalt not bear false witness against thy neighbour.'

> But enough. There is little more that I could say to induce you to give up your Quixotic fight against the windmills of 'priestly dictatorship'. It is pure hallucination.[41]

Hertz had his facts right, but as the war drew to a close, he was an old and tired man. Not just physically overwhelmed by the pace he still set himself, but mentally exhausted by the horrors of the Holocaust which were now so clear to everybody. Regrettably, even as the war ended in Europe, the battle for supremacy continued and Waley Cohen had the United Synagogue battalions well organised.

The destruction of the Hampstead Synagogue sermon reprint was a case in point. The power in that community was Henry Gledhill, who was the United Synagogue treasurer responsible for District Synagogues. The Warden would have accepted the orders of such a figure. The minister might have prevented it happening, but the minister was the same Mark Gollop who was involved in being senior chaplain to the Forces and wasn't well anyway. Hertz was isolated.

Hertz had been fighting other battles as well. At this point the British authorities in Palestine had to deal with terrorist attacks from Jewish extremists in the Stern Gang and Irgun Zvei Leumi. The authorities tried to shame the community into lobbying for these to stop. Their strictures were, however, far too general and the Chief Rabbi wrote to *The Times* to complain.

> The wording of the warning [to the community to stop the attacks] is most unfortunate. No responsible Jew anywhere endorses the senseless crimes of terrorists ... moreover, they assert that these crimes bring dishonour upon the Jewish people as a whole. This is the first time to my knowledge that a British administration anywhere has condemned an entire people for the acts of a repudiated few ... the Mufti of Jerusalem directed the Arab terrorist campaign in Palestine and has now, for some years, been in Berlin collaborating with Hitler. But no official British representative has ever declared that his misdeeds bring shame and dishonour to the Arab people as a whole.[42]

It was not surprising that Zionists were being attacked, even though thousands had joined up in Palestine to fight for the Allies. One writer to *The Times* denounced them as atheists and said that the Jews had only ruled in the Holy Land for 500 years. Hertz identified over 1,000 years of Jewish rule. He even quoted Gibbon as saying that 26,000 Jewish troops fought for the Persians when they invaded the country in

614CE. Moreover, he made it quite clear that he was a lifelong Zionist and certainly not an atheist.

Towards the end of 1945 another row erupted. The plight of concentration camp survivors was pitiful and Hertz designated 6 October 1945 as a 'day of Jewish solidarity' with the remnants of European Jewry. He argued that the Jews of England expected the government to keep faith, in regard to Palestine, as the only haven of refuge for survivors of Nazi bestiality, and he asked Jewish ministers to preach a sermon, pleading for the remnants of European Jewry to be allowed to obtain refuge in the Holy Land.

When Waley Cohen heard of this proposed criticism of the government's policy on Palestine, he sent telegrams to the ministers, ordering them to do no such thing. He felt that such a plea would introduce politics into the synagogue and he was angry that Hertz hadn't consulted the Honorary Officers before coming to the decision.

Waley Cohen's behaviour now seems scarcely credible. The newsreel pictures of the emaciated survivors, with mounds of unburied human remains behind them, had been the most appalling images that most people had ever seen. Common humanity demanded a home for the wretched remnant, many of them struggling to overcome the effects of malnutrition, tuberculosis, dysentery and other diseases. How could the dignity of the United Synagogue Honorary Officers take precedence over the plea of the Chief Rabbi? What is more, they still chose to ignore the United Synagogue constitution which left the authority for synagogue services totally in the hands of the Chief Rabbi.

In fact, the Jewish lay leadership merely wanted to tread warily and thought that discussions with government ministers in private about the survivors might be more productive than exerting public pressure. The Jewish lay leadership was concerned about an anti-Semitic backlash in Britain and didn't want to give propagandists any ammunition. They were pragmatic where Hertz was more emotional, but if ever emotion could be excused it was at that dreadful time. Hertz had always held that Palestine was a religious issue and pointed out that, if it were political, then all references to Zion in the prayer books would have to be excised.

Waley Cohen could well say that the Halacha insists on loyalty to the government of the country, but the condition of the survivors seemed to Hertz to demand urgent action. Nonetheless: 'gradually Sir Robert had come to personify all the various tendencies in Anglo-Jewry which Dr Hertz most feared'.[43] In the Chief Rabbi's circle it was considered spiteful of Waley Cohen to humiliate Hertz, but Waley Cohen felt that Zionism was a political issue and should be kept out of the pulpit. For Hertz, the pulpit was one of the best arenas in which to promote Zionism. When he had used it in South Africa forty years before to support the British position, nobody had complained about politics then.

The *Jewish Chronicle* normally reflected the views of the mainstream in the Jewish community and there was no question of how the community reacted to Waley Cohen's action: 'An instant explosion of anger reflected in the letters of protest that have poured into this office.'[44]

The leader writer insisted that Waley Cohen had attempted a pure usurpation of the Chief Rabbi's authority, and went on to say: 'Over a long period the Community has closed its eyes to the manifest anomaly of an institution for the maintenance of Orthodox Jewry being run by men who were themselves not only non-Orthodox – that would be difficult enough – but as they have shown in a hundred different ways, actually anti-Orthodox.'[45]

Waley Cohen and the other similarly minded Honorary Officers were invited to stand down as unfit to lead the organization. Waley Cohen took no notice and continued in office till he died in 1952. There can be little doubt, however, that the concerted opposition of the Honorary Officers to the wishes of the Chief Rabbi must have had an effect on Hertz's constitution, which was already under severe pressure.

The Honorary Officers of the United Synagogue now bent before the wind. They called a Council Meeting in November, knowing that Hertz was fading away. Waley Cohen left Ewen Montagu, the vice-president, to chair the meeting and mend the hole in the dike. Montagu was well able to achieve this and would be the last of the Cousinhood to become president of the United Synagogue after Waley Cohen died. He ensured that the minutes of the Council meeting[46] made it clear that the United Synagogue considered the Chief Rabbi the only authority in religious matters, and that ministers had the freedom of the pulpit and could preach what they wanted.

He apologised if Waley Cohen's overruling of the Chief Rabbi had been misunderstood. He envisaged a meeting with the Chief Rabbi to resolve any outstanding differences. By a slim majority the Council defeated a motion of no confidence in Waley Cohen and the Honorary Officers, pending the results of a meeting, knowing that this would comfort Hertz, even if the meeting was never likely now to take place.

It was just as well that the *Jewish Chronicle* defended the Chief Rabbi, as he was finally unable to do so for himself. As Leon's wife, Irene, wrote:

> At the beginning of 1946, Josephine's letters from London became urgent. Chief Rabbi Hertz had been ailing for some months and she alone was there to care for him. Judith had been moved to Harlow with her son, Victor, and Ruth had got married to her American cousin, Ted Hecht. They were now living in New York. Samuel was in the British army in Lagos ... In her correspondence Josephine told us that if we wanted to see Opa London alive, we must come soon.[47]

Leon and Irene couldn't get priority permits for the journey and in January 1946 the Chief Rabbi died without them seeing him again. When they eventually reached Hamilton Terrace:

> It was quite dismal with hardly any bulbs to lighten the gloom. In the pre-war days there had been a cook, parlour maid and cleaning woman ... Now there were no helpers ... Jo and I shared the cooking. Later on ... the telephone room became Jo's bedroom ... Ruth had followed her husband, Ted, to New York as a 'GI Bride' ... Samuel was in charge of the thousands of books ... Leon and I ... salvaged all the papers relating to Palestine, the Balfour Declaration and the Hebrew University.[48]

The Chief Rabbi died in his sleep on 14 January. He left £16,000 in his will (in terms of today's money, about £500,000). A substantial proportion of this came from royalties for his books, which would serve his children well in the future. His fine collection of first edition and early books was sold by Rosenthal of Oxford. He had ensured that many were beautifully bound and preserved. They included at least one piece of the Cairo Genizah.

He did not live to see his one-volume *Authorised Daily Prayer Book* published, but he had told Samuel that the only memorial he wanted was one that would spread Jewish knowledge. His son wrote in a foreword in July 1946:

> The Chief Rabbi, Dr J.H. Hertz, C.H., was not spared to see the completion of this one-volume edition of his Prayer Book. He had, however, carried out all the proof corrections until p 1064, 'Confessions on Deathbed', which happened to be the last page he corrected; closing there his great Jewish leadership.
>
> It is hoped that this work – the first of its kind in English – will enable the prayers of its distinguished author to be fulfilled, that his labours therein 'lead to a deepening of devotion in the tents and sanctuaries of Israel in English-speaking lands'[49]

Once again, there was no sign that his mind had been affected by the bombing in Harrogate or by his ageing in general.

Even at the end Hertz was trying to campaign. He left instructions for Samuel, who was by now a captain in the army, to communicate his input to the Anglo-American Committee on Palestine. He left one last message in a letter which was never sent. He wrote: 'My only object is to transmit to my successor the constitutional rights of my high office undimmed and undiminished.'[50]

NOTES

1. *Daily Worker*, 18 October 1943.
2. *Daily Worker*, 12 December 1942.
3. Wernher E. Mosse (ed.), *Second Chance: Two Centuries of German-speaking Jews in the United Kingdom* (Tubingen: J.C.B. Mohr, 1991), p.97.
4. Ibid., p.98.
5. Pamela Shatzkes, *Holocaust and Rescue: Impotent or Indifferent? Anglo-Jewry 1938–1945* (Basingstoke: Palgrave, 2002), Chapters 6 and 7.
6. Ibid.
7. Ibid.
8. Bernard Wasserstein, *Britain and the Jews of Europe, 1939–1945* (London: Institute of Jewish Affairs, 1979), p.169.
9. *Jewish Chronicle*, 26 February 1943.
10. *Jewish Chronicle*, 8 January 1943.
11. W.W. Simpson, *Common Ground* magazine. Jeremy Schonfield private family archive.
12. Joseph Herman Hertz, *Early and Late: Addresses, Messages, and Papers* (Hindhead: Soncino Press, 1943), p.197.
13. Ibid., p.214.
14. *The Times*, 6 February 1943.
15. *The Times*, 23 May 1942.
16. Hertz, *Early and Late*, p.7.
17. Jeremy Schonfield private family archive.
18. *Manchester Guardian*, 1 January 1943.
19. Aubrey Newman, 'Chief Rabbi Dr Joseph Herman Hertz, CH' (London: United Synagogue, 1972), p.23.
20. Letter to Jewish War-Service Committee from the Chief Rabbi, 29 November 1943.
21. *Jewish Chronicle*, 20 October 1946.
22. *Jewish Chronicle*, 31 December 1943.
23. Bernard Homa, *Footprints in the Sands of Time* (Privately printed, 1990), p.208.
24. Dayan Lazarus to US Honorary Officers 1944, Memoranda 2206, United Synagogue Archive, London Metropolitan Archives.
25. Letter dated 5 April 1943, File 86/9, J.H. Hertz Archive, Hartley Library, University of Southampton.
26. Ibid.
27. Ibid.
28. Ibid.
29. *Jewish Chronicle*, 20 January 1945.
30. *Jewish Chronicle*, 21 February 1945.
31. *Jewish Chronicle*, 18 June 1945.
32. *Jewish Chronicle*, 17 June 1945.
33. *Jewish Chronicle*, 20 July 1945.

34. Hertz, *Early and Late*, p.182.
35. *Jewish Chronicle*, 15 December 1944.
36. Ibid.
37. Joseph Herman Hertz, 'The Battle of Warsaw', The Chief Rabbi's sermon, 22 May 1944. Office of the Chief Rabbi, London. p.2. London Metropolitan Archives.
38. Ibid., p.3.
39. Ibid., p.4.
40. Ibid., p.7.
41. Letter to the Honorary Officers of the United Synagogue, 9 April 1945, Ms 175, Hertz Papers, London Metropolitan Archives.
42. *Jewish Chronicle*, 20 October 1946.
43. Aubrey Newman, *The United Synagogue, 1870–1970* (London: Routledge and Kegan Paul, 1976), p.157.
44. *Jewish Chronicle*, 19 October 1945.
45. Ibid.
46. Minutes dated 14 November 1943, File 86/9, J.H. Hertz Archive, Hartley Library, University of Southampton.
47. Irene Hertz-Majerczik, *Through Life My Way* (Ra'anana: Docustory, 2003), p.133.
48. Ibid.
49. Joseph Herman Hertz, *Authorised Daily Prayer Book* (New York: Bloch Publishing, 1946), Prefatory note.
50. Newman, 'Chief Rabbi Dr Joseph Herman Hertz, CH', p.25.

Epilogue

Both inside and outside the community there was genuine regret at the passing of the Chief Rabbi. *The Times* said: 'side by side with the heads of the churches, he sat on all the important national committees and shared with his colleagues of other faiths in the work of national movements'.[1] In those surroundings he gained regard and affection. The Free Church Council wrote to the Hertz family after his death: 'you would all have been deeply impressed, we are sure, had you been present, by the real respect and esteem for your father which was expressed at the meeting'.[2]

There was a massive funeral at Willesden Cemetery. Six United Synagogue ministers brought in the coffin and Revd Harris Swift gave the funeral oration. All the dayanim took part, and it was good of Sol Bloom to attend. Now the chairman of the Foreign Affairs Committee of the American House of Representatives, he had worked with the Chief Rabbi on defeating the attempt to reform the calendar nearly twenty years before. The only missing faces of note were Ewen Montagu and Frank Samuel from the United Synagogue.

Waley Cohen did attend and turned his attention immediately to the spiritual leadership of the community in the interregnum before the appointment of a successor. Two days after the funeral, without consulting the United Synagogue Council, he asked Dayan Lazarus to act as Chief Rabbi and wrote to all the congregations who recognized the office to ask them to give him their support in the circumstances. This was immediately misinterpreted. *The Times* announced: 'A successor to Dr Hertz' and the *Daily Mail* said a new Chief Rabbi had been appointed.[3]

The *Jewish Chronicle* was incensed: 'A barefaced attempt is afoot to establish control of the Chief Rabbinate by the United Synagogue ... if the intrigue should succeed and the Chief Rabbinate should pass under the thumb of an aspiring and dictatorial layman, it will be stripped of all its dignity.'[4] The interregnum still lasted for nearly two and a half years before the installation of Rabbi Dr Israel Brodie.

When Hertz died, members of the community were not equally loyal to the Honorary Officers of the United Synagogue:

> there developed an incursion at first into the Council and then into the Executive Committee, of individuals increasingly reluctant to accept without question rulings by Honorary Officers. Increasingly, the Honorary Officers found it difficult to persuade the Council or even the Executive to follow their advice ... Honorary Officers had increasingly to make various votes issues of confidence in order to get their way ... There was also a growing groundswell of opposition in the Council to the 'undemocratic' leadership of the Honorary Officers and increasing attempts made to curb the President's powers.[5]

As this assessment is from the authorized history of the United Synagogue, it presumably gives a more balanced view of the state of the organization, although it is far from complete. After Hertz died, some trouble was taken by Goldberg, the secretary of the United Synagogue, to undermine his reputation. Goldberg, an acolyte of Waley Cohen, wrote that the rows with him were because Hertz: 'no longer had the robust health, mobility, the clarity of vision, deep insight, patience and understanding which are all necessary to smoothing away the difficulties [in] ... conditions ... far different from those of normal years'.[6]

He does not, however, fault Hertz for objecting to Lily Montagu being chosen by Waley Cohen to chair a committee dealing with the religious education of Orthodox Jewish children. Nor does he discuss why the president of the Board of Deputies in 1941 praised the Chief Rabbi's relevance, lucidity, forcefulness and objectivity, only a few years before his death. Or how the *Jewish Chronicle* could praise the vigour of Hertz's wartime sermons and radio broadcasts. Goldberg's criticisms do not hold water.

Ignoring the definition of Hertz's official status, based on the original deeds of the United Synagogue, Goldberg went on: 'There is not, and cannot be, a Pope in Israel', echoing Waley Cohen's insinuation made many years before. Goldberg was, however, right to continue that:

> The extent to which the Chief Rabbinate in this country and the Empire will be assured of loyal support and respect, depends entirely on the hold which the individual ... is able to establish by his high ideals, his exemplary character and life, his ability to promote co-operation and concord in the Communities, and the maturity and wisdom of his judgement in dealing with the affairs of British Jewry.[7]

All these qualities Hertz had shown in full measure for thirty-three years, and the United Synagogue community and the Empire had been loyal to him as a result.

An alternative view of Hertz was given by one of his senior ministers: 'He bore with extraordinary resilience the obstacles which his ideas sometimes encountered, but he never weakened in his unswerving loyalty to the principles for which he stood. He was ever faithful to the great tradition he had inherited from the past.'[8]

The *Jewish Chronicle* commented: '[The Chief Rabbi] exemplified, as never before, the vital function of the Chief Rabbinate with its absolutely indispensable ability to [foster] the welfare of Judaism in Great Britain and the Empire. It would be the crassest folly, therefore, to contemplate abolishing this precious office, or reducing its power.'[9]

If Hertz had to accept failure in any area, it would have been his lack of success in improving academic standards in the United Synagogue to a level closer to those common in Europe before the war. It wasn't for a lack of trying; the Chief Rabbi's literary output exceeded that of all of his predecessors put together.

The attempt to find funds to improve education after the First World War had been unsuccessful and there were no great teachers for a Rabbinics course at Jews' College; during Hertz's thirty-year ministry there had been fewer than a dozen Jews' College students who had been awarded a *semicha*. Hertz had managed to strengthen the college by appointing Dr Isidore Epstein, initially as director of studies, and in 1945 as acting principal. Only a month after Hertz's death, it was Epstein who at last found the right man to raise students to a level at which they could be awarded *semicha*: Rabbi Koppel Kahana, an exceptional Talmudic scholar, who had come to Britain as a refugee before the war and taken a degree at Cambridge in Roman Law.

Kahana wanted to go on to obtain a PhD and when told that he would have three years to provide a suitable thesis, produced a work in three months. The university wasn't expecting this level of enthusiasm and expertise. It awarded him an M.Litt.

The rabbi was in his forties when he studied at Cambridge and he suffered from being extremely short sighted. His memory, however, was formidable, allowing him to quote the exact words of the Babylonian Talmud on any page. An obituary in 1978 quotes him as having said: 'There are only three outstanding Jewish scholars in the country; Dayan Abramsky, Rabbi Rabinow and myself – and not necessarily in that order.'[10]

Epstein persuaded Kahana to take over the Codes section of the rabbinical diploma course at Jews' College, and, over the years, he taught and gave *semicha* to some of the ablest ministers in Britain and overseas.

The Rabbinic Examining Board was finally busy. Its membership originally included the Chief Rabbi, the dayanim and representatives of Yeshiva Etz Chaim, Jews' College and the provinces. But, as Hertz had recognized from the very beginning of his ministry, the central problem in moving the community forward was a lack of really good teachers in any real depth. To make matters worse, with so many continental *yeshivot* destroyed, the need for British rabbinic leadership was far more important than before.

The obsequies over Hertz had hardly been completed when Waley Cohen set out to achieve what the Chief Rabbi had always denied him. In the process of choosing a successor, it was agreed that in future there would be a Consultative and Advisory Committee for the Chief Rabbi. Also that the Chief Rabbi would be forbidden to be associated with any appeal for funds unless that Committee had given its approval, and the name and title of the Chief Rabbi could no longer be embodied in the name of any organization or charity.

Waley Cohen even set out to reduce the Chief Rabbi's authority to be the final decision-maker on religious matters. This was now to be the province of the Beth Din. The Chief Rabbi might be its chair, but if the Beth Din decided they did not agree with his opinion, the Beth Din's view would prevail.

These changes were made before a new Chief Rabbi was appointed and if the candidate had not agreed to them, another candidate would have been found. Israel Brodie, who became Chief Rabbi, was:

> not all that happy, however, about what seemed to be restriction on his powers, particularly by the terms of reference which seemed to introduce 'shackling and restraint' of 'the unfettered and ultimate decision of the Chief Rabbi.' Sir Robert's reply was friendly, conciliatory but quite firm, insisting that there could be no alteration in the conditions of appointment ... given verbal assurances and written confirmation that his authority was unfettered, Dr Brodie agreed to accept.[11]

Whether these new provisions would have been followed in practice would always depend on the strength of the Chief Rabbi himself. After Waley Cohen's death in 1952, the contrasting philosophies of Spiritism and the Halacha were little discussed. The new Honorary Officers from the nineteenth-century immigrant families were differently inclined.

The *Jewish Chronicle*'s obituary for Waley Cohen said his passing: 'evokes ... universal feelings of bereavement and grief'.[12] From a newspaper which had criticized his methods, often savagely, for at least thirty years, this was, perhaps, taking not speaking ill of the dead to a new level.

His efforts were more credibly recorded by the minister of the Edgware Reform Synagogue who described him as: 'A great guardian of religious Judaism against the infringements of political Judaism and as a defender of the priestly independence of every Jew against ecclesiastical tutelage and centralism.'[13] This was certainly Waley Cohen's aim, but he was not successful in foisting on the United Synagogue any changes the vast majority did not support. Furthermore, to suggest that Waley Cohen was against centralism would be extremely hard to justify.

In the greatest domestic cause célèbre after the war, when Brodie was asked by the New West End Synagogue to allow Rabbi Louis Jacobs to resume his former pulpit, he refused to agree and Jacobs was cast into the wilderness, arousing great controversy. Subsequent Chief Rabbis would also speak for the community on occasions without consultation, but neither the United Synagogue nor the Beth Din would contradict them on important matters. At the end of the day, the Chief Rabbi remains the leader of the community in the eyes of both the community and the outside world.

Studies of Hertz's ministry written since his death have presented a picture of a Chief Rabbi often in abrasive conflict with the United Synagogue Honorary Officers, and particularly with Waley Cohen. It presents a depressing litany of a dysfunctional administration over no less than thirty years. The question arises of how near those Honorary Officers came to replacing the Chief Rabbi's religious authority with their own.

The protagonists are often presented as an irresistible force meeting an immovable body. The truth is that they were not equal at all in the eyes of the Anglo-Jewish community. The respect and deference given to Hertz was far greater than that accorded to the Honorary Officers of the United Synagogue. If the latter had tried to dictate to the synagogues in anything more than the detailed running of their finances, they would have encountered major opposition.

Furthermore, the United Synagogue was largely a London-based organization and many of the provincial communities were associated with it only loosely. Montague Burton, the clothing magnate, ran the Harrogate community. Meyer Goldstone, of Ward and Goldstone, ran Arnside Road in Southport, and Arnold Jaffe, the linen magnate, ran the Belfast community. In London it was the Rothschilds who ran the

Great Synagogue and the Freedman family who served as Honorary Officers in a wide range of boardrooms.

Waley Cohen may have controlled the Honorary Officers of the United Synagogue, but he had no means of influencing the powerful men in the provinces, who were voted in annually by their congregations to run individual *shuls*. Waley Cohen had been a senior businessman, but so were the provincial leaders. In many cases, after Waley Cohen left Shell, they were more powerful in business than he was. If they didn't agree with his views on religious practices, they could ignore him. And they wouldn't have opposed the Chief Rabbi because they were Anglo-Jewish Orthodox to a man, and were fully prepared to recognize the religious authority of the Chief Rabbi.

They knew of Waley Cohen's view that there should be closer links between the Progressives and the United Synagogue, but, if it had come to a vote, they wouldn't have supported him for a moment. The synagogues didn't even have uniform practices within the United Synagogue; there was the mixed choir at Hampstead, for example, and the congregation wouldn't give it up. Hertz didn't press them to do so, though his successor, Israel Brodie, abolished it in his time.

There was another factor. Waley Cohen was a member of the Cousinhood, whose families had run the United Synagogue since its inception, and would continue to do so until Sir Isaac Wolfson was elected president in Brodie's time. Men like Burton, Goldstone and Jaffe had come up the hard way, as had Wolfson. They had little in common with the established Cousinhood families. Supporting the Chief Rabbi who, unlike Hermann Adler, was an independent force, might have been a form of revenge for their not being admitted into the Cousinhood's magic circle. The simpler the origins from which they sprang, the more deference they were likely to show to the Chief Rabbi.

The number of occasions on which Waley Cohen took unilateral action without consulting the United Synagogue Council was a major irritant to its members. Waley Cohen often said that if the Honorary Officers were not supported, they would have to resign. They actually did so in July 1939, but nobody is irreplaceable and there is little point in having a Council if they merely approve without argument the decisions of the Honorary Officers.

Waley Cohen may have had more influence with the synagogues that needed the financial support of the United Synagogue but in religious disputes it is likely that they would, at best, have abstained. It was generally agreed across the Anglo-Jewish board, that if it was a religious matter, then it was up to the Chief Rabbi to decide. Hertz was generally popular and his reputation as an international authority grew substantially during his ministry.

To make matters worse for the Honorary Officers, the United Synagogue sometimes had to make financial decisions which were not in accordance with the wishes of the congregations concerned. As a consequence, they bore the opprobrium which commonly applies to the Treasury and the Chancellor of the Exchequer.

What was the root problem between Hertz and Waley Cohen? A psychiatrist might suggest a rationale for Waley Cohen's approach to the Chief Rabbi over the years, although jealousy would be one simple way to explain his behaviour. In the early days, during the First World War, Hertz could be regarded as a poor Hungarian refugee who had come to his elevated post from the obscurity of South Africa. Waley Cohen was rich, from a prominent family, a powerful executive in one of the foremost British companies, and given senior responsibility by the government in a crucial area of the war effort. He would later be awarded a knighthood, he understood the general attitude of the British Jewish community and was a senior officer of its most powerful organization. As a consequence he expected to take the leading role in the community.

By the time of Hertz's death, the Chief Rabbi had overtaken Waley Cohen in area after area. He was a far better speaker and had written highly regarded books. He had become a Companion of Honour, which rates higher than a knighthood, and was an international figure through his pastoral tour, his work on the Chumash and his battle against calendar reform.

Hertz was respected throughout Britain following his visits to provincial communities and was more important and better liked by the community than Waley Cohen. In the end Waley Cohen had no meaningful role in the 1939–45 war effort, had lost his senior position in British business, had no international reputation, no publications and was constantly criticized for his overbearing manner.

Waley Cohen was not accustomed to being thwarted and his prime reaction was known to be to lose his temper. While this impressed and intimidated many people, it didn't work with Hertz, and it must have been frustrating to lose so many communal battles to a man he considered his inferior. As Hertz grew steadily in terms of public and communal regard, by playing his part on the world stage and winning honour in his adopted country, Waley Cohen must have become increasingly incensed.

Waley Cohen's discourteous treatment of Hertz, together with the constant attempts to diminish his authority, were the actions of a man filled with dislike for a Chief Rabbi who often stood in his way. It must have annoyed Waley Cohen intensely that, as his own star waned, the Chief Rabbi's star waxed. He could rationalize his behaviour because his capacity for self-delusion was immense. There was his comment to a friend: 'I am sure you would be the last person to agree that my mild and patient method of argument [with the Chief Rabbi] is in any way rightly described as "pressure".'[14]

Looked at from Waley Cohen's point of view, the results he achieved in opposing the Chief Rabbi were depressing. When he took office as treasurer, the United Synagogue was an organization in which the president and the Chief Rabbi had worked together harmoniously. Hermann Adler had not embarrassed Lord Rothschild, and his Lordship's level of observance had been the accepted norm for United Synagogue members. With Hertz, the situation changed. Not only did Hertz attack the Liberals, who included some of Waley Cohen's friends, but he made scathing attacks on the leadership of the community – 'inimical to Orthodoxy' etc. – which could only be seen as a rejection of Waley Cohen's standards and those of the other Honorary Officers.

As far as Hertz was concerned, if Waley Cohen chose to drive to synagogue or not keep kosher, that was his right, but it was not acceptable in the president and Honorary Officers of the United Synagogue. He couldn't stop him, but he could make his disapproval abundantly clear.

Waley Cohen, however, thought that Hertz had altered the rules, as he understood them when he accepted office, and he felt Hertz had done so without forewarning or consultation. Titularly, Hertz may have been appointed to uphold the law but, disconcerting to some, that was exactly what he did. A degree of lip service might once have been acceptable, but now attracted public criticism.

That Hertz succeeded in his main objective of keeping the community Orthodox against the odds is a remarkable testimony to his courage and ability. He was not just a powerful speaker; he never allowed himself to become isolated in remote scholarship, leaving the present to take care of itself: 'He went down into the dust and battles of his fellow man's daily life and brought to it the teachings and the guidance and the interpretation which Judaism has so pre-eminently to offer'.[15]

In reviewing Hertz's ministry in spiritual terms, the accusation is often made that he was unsuccessful because he presided over a steady decline in the level of observance in the community. That there was such a decline is not in question, but the level of observance of the core Jewish community in Britain before the flood of immigrants in the late nineteenth century was already seriously in decline. The complaints of newcomers from Eastern Europe were always centred on the inadequacies of general observance compared to their own, but the pressures in Britain differed from those in their home lands.

In the *shtetl*, the only escape for a religious Jew from the grinding daily poverty was Talmudic study, or the freedom to pray for deliverance from twenty-five years in the Russian army, the next pogrom, or special taxes on the Jewish community.

If someone was not Orthodox in their behaviour, it was soon well known to the community. There was nowhere to hide in the *shtetl*, unlike in London between the wars. Nor were there alternative attractions like radio, the cinema, free libraries, or Arsenal or Manchester United. To this day, if the two teams are playing on Yom Kippur, a mass of season ticket seats remain empty.

Rescued from the threats of discrimination, with less need to call on the Almighty for help, with alternative attractions and no communal sanctions inflicted for backsliding, there was bound to be a drop in the standard of religious observance. When towards the end of the twentieth century there began to be a revival, it was because the people concerned were satisfied that the traditional way of life was superior to current fashion.

The very Orthodox would give up television for fear of having their children corrupted, and turn to a stricter level of observance as a defence against hedonism, and indifference to the decline of the family unit. A considerable number of the core United Synagogue members became more observant.

What remains remarkable about Hertz's achievement is that, in spite of the new challenges, he was able – with other Orthodox leaders in the Federation and the Union of Orthodox Hebrew Congregations – to keep the majority of the community within the Orthodox camp. Between 1921 and 1948 nearly all Jewish marriages were central Orthodox and the total for both the Left and Right Wings was insignificant. His influence was such that: 'to the ordinary Jewish layman the Chief Rabbi became not so much a decider in matters of Halacha as the virtual embodiment of the Halacha'.[16]

Another accusation against Hertz was that he was vain. As Robert Henriques wrote: 'He tended to seek publicity for himself on all occasions and to discover a denigration of his office in almost any incident or encounter which did not feed his vanity.'[17]

No examples are provided, but Henriques neglects to mention that respect for the office is also respect for what the office stands for. Once a religious leader is considered or treated as an ordinary citizen, the importance of the rulings and guidance he provides is diminished. When the judge enters the court, all rise, not because that particular judge is so eminent, but because the importance of the office is vital to acknowledge publicly. In defending the status of the Chief Rabbinate, Hertz was defending what it stood for. He would not cower from the attacks by left and right but would give as good as he got.

It is only natural that when historians write of the British-Jewish community in the twentieth century, Hertz is considered a key factor. But so impressed has everyone been by his achievements that they have wanted to claim Hertz for their own. As he went to the Jewish Theological Seminary, was he a Conservative Rabbi, as the institution is today? As he was a student of Morais, did he really belong to the ultra-Orthodox? As Chief Rabbi, was he middle of the road? As he was prepared to consider the best of modern scholarship, did he have Reform leanings?

It certainly isn't easy to decide on the basis of early twentieth-century labels, such as 'positive Conservatism' or 'Orthodox fundamentalism'. Meanings and cultures change. Only on specific topics can one be sure. For example, the Conservative movement in America has now agreed that openly gay men can become ministers. In Britain in Hertz's time, homosexuality was a criminal offence, apart from being against the *din*. Whatever the position today – greater tolerance, greater indifference, higher standards of humanity, lower standards of morals – it's a free country, but it's safe to assume that Hertz would not have approved of homosexual rabbis.

In general Hertz kept to the traditional Orthodox commitment he identified in Morais: 'We were thrilled by the clear, clarion notes of his call to the Wars of the Lord; by his passionate and loyal stand that the Divine Law was imperative, unchangeable, eternal. He made rigorous demands ... [for] ... the courage to stand alone, if need be, in the fight against unrighteousness and un-Judaism.'[18] All the evidence is that this remained Hertz's position throughout his ministry and, when he died, a large majority of the Jews in Britain agreed with him and still do.

In the lecture he gave on the occasion of the centenary of Hertz's birth in 1972, Dr Aubrey Newman said: 'He saw his path clearly; as teacher of the Book to the people of the Book; as interpreter of Israel, the great misunderstood of history, to the larger, often hostile, world around him; as champion of my people, guarding the honour, upholding the prestige of Anglo-Jewry; as defender of the Faith, who cannot permit any cutting of the dikes.'[19]

There is no doubt that Hertz faced more entrenched opposition from within his own camp than any other British Chief Rabbi before or since. That it only came from a small coterie of United Synagogue Honorary Officers did not make it easier to resist. While some of the Honorary Officers during his ministry were very supportive – Joseph Freedman who financed the Chumash was only one example – the majority accepted Waley Cohen's fiat.

In former years the lay leaders of the community had very happily left religious decisions to the Chief Rabbi. It was their wish to do so which inspired the creation of the position in the first place, and the embodiment of that authority in the United Synagogue Constitution.

The first Chief Rabbi, Aaron Hart, had had little trouble because the principal lay leader in his day was his brother. Hart Lyon didn't stay long enough to make it an issue. David Tevele Schiff had one of the most respected *Batei Din* in Europe and none of his lay leaders disputed the scope of his role. Nathan Mayer Rothschild was so happy with Solomon Herschell that he probably was influential in making him the richest of all Chief Rabbis. Sir Moses Montefiore worked hard to ensure that Nathan Marcus Adler was the supreme religious authority throughout the country. Lord Rothschild cooperated very well with Hermann Adler.

The religious position of mainstream Orthodox Jews in 1913 when Hertz took office was indistinguishable from their attitude when Aaron Hart was appointed over 200 years before. It was only in Hertz's time that important Orthodox practices had to be vigorously defended and Hertz proved himself up to the task.

The example Hertz gave his successors was crucial. His ministry of over thirty years showed that it was possible to uphold the *din* even against the entrenched opposition of United Synagogue Honorary Officers, led by one of the most powerful businessmen in the country. Hertz had been entrusted by Rothschild with the care and safe custody of the ancient law and the community's religious guidance. He did not betray the trust.

NOTES

1. *The Times*, 15 January 1946.
2. Jeremy Schonfield private family archive.
3. *Jewish Chronicle*, 25 January 1946.
4. Ibid.
5. Goldberg papers, Anglo-Jewish Archives, University College London.
6. Ibid.
7. Aubrey Newman, *The United Synagogue, 1870–1970* (London: Routledge and Kegan Paul, 1976), p.175.
8. Revd S. Levy, 'Very Reverend Joseph Herman Hertz, Chief Rabbi', *Proceedings of the Jewish Historical Society of England*, Vol. 16 (1945/51), p.238.

9. *Jewish Chronicle*, 18 January 1946.
10. Robert Henriques, *Sir Robert Waley Cohen, 1877–1952* (London: Secker and Warburg, 1966), p.348.
11. Ibid., p.10.
12. *Jewish Chronicle*, 21 July 1978.
13. Norman Cohen, Jewish Historical Society of England Transactions, Vol. 21, p.304.
14. Henriques, *Sir Robert Waley Cohen*, p.348.
15. Aubrey Newman, 'Chief Rabbi Dr Joseph Herman Hertz, CH' (London: United Synagogue, 1972), p.8.
16. Henriques, *Sir Robert Waley Cohen*, p.182.
17. *Jewish Chronicle*, 5 December 1952.
18. Joseph Herman Hertz, *Sermons, Addresses and Studies* (London: Soncino Press, 1938). p.361.
19. Jeremy Schonfield private family archive.

Appendix A

Honours, Qualifications and Offices

Honours and Qualifications
Companion of Honour
Commander of the Order of Leopold II (Belgium)
JP (South Africa)
PhD (Columbia)
LL.D (Hon), London University, Doctor of Hebrew Literature (Hon), Jewish Theological Seminary
MA (Capetown)
BA (College of City of New York)
Columbia Medal for Outstanding Service
Riggs Gold Medal (College of City of New York)
Chief Rabbi of the United Hebrew Congregations of the Commonwealth

Offices

1893–98	Rabbi of Congregation Adath Yeshurun, Syracuse, New York
1898–1911	Rabbi of Witwatersrand Old Hebrew Congregation, Johannesburg
1899–1904	Vice-President, South Africa Zionist Federation
1900	Member of High Commissioner's Consultative Committee, South Africa
1903–11	Administrator, Johannesburg Public Library
1906–08	Professor of Philosophy, Transvaal University
1911–13	Rabbi of Congregation Orach Chaim, New York
1911–46	Chief Rabbi of the United Hebrew Congregations of the British Empire

Community Offices
President, Aria College
Bachad Fellowship
Central British Fund for Jewish Relief and Rehabilitation
Chairman, Chief Rabbi's Kosher Canteen Committee
Chairman, Chief Rabbi's Religious Emergency Council
Chairman, Committee of Ministers
Chairman, Conference of Anglo-Jewish Preachers
Co-Chairman, Council of Christians and Jews
Chairman, Council for Jewish Adult Education
Federation of Czech Jews
Federation of Jewish Relief Organisations
Institute of Jewish Studies, Hebrew University, Jerusalem
Jewish Higher Education Committee
Jewish Institute for the Blind, Jerusalem
President, National Council for Jewish Religious Education
Jewish Peace Society
Chairman, Jews' College
Chairman, Kashrut Commission
London Jewish Hospital
Old Yishuv War Fund
Polish Jewish Refugee Fund
Chairman, Rabbinical Committee for Licensing *Shochetim*
Sabbath League of Great Britain
Solomon Wolfson Jewish School
Talmud Torah Trust
Torah va'Avodah Organisation
United Jewish Relief Appeal

Bibliography

Archives

British Library Sound Archives, London, UK.
Goldberg Papers, Anglo-Jewish Archives, University College London, UK.
J. Schonfield, Private family archive.
J.H. Hertz Archive, Hartley Library, University of Southampton, Southampton, UK.
London Metropolitan Archives, London, UK.

Publications

Adler, C. (ed.), *The Jewish Theological Seminary of America* (New York: Jewish Theological Seminary of America, 1939).
Alderman, G., 'The Holocaust. Why Did Anglo-Jewry Stand Idly By?' (New York: Touro College, 2001).
Alderman, G., *Controversy and Crisis: Studies in the History of the Jews in Modern Britain* (Boston, MA: Academic Studies Press, 2008).
Bermant, C., *The Cousinhood: The Anglo-Jewish Gentry* (London: Eyre and Spottiswoode, 1971).
Cesarani, D., *The Jewish Chronicle and Anglo-Jewry, 1841–1991* (Cambridge: Cambridge University Press, 1994).
Cesarani, D. and Kushner, T., *The Internment of Aliens in Twentieth Century Britain* (London: Frank Cass, 1993).
Cohen, S., 'The Zionists and the Board of Deputies in 1917', *Jewish Journal of Sociology*, 1977/78.
Drachman, B., *The Unfailing Light. Memoirs of an American Rabbi* (New York: The Rabbinical Council of America, 1948).
Elton, B.J., *Britain's Chief Rabbis and the Religious Character of Anglo-Jewry, 1880–1970* (Manchester: Manchester University Press, 2009).
Epstein, I. (ed.), *Joseph Herman Hertz: In Memoriam* (London: Soncino Press, 1947).
Ferguson, N., *The World's Banker: The History of the House of Rothschild* (London: Weidenfeld and Nicolson, 1998).

Finestein, I., *Scenes and Personalities in Anglo-Jewry, 1800-2000* (London and Portland, OR: Vallentine Mitchell, 2002).
Finestein, I., *New Dictionary of National Biography* (Oxford: Oxford University Press, 2010).
Freud-Kandel, M., *Orthodox Judaism in Britain since 1913* (London and Portland, OR: Vallentine Mitchell, 2006).
Henriques, R., *Sir Robert Waley Cohen, 1877–1952* (London: Secker and Warburg, 1966).
Hertz, J.H., *Bachya, The Jewish Thomas a Kempis* (New York: Jewish Theological Seminary, 1898).
Hertz, J.H., *A Book of Jewish Thoughts* (London: Eyre and Spottiswoode, 1917).
Hertz, J.H., *Transactions of the Jewish Historical Society of England*, Vol. 9 (London: JHSE, 1918/20).
Hertz, J.H., *Transactions of the Jewish Historical Society of England*, Vol. 10 (London: JHSE, 1921/23).
Hertz, J.H., 'Opening Address in 1923 at the Conference of Anglo-Jewish Preachers' (London: Oxford University Press, 1923).
Hertz, J.H., *Affirmations of Judaism* (London: Oxford University Press/Humphrey Milford, 1927).
Hertz, J.H., *Pentateuch and Haftorahs* (London: Oxford University Press, 1929–36).
Hertz, J.H., *Transactions of the Jewish Historical Society of England*, Vol.13 (London: JHSE, 1932/35).
Hertz, J.H., *Sermons, Addresses and Studies* (London: Soncino Press, 1938).
Hertz, J.H., *Transactions of the Jewish Historical Society of England*, Vol.15 (London: JHSE, 1939/45).
Hertz, J.H., *Early and Late: Addresses, Messages, and Papers* (Hindhead: Soncino Press, 1943).
Hertz, J.H., *Pentateuch and Haftorahs* (Hindhead: Soncino Press, 1960).
Hertz-Majerczik, I., *Through Life My Way* (Ra'anana: Docostory, 2003).
Homa, B., *Footprints in the Sands of Time* (Privately printed, 1990).
Janner, G. and Taylor, D., *Jewish Parliamentarians* (London and Portland, OR: Vallentine Mitchell, 2008).
Kershen, A. and Romain, J., *Tradition and Change: A History of Reform Judaism in Britain, 1940–1995* (London and Portland, OR: Vallentine Mitchell, 1995).
Lacqueur, W., *A History of Zionism* (London: Weidenfeld and Nicolson, 1972).

Landman, S. (ed.), *Essays Presented to Dr J.H. Hertz, Chief Rabbi* (London: Edward Goldston, 1942).
Langham, R., *250 Years of Convention and Contention. A History of the Board of Deputies of British Jews, 1760–2010* (London and Portland, OR: Vallentine Mitchell, 2010).
Levin, A.L., *Letters from South Africa* (New York: Herzl Press, 2005).
Levy, Revd S., 'Very Reverend Joseph Herman Hertz, Chief Rabbi', *Proceedings of the Jewish Historical Society of England*, Vol.16 (1945/51), p.238.
London, L., *Whitehall and the Jews, 1933–1948: British Immigration Policy, Jewish Refugees and the Holocaust* (London: Oxford University Press, 2000).
McMeekin, S., *The Berlin–Baghdad Express: The Ottoman Empire and Germany's Bid for World Power, 1898–1918* (Cambridge, MA: Harvard University Press, 2010).
Marcus, M., *The Unwanted: European Refugees in the Twentieth Century* (London: Oxford University Press, 1985).
Morris, B., *Righteous Victims: A History of the Zionist–Arab Conflict, 1881–2001* (London: Random House, 2001).
Mosse, W.E. (ed.), *Second Chance: Two Centuries of German–speaking Jews in the United Kingdom* (Tubingen: J.C.B. Mohr, 1991).
Newman, A., *Lecture on the Centenary of the Birth of Joseph Herman Hertz* (London: United Synagogue, 1972).
Newman, A., 'Chief Rabbi Dr Joseph H. Hertz, CH' (London: United Synagogue, 1972).
Newman, A., *The United Synagogue, 1870–1970* (London: Routledge and Kegan Paul, 1976).
Persoff, M., *Faith Against Reason: Religious Reform and the British Chief Rabbinate, 1840–1990* (London and Portland, OR: Vallentine Mitchell, 2008).
Rabinowicz, H., *A World Apart: The History of Chasidism in England* (London and Portland, OR: Vallentine Mitchell, 1996).
Sarna, J. (ed.), *People Walk on their Heads: Moses Weinberger's Jews and Judaism in New York* (New York: Holmes Meir Publishing, 1982).
Saron, G. and Hotz, L., *The Jews of South Africa: A History* (London: Oxford University Press, 1955).
Schonfeld, S., *Jewish Religious Education* (London: Jewish Secondary School Movement, 1943).
Schonfeld, S., *Message to Jewry* (London: Jewish Secondary School Movement, 1958).
Shatzkes, P., *Holocaust and Rescue: Impotent or Indifferent? Anglo-Jewry 1938–1945* (Basingstoke: Palgrave, 2002).

Stein, L., *The Balfour Declaration* (London and Portland, OR: Vallentine Mitchell, 1971).
Taylor, D., *British Chief Rabbis, 1664–2006* (London and Portland, OR: Vallentine Mitchell, 2007).
Taylor, D., *Solomon Schonfeld. A Purpose in Life* (London and Portland, OR: Vallentine Mitchell, 2009).
Wasserstein, B., *Britain and the Jews of Europe, 1939–1945* (London: Institute of Jewish Affairs, 1979).

Index